I0520722

THE LIGHTHOUSE EFFECT

Skillful Recovery Program Training Manual

Practicing Your Way From Survival to Revival

by

Faith Burrington Jones

Copyright © 2025 Faith Burrington Jones
All rights reserved.

ISBN: 979-8-9904262-1-4

Printed in the USA

Cover Image & Interior Graphics Canva Pro | Edit & Graphic Design Linda Black

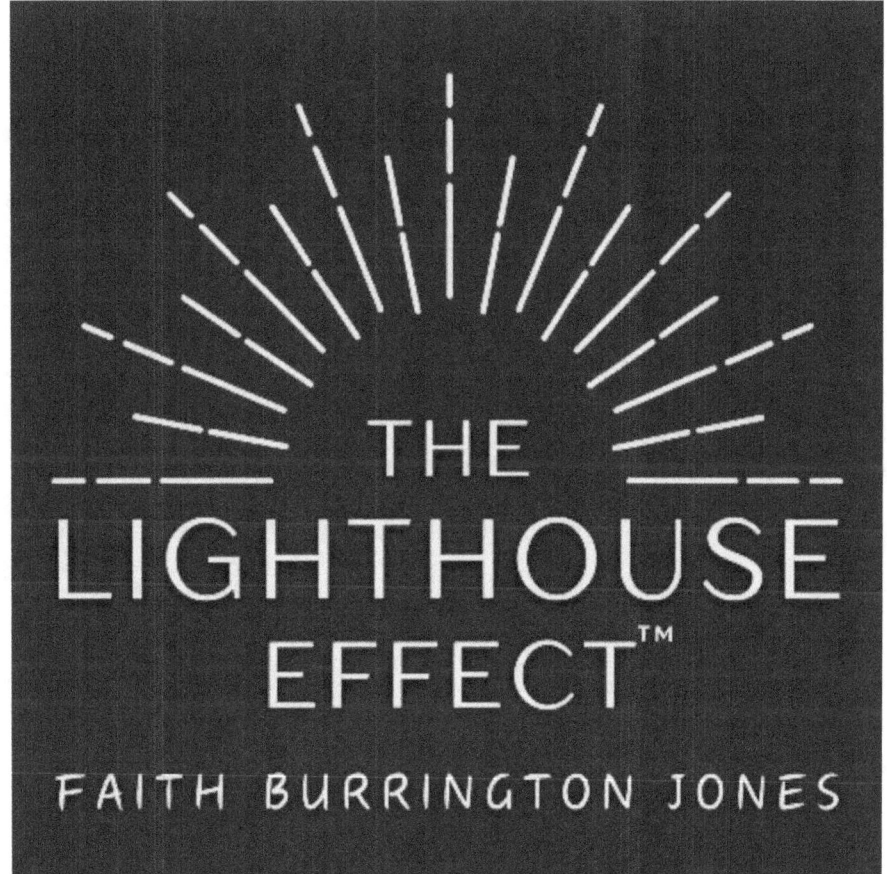

THE
LIGHTHOUSE
EFFECT™

FAITH BURRINGTON JONES

In loving memory of my dear friend and mentor Robert "Bob" L. A. Cote,
a devoted and inspirational leader in addiction and recovery in New England.

In loving memory of Joseph R. Botz and Living in Recovery,
the recovery center in Pittsfield, Massachusetts, founded in Joseph's memory.

ACKNOWLEDGMENTS

I thank the late Bob Cote, who I and many others think of as 'the father of addiction and recovery,' not just for his extensive wealth of knowledge and experience in the field, but for his integrity, compassion, fierce honesty, and kindness. Among other significant achievements in the addiction and recovery field, Bob co-founded the Thomas McGee Substance Abuse Unit at Hillcrest Hospital in Pittsfield, Massachusetts, was a consultant for the Jones Medical Center in Pittsfield, and created the Addiction Counselor Education Program at Westfield State University. I worked with Bob at The Brien Center in North Adams, Massachusetts, where he was senior clinician for sixteen years. He also led men's spiritual workshops and retreats throughout the country. He was influential in guiding me in my development of The Lighthouse Effect Skillful Recovery Program. Bob was an exceptional man in every way, and for me, modeled the Divine Masculine; he was the real deal.

I could not publish this training manual without acknowledging my connection with a former client, Joseph Botz, who sadly passed away in 2017 after a long battle with alcohol dependence and severe anxiety. His family--his mother and stepfather, Donna Herbert Darcy and David Darcy, his sons Dylan Botz and Joe "Joey" Botz, and their mother, Teva O'Rourke Lacuessa--wanted to give meaning to Joe's shortened life by providing a safe and supportive community-based recovery center in the town of Pittsfield, where he grew up. They entrusted me to find a way to make it happen. After a lot of networking and meetings, the family decided to join forces and collaborate with ServiceNet, a mental health and human resources agency in Northampton, Massachusetts, with a satellite behavioral health office in Pittsfield. The family provided the seed money for a significant grant from the State; it wouldn't have been awarded to ServiceNet without the family's generous donation.

Much to their joy, Living in Recovery was founded in 2018 in Joe's memory. The Center is a peer-driven community organization for all pathways and stages of recovery. I served in a part-time position at the center for about one-and-a-half years, during which I ran my Skillful

Recovery Program as training for staff members and provided ongoing support in recovery, skill-building, self-empowerment, and conscious communication. As the Program was one of the most popular there and at other agencies I worked for, it became my passion and vision to create a manual that could provide comprehensive training for group facilitators in recovery centers and mental health centers, far and wide.

I also thank and honor mentors who, for me, model the Divine Feminine: Margaret O'Connor, a psychotherapist who specializes in integrating the "inner landscape" by going within to explore the parts of us that get repressed and neglected; Jacquelyn Small, author of *Becoming a Practical Mystic* (among other inspirational books) and founder of Eupsychia Institute, whose work in bringing integrative breathwork and soul psychology into recovery centers and personal-growth retreats across the country inspired me to work in the addiction field and to facilitate integrative breathwork workshops; Lynne Forrest, who is an exceptional experiential group-facilitator for "shadow work" and family-of-origin workshops, and author of *Guiding Principles for Life Beyond Victim Consciousness* and "The Three Faces of Victim," in which she takes a detailed look at the three main defense strategies of victim consciousness. These extraordinary women are wayshowers for experiential inner work, shadow work, self-inquiry, and the transforming of victim consciousness into integrative consciousness, integrating the ego within the soul. Thank you for encouraging my personal journey of recovery from codependency and childhood negative core beliefs, and for modeling self-empowerment, self-awareness, and self-realization.

Thank you to Tae Kwon Do Grandmaster *(Kwan jang nim)* Roger Lynch, Master Lindsey Fletcher-Lynch, and the entire Tae Kwon Do community––especially Master Bob Markey, Master James White, Master Abbot Cutler, Master Pat Daily, and the late Master Joseph Scalice. Thank you for teaching me to literally stand in my power no matter what gets "thrown" at me or "blocks" my way, and for being models of great inner strength, integrity, and heart!

Thank you all for helping me to understand how essential it is that we each take responsibility for ourselves and for how we choose to navigate our life path. I bow to you, in honor of all that you are and all that you contribute as beacons of guidance and light--the various ways you positively impact those who cross your path, your careful attention and service to community, and your cultivation of mind-body-spirit alignment, self-empowerment, and respect for all sentient beings.

Special appreciation to those who came together as a team to bring this book and The Lighthouse Effect series to fruition. I couldn't have accomplished this without you and the expertise and support you provided: John Coster, for your ongoing encouragement, editorial contributions, and consulting; Drew Hutchison, for your videography work and championing my vision; Paul Costello for your unwavering moral support and editorial and proofreading expertise; and Linda Black, for your multilateral contributions as editor, writing coach, graphic and web designer, and hybrid publisher, walking me through the maze of the publishing process.

And cheers to Mocha Maya's Cafe in Shelburne Falls, to owner-manager Christian King, his amazing staff, and the many wonderful village patrons and fellow customers I crossed paths with. I spent a lot of time at the cafe during the couple of years I was writing this book series; I'd be there most mornings, rain, snow, or shine, drinking their delicious coffee and being cheered on.

Thank you to my family, especially my sons Riley and Rowan Jones, for your ongoing love and support!

Last but not least, deep appreciation and gratitude to the participants who graduated from The Lighthouse Effect Skillful Recovery program and those who courageously volunteered to participate in the filming of live sessions (15 hours) of the modules. It is such a gift to others who choose to be on the path of recovery to be able to witness your process in "real time," moving through exercises, practicing skills and tools, and engaging in group dynamics.

FOREWORD

By Diane Kurinsky, PhD

When Faith Burrington Jones came to the Clinical Mental Health Counseling Program at Antioch University in 2005, she brought with her a wealth of professional experience, having worked as an Integrative Acupressure practitioner and having engaged in a lifelong healing process from her own traumatic childhood health challenges. Faith touches on her experiences as a child and young adult in the "My Story" chapter of this manual, how they led her down the path of the wounded healer and inspired her to seek meaning and relevance in life. She found meaning through spiritual explorations (including completing the Soul Psychology Program at Eupsychia Institute) and training in acupressure and martial arts.

As is often true of people who work with the body, she found that unlocking physical pain is often difficult or impossible without addressing the mental distress that accompanies it. Faith wanted to build on her comprehensive understanding of bodywork, which brought her to enroll in Antioch's graduate program to become a mental health counselor. At that time, I was Director of the Mental Health Counseling Program and Coordinator of the Substance Abuse/Addictions Concentration, as well as Faith's Professional Seminar leader.

During her time as a student, when I knew her best, I found her to be an intelligent, deeply committed student and a gifted practitioner. She delved into the practice of counseling with the same intensity and dedication that she had brought to her earlier studies and practices. As part of the program, Faith did an internship as a substance abuse clinician at the Brien Center (which later hired her.) She graduated with a master's degree in counseling psychology with a concentration in addiction, prepared to engage in an integrated wellness practice that would include mind, body, and spirit in the healing process.

The publication of The Lighthouse Effect Skillful Recovery Training Program Manual demonstrates the degree to which that practice has matured and deepened. This manual is

iv

an invaluable aid to practitioners who use group therapy and "group process" to facilitate healing from trauma and addiction. Faith translates her understanding of the complex issues that make healing so difficult into a straightforward yet creative approach that provides a transparent, accessible, and manageable recovery roadmap. For so many people suffering from trauma and addiction, the challenges are overwhelming and unmanageable. Faith unlocks the recovery process in a step-by-step way that enables practitioners to help their clients develop essential skills and daily practices to support them on the road to recovery, or as Faith puts it, on the path from survival to revival. The program is organized into four comprehensive modules, each focused on an integral aspect of the healing process. The modules can be offered singly or together as a year-long program, with each module building upon the others.

Faith provides the particular amalgamation of skills and practices that have been so deeply beneficial to her clients and herself, and that evolved into The Lighthouse Effect Skillful Recovery Program. The incredible effort she has taken to make the program accessible to the broad wellness field demonstrates her dedication to helping others. Her insight, intelligence, and skill as a wellness clinician shine through. Those of you who have found your way to this book have found an indispensable guide and aid. I am confident this training manual will expand your understanding of the process of healing from trauma and addiction and enhance your practice, whatever your therapeutic focus. This book expands the knowledge base in the wellness field and will be a valuable tool to all who use it.

CONTENTS

MY STORY

The Lighthouse Effect is the culmination of my life's work, professionally and personally, as the two paths are intimately intertwined, to the extent that I'd say my story is that of the wounded healer. I speak more to my story in *The Lighthouse Effect: Practicing your Way from Survival to Revival*, but what is relevant here is that I had to grapple through physical and mental health challenges at an early age, and continued to do so into adulthood. Not finding a healing path that worked for me in the traditional Western Medicine landscape, I was driven to seek out and learn alternative healing modalities and practices, many of which would become part of my professional repertoire. I've come to see my own struggle from a more spiritual perspective, how it is perhaps my life's purpose to be a wayshower for others trying to overcome physical and emotional barriers to wellbeing.

Perhaps by easing the pain of others on their journey and helping their lives to be more fulfilling, I am fulfilling my own quest. Part of that quest has been to get to the "truth" of our existence, to gain insight into what purpose our pain and suffering might serve, to answer, even in part, the grand, existential question: *What exactly is this human experience all about*? I don't know that we can ever fully answer that question, and maybe we don't need to; maybe the quest for the answer is what sets us on our paths of healing.

Through my own journey and in working with clients over the years, I've come to see that who we are and how we manage our emotional system as adults has everything to do with our earliest experiences. I see conditions like depression, anxiety, addiction, and so on as essentially symptoms that all tie back to our childhood programming and how we learned to navigate the often stormy waters of life within our family of origin. (Origin not necessarily meaning birth, but the family in which we were raised and had our first experiences.)

My early training was as an Integrative Acupressure practitioner, and while it was body focused, it also inspired me to explore how the mind impacts the body. In other words, I got interested in the mind-body complex, and then, how we might bring our mind and body into alignment with spirit, or what we might think of as our higher self. Martial arts training had a big impact on my understanding of the mind-body complex; it taught me self-discipline and self-confidence, and built inner strength. The Lighthouse Effect Skillful Recovery Program is an amalgamation of all of that training, plus two decades of hands-on experience working with clients.

My clients have been my greatest teachers and inspiration, witnessing their journeys moving out of suffering from trauma and addiction toward healing and self-empowerment. I see them as unsung heroes who are doing the hard work of *being* in the human experience. They have deepened my belief that untangling our childhood programming and core beliefs, looking at our addictions, attachments, and dependencies as symptoms, and treating ourselves with patience, kindness, and understanding are all essential to our wellbeing and facilitate us in coming home to who we truly are, to our "Authentic Self."

Some of my program's graduates generously share their stories and processes of recovery in *The Lighthouse Effect: Practicing Your Way From Survival to Revival*, and you will see excerpts from those interviews in this training manual. (These are the same clients who participated in the creation of The Lighthouse Effect videos on my website: innerfaiththerapy.com.)

My hope with this manual is that you, the therapist, recovery coach, or group facilitator, can use The Lighthouse Effect Skillful Recovery Program with your clients, and that together, we might begin to heal our collective trauma and programming, from the inside out.

THE LIGHTHOUSE EFFECT EXPLAINED

The "lighthouse effect" is an experiential therapeutic process of healing into wholeness by aligning vertically, mind, body, and soul, to be able to shine our unique expression of the divine. It is a process for navigating the human experience with intention and mindfulness, as a sovereign being. The process doesn't end upon completion of The Lighthouse Effect Skillful Recovery Program; rather, the skills introduced in the program can be integrated into our daily lives, essentially, as an ongoing lifestyle.

The Lighthouse Effect is about learning to deprogram trauma memory and negative core beliefs that were internalized in childhood, encoded into our cellular memory, and then manifested as addictions and other maladaptive ways of coping: *survival*. It's about looking within to the origin of our addictions and dependencies in order to consciously change and repattern those default behaviors. It is a journey of self-exploration and self-actualization, for gently and skillfully transforming core beliefs and returning us to our Authentic Self: *revival*. I would say the Lighthouse Effect is a gradual awakening into a higher state of consciousness, from where we can radiate our unique way of being in the world and truly be in service to ourselves and others.

HOW TO UTILIZE THIS MANUAL
& THE LIGHTHOUSE EFFECT SKILLFUL RECOVERY PROGRAM

The Program

I developed The Lighthouse Effect Skillful Recovery Program as a year-long group program, with four core modules: Module I Mindful Recovery: The Bedrock of your Lighthouse ~ Anchoring Awareness; Module II Tolerance Building: The Structure of your Lighthouse ~ Developing Resilience; Module III Emotional Balancing: The Power Source of your Lighthouse ~ Authentic Power; Module IV Conscious Communication: The Visible Shine of your Lighthouse ~ Transmitting your Light. The modules run for twelve weeks each. In the last session of the module, participants are provided with a Putting it All Together (PAT) packet, which is designed to help integrate the discoveries, processes, and practices gained throughout the program and apply them as an ongoing daily practice.

I introduce the "stages of change" in Module I, and we explore it throughout the program, as it is a core component. Though I developed The Lighthouse Effect as a second-stage-recovery group process, I came to see that it could be more than that, that it *is* more than that. It serves as a road map for people in recovery who aspire to become recovery coaches, while enhancing their ability to maintain recovery and heal childhood wounds and negative core beliefs. The Lighthouse Effect Skillful Recovery Program could also be highly beneficial to those working in trauma and addiction (any form of addiction, including gambling, eating disorders, and sex) and to the broader community of the wellness field, as it can provide a pathway for healing into wholeness. It is really a template for unveiling our Authentic Self, reclaiming our power, and healing from the inside out.

Each of the modules in the program is meant to be experienced on its own merit *and* to be part of an evolving, integrative, and even circular process, as all of what we learn and practice in one module gets reinforced in the next module, and the next, and the next, rather like weaving a tapestry. We are weaving together all aspects of the self (mind, body, and spirit) to embody and embrace our unique and divine nature within the human experience. When we learn any new material, we first need to understand it and we all have different ways of learning, which is why I support the written content in the book with a series of videos that you can view or download on my website (innerfaiththerapy.com). You can watch a group move through a condensed version of the program in a month-long (four weekends) workshop that includes each of the modules. (See the template on my website for condensing the program into workshops.) There are also videos and audio recordings of meditations, exercises, and self-care practices.

While the program is designed as a group process, I invite each participant to focus on their own journey: *You are the best person and ultimately the only person who can do what is required on your courageous journey from addiction into recovery.* I also often point out to participants that if we got "really good" at our addiction, then we have the potential to be really good at developing healthier ways of coping. We have the ability to reclaim our power and come home to our Authentic Self.

I cannot say enough about the power of self-reflection for supporting self-care, self-respect, and self-acceptance and I always encourage participants to keep a journal. It helps in committing to a daily practice, and provides essential self-validation: *When you put your thoughts and feelings on paper, you are "seen" by the most important person in your journey--you!*

As the Lighthouse Effect is about coming into vertical alignment, I also encourage participants in the program to engage in a spiritual practice (meditation, prayer, yoga, or qigong, for example) to develop a connection with their higher power, spirit, God of their understanding--whatever resonates with them or their belief system. This program is designed to be inclusive, and in that sense, it works well with other recovery programs, such as Twelve Step or Refuge Recovery, the latter of which is based on the core tenets of Buddhism.

Moving Through Modules & Sessions

Provide participants with The Lighthouse Effect Skillful Recovery Program Group Rules at the onset of every module and review the rules together. It is essential for creating a safe container and trust within the group, with confidentiality being a priority. In the spirit of an open-door policy, with no discrimination and no exclusion, I designed the program to be iterative and circular or cyclical, so a new participant can join the group at any time during the year-long program. And if you are running a group in a facility, you may very well have participants coming and going for various reasons, such as court mandates.

Thus, I encourage you to review group rules at the start of every module and *at any point* when a new member joins, in order to foster group cohesion. You want to provide the group with an opportunity to address concerns they might have about the change to the group dynamic. I encourage having a conversation with the new person *before* introducing them to the group, to prepare them for the group dynamic and bring them up to speed about the program. There may be participants who will not engage in the full year-long program, but I would strongly encourage them to commit to moving through the entire module they have entered.

As you move through a given module, you might review or refer back to content from previous modules if you assess that it would benefit your group. Essentially, you can facilitate the integration of content and skills as you go, using your intuition, and with careful attendance to the group dynamic.

I also provide a syllabus at the onset of each module, outlining what will be covered in each of the twelve sessions of that module. (They are one-and-a-half hour sessions.) The syllabi serve as guideposts or buoys, providing a malleable, soft trajectory for moving through the modules. I encourage you to use your own intuition as the facilitator to mindfully attend to the collective needs of the group, and focus each session on the skills, exercises, role-plays, and so on that best meet those needs. I include homework suggestions, but use your intuition here too, and offer homework to support what was covered with the group; it might simply be to practice the skill or skills that were introduced, or it could be a journal prompt or worksheet exercise.

Guided Meditations: You'll see that I provide a suggested opening meditation and suggested closing meditation for each session. The meditations are designed to underscore the skills, exercises, and concepts presented in each session and throughout the module to help reinforce them on a deeper level. (You can find a complete set of meditations on my website.)

These are meant to be guided meditations with you, the facilitator, speaking in a calm, soothing tone of voice. I also use a singing bowl or chime at the open and close of each meditation, and each session. It helps to set the tone and models the importance of developing a daily mindfulness practice using the skills we are learning. It is a gentle way of bringing our attention to the center of our being and to the present moment: We are vibrational beings and sounds resonate within us and attune to our energy field.

Check-Ins & Q&A: At the onset of each session, we do a group check-in and a Q&A. (In a one-and-a-half-hour session, this would take a total of twenty to thirty minutes.) During the check-in round, each person takes a moment to talk about what is currently happening in their lives and what is of importance to them. The check-ins can take on a life of their own, which can be good for group cohesiveness and for getting participants fully engaged. When events occurring in real time in their lives are relevant to the theme or content of the session, they are all the more motivated to apply the skills and do role-playing exercises to help them overcome those challenges. However, I recommend that you ask someone in the group to act as a timekeeper, to keep each person's check-in to two minutes or less. If a participant has a tendency to take up more check-in time, it might be an indication that they need more individual support.

The Q&A provides an opportunity for participants to ask questions about the previous session's homework or about other aspects of the program, concepts, or skills that have been introduced--before moving on to new material.

Whiteboard: I encourage using a whiteboard at every session to underscore concepts and engage participants in group exercises. It helps to make the *conceptual* more *experiential*, supporting and reflecting back participants' insights in "real time."

Encouraging Peer Leadership: As a facilitator, it is important to invite each participant to share their wisdom and their lived experiences, with your discretion and within the bounds of your agency. It is empowering for each participant to have the opportunity to be a peer leader, where they model aspects of recovery. Peer leadership benefits everyone in the group, helping all participants to appreciate their own value and worth as an integral part of the group experience. (Hence, the popularity of peer-driven recovery groups in the recovery field.)

Handouts & Resources: I provide you with a complete set of handouts for each module at the end of the module. (You can download worksheets and handouts on my website: innerfaiththerapy.com.) You will see that some of the handouts and worksheets appear as content in that module when they are primary components or skills of the session that are to be addressed in real time with the group. But again, the thinking behind the program is that it is meant to be iterative and intuitive, so as you move through a module, you might discuss any concept, handout, or worksheet with your group as the need or interest arises in the moment. I also provide recommendations for websites, books, audio recordings, and videos in the resources section.

—

Repeat Handouts: At the onset of *every* module, the group receives the following "repeat handouts." (They are provided at the back of the book, and can be downloaded from innerfaiththerapy.com.) Participants also complete a Stages of Change Addiction/Recovery Pros & Cons Worksheet twice during each module, in the first or second session, and again, in the eleventh session.

The Lighthouse Effect Group Rules
Stages of Change: Metamorphosis from Survival to Revival Lifestyle
Stages of Change Addiction/Recovery Pros & Cons Worksheet
The Role of an Accountability Partner & How to Give Constructive Feedback
Relapse Prevention Plan Worksheet
*Post-Acute Withdrawal Syndrome (PAWS) Self-Assessment
*How to Manage Emotional Denial

*If there are new members in the group, they also get the PAWS Self-Assessment and How to Manage Denial handouts. It's a good idea to keep extra copies of both of these on hand, as it may benefit participants to review them again. I also encourage participants to bring the PAWS and Denial handouts to their therapist or others in their recovery network, to provide for more focused work. In general, use your discretion regarding what handouts that would be appropriate, based on your individual assessment of each group member.

Whether you are meeting in person or are working remotely and engaging with your group by an online meeting forum, all of the handouts are available to download from innerfaiththerapy.com as PDFs to be printed or shared electronically.

TIPS: Look for helpful tips as you move through each module of the program. For example, my first "TIP" would be to provide each participant in your group with a folder with pockets on the inside covers, where they can keep all of the handouts and diagrams provided throughout the program.

Suggested Homework: I provide suggested homework at the close of each session. It's based on the content, concepts, and exercises presented in that session, but I do encourage using your intuition and professional instincts about the direction a session needs to go. So if the suggested homework doesn't quite line up with what actually occurred during the session with your group, improvise! That said, where the homework is to complete a new Stages of Change Addiction/Recovery Pros & Cons Worksheet, it will benefit you and your group to follow that direction, as it is important that each participant track their progress through the worksheets, which they complete twice in each module.

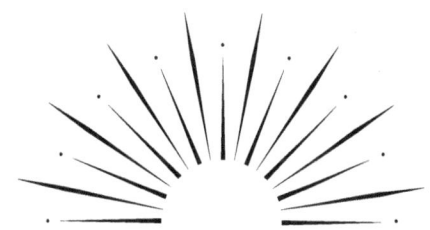

THE LIGHTHOUSE EFFECT
SKILLFUL RECOVERY PROGRAM MODULES

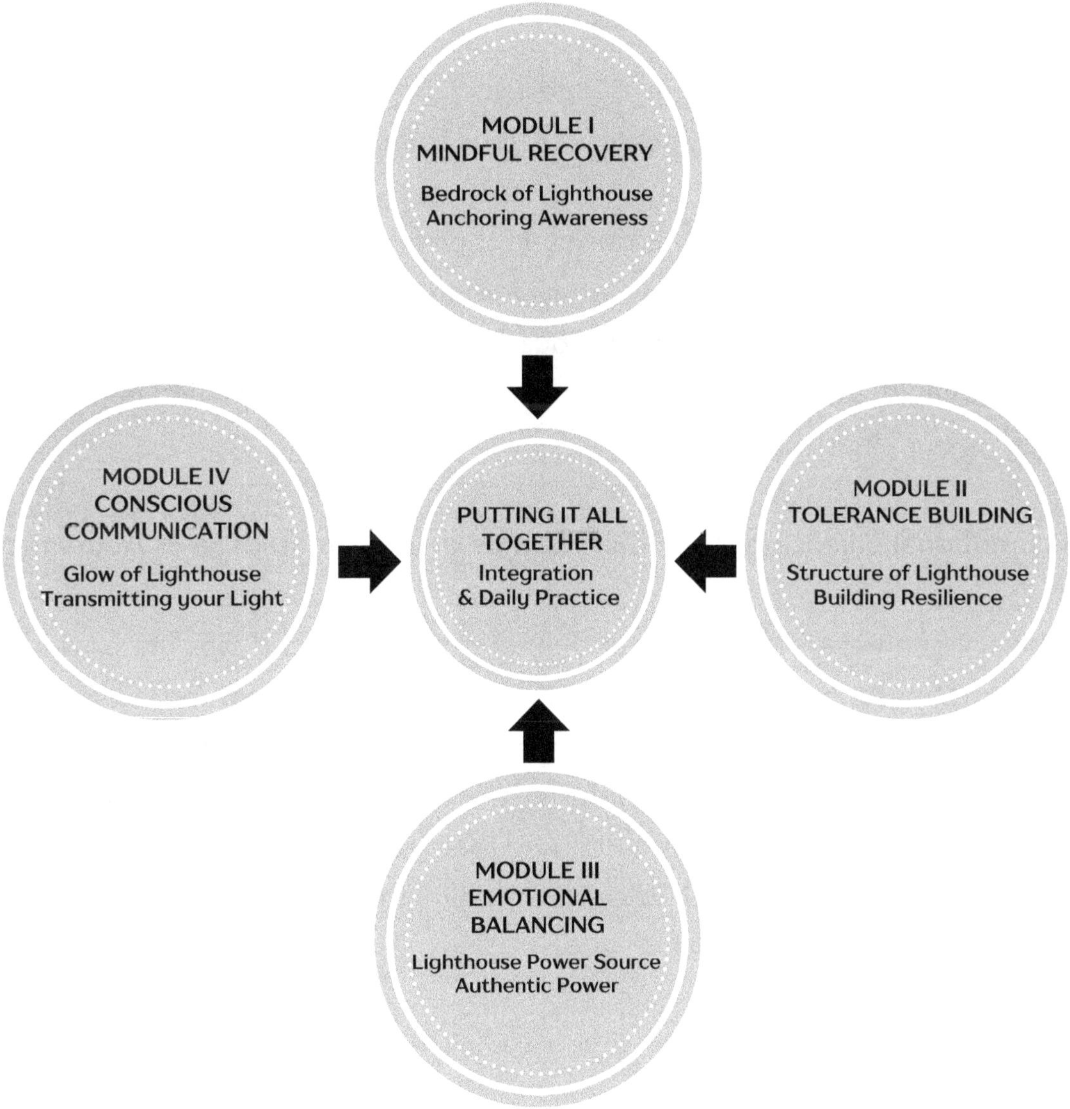

MODULE I
MINDFUL RECOVERY

Bedrock of Lighthouse
Anchoring Awareness

MODULE IV
CONSCIOUS
COMMUNICATION

Glow of Lighthouse
Transmitting your Light

PUTTING IT ALL
TOGETHER

Integration
& Daily Practice

MODULE II
TOLERANCE BUILDING

Structure of Lighthouse
Building Resilience

MODULE III
EMOTIONAL
BALANCING

Lighthouse Power Source
Authentic Power

11

SUMMARY OF MODULES

Module I Mindful Recovery: The Bedrock of your Lighthouse ~ Anchoring Awareness

Mindfulness or presence practice is the core component of the program. It is essential to our ability to come into awareness, be in the moment, and step back from our addiction, dependency, or attachment in order to make conscious choices in support of our wellbeing. It is about bringing the mind into focused attendance, so that we have firm ground upon which we can build our lighthouse.

Module II Tolerance Building: The Structure of your Lighthouse ~ Developing Resilience

The second module has to do with the brick and mortar of the lighthouse. It's about gaining skills and practices to build tolerance to whatever internal resistance and barriers we might face in our recovery journey. It's where the puzzle pieces start fitting together, with "radical acceptance of what is" as the core component. It is where the heavy lifting happens, building the "muscles" of our inner core.

Module III Emotional Balancing: The Power Source of your Lighthouse ~ Authentic Power

Our emotions, when we are grounded and emotionally balanced, are the power source of our internal lighthouse. It's about building on the skills we've learned while adding new techniques and practices for approaching our emotions with compassion and understanding in order to be fully in our hearts and in control of our emotional system. Developing a deeper understanding of the power of our emotions and their purpose and function in our daily lives helps to bring us into alignment with Wise Mind, what I think of as "heart-mind coherence."

Module IV Conscious Communication:
The Visible Shine of your Lighthouse ~ Transmitting your Light

This module is about radiating and expressing our Authentic Self, both verbally and nonverbally. While we are sovereign beings, we are also interconnected and need each other to thrive. This module is about learning to be *inter*dependent instead of *co*dependent. It's about standing in our truth, and not losing ourselves in relation to others. When we have a healthy relationship with the self, we don't need validation from anyone else; we radiate our own light and can be fully conscious and loving in our relationships. It's about holding our own value and worth, while simultaneously honoring the value and worth of the other person. *By radiating our light, we move out of survival and into revival.*

Graduation & "Putting it All Together" (PAT):
Embodying the Lighthouse Effect ~ Self-Mastery

Along with their graduation certificates, at the final session of the program I provide participants with the "Putting It All Together" (PAT) Packet. In recognition of the commitments they made and skills they've gained and to encourage integrating them into their daily lives, it provides additional inspirational handouts and worksheets that encourage and support integrating the Lighthouse Effect as a daily practice and lifestyle.

The PAT Packet also references *Bookending Your Day: The Lighthouse Effect Self-Care 30-Day Challenge* workbook, and encourages taking the thirty-day challenge as a follow-up to the program. It is about beginning, moving through, and ending our day with mindfulness in order to ground ourselves in our daily experience and foster mind-body-spirit alignment. It underscores the power of keeping a journal to support us in our self-care journey. I created the workbook for that reason. The thirty-day time frame is important, as it takes two to four weeks for the brain to disconnect the neural network of old patterns and create new neural pathways. (You can order *Bookending Your Day* from my website, Amazon, and other online booksellers.)

I always offer this encouragement to group participants at the onset of the program, and you are welcome to use it: *Your return on this investment is getting your life back on track. As the AA encouragement goes, "I will believe in you until you can believe in yourself." Come with me as we move through this journey together! It's about practice not perfection!*

MODULE I MINDFUL RECOVERY:

THE BEDROCK OF YOUR LIGHTHOUSE ~ ANCHORING AWARENESS

Where are you?
"Here."

What time is it?
"Now."

What are you?
"This Moment."

-- Dan Millman, *Way of the Peaceful Warrior*

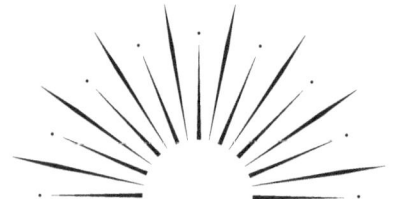

THE LIGHTHOUSE EFFECT MODULE I SYLLABUS
Mindful Recovery: The Bedrock of Your Lighthouse ∽ Anchoring Awareness

Session #1 Welcome & Introduction: Group Rules, Confidentiality, Building Group Cohesion; Developing Mindfulness Practice; Introducing Stages of Recovery; Group Exercise ∽ Stages of Recovery

Session #2 Stages of Change (SOC): The Lighthouse Effect Stages of Change Metamorphosis from Survival to Revival Lifestyle; Group Exercise ∽ SOC Pros & Cons Worksheet

Session #3 Anchoring and Following the Breath: Coping Skills for Strengthening the Foundation of your Lighthouse; Group Exercise ∽ Anchoring the Mind, Body, and Spirit

Session #4 Developing Observer Self: Coming back into Alignment (nonjudgment practice); Group Exercise ∽ Observer Self Perspective

Session #5 Understanding Mind States: Understanding the interplay between Mind States (Rational Mind, Emotional Mind, Wise Mind); Keeping a Daily Journal; Group Exercise ∽ Mind State Traits

Session #6 Dialectical Behavior Therapy ∽ The Interplay of Opposing Views: Understanding the Concept of Both/And; Dialectics & The Human Condition Model; Group Exercise ∽ Understanding Dialectics (demonstrate & engage by using participants' own experiences)

Session #7 The Art of Acceptance: The Serenity Prayer; Group Exercise ∽ Decoding The Serenity Prayer

Session #8 What & How Skills: What & How questions versus Why questions (taking a nonjudgmental stance); Group Exercise ∽ What & How Skills (Observe, Describe, Participate, One-Mindfully)

Session #9 Attachment to Detachment: Attachment versus Detachment/Nonattachment; Urge Surfing; Group Exercise ∽ Zoom Out (using camera-lens analogy to demonstrate the art of stepping back)

Session #10 Movement Meditation: Body-Movement Meditation Practices (Qigong); Group Exercise ∽ LaQi Power to Heal

Session #11 Stages of Change Reflection & Progress: Charting "mindful recovery" progress over the course of the module; Group Exercise ∽ Stages of Change Review, Repeat, Reflect

Session #12 Closing Ceremony & Graduation: Certificates of Completion; Appreciation/Gratitude Circle; Invite group to continue on to the next module (Tolerance Building)

Module I (Mindful Recovery) Session 1:
Developing Mindfulness Practice & Introducing Stages of Recovery

In bookending each session with a short meditation, the idea is to set the tone for the session, and also to help participants embody the skills and practices they are learning. Be sure to speak slowly and mindfully, and with a soothing, calm tone of voice. As mindfulness is the anchor of the Lighthouse Effect Program, I open the first session with the Anchoring Awareness Meditation.

Suggested Opening Meditation ~ Anchoring Awareness Meditation

Get into a comfortable position, and close your eyes or lower your gaze. (Sound chime or toning bowl.) Take three long, slow, deep breaths, allowing your entire respiratory system to gently fill and then slowly and fully empty. Take another deep breath; focus your attention on the question, *Where are you*? As you exhale, consider the answer: *here*. Inhale, breathing the felt sense of the word *here* all the way through your body. Exhale, allowing yourself to be here, fully present. Take another deep breath; focus your attention on the question, *What time is it*? Don't look for the answer from a place outside of you. As you exhale, consider the answer: *now*. Breathe deeply into the felt sense of the word *now*. Allow yourself to be here, now, fully present. Feel the emerging awareness from within. Take another deep inhalation; focus your attention on the question, *What are you*? As you exhale, consider the answer: *this moment*. Breathe fully into the felt sense of you as *this moment*. Allow yourself to be *here, now, this moment*, fully present. Take one more full inhalation as you anchor yourself fully in this gift of presence that is you, and slowly exhale, releasing all resistance. (Sound chime.) Slowly open your eyes. Carry this feeling of being anchored *here, now, this moment* throughout your day.

Check-Ins and Q&A: Facilitate a brief check-in round, where you invite participants introduce themselves in order to create group cohesion. Encourage participants to keep check-ins brief, two minutes, tops. You might want to appoint a timekeeper, especially as sessions progress and new content and concepts are introduced. Allow time for group members to ask questions, express concerns, and share reflections, and then introduce group rules to create a safe container for the entire module.

Repeat Handouts: Group Rules, Stages of Change Model, Stages of Change Addiction/Recovery Pros & Cons Worksheet, Stages of Change: Metamorphosis from Survival to Revival Lifestyle, The Role of an Accountability Partner & How to Give Constructive Feedback Relapse Prevention Plan Worksheet, PAWS Self-Assessment, How to Manage Emotional Denial Evaluation

Handouts: Module I Syllabus, Stages of Recovery Model, Victim (Inverted) Triangle Model, Higher Power (Upright) Triangle Model

Mindfulness Practice

Mindfulness practice is one of the most powerful and effective tools for healing and moving toward wholeness--from any addiction, unhealthy habit, or psychological programming. It is the foundational practice for all of the modules in The Lighthouse Effect Skillful Recovery Program. I equate it to being the bedrock of our lighthouse, as it is the practice upon which we build other skills and practices in order to come into alignment, mind, body, and spirit, and heal into wholeness. I think of mindfulness as consciously focusing the mind on our sensory perception in a given moment--felt-sense, smell, taste, sight, and sound--in order to center and anchor ourselves. It is focused attendance to the present moment in the present context, and it can be done with eyes closed or open. We can practice mindfulness washing the dishes, folding clothes, or attentively listening to another person. We can even practice mindfulness while driving our car, as it is extremely important to *be* driving the car and not thinking about what we are going to do when we arrive at our destination. It is about attending to the present moment without judgment, interpretation, or commentary.

Through mindfulness, we develop the skill of observing and to step into our "Observer Self," where we can witness or "be with" whatever arises in a given moment, without judgement. We can do this by stimulating any of our senses, including our sixth sense. We might think of our sixth sense as our intuition or intuitive knowing--the vibrational connection we have with the nonphysical. It is one of the components of the self that we lose when we are not in alignment, when we are not "whole." But when we come into mindful presence, when we are present in the moment and activating all senses, we have access to everything we need (both physical and nonphysical) to return to wholeness.

In any recovery process, there is potential to lapse back into maladaptive but familiar ways of coping. These patterns, which are hardwired in the brain, are the essence of addiction. Mindfulness practice is essential to managing this potential and for moving out of a relapse, if it happens. Once we recognize the automatic reactive patterns that unconsciously lead to relapse, we can make conscious choices to move forward. Mindfulness practice is also an effective intervention for mind chatter or "monkey mind." The mind is easily seduced into ruminating about the past or projecting into the future, both of which can cause emotional instability and imbalance. Mind chatter is a driving force of our moods, feelings, and emotions, and thus, in determining reactions and behavioral patterns. "*E-motion* is energy in motion," as the maxim goes.

Disciplining and quieting the mind allows for emotional stability and fosters inner strength. Western medicine sees emotional conditions such as anxiety and depression as the problems, thus, treatment, rather than prevention, is the point of focus. I take an integrative approach to health and healing and draw from the best of both disciplines. As I noted earlier, I see such conditions as symptoms or what I think of as "indicator lights" that are calling us to take a deeper look at the underlying narratives and beliefs.

Clients will often begin a session lamenting about how they want help "getting rid" of their anxiety or depression, without understanding the underlying cause of those symptoms. But again, the symptoms are a call to *attend* to the inner self with loving kindness and compassion, rather than medicating, avoiding, or judging ourselves. Our mind states are consequences of our mind's experiences of traumatic memories and/or of our mind projecting a re-traumatization into an imagined future outcome. Our state of mind either sedates the central nervous system or it over-stimulates and triggers it. The grounding and centering effect of mindfulness practice helps to stabilize the emotional system. As another wellbeing maxim suggests, "where attention goes, energy flows."

Introducing Stages of Recovery ~ One Stage at a Time

The notion that there are three stages of recovery, introduced by Dr. Judith Herman in her 1992 book *Trauma and Recovery*, has become entrenched in the recovery field. I was introduced to the stages of recovery when I was working with Jacquelyn Small at Eupsychia Institute. Essentially, there are three levels of readiness or tolerance an individual moves through to come into recovery from major life transitions, especially regarding an addiction or behavioral pattern. Jacquelyn takes it further, bringing in soul psychology, dynamic group "shadow work," and inner work as essential components in the healing process.

My personal psychotherapist and mentor, Margaret O'Connor, taught me the critical importance of self-assessment, how people need to assess their own readiness to move from one stage to the next in their recovery and to look to mind-body-spirit integration as essential to that process. She taught me the value of going within to allow the body and mind (creative imagination) to work in concert to reveal the source of our trauma and programming and empower us to change. I can't emphasize enough with my clients and my group that it doesn't work to try to cut corners and bypass the inner work. Jacquelyn Small refers to this as "Spiritual Bypass," a phenomenon where the person avoids the pain as a way of coping, rather than facing and feeling through the pain, with support.

The body will let us know if we are moving too fast; the key is to deeply listen and allow the healing process to happen naturally. Recovery is not a competition, it's a process of acceptance and integration for healing all aspects of the self. It needs our utmost respect, care, and patience. It's about self-awareness and gaining self-mastery of skills and practices that support the recovery process. It's also about shining a light on the dark shadows of neglect and repression in order to heal what was never seen or heard. This healing process is essential to becoming whole, to coming home to our Authentic Self, to shine our unique expression of light, love, and truth, as only we can.

First Stage Recovery: In first stage recovery, we abstain from the addictive substance, behavior, or attachment and begin to understand that it is a coping mechanism for surviving childhood dynamics and programming, trauma, and so on. We can support our abstinence by learning intervention skills that foster healthier ways of coping and by building a recovery support system and network.

Second Stage Recovery: In second stage recovery, we are maintaining abstinence and practicing the recovery and mindfulness skills we've learned, such as DBT, Observer Self, and Radical Acceptance. As we become more mentally and emotionally stable, we naturally choose long-term wellness rather than the short-term relief of substances and/or maladaptive behaviors. We are willing to commit to doing the inner work because we have become acutely aware that it is essential to us experiencing inner peace. We understand that it's an "inside job!"

Third Stage Recovery: In third stage recovery, we are achieving self-mastery in mind-body-spirit integration, building inner strength, and experiencing self-empowerment. Being mindful and alert to life's unexpected challenges, we continue to practice inner work, to be vigilant, and to not become complacent. We are radiating our Authentic Self: This is "the Lighthouse Effect." My own practice, which I share with my group, is to also remain humble and accountable and to continuously effort to "radically accept" life on life's terms.

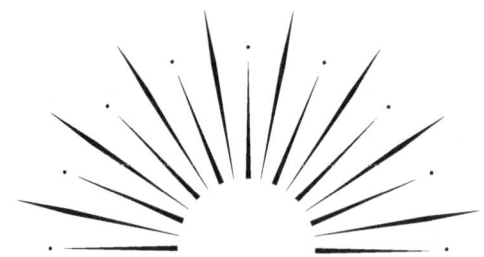

THE LIGHTHOUSE EFFECT STAGES OF RECOVERY MODEL

THIRD STAGE RECOVERY

**Ego & Soul Integration
The "Lighthouse Effect"**

THIRD STAGE

- Self-mastery & mind, body, spirit integration
- Inner strength & self-empowerment
- Radiating the Authentic Self

SECOND STAGE RECOVERY

**Maintaining Abstinence
Practicing Skills**

FIRST STAGE RECOVERY

**Abstinence
Harm Reduction**

SECOND STAGE

- Deprogramming negative core beliefs
- Maintaining abstinence or harm reduction and practicing recovery and mindfulness skills daily
- Choosing long-term wellness over short-term relief

FIRST STAGE

- Abstaining from addictive substance, behavior, or attachment
- Recognizing it as a coping mechanism for surviving childhood dynamics, trauma, and life
- Building a recovery support system and network, learning tools, and applying healthier ways of coping—ongoing

Group Exercise ~ Stages of Recovery

Use your whiteboard to draw the Stages of Recovery Model, and then ask participants to offer examples from their own lives and experiences.

Deepening our Understanding of Stages of Recovery

It's essential for us to understand that transitions between stages are bound to be imbued with some level of ambivalence and uncertainty, and thus can be confusing and even chaotic. We might view these transitions as *bridges*, which means we can go back and forth between stages. We might be transitioning to the next stage or already be in it, and could still take an occasional step backward. Perhaps some inner, vulnerable, child self gets pulled back, while another part, the emerging, wiser Authentic Self, has a foot in the next stage. From that perspective, our wiser self is able to acknowledge and accept our child self, and can lead us to a healthier way forward, that being the next stage. Such is the process of healing and integration.

First Stage Recovery

First Stage is the most challenging in terms of any addiction, whether drugs, alcohol, nicotine, sugar/carbs, love/sex, gambling, codependency, work, or whatever it might be. To begin the process of recovery, we need to be honest with ourselves and acknowledge that we have unconsciously given our power away to the substance, attachment, or pattern of behavior that has been encoded in the brain. It is up to us (with the support of our recovery network) to reclaim that power. Awareness is the first step, followed by accountability, which means being responsible for our decisions and actions.

Second Stage Recovery

Second Stage has more to do with *process,* with the development and practice of skills that support abstinence and healing. It can occur simultaneously with first stage recovery, which can be both beneficial and potentially more confusing. Thus, it is all the more important to have a sponsor, recovery coach, or accountability partner to hold us accountable to our recovery plan, which we can create using the Relapse Prevention Worksheet. The mind-body complex needs to heal one day at a time and one step at a time, with our body guiding the way. The body is like a barometer, especially when there is a trauma history, yet symptoms can easily be misinterpreted, amplified, or ignored, which is why grounding ourselves through daily mindfulness practice is essential.

This stage of recovery is about listening to our bodies and paying attention to our symptoms (indicator lights) and then engaging in a process of self-inquiry to assess the narrative our mind is running or broadcasting. I liken the mind chatter that feeds our negative narratives to an internal reporter who lives for drama and is incessantly broadcasting our fear-based ticker tape. The challenge is to step back, question the instigator (broadcaster), and think critically about the story it is telling. When we think of anxiety, depression, addiction, and so on as indicator lights, we can approach them with understanding and acceptance, rather than throwing them under the bus and finding ways to neglect, hide, or silence them. The key is to learn and apply interventions to interrupt these automatic, negative narratives and, ultimately, the underlying core beliefs that are feeding them.

Second stage recovery is about creating a safe space where these core beliefs or secrets can be aired, integrated, and released in the presence of love. It is a process of *uncovering* and *discovering*--of getting to the root of why we became vulnerable to addiction, dependency, or attachment in the first place--one stage at a time. As I expressed previously, we are *all* recovering from something and we could all benefit by being on a path of healing into wholeness. In this stage, we deepen our mindfulness practice to customize a recovery and healing path that works best for us. What I have come to understand, and what much of The Lighthouse Effect program emphasizes, is how deeply we are influenced by our experiences in our family of origin and the roles we played within them.

Lynne Forrest, who I've mentioned was a mentor for me, underscored the importance of doing deep inner work in any healing journey in order to explore, reveal, and bring to light negative core beliefs. As we heal and transform them, we rise out of the "victim consciousness" programming that came from our early experiences in our families of origin. We delve more deeply into victim consciousness in Module II (Tolerance Building), but I introduce the Victim (Inverted) Triangle Model here, in this session of Module I.

It helps to provide context for how early programming in our families of origin and the roles we take on in them play out in our adult lives, which is highly relevant to the second stage recovery process. Many of us do not grow up with the idea of a "higher power" existing within us; we've been taught that any such power is "up there," away and separate from us. So introducing the concept of our Authentic Self, our internal higher power, at this early point in the program helps participants to see the path forward and out of victim consciousness.

We need to understand that Victim Triangle and Higher Power Triangle perspectives and dynamics are always in flux and mutable; we go back and forth between them. We will also look at victim consciousness further along in the program in terms of relationship dynamics and how the predominant role that played out in our family of origin will show up in our relationships throughout our life.

THE LIGHTHOUSE EFFECT
Victim (Inverted) Triangle ~ Victim Consciousness

A state of mind, an archetype (pattern of behavior)
in a lower state of consciousness

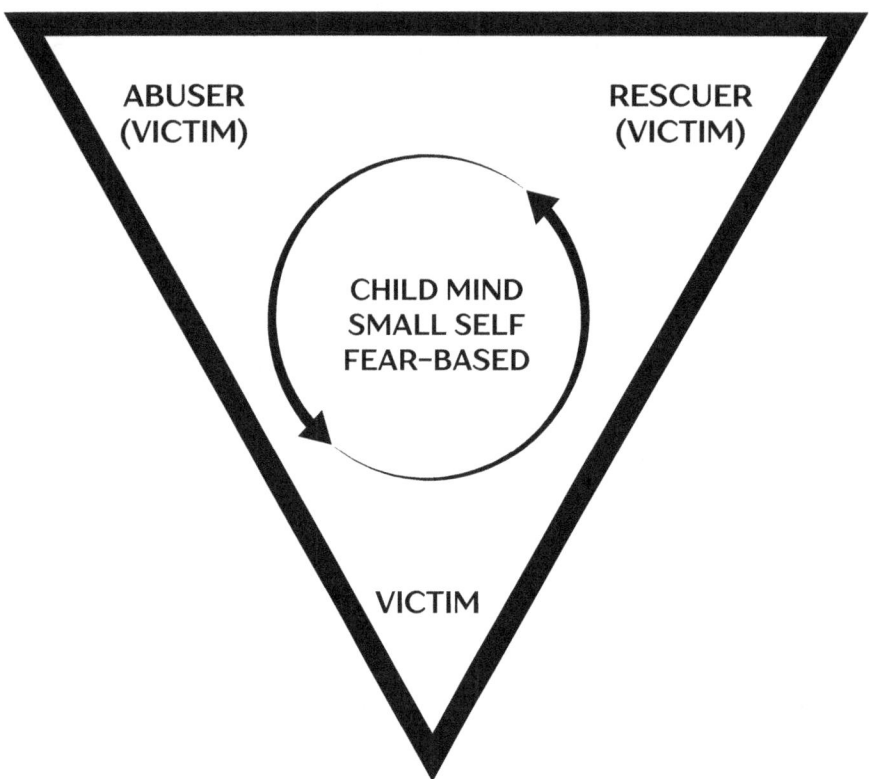

This is the human condition, the dynamics we are born into: We are born upside down and move through the world to become righted. We may be habitually drawn to one role, perspective, or dynamic, depending on our childhood programming. It is through the integration of the ego and the soul that we move into wholeness to become our higher selves, our authentic selves.

THE LIGHTHOUSE EFFECT
Higher Power (Upright) Triangle ～ Ego/Soul Integration

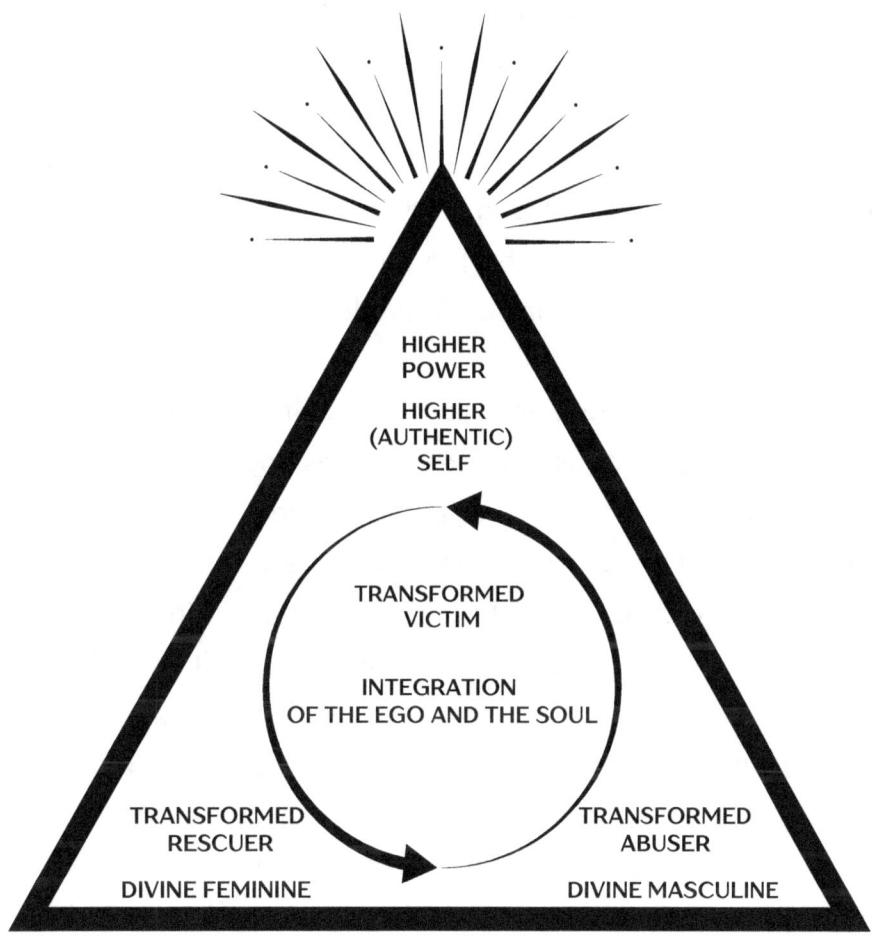

HIGHER POWER

HIGHER (AUTHENTIC) SELF

TRANSFORMED VICTIM

INTEGRATION OF THE EGO AND THE SOUL

TRANSFORMED RESCUER

TRANSFORMED ABUSER

DIVINE FEMININE

DIVINE MASCULINE

Divine feminine and divine masculine are not gender-based, but rather spiritual qualities that anyone of any gender might possess. In the process of moving from survival to revival, through daily mindfulness practice and application of intervention skills, the "victim" is transformed and the ego and the soul become integrated.

Third Stage Recovery

Third Stage is about self-mastery: It is mastery of the self (mind, body, and spirit) with self-reflection, accountability, and self-empowerment as ongoing practices. It is about the integration of the ego and the soul. It is about learning to trust whatever happens. This is where we hone our ability to center and ground ourselves in order to meet whatever arises in a given moment with understanding and "radical acceptance." (Radical Acceptance is a DBT practice introduced a little further along in Module I and we explore it more deeply in Module II, as it is the core component for building tolerance.)

In third stage recovery, we continuously adapt our mindfulness practice, as our consciousness expands and our awareness grows. It is a process of revisiting and cycling back through what we learned in our first and second stages of recovery, and applying the various skills and interventions in our toolkit to reclaim our power and release our dependency from anything or anyone outside of ourselves. It is the continued practice of calling ourselves back to center from whatever might be trying to lure us into thinking we need it, in order to carry on.

We do so by stepping into the stance of Observer Self, serving as a witness to our own thoughts and mindfully choosing to reject the quick fix or temporary relief we might gain from an addictive substance or pattern of behavior. This isn't a "one and done" deal. It is a lifelong practice and sacred commitment to personal and spiritual growth. We naturally cycle through reactive patterns, behaviors, and narratives. So, while The Lighthouse Effect program focuses on second stage recovery, first and third stage elements and skills are woven throughout. I see it as a process of human evolution, a process of "be-coming" and "re-membering" toward integrating all parts of our Authentic Self.

Suggested Closing Meditation ~ Basic Mindfulness Meditation

Get into a comfortable position, and close your eyes or lower your gaze. (Sound chime or toning bowl.) Take three long, slow, deep breaths. With each inhalation, follow the cool air up through your nostrils and down into your lungs. Feel your breath expanding fully into the abdomen, and all the way through to your back. Now, slowly exhale through your mouth, completely emptying your lungs; notice the muscles softening in your shoulders, jaw, face, and back. With each exhalation, follow the softening of each muscle group down through your entire body. Continue to inhale and exhale, extending the breath each time, noticing how your body softens even more with each elongated exhalation. Notice how the movement of the breath gently rocks your body. Breathe in, breathe out; breathe in, breathe out; breathe in, breathe out. (Sound chime to bring the group to presence.) Slowly open your eyes and come back into presence. Allow yourself to carry this deep relaxation of your body throughout your day.

Suggested Homework: Reflect on the Victim Triangle Model and write in your journal about what role you predominantly play in your family of origin and in your circle of friends. Reflect on how it is part of the human condition to move between the three points on this triangle, which we all do, depending on the relationship dynamic. Notice what role you play in different situations and relationships.

Under what circumstances do you tend to be a Rescuer, an Abuser, a Victim? Under what circumstances do you switch from one to the other? You might tend to be aggressive (Abuser) with a person who is younger than you, yet with a person of authority you might be more shy or timid (Victim). Be prepared to share your reflections and deepen your understanding about this conceptualization of the human condition at the next session.

Module I (Mindful Recovery) Session 2:
Cycles of Addiction and Recovery & Introducing Stages of Change

Suggested Opening Meditation ~ The Five Senses Meditation

Get into a comfortable position, and close your eyes or lower your gaze. (Sound chime or toning bowl.) Take three long, slow, deep breaths to bring your attention inward. Now, as you slowly inhale, and slowly exhale, notice what you smell and continue to focus on your sense of smell as you breathe deeply. Now, bring your attention to your salivary glands; notice any taste sensations. Continue to breathe deeply, breathe in and breathe out, without judgment or commentary, focusing on any hint of taste. Move on to what you "see" behind your eyelids; notice shapes, colors, patterns, symbols, as you continue to slowly inhale and exhale. Now, as you continue to breathe deeply, move your attention to what you hear, in the room or outside of the room. Listen to the sound of your own breathing, hear the air moving in through your nose, and out through your mouth.

Continue to breathe slowly and deeply, as you move your attention to what you feel. Bring your attention back to the function of the breath. Breathe in through the nose, noticing how the breath feels as it moves down into your lungs. Feel the expansion of your diaphragm and allow your lungs to fill completely. Now, exhale, slowly and gently, following and feeling the sensation of the outflow of breath through your mouth. Feel into the deep peace of the breath. (Sound chime.) Slowly open your eyes and return to presence. Carry this felt sense of deep peace and relaxation throughout your day.

Check-Ins and Q&A: Encourage group participants to keep check-ins brief and concise in order to have time to introduce new content. Take clarifying questions about the Stages of Recovery and any other content from the previous session.

Handouts: Cycles of Addiction & Recovery Models

Regarding Addiction

When I speak about addiction, I include substance, behavioral, and spiritual aspects of addiction. I don't see these as separate or unrelated; all addictions have physical, mental, emotional, and spiritual impact. Whether the addiction or dependency is to alcohol or an unhealthy relationship, it impacts the brain and the central nervous system, creating and/or reinforcing reactive patterns, obsessions, or compulsions. I believe that all addictions are symptoms, pointing to negative core beliefs from our early-childhood programming and social conditioning. Addictions are coping mechanisms for managing trauma, whether mild or severe, and are fear-based at their core. And just as we might experience transgenerational trauma, we can inherit transgenerational ways of *coping* with trauma. The first step toward stopping the pattern is coming into awareness; the second, having the willingness to change; and the third, following through by learning and applying intervention skills as daily practices, with, I can't emphasize enough, a support system and network.

How Care Energy Flows

In learning to address conflict skillfully and gracefully, without fear of being judged or rejected, we can even come to see challenges as opportunities for honing our skills. To be fully sovereign, respectful, and kind to the self is a choice, and one that is essential to creating and maintaining supportive and healthy relationships with others. When we take care of ourselves, our care energy flows to those around us. In third stage recovery, we deepen our understanding of the law of attraction and the *law of allowing*, which is about raising our energy frequency or vibration to gain a higher, wider perspective and come into alignment, mind, body, and spirit.

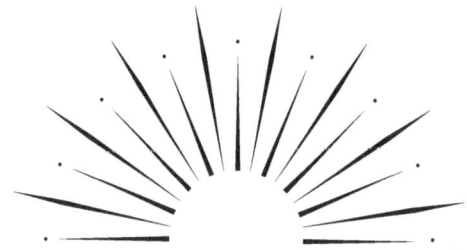

THE LIGHTHOUSE EFFECT CYCLE OF ADDICTION MODEL

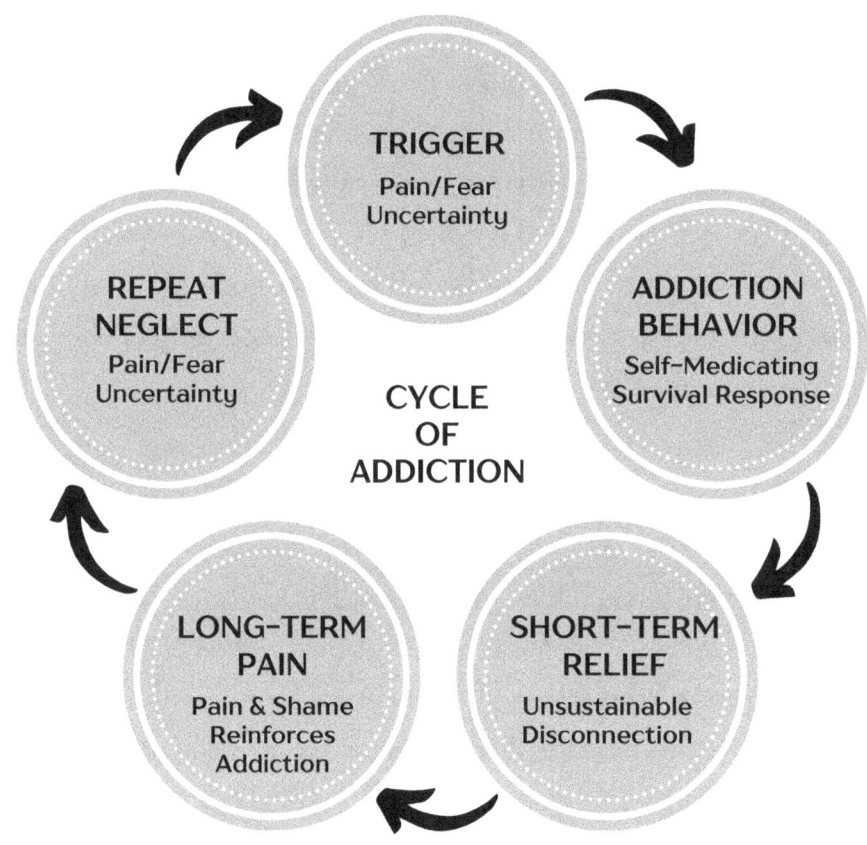

TRIGGER
Pain/Fear
Uncertainty

ADDICTION BEHAVIOR
Self-Medicating
Survival Response

SHORT-TERM RELIEF
Unsustainable
Disconnection

LONG-TERM PAIN
Pain & Shame
Reinforces
Addiction

REPEAT NEGLECT
Pain/Fear
Uncertainty

CYCLE
OF
ADDICTION

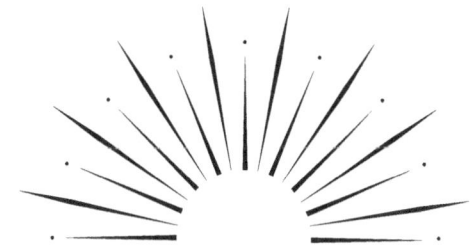

THE LIGHTHOUSE EFFECT CYCLE OF RECOVERY MODEL

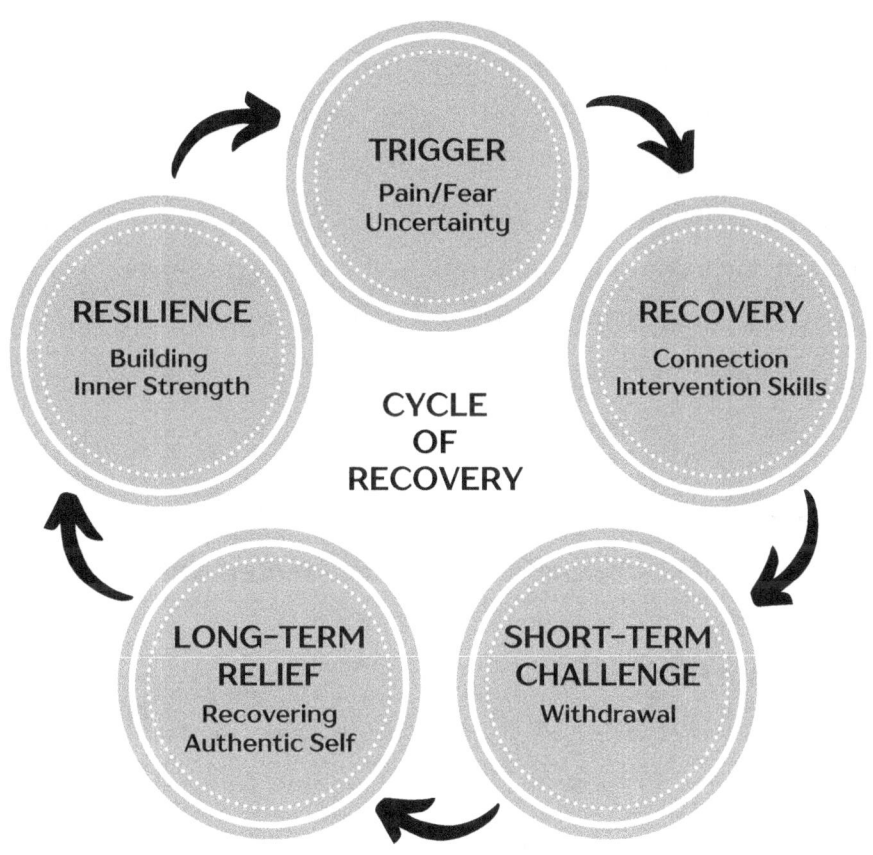

CYCLE
OF
RECOVERY

TRIGGER
Pain/Fear
Uncertainty

RECOVERY
Connection
Intervention Skills

**SHORT-TERM
CHALLENGE**
Withdrawal

**LONG-TERM
RELIEF**
Recovering
Authentic Self

RESILIENCE
Building
Inner Strength

Introducing Stages of Change

If you work in the addiction and recovery field, you are quite likely familiar with the Stages of Change (SOC) Model, but let's do a quick review. It was created by James DiClemente and Carlo Prochaska in 1982, funded by a grant from the federal government to address smoking cessation. It became such an effective aid in the smoking-cessation crusade that it has been broadly adopted by other substance abuse and addiction treatment programs, not just in the United States, but internationally. It has been modified over the years, undergoing various translations and adaptations. DiClemente and Prochaska's original Model of Change includes five stages that one undergoes when moving (or trying to move) through a change: Pre-contemplation, Contemplation, Preparation, Action, and Maintenance.

I work with the Transtheoretical Model, which is an evolved version of the DiClemente and Prochaska model that includes an additional potential experience: relapse. Though not everyone will experience relapse, it remains a possibility, given the nature of addiction and our animal brain's inclination to instinctively fall back to familiar ways of coping.

Importantly, the relapse *phase* (it is not technically considered a "stage") provides the contrasting experience of how short lived "pros" of addiction swiftly become long term "cons," as conveyed in the SOC Chart and SOC Addiction/Recovery Pros & Cons Worksheet.

Group Exercise ~ Stages of Change

Walk the group through the Stages of Change: Metamorphosis from Survival to Revival Lifestyle handout and have them complete the SOC Addiction/ Recovery Pros & Cons Worksheet together as a group, using your whiteboard to draw the columns and fill in responses. (The handout and worksheet are in the "Repeat Handouts" section of How To Utilize This Manual & The Lighthouse Effect Program. You can also download PDFs from innerfaiththerapy.com to print or distribute electronically.)

You'll see that the SOC Addiction/ Recovery Pros & Cons Worksheet is included as individual homework, below. Let your group know that they will be completing the worksheet again at the end of the module and at the start and close of each module, as a process for tracking and reflecting on their progress from the beginning to the end of each module and from one module to the next. Encourage them to pay particular attention to the "pros" column of addiction and the "cons" column of recovery, to help assess where they are within the stages of change at any given point. As I often tell people on a recovery journey, *Short-term relief equals long-term grief, while short-term pain equals long-term gain*. I also encourage each person to share their worksheets with their recovery network (sponsor, recovery coach, therapist, accountability partner or partners) to help support them in their journey to wholeness and to update their Relapse Prevention Plan Worksheet accordingly.

Suggested Closing Meditation ~ Metamorphosis Meditation: This meditation helps to reinforce Stages of Recovery and Stages of Change Models and concepts.

Sit comfortably with your eyes closed and your body completely open and relaxed. (Sound chime or toning bowl.) Take three slow, deep breaths to breathe your way into this present moment. Imagine the process of transformation from a caterpillar into a butterfly, the magic and wonder of it all. Now consider the perspective of a caterpillar compared to the perspective of a butterfly. The caterpillar is unaware of the process of change that it is soon to experience, while the butterfly is the outcome of that change. Continue to breathe deeply, as you turn your mind's eye to the butterfly emerging from its cocoon and taking flight; imagine you are the butterfly. Breathe in; breathe out. Imagine the wisdom you carry now, having completely changed your form and having shed your old self. Breathe in; breathe out. Imagine what advice your butterfly-self could offer the caterpillar from this "higher" perspective.

Ponder what advice you might offer to comfort and encourage that caterpillar-self. Take another deep breath, and as you inhale, breathe in the courage and faith to face whatever changes are before you and view them from this higher perspective. As you exhale, release any resistance to change you might be holding. Take one more long, slow inhalation, and one more long, slow, exhalation. (Sound chime.) Slowly open your eyes and come back to the present moment. Allow yourself to be open and trust your personal journey of transformation and expansion. Consider how your butterfly-self feels, the power of your wings, and the liberty to fly free. Carry that feeling with you through your day.

Suggested Homework: Complete your individual Stages of Change Addiction/Recovery Pros & Cons Worksheet and be prepared to share insights at the next session. You will complete the worksheet again at the end of the module, and then compare it to this one to assess your progress. (You will be repeating the process at the beginning and end of each module. Please keep all of your SOC Worksheets in your Lighthouse Effect Program folder or binder, so that you can continue to assess your progress along the way.)

TIP: As noted, the SOC Worksheets are for the benefit of participants, for evaluating their progress and to inform their self-care. Also, depending on your agency's protocols, they can provide information that would be helpful in evaluating the effectiveness of the program. Your agency may want you to do a basic evaluation at the end of each module and/or for the entire year-long program.

Module I (Mindful Recovery) Session 3:
Anchoring the Mind, Body, and Spirit ~ Following the Breath

Suggested Opening Meditation ~ The Gravity of Relaxation: Carry the thread of last week's session into this session's opening meditation.

Get into a comfortable position with your feet on the ground or floor, and close your eyes or lower your gaze. (Sound chime.) Take three long, slow, deep breaths down to the bottom of your lungs and all the way through into your back. As you breathe, feel your body softening; notice and allow the weight of gravity to gently soften your whole muscular system. Continue to breathe deeply. Notice any place in the body where you may be holding tension. Now, as you inhale, breathe directly into that area; as you exhale, feel the softening and relaxing of those muscles. Take another slow, deep breath, noticing the weight of your feet on the floor.

Continue to breathe deeply, sending your breath, your attention, further down, deep into the earth beneath the floor or beneath your feet. Notice the solid foundation of the earth, supporting and stabilizing your body. Feel the weight of gravity and how it grounds your entire being. Breathe in, *I am present*; as you breathe out, feel your muscles softening. Breathe in, *I am allowing*; as you breathe out, feel your tension easing up. Breathe in, *I am becoming more relaxed and aware, one breath at a time*; as you breathe out, feel your body opening. (Sound chime.) Slowly open your eyes and bring your relaxed presence back to the group.

Check-Ins and Q&A: Encourage participants to keep check-ins brief and to focus on the previous session's content about cycles of addiction and recovery, and the Victim Triangle. Invite them to share reflections from their homework with the group to build group cohesion.

Handouts: Anchoring the Mind, Body, and Spirit: Coping Skills for Strengthening the Foundation of your Lighthouse

Grounding (Anchoring) as a Practice

The practice of grounding helps us to fully experience ourselves, our Authentic Self, through all of the five senses, to be open and in a state of surrender, thus, to be fully engaged in the present moment. We naturally merge with the energy of *unification* and come into full alignment with the earth, our environment, and our higher selves. Being intentional with our physical stance, posture, and positioning of our bodies facilitates self-empowerment. It also opens us up to or aligns us with higher energies. When we intentionally position ourselves between the earth and the sky (think: lighthouse) we gain access to our sixth sense, felt sense, or what many in recovery refer to as our "higher power." Most of us have experienced some degree of trauma in our lives and have felt unstable, vulnerable, or afraid. We are far more similar than different, and sharing our experiences helps us to support each other, while fostering self-care and self-acceptance.

When I'm working with a group, I often share my own experience of what works for me and how those tools are integrated into the program. I find that moving or positioning my body with intention and mindfulness--walking in nature, doing qigong or yoga, dancing, martial arts--will energetically signal my central nervous system that I am not alone and I am safe. It takes me home in an instant to my center, to my essential self within. It reduces uncertainty and calms my vulnerable inner child. For example, I might imagine and model a majestic oak tree planted in the earth, its deep roots holding it steady, while its huge canopy of branches reaches to the sky. In a standing or sitting posture, I will breathe deeply into the feeling of the ground beneath me, feel myself rooting in the earth, and simultaneously feel myself expanding beyond my body and up into the ethers. In merging with the environment, I gain a broader, higher perspective and can perceive a full 360 degrees around me.

It's as if I changed my lens from telephoto to wide angle and with that wider perspective, I'm not hyper-focused on whatever I was obsessing about that caused me to be ungrounded. I experience this when I hike up a hill or mountain. Once I reach the summit and take in the panoramic view, all of my worries and stressors simply vanish. I am in "experience" mode and I stop overthinking. I am overcome with awe and gratitude at the incredible power and beauty of it all; I feel free. Now, when I watch an eagle fly overhead or observe a butterfly, I am reminded that I can take that "higher" perspective whenever I feel out of balance. Mindful grounding practices help the mind attend to the body, allowing us to be in the flow of the energetic systems all around us. In turn, the mind will follow the body and let go of ruminations and projections that are not current, supportive, or true.

In addition to being psychologically beneficial, there are studies suggesting that direct contact with Earth's surface (grass, dirt, sand) can positively impact physical and mental wellbeing, including reducing inflammation, improving sleep quality, and decreasing anxiety and depression. (You might want to watch "The Earthing Movie" documentary: earthingmovie.com.)

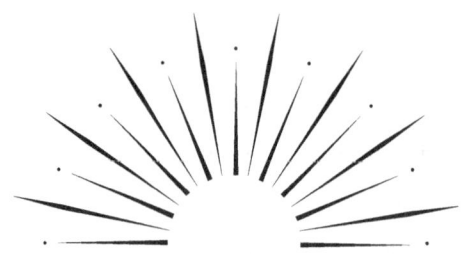

THE LIGHTHOUSE EFFECT
Anchoring the Mind, Body, and Spirit
Coping Skills for Strengthening the Foundation of your Lighthouse

These coping skills can be applied as daily practices or at any time you need to anchor yourself: when you are triggered; when you are trying to resolve a conflict; when you feel disconnected; when you feel overwhelmed; or in any other situation where you feel out of alignment. Anchoring or grounding ourselves is about bringing the mind, body, and spirit into alignment, with intention, through mindfulness practice. Think of the mind as the mental component, the body as the physical and sensory component, and spirit as the nonphysical component, that which connects with non-3D reality or our higher selves. While grounding is predominantly about being aware of our physical selves in physical reality, all three components of the mind-body-spirit complex are integral to the human experience and essential to being fully present and in "the here and now."

MIND: Mental Grounding Practices

Describe your environment through your senses. Observe and describe what is around you, wherever you are, at any time. If you are walking down a street, for example, notice and describe the buildings and the architecture; notice and describe the sounds, smells, colors, and temperature of the air. If you are sitting in a waiting room at your dentist's office, instead of worrying about the procedure, notice and describe (to yourself, in your mind) the art on the wall, decorative objects, plants. Focus on and describe the colors in the room or the music playing in the background.

Play mind-recall games. Challenge your mind by naming various favorites: favorite songs and the artists who wrote them; movies and the actors who played in them; books and their authors; sports teams and their players; foods and recipes you love; your favorite places to travel and what you love about them. Turn your mind to joyous or poignant memories and moments you experienced in physical reality.

Timeline progression. Go back to your earliest memory and then add five years to whatever age you were at that time, and another five years, and another five years, and so on. Challenge your mind to remember what you were doing at each point on your timeline and write something about it. It's not about evaluating or assessing, but simply noticing the progression of your life. Add a future point five years from now and imagine where you will be then, with you living your best life.

Describe a daily routine in great detail. You might describe your morning ritual from when you wake up, or describe how you prepare a favorite meal, or how you organize your day to keep yourself focused and grounded. Example: *When I first wake up, I do some gentle stretches in bed and then I get my Bookending Your Day journal and do the morning Body, Mind, Spirit exercises.*

40

Imagine creative ways to release pain. Go into your pain, whether physical, mental, or both, and describe it in detail, and then imagine that it is dissipating. Avoid checking to see if it worked, simply stay with the imagery. Examples: *I put my anxiety in a balloon and released it. Now, I'm watching it as it gets smaller and smaller and begins to disappear in the sky.* OR: *My back pain is a jackhammer against my spine. I loaded the jackhammer and the pain it's causing onto a train. Now, I'm watching the train travel away down the tracks, getting further and further away.*

Repeat a mantra or supportive statement. You might say it out loud, or in your mind. Examples: *I am growing, learning, and becoming more aware, one day at a time; I am free to be me, to be my authentic self. I am practicing mindfulness, right here, right now, without self-judgment. I am (your name) and I am a unique expression of spirit, not to be compared to another.*

Read or sing out loud. Read aloud passages that help you feel anchored in your body and make you feel empowered. Sing out loud lyrics that help you to feel healthy and strong in your mind and body.

Change your mood with a joke or animal antics. Shift your mind and change your mood by reading or recalling a joke that made you laugh, or by watching animal antics. Smiling is highly therapeutic!

Count or say the alphabet out loud. Count out loud from at least one to ten, or to a higher number; say the alphabet out loud, maybe even backwards, to really get your mind focused and charged!

BODY: Physical Grounding Practices

Use cold water. Cold plunge with your entire body: in a tub, shower, lake, or ocean; run cold water on your wrists; splash cold water on your face.

Use objects in your environment. Grab the sides of your chair as hard as you can. Put a rubber band around your wrist and snap it. Play with a stress ball. Roll a stone in your hand or hold a crystal and mindfully notice the texture, color, weight, and energy.

Use your own body. Tap your legs or arms in a right leg/left leg pattern. Tap your head and face with your fingertips and then gently slap your arms, abdomen, and legs.

Connect with physical reality. Dig your heels into the floor and notice the tension in your heels. Imagine the energy as roots winding down through the floor and into the earth, literally grounding you. Jump up and down ten times, noticing how your mind shifts its attention toward the action. Simply feel the physicality of your body: the weight of your clothes or shoes, the surface of the chair against your back, the wind brushing your skin, the sun on your face. Mindfully eat a piece of fruit or any food, chewing very slowly and noticing in detail the flavors, textures, and smells.

Engage in a body meditation practice. Qigong: Notice the "qi" or energetic system of your body; connect with the energy around you; feel it rising from the earth and through you and out into the cosmos. Yoga: Feel your body as it takes each yogic position and use your breath to fully ground yourself in the position, in the moment.

Follow the breath. Following the breath means to mindfully engage in this most natural of processes. Inhale, slowly and deeply, and follow the breath all the way through, and then follow it through a full and elongated exhalation, relaxing and softening your jaw and shoulders. As you exhale, you might think of a soothing mantra or phrase to help foster inner peace and wellbeing.

SPIRIT: Spiritual Grounding Practices

Encourage yourself as you might a child. Soothe your inner child by saying something encouraging and compassionate to yourself. Examples: *You are doing the best that you can in your situation; You have a legion of guides and angels watching over you; You are not alone, I am right by your side.*

Encourage yourself from Wise Mind or Higher Self. Remind yourself of who you are, as a unique expression of Spirit. Remind yourself that you have what you need to navigate your life. Example: *I've been here before and found my way with help. Though this moment is challenging, I've got this.*

Think about things that bring you joy. In the *Sound of Music* sense of "these are a few of my favorite things," think of your favorite spots in nature, favorite season, and favorite seasonal festivities; favorite songs, movies, and books; favorite sports, teams, and players; favorite colors; favorite art, artists, and galleries; and so on.

Describe your happy place. Where is it that brings you a sense of deep calm? Perhaps it is being in nature: at the beach or by water in any form, in the mountains or hiking in the woods, lying in a field or meadow. Perhaps it's a point or place in time or a memory: being in your grandmother's kitchen, sitting on the back porch at your childhood best friend's, that moment when you held your baby for the first time. Wherever it is, go there in your mind and notice all of the felt senses you experience in that place.

Treat yourself to a soothing activity. Run a warm bath or sit in a hot tub; enjoy a candlelit dinner; get a massage or do a self-massage; go to a yoga class; listen to comforting music or a guided meditation in a quiet, calm place.

Visualize and express the changes you want to experience in your life. Be clear about what you need and the changes you want to make. Examples: *I want to feel grounded and stable in my body and my mind, no matter what is happening in the world; I want to feel stable in my body in any life situation that challenges me; I want to feel aligned in my mind, body, and spirit and grounded in my authentic self.*

Recall prayers or spiritual wisdoms. Recite prayers or sayings that help you feel connected. For example: The Serenity Prayer, The Lord's Prayer, Don Miguel Ruiz's Four Agreements, an Indigenous American blessing, or any spiritual saying or wisdom that resonates with you.

Listen to spiritual messages that inspire and empower you. Listen to a talk, radio show, or podcast on your spiritual philosophy. Listen to an audio book by an inspirational speaker or spiritual leader whose teachings resonate with you. Listen to audio recordings of inspirational quotes, stories, poetry, or guided meditations. Consider asking your therapist, recovery coach, sponsor, or a trusted friend for recordings that might resonate with you.

Consider why spiritual grounding works. Why might it be that by focusing on your connection to the natural world and the unseen, you begin to find a sense of inner peacefulness? As you practice these spiritual grounding exercises, notice the methods that work best for you, and consider why they might be more powerful for you than other methods. Consider journaling about your experiences and all of the felt senses that arise.

Alignment as a spiritual anchor. Grounding is a spiritual practice that happens in physical reality. It is about choosing to live your life with purpose and intention while being fully present in your human body. When we engage in a daily practice for aligning mind, body, and spirit, we strengthen the foundation of our lighthouse and can shine as our authentic selves.

Group Exercise ~ Anchoring the Mind, Body, and Spirit

Guide the group through the handout, using your whiteboard. Ask them to come up with their own mantras, in addition to the examples provided.

The Value of Attending to the Breath

The power of "attending to the breath" is in its simplicity and accessibility; it is a direct connection to the life force, our own, and beyond. In other words, it bridges the mind through the body, and from there, opens to the nonphysical or spiritual realms. In attending to the breath, we call our mind back from its ruminations about the past or projections of the future. The breath is the central conduit for aligning our entire being, mind, body, and spirit. At our very core, we are "spiritual beings having a physical experience," as philosopher Pierre Teilhard de Chardin expressed it. This is why I have highlighted attending to the breath as integral to the whole program. Following the inhalation and exhalation of the breath is a simple and effective way to practice mindfulness--and one that is always available, as demonstrated in the Attending to the Breath meditation, which I offer as the suggested closing meditation for this session.

Through the spirit or "qi" (life force), the body simply *breathes* and the mind simply *thinks*. The practice is not to try to change the thinking process, but to accept what it does, turn our attention to our breath, and then just *notice*. Becoming adept at the skill of observing (Observer Self) is to become adept at quieting our monkey mind, to consciously allow our ruminations about the past and projections into the future fall away in the context of the moment, and to then make conscious decisions for moving forward. It's about managing our thoughts more skillfully, and not allowing them to take us on wild goose chases.

Meditation is *mindful attendance* in action. The goal is not to force the mind to behave correctly, but rather to *move the mind* away from its reactive commentary. It is like the mind and its thoughts are a fast-moving train, and we can make the choice to *not* jump on the thought train and instead, watch it pass by. After a time, we learn to smile at the animal brain and its attempts to control us, as a mother might with her child. Recognize that the primordial brain's survival instinct is on automatic pilot; it is wired to protect us. As we practice surrendering to the present moment, we will increasingly feel more centered and peaceful. It is from this more centered place or still point that emotions can be stabilized and balanced, which, in turn, sets us up to flow through our day without expectations and in readiness for whatever might be presented.

Developing a customized daily practice of mindfulness is how we come to self-mastery of the mind-body-spirit complex. This excerpt is from a client interview in *The Lighthouse Effect: Practicing Your Way From Survival to Revival*. I'm sharing it here, as Nancy talks about how mindfulness practice, and in particular, meditation, was so important to her recovery process.

It makes so much sense that meditation would work for people with addiction. Because you are becoming aware of all the sensations in your body, and cultivating the ability to be equanimous or not be in resistance or attachment to whatever you're feeling in the moment. That was the whole answer for me, because I was addicted to opiates to numb what I was experiencing in my body. And when I say what I was experiencing in my body, yeah, I mean like physical pain, like back pain, but I also mean emotions because we experience emotions in our physical bodies. For me, that was really true. I understood that I was experiencing emotions in my mind, but also, greatly, in my body. You've got to connect to your body because there's all sorts of stuff going on, so it made total sense to me that cultivating the ability to be present and equanimous with all those emotional sensations would help me to not want or need to find relief.

Suggested Closing Meditation ~ Attending to the Breath Meditation

Get into a comfortable position, and close your eyes or lower your gaze. (Sound chime or toning bowl.) Take three long, slow, deep breaths. With each inhalation, sense the temperature of the air, feel the sensation of the air as it enters your nostrils, and follow the flow into your lungs. Notice how your chest rises with each "in" breath and relaxes with each "out" breath, as if the process of breathing is gently rocking you. Feel into this subtle rocking motion, noticing your "in" breath and "out" breath as you continue to breathe deeply. Notice how soothing it feels to attend to your breathing. If your mind tries to comment or judge and distract you from the present moment, simply acknowledge that it is what the mind does. Breathe into it and just observe it, without worry, without engaging, and let it go. Just continue to follow the rocking rhythm of your breath. One more deep inhalation; one more full exhalation. (Sound chime.) Slowly open your eyes, and gently begin to move your body. Take your time. Slowly bring your attention back to the group.

Suggested Homework: Practice in real time some of the coping skills in the Anchoring the Mind, Body, and Spirit: Coping Skills for Strengthening the Foundation of your Lighthouse handout. Reflect in your journal on how Nancy's excerpt resonated with you. How does her experience inspire you? What do you think about as you reflect on your own personal experience of using mindfulness or various types of meditation to support your recovery?

Resources: I often reference Dan Millman's renowned book *Way of the Peaceful Warrior* (peacefulwarrior.com) and recommend that participants read it or watch the movie, *Peaceful Warrior*. Both are based on a true story about training the mind of an Olympic gold medalist known as "Lord of the Rings." What the story conveys is that arduous physical training is a primary part of an Olympian's training, but equally important is training the mind. The goal is to gain self-mastery of the mind, in order to detach enough from the ego to release negative emotions, and in turn, allow the mind and body to be in complete alignment with the still point of *now*. This point of focus is free of fear and doubt, and provides access to sheer authentic power, where all possibilities are available. It is where Spirit or God (as you understand it) is fully experienced, without any sense of separateness. It is the flow state of consciousness, a most powerful place to be, yet it takes lots of practice to get there!

Module I (Mindful Recovery) Session 4: Developing the Observer Self

Suggested Opening Meditation ~ Butterfly View Meditation: As this session is about developing the Observer Self, I suggest the Butterfly View, which is a modified version of the Metamorphosis Mediation presented in the previous session. Or choose another meditation that encourages distancing oneself from a conflict or challenge.

Get into a comfortable position, and close your eyes or lower your gaze. (Sound chime or toning bowl.) Take a long, slow, deep breath. As you inhale, in your mind's eye, take the caterpillar view and zoom in on a current life challenge; now, as you slowly exhale, zoom out, like a butterfly rising above the conflict. Continue to take long, slow, deep breaths and observe from this higher perspective; simply observe, without judgment or resistance. Notice changes in your emotional body and your physical body; notice any softening or lightening sensations. Take one more deep inhalation, and slow exhalation. (Sound chime.) Now, slowly open your eyes and bring yourself back to the present. Know that you always have the ability to zoom out to the butterfly view to gain a higher and more expanded perspective at any given moment. Practice this skill throughout your day and make it a daily practice.

Check-Ins and Q&A: Encourage group participants to keep check-ins brief and to reflect on grounding and anchoring concepts from the previous session. They might also share their reflections from their journals on what resonated for them about Nancy's recovery experience, which was also presented in the previous session.

Handouts: No new handouts. (You might review previous handouts that support group process.)

Who or What is the Observer Self?

As we practice mindfulness, we become aware of the observer within, as if there is a presence watching us. We might find ourselves asking, *If I am me, then who or what is watching me and how are they, the watcher, so intimately connected with me*? The best answer to this inquiry I have found is *consciousness*. This Observer Self is a witness to our behaviorisms and our antics. It doesn't judge, it notices without an emotional charge. It is a state of consciousness where we can perceive from a distance, in order to see with clarity and without judgment.

We might even be practicing mindfulness without realizing it, in that we do it instinctively, as with my earlier example of driving a car on a busy highway, where we are present and focused and all senses are activated. A primary benefit of practicing mindfulness is that we more easily step into Observer Self. When we develop the vantage point of the observer, we are more likely to respond skillfully and gracefully to unexpected challenges, as it provides a moment of pause, even a nanosecond--just enough that we can be conscious with our response, rather than responding reflexively. That said, we often act reflexively in *positive* ways, without running narratives in the moment. For example, something falls off the counter, and we grab it. The same is true when something more significant happens, where we act reflexively in the moment and it's only *afterward* that dramatic narratives arise, as we attempt to cognitively understand what just happened.

For example, when you're driving and someone cuts you off or an animal darts out across the road in front of you, most of the time, you react instinctively by swerving around the car or animal. You are not rattled until after you averted the close call, and then you run all of the worst-case scenarios of what *could* have happened. We navigate these things and naturally do what is needed in the moment, sometimes quite artfully, throughout our day. The narrative that floods in once the moment has passed comes from Ego and our fear of what might have happened. It is important to allow the mind to catch up to what the present part of us handled effortlessly and skillfully in the moment. Observer Self helps us to acknowledge what *actually* happened so that we can more easily let go of would have/should have/could have narratives.

Group Exercise ~ Observer Self Perspective

Invite participants to share examples of situations where they automatically acted and then ran negative narratives afterward, and how taking the perspective of Observer Self could have minimized those worst-case-scenario narratives. I have observed that using metaphors, analogies, and visual displays on the whiteboard helps to reinforce the lesson. During this session, I might use one of my analogies for gaining a higher or broader perspective to demonstrate Observer Self, such as the butterfly view. Another that I use is the camera lens, how we can choose to move from the zoomed-in "telephoto" view to the zoomed-out "wide angle" view.

The more we practice being present, aware, and focused, the more grounded we are, and in turn, the more we are able to respond to challenging events and dynamics with resilience and ease of being, without going into the drama. When we are rooted in our physical body, our minds become clearer and we are better able to manage the flow of our emotions. Eventually, our very presence will emanate strength, solidarity, and flexibility. Presence is the foundation for alignment and resiliency. Command your mind from Observer Self: Be in present time and the body will serve as a conduit for "the now," in alignment with Spirit or "all that is."

Suggested Closing Meditation ~ The Lighthouse Effect Theater of Life Meditation

Get into a comfortable position, and close your eyes or lower your gaze. (Sound chime or toning bowl.) Feel your feet on the floor, your back against your chair; relax your shoulders and jaw. Take three long, slow, deep breaths. Each time you exhale, feel your body softening and relaxing more deeply. Now, as you continue to breathe deeply, bring your attention to a conflict that is occurring in your life or a recurring challenge in a close relationship. Imagine you are sitting in a theater, in the front row, watching this scene play out on the stage. Feel yourself sitting there, simply observing the drama as it unfolds in front of you, just a few feet away. Watch how the actor playing you interacts with the person causing you discomfort. Take another slow, deep breath; as you exhale, imagine you are moving from the front row to the very back of the theater. Notice how you feel as you observe your drama playing out from a greater distance. Continue to breathe, letting go of judgment, negative thoughts, and emotions with each exhalation. Now, imagine yourself moving up into the balcony of this life theater. Notice what it feels like to view the scene from a bird's eye perspective; notice you are more detached from your emotions. Take another slow, deep breath all the way into your back, and slowly exhale, allowing your body to fully relax. (Sound chime.) Slowly open your eyes and begin to move your body, as you return to the present moment. Carry this sense of relaxation with you throughout your day.

Suggested Homework: Continue to practice the skills from the Anchoring the Mind, Body, and Spirit: Coping Skills for Strengthening the Foundation of your Lighthouse handout. (Shared in the previous session.) Focus on those that resonate most with you. Did any of the suggestions inspire other ways to practice grounding that aren't listed? Also practice distancing yourself from triggers, not as a way to minimize your feelings but to give yourself the space you need in order to think more clearly.

Module I (Mindful Recovery) Session 5: Understanding Mind States

Suggested Opening Meditation ~ Following the Sound Meditation

Get into a comfortable position, and close your eyes or lower your gaze. (Sound chime or toning bowl.) Take a long, slow, deep inhalation and exhalation, as you follow the sound of the chime, listening intentionally and intently until it fades completely. (Sound chime.) Take another full, deep, inhalation through the nose as you focus on the sound: feel the air moving through your nose, down into your lungs, expanding into your abdomen, and all the way into the back. Slowly exhale through the mouth, completely emptying your lungs as you continue to listen intentionally. (Sound chime.) Follow the sound as you breathe in through the nose, all the way down through your lungs and into your back. Now slowly exhale, releasing through your mouth, following the sound as it fades. (Sound chime again.) Slowly open your eyes and mindfully return to the present moment.

Check-Ins and Q&A: Encourage group participants to keep check-ins brief. Invite them to share their homework and reflections on developing the Observer Self and the Theater of Life Meditation. Reinforce the importance of sharing their personal interpretations, as it builds group cohesion and deepens their understanding of the content.

Handouts: DBT Circles Model, Hegel's Triangle Model, The Lighthouse Effect Mind States Model

THE LINEHAN DBT MIND STATES CIRCLES MODEL

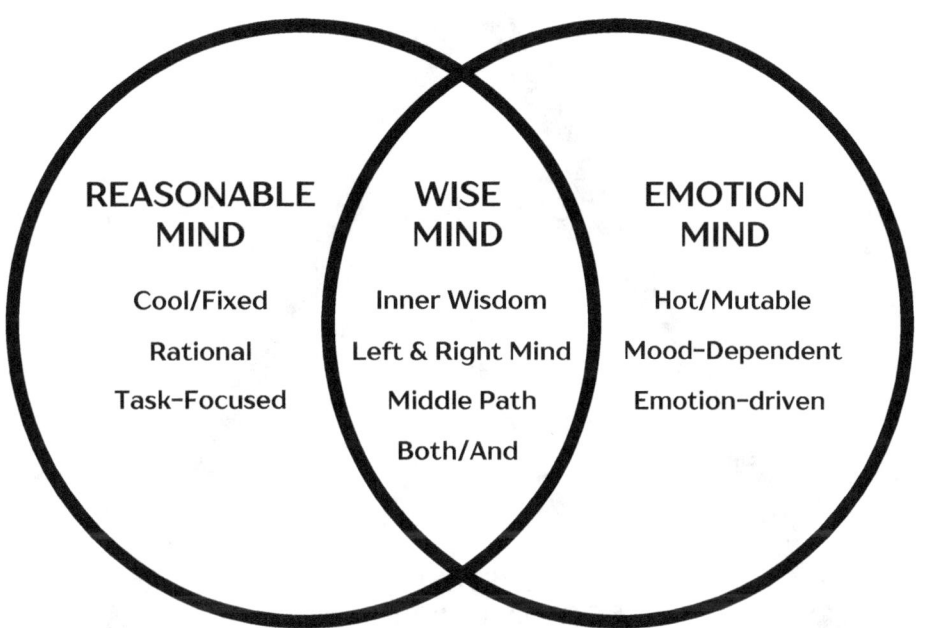

REASONABLE MIND

Cool/Fixed

Rational

Task-Focused

WISE MIND

Inner Wisdom

Left & Right Mind

Middle Path

Both/And

EMOTION MIND

Hot/Mutable

Mood-Dependent

Emotion-driven

HEGEL'S TRIANGLE MODEL

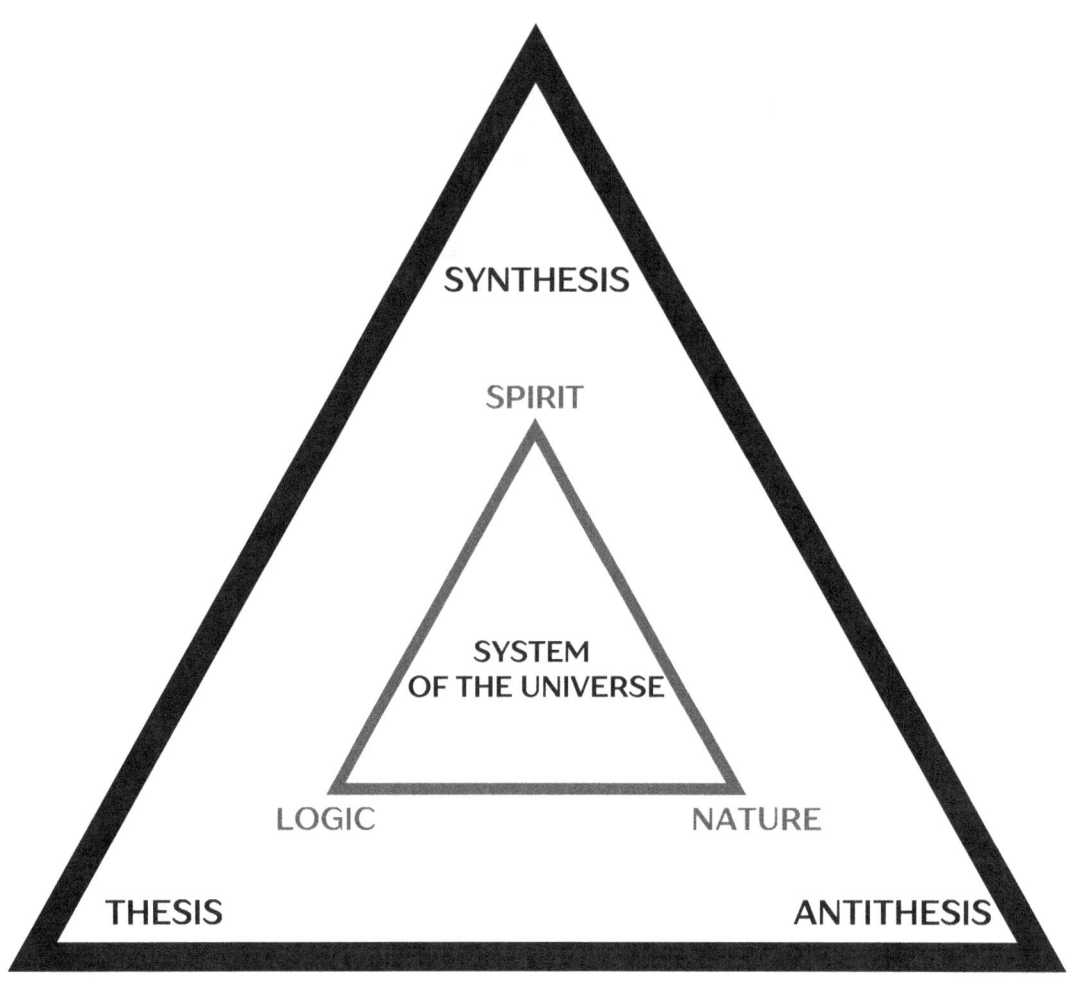

Thesis/Antithesis/Synthesis & Logic/Nature/Spirit

States of Mind

Our states of mind play a part in reactive behavioral patterns, how the right brain and left brain function, and how our thoughts and narratives drive our emotions and moods. The Lighthouse Effect Skillful Recovery Program is an amalgamation of my own concepts and models and concepts introduced by others, including Byron Katie, Lynne Forrest, Dr. Marsha Linehan, and Hegel. Dr. Linehan (the mother of DBT) presents the mind states as Reasonable Mind, Emotion Mind, and Wise Mind. Alternatively, we might refer to the first two as "Rational Mind" and "Emotional Mind" or "Child Mind."

I interweave Linehan's overlapping circles model of mind states with Hegel's logic/nature/spirit and thesis/antithesis/synthesis triangle models to create my version of mind states, where I see "synthesis" as the integration of opposites and embodiment of the concept of Both/And.

Emotional Mind is at the base of the left side, indicating the feminine and more intuitive side, while Rational Mind is at the base of the right side, indicating the masculine and more practical side. Wise Mind is at the pinnacle of the triangle, indicating the *integration* of Emotional Mind and Rational Mind perspectives. It synthesizes opposing views so a compromise can be made and/or promotes acceptance of and respect for the opposing view, as in a true democracy and in healthy, conscious relationships.

My definition of mind states borrows from Neale Donald Walsch's maxim "wisdom is knowledge experienced." I align Rational Mind with knowledge, Emotional Mind with experience, and Wise Mind with wisdom. Hence, wisdom (Wise Mind) is knowledge (Rational Mind) experienced (Emotional Mind). We come to Wise Mind by way of mindfulness practice, as it is about integrating our intelligence with our emotions and sensory field, in alignment with "the now" or " this moment."

THE LIGHTHOUSE EFFECT
MIND STATES MODEL

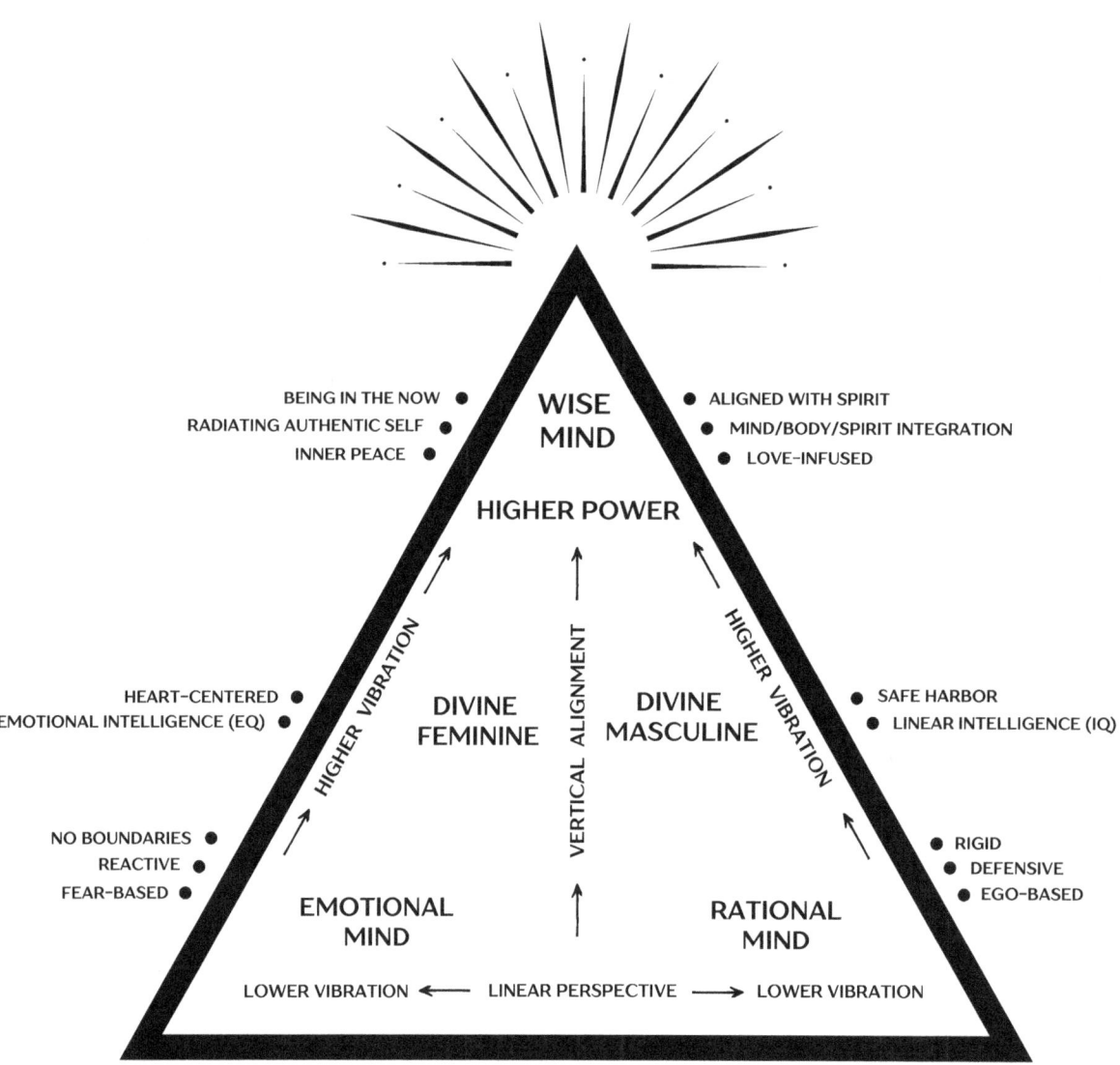

Divine Feminine and Divine Masculine are not gender-based. They are spiritual qualities that can be embodied by anyone of any gender.

Group Exercise ~ Mind State Traits

Draw the Mind States Model on your whiteboard. As you walk the group through it, ask them for examples of traits they might associate with each mind state.

Rational Mind has a left-brain, linear perspective. It is about structure, planning for the future, and needing to know what is happening; it loves to be in control. It navigates our physical and material world in a very systematic and practical way and operates in the linear time frame of daily experience. It remembers and collects data from our personal and environmental history, and chronicles events along a timeline from birth to present. It has a tendency to store (the hippocampus) a negative experience and unconsciously react from that place. On the other hand, Rational Mind grounds us and helps us to feel safe (at least on a surface level) as its black-and-white or self-versus-other perspective helps to delineate self-image (individualism and separatism) and our sense of belonging. It is our cognitive control center, if you will, the prefrontal cortex or executive functioning part of the brain. In terms of the Lighthouse Effect, it is akin to the shore.

Emotional Mind has a right-brain, more intuitive, nonlinear perspective. It is unstructured and lacks boundaries. It is gray as opposed to black-and-white, and yet can also be quite colorful as it exists predominantly within the world of the creative imagination and the *felt* sense. It is also more childlike in that it can be theatrical, expressive, dramatic, and adventurous: Child Mind. It exists in direct opposition to Rational Mind, forming the left baseline of the triangle. Emotional Mind is composed of two opposing experiences within its own sphere, with the lower vibrations being fear-based and higher vibrations being soul- and/or love-based. It carries its own unique kind of intelligence, what we might refer to as *emotional intelligence*. I get more into that in *The Lighthouse Effect: Practicing your way from Survival to Revival*, but we do touch on it in Module III Emotional Balancing: The Power Source of your Lighthouse ~ Authentic Power. In terms of the Lighthouse Effect, think of Emotional Mind as the sea or our emotional waters, which can be quite dramatic and even dangerous!

Wise Mind is *a state of being* rather than a goal or destiny we might try to reach. It is *how* we are and *who* we are when we simply allow ourselves to *be*. It is to experience life from the fullness of our being, integrated in mind, body, and soul, with Rational Mind and Emotional Mind working in concert. We can come home to Wise Mind through daily mindfulness practice, self-reflection, and applying emotional balancing techniques, such as DBT, Emotional Freedom Technique (EFT), and Cognitive Behavioral Therapy (CBT).

By integrating our Emotional Mind (right-brain experience) and our Rational Mind (left-brain experience), we raise our vibration and come into our wisdom, i.e., Wise Mind. Interestingly, there is a crossover dynamic in our right-brain/left-brain mapping, where the right brain controls the left side of the body and the left brain controls the right side of the body. To achieve a state of balance, it is all the more essential to harmonize both aspects within the mind-body complex. When we do, we radiate from the inside out: this is the premise of "the Lighthouse Effect."

Many of us are taught to avoid or repress our emotions and even to be ashamed of our emotions. As a result, we subconsciously store our emotions in the denser, lower vibrations of our Emotional Mind, where fear-based Ego works to ignore or numb them. Talk therapy can be helpful in restoring a healthy understanding, as engaging in a therapeutic relationship of trust and connection is, in and of itself, cathartic. However, it primarily works with Rational Mind on the surface layers of our wounds and negative core beliefs, and might not get to the root causes, thus, it might not be fully effective for deprogramming those long-held beliefs and default reactions.

I believe the most effective regimen for mental health healing is one that includes *experiential* therapies, such as mindfulness practice, that help in accessing altered states of consciousness. When we engage the mind-body complex in practices from multiple healing modalities, we are better able to face and embrace our emotional selves and come into alignment. I encourage cultivating a conscious relationship with our higher power, whatever that is for each one of us.

This brings us back to Observer Self and how taking a wider perspective can benefit us in any life situation. What we might deem as less desirable emotions actually serve as a guidance system, tripping imprinted narratives that need our attention. Our emotions are vital to our human experience and those vulnerable parts of ourselves need to be seen. Our innocence is precious and essential to restore if we are to overcome our deepest traumas and fears; it's about self-love. Attending to our feelings is about summoning Rational Mind and asking it to meet Emotional Mind with patience and understanding in order to deprogram emotions held in the body as cellular memory. This action synthesizes Wise Mind and creates inner peace. When we are in Wise Mind, we are the lighthouse. We shine our personality, our aliveness, our light, without apology; our spirit is liberated within the context of the human experience.

Teflon Mind is another mind state in the DBT model. It is a component or sub-mindset of Rational Mind, as it is not emotional. It is about letting go of uncomfortable, painful, or sticky feelings and emotions. Teflon Mind acts as a sort of protective body armor that deflects the penetrating thoughts coming at us (whether from outside or from within) and keeps them from sticking. We can then do our inner work in a safe container, which is crucial to building self-confidence and resilience in order to heal from the inside out.

TIP: When you present any of these models to the group, you might underscore that they are not meant to be static; they are mutable. We tend to fixate on symbols as being fixed representations of a truth, but this program is about coming to our own understanding of what is true; it's about self-empowerment, self-realization, and self-care. We might think of these models as templates or maps, that might inform and guide our understanding of the human condition, human behaviors, and states of mind.

Suggested Closing Meditation ~ Mind States Meditation: I suggest this meditation, as our states of mind are part of the human condition and need to be met with understanding and compassion.

Get into a comfortable position, and close your eyes or lower your gaze. (Sound chime or toning bowl.) Take three slow, deep breaths. As you slowly inhale and exhale, in your mind's eye, imagine the sphere of Rational Mind as the shore. Consider how Rational Mind satisfies our human need for structure, boundaries, plans, and information, how it is something to depend on, stand on, and feel safe with, like the shore. Now, as you continue to breathe deeply, shift your focus to the sphere of Emotional Mind, and imagine it as the sea. Consider how the rolling waves of Emotional Mind satisfy our human need to feel and express our vast spectrum of emotions: love, joy, gratitude, fear, anger, frustration.

Continue to breathe deeply. Now, imagine Rational Mind as a being, embracing Emotional Mind without judgement. Imagine Emotional Mind as a being, allowing Rational Mind to embrace it, without sabotaging or rejecting it. Imagine Rational Mind allowing Emotional Mind to soften and be humbled, to surrender, to come into acceptance and deep understanding. Notice how your body feels, how your lung capacity expands, as you allow this integration to occur within you: This is Wise Mind. Notice how your body, mind, and spirit align in this moment. (Sound chime.) Slowly open your eyes and return to presence, feeling the full power of Wise Mind and carrying it into your day.

Suggested Homework: Reflect on your understanding of mind states and how you relate to each state. When are you in Rational Mind, Emotional Mind, and Wise Mind? Under what conditions do you move between them? Reflect back to the last session and Theater of Life Meditation; how do mind states come into play in developing Observer Self? Focus on the cast of characters: Emotional Mind, Rational Mind, and Wise Mind. Which character is observing from the balcony? What quality of being does the character embody? Who or what is your Observer Self voice? Be prepared to share your insights at the next session.

Module I (Mindful Recovery) Session 6:
Dialectical Behavior Therapy ~ The Interplay of Opposing Views

Suggested Opening Meditation ~ Body Scan & Sensory Meditation

Position your body to be comfortable, relaxed, and open. Close your eyes or lower your gaze. (Sound chime or toning bowl.) Take a slow, deep breath, utilizing your entire lung capacity, moving the breath down into the belly and all the way into the back. Now, slowly exhale. Continue to breathe deeply, allowing your entire body to soften a little more with each exhale. Notice how you are completely supported. Notice how your body naturally rises and falls with each breath, as if the breath is rocking you ever so gently and consistently.

Now, as you continue to breathe deeply, slowly scan your body beginning at the crown of your head and moving all the through to the tips of your toes. Simply notice each area of your body without judgment or commentary. If you notice any tension or tightness, bring your attention to that area and breathe into it to help open and release it. If there are thoughts trying to distract you, move your attention back to the breath. Feel the coolness of the breath as you inhale, the warmth of the breath as you exhale. Move your attention to any sounds that you hear and simply notice them as you continue to breathe deeply. Now bring your attention to what you see behind your eyelids, whatever colors, shapes, or patterns appear; just notice as they appear and fade away. Continue to breathe deeply. Turn your awareness to your sense of taste, and simply notice any taste sensations, however faint. Now, move your focus to your sense of smell, as you breathe in, slowly and fully. Simply notice with curiosity and openness, as you slowly exhale.

Move your attention to the sensations you are feeling on your skin. Notice the movement and temperature of the air; notice clothing or textures against your skin. Sense your feet in your shoes, and the floor beneath you. Now, slowly move your attention back to your breath as you step into Observer Self. Observe the process of breathing as you take one more full, deep inhalation all the way down through your lungs and into your back. Breathe in awareness and gratitude. As you exhale, feel your body release and relax fully. (Sound chime.) Slowly open your eyes and return to the room. Offer gratitude to your breath and your mind-body-spirit complex. Send yourself a blessing of full acceptance for you, just as you are!

Check-Ins and Q&A: If necessary, remind the group to keep check-ins brief (under two minutes). As this is the hallway point of the module, encourage participants to base their check-ins on the skills and practices they've learned and how they apply them in their lives. Invite them to share their homework, journal reflections, or insights they've gained over the past six weeks of the module. Have them reflect on the mind states and any other content they might want to expound on. A prompt might be, *How does learning about mind states help in developing Observer Self?*

Handouts: Dialectics & The Human Condition Model, Both/And Model

In this session, we look at the Dialectics & Human Condition Model and Both/And Model, starting with Dialectics. Use your whiteboard to convey primary concepts and to help participants connect what they are learning with what they are experiencing in their lives.

Dialectics & The Human Condition

It is essential for moving into wholeness that we understand the polarity of opposing views, forces, or experiences, and how to move between these often dramatic and opposing *ways of being* in the human experience. It is rather like learning to dance with a partner, which requires coming into alignment with their "opposite" steps. As we've discussed, Rational Mind is more structured and practical by nature and possesses a masculine quality, whereas Emotional Mind is more intuitive and unpredictable and embodies a feminine quality. It's not about gender, but rather qualities that any of us might possess and access, as we interact with people, places, and life circumstances.

We have surely all experienced the inner power struggle between the part of us that feels irrational and rebellious and the part that feels more practical and grounded. The goal is for the opposing mindsets of Emotional Mind and Rational Mind to come into balance, in order to come into alignment with Wise Mind. This is tricky because, as noted, there are higher and lower vibrations within the Emotional Mind sphere. Where Rational Mind is neutral and fixed, like the shore, Emotional Mind is in motion, mutable, and everchanging, like the ocean.

Lower vibrational emotions are fear-based (the bottom half of the Emotional Mind sphere) and carry a density or a heaviness that negatively impacts the mind-body complex, diminishing its ability to maintain good health. For example, when we are in the lower vibration fear state of Emotional Mind, our decision-making typically bifurcates. We are less able to think critically or use discernment, which leads to a perception that a black-and-white option is the only safe option. The more we are triggered, the less able we are to make rational decisions. To move out of that, we want to access Rational Mind to evaluate from a pragmatic perspective. By *noticing* when we are emotionally triggered, we can manage our emotions and apply the skills we are learning, which are found in Rational Mind.

Higher vibrational emotions are love-based and lighter (top half of the Emotional Mind sphere), thus have a positive impact on the mind-body complex and promote good health and overall wellbeing. When we are in that higher frequency, our decision-making tends to become naturally harmonious and aligns more with unity consciousness, as in the "Both/And" concept. The healing process takes willingness and a commitment to daily practice; it is a learning curve, so we need to be patient with ourselves and each other.

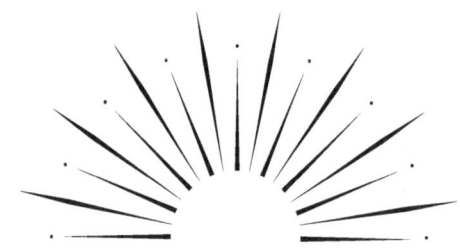

THE LIGHTHOUSE EFFECT BOTH/AND MODEL

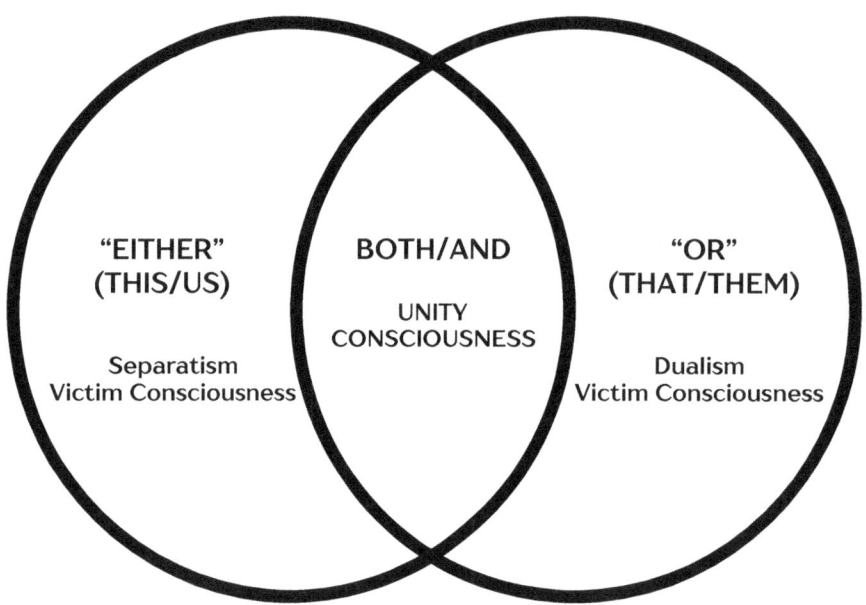

"EITHER"
(THIS/US)

BOTH/AND

"OR"
(THAT/THEM)

UNITY
CONSCIOUSNESS

Separatism
Victim Consciousness

Dualism
Victim Consciousness

THE LIGHTHOUSE EFFECT
DIALECTICS & THE HUMAN CONDITION MODEL

WISE MIND

HIGHER POWER

AUTHENTIC SELF

Emotional Mind
& Rational Mind in Harmony

INVERTED "DRAMA" TRIANGLE

Emotional Mind &
Rational Mind in Low Vibration
Reinforce Negative
Core Beliefs &
Attachment
Patterns

EMOTIONAL
MIND

Childlike

Imaginative

Creative & Expressive

RATIONAL
MIND

Intellectual

Structured

Rules & Order

Emotional Mind raises vibration when Rational Mind meets it with radical acceptance and understanding.

Group Exercise ~ The Dialectics Model

Draw the Dialectics Model on your whiteboard and convey key points as you walk participants through the content, and invite them to share their perspectives on each state.

The Both/And Concept

"Both/And" is a DBT concept that has its roots in Chinese philosophy, as in yin/yang. It is to experience the interconnectedness of opposites, rather than the more binary or dualistic experience of either/or. Integrating our opposing ways of thinking is how we free ourselves from internal and external conflict; mindfulness practice is essential to that process, thus, it is the core practice in the program. Through mindfulness and such practices as Observer Self, we are better positioned to make wise decisions.

Our cultural programming tends toward dualism, as in the adage, *Would you rather be right or happy*? Whereas Both/And is about accepting that two things can be true/valid at the same time: *That is true, and this is also true*; or, *I hear your perspective and it is valid, and this is my perspective, and it is also valid*. When we come from Both/And, we can experience compromise, harmony, and balance.

The Both/And way of being in the world is about walking between the "tension of opposing forces," as Carl Jung coined it, to find the middle path. It's a delicate balance that takes awareness, perseverance, and practice to maintain, and when we do, it is invaluable in helping us navigate the storms of life. Both/And allows us to meet our inner rebel, inner critic, and inner judge with understanding. We can listen to and at least *consider* that opposing view, even if we don't agree; again, it's about acceptance and compromise. As we build our toolkit, we begin to use recovery skills in concert with each other. Observer Self and Both/And go hand in hand. Another complementary skill is Turning the Mind, which we go into more in Module II. We don't have to solve a conflict in the moment it arises, we can simply turn our mind away from obsessing or fixating on the issue.

We might go for a walk, write the conflict down in our journal, or bring it to our sponsor or therapist to help us brainstorm what underlying feelings are at play and what the resistance or fear might be. When we return to the conflict, we are able to see it with clarity and can negotiate a compromise, rather than spending more time in a losing battle. This is true regardless of whether it's an internal conflict or one that has been projected onto someone else.

The Still Point ~ Eye of the Hurricane & Alignment with Love

The "still point" is broadly used in the wellness field; it essentially means to center or go within. It is the inner place that we settle into when breathing into the present moment during a meditation, practicing mindfulness in real time, consciously engaging in a challenging situation, and when we maintain equanimity in chaotic environments. Rather than chasing and amplifying the storm or feeding the ticker-tape of ingrained internal storylines, it is the stance we can take when the storms of life hit us. If we think of the lighthouse as representing vertical alignment between earth and the cosmos and between our bodies and our higher selves, we might think of our emotions as the ocean, as previously suggested. They can change from smooth sailing and calm, sunny moods to the stormy seas of emotional upheaval, the white squalls of violent waves rising and crashing within, often without warning. When we are in alignment, our emotions are the power source of our lighthouse. They carry the frequency of love, gratitude, and compassion. It's like the emotions are the *way* to Wise Mind, the portal or the part of us that expands into a broader energetic field where we can manifest higher states of consciousness.

The Lighthouse Effect is about learning how to masterfully center ourselves and manage our emotions, reactions, and responses when we are triggered, in order to anchor and channel our light and radiate our Authentic Self from the inside out. We do this by integrating and putting into practice all of our Lighthouse Effect skills with mindful focus, presence, and daily practice.

Suggested Closing Meditation ~ The Eye of the Hurricane Meditation

Get into a comfortable, receptive position and close your eyes or lower your gaze. (Sound chime or toning bowl.) Breathe slowly and deeply, low into your belly and all the way into your back; engage your entire lung capacity. Exhale slowly and fully. Continue to breathe deeply, as you drop your jaw and shoulders. Notice any tension in your body and send your attention and your breath into those areas. Notice the tension leaving your body with each exhalation. Now, imagine that you are a lighthouse and there is a hurricane swirling about you; imagine how you stand within the eye of the hurricane—still, calm, and centered even as the storm rages around you.

Continue to be the lighthouse as you breathe. Feel the strength of your body. Feel your feet planted firmly on the ground where you stand, or your back against the chair where you sit. Notice how you are completely supported. Allow yourself to be held in the embrace of the present moment. Call in your higher power and take another full-body breath into this vision of you, the lighthouse. Imagine that higher power as warm light emanating both from within you, and from all around you. As you exhale, allow your entire body to feel the warmth and safety of this nonphysical connection within your physical being.

Continue to breathe deeply. Now, notice the sea, your emotional waters; simply notice from a distance, from your lighthouse tower; observe any worry-thoughts stirring the waters. Notice what happens when you send those thoughts loving attention. Notice the calming effect. Notice how it is easier to see and feel them from a distance. Continue to breathe deeply, as you allow yourself to simply be with them in this way, observing without resistance, without fear, and with loving acceptance. Now, slowly turn your attention back to your foundation, your lighthouse-self, and allow yourself to fully align with your center, your still point within. Notice how it feels to be sovereign--to stabilize and anchor your mind, in alignment with the moment, in alignment with your authentic power. Take one more deep inhalation, and one more full exhalation. (Sound chime.) Slowly open your eyes and come into the present moment. Carry this sense of yourself as the lighthouse, your own safe refuge, rooted in bedrock and sheltered from life's stormy seas with you. Call it up whenever you face challenges or sudden storms in your life!

Suggested Homework: In your journal, reflect on how the Dialectics & The Human Condition Model and Both/And Model help you to come into balance. Think of examples in your own life where the Both/And concept might help you shift your state of mind. Be prepared to share your answers at the next session.

Suggested Opening Meditation ~ Both/And Meditation

Get into a comfortable position, and close your eyes or lower your gaze. (Sound chime or toning bowl.) Take three long, slow, deep breaths, filling your lungs and expanding into your abdomen. Imagine a challenge you currently face. Notice what happens to your body when you bring this conflict to mind. What stress level does it carry? Now, take another long, slow, deep breath to clear the mind, and zoom out to observe the same conflict from a distance. Notice the stress level of your body now. Notice how it is the same conflict, but looks different from another perspective. Continue to breathe deeply, as you consider the change in perspective. Neither perspective is wrong, you are just seeing things in two different ways: both/and. Maybe you see details in the closer perspective that you don't see in the broader perspective; maybe you can detach from your emotions from the broader perspective.

Continue to breathe deeply, allowing the "both/and" concept to settle in. Instead of looking for an either/or resolution, consider a compromise where you are stepping back enough to be the mediator of your own conflict. Consider both points of view. Notice what happens to your stress level when you allow and integrate the best of both perspectives. Take one more deep inhalation through the nose, and one more exhalation through the mouth. (Sound the chime) Now slowly open your eyes and stretch your body returning to your day with a sense of ease. Practice this both/and concept with any conflict that presents itself.

Check-Ins and Q&A: Encourage group members to focus check-ins on how their current life situations can be better navigated by applying the mindfulness practices and concepts they have learned so far in this module. Field questions to make sure that everyone clearly understands the material presented; all questions are welcome.

Handouts: The Serenity Prayer

What is the Art of Acceptance?

I introduce the Art of Acceptance in this module, as a precursor to Radical Acceptance, which we get into in the Tolerance Building module. It is essentially a guidepost for flagging what we are resisting or in conflict over in terms of mindfulness, or generally, in any given moment or life situation. Being in acceptance is about being without judgment; it is a way to ride the wave of life on life's terms. In any practice, we might instinctively attempt to counter our effort to change. Resistance isn't wrong or bad, it just *is*; it is a function of the ego, of our animal instinct and survival nature, and needs to be met with understanding. It ties to mindfulness practice in that it is through the practice of mindfulness that we can gain a perspective that is *observant* rather than *reactive*. We come to this detached, neutral, Zen stance and place of physical alertness by going within and providing ourselves with a moment of pause before taking action.

Through my years of martial arts training, qigong, and mindfulness practice, I have come to believe that all humans are capable of taking this inner stance, to be able to experience inner peace and serenity; it is actually a choice. The only thing any of us can really control is how we accept, tolerate, or respond in any given moment, and especially, challenging moments, which might be why the recovery culture has adopted The Serenity Prayer as a creed. "One day at a time" is another wise adage often used in recovery; it encourages us to be fully present in the moment and underscores how mindfulness practice can be a powerful relapse-prevention tool. To "be with" urges and cravings that are wired into the brain or to move through symptoms of withdrawal, we have to make the choice to implement an intervention process. To do that, we have to be in a state of awareness, which we can develop and achieve through mindfulness practice. You might do a group round, asking the group what they see as the value of that adage.

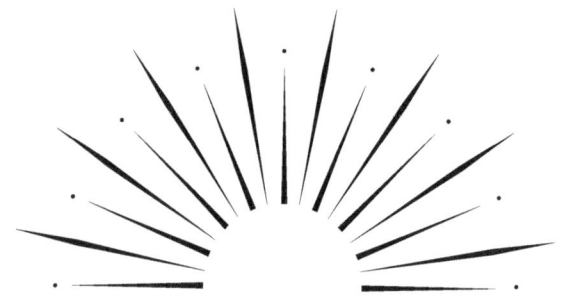

The Lighthouse Effect ∼ The Art of Acceptance

The Serenity Prayer

*God grant me the serenity
to accept the things I cannot change,
courage to change the things I can,
and wisdom to know the difference.*

*Living one day at a time,
enjoying one moment at a time,
accepting hardships as a pathway to peace.*

*Taking this world as it is,
not as I would have it;
Trusting that all things will be right;
if I surrender to Higher Power,
I will be happy in this life.*

Adaptation of "The Serenity Prayer" by Reinhold Niebuhr

Group Exercise ~ Decoding The Serenity Prayer

Review the prayer line by line. Ask participants to consider it in terms of challenges in their lives and their own issues with acceptance. Prompts might be: *What is happening in your life right now that you cannot change? What can you change about it?*

When we are chemically dependent--either internally, to hormones like adrenaline, or externally, to drugs or alcohol--to even come to believe there is such a thing as choice, we first have to move through the stages of change, and for that, willingness is key. The mind-body complex has acclimated to whatever habit we have formed that we are trying to change. As Dr. Bessel van der Kolk coined it, "the mind follows the body." It can be incredibly difficult for someone who is wired for addiction to actually slow down their mind-body complex. It's my experience that one of the most effective ways to do so is with movement, which is why I include qigong into The Lighthouse Effect Mindful Recovery Program. It's the Move a Muscle/Change a Thought premise, and whether it's qigong, yoga, gentle stretching, or taking a mindful walk, when we "move" our bodies, we shift our mindset.

Suggested Closing Meditation ~ Serenity Prayer Meditation

Close or lower your eyes and get comfortable in your body. (Sound chime.) Take three long, slow, deep breaths to bring yourself fully into presence. Focus your mind on the Serenity Prayer concept: *I will accept the things I cannot change, and I will change the things I can.* Take another slow, deep inhalation, feeling the breath move all the way through your lungs and into your back, breathing the truth of this wisdom into your being. Now slowly exhale, releasing tension and resistance. Take another slow, full inhalation, breathing in acceptance; feel the serenity of acceptance flowing through you. Now slowly exhale, releasing resistance. One more time, inhale deeply, breathing in courage; notice how it feels in your body, the energy of courage. Now slowly exhale, releasing all remaining resistance. (Sound chime.) Slowly open your eyes and return to presence. Allow yourself to feel the serenity of this truth of acceptance as you move through your day.

Suggested Homework: Reflect on the word "acceptance" and write about what it brings up for you. Consider the opposing word to acceptance: "resistance." Write about what happens to your mind-body-spirit complex when you focus on acceptance and what happens when you feel resistance. What would you need for support in order to move from resistance to acceptance? Be prepared to share your answers and reflections at the beginning of the next session during group check-ins.

Module I (Mindful Recovery) Session 8: What & How Skills

Suggested Opening Meditation ~ Gravity of Relaxation Meditation

Get into a comfortable position with your feet on the ground or floor, and close your eyes or lower your gaze. (Sound chime.) Take three long, slow, deep breaths down to the bottom of your lungs and all the way into your back. As you breathe, feel your body softening; notice and allow the weight of gravity to gently soften your entire muscular system. Continue to breathe deeply. Notice any place in the body where you may be holding tension. Now, as you inhale, breathe directly into that area; as you exhale, feel the softening and relaxing of those muscles. Take another slow, deep breath, noticing the weight of your feet on the floor.

Continue to breathe deeply, sending your breath, your attention, further down, deep into the earth beneath the floor or beneath your feet. Notice the solid foundation of the earth, supporting and stabilizing your body. Feel the weight of gravity and how it grounds your entire being. Breathe in, *I am present*; as you breathe out, feel your muscles softening. Breathe in, *I am allowing*; as you breathe out, feel your tension easing up. Breathe in, *I am becoming more relaxed and aware one breath at a time*; as you breathe out, feel your body opening. (Sound chime.) Slowly open your eyes and bring your relaxed presence back to the group.

Check-Ins and Q&A: Invite group participants to focus their check-ins on the Art of Acceptance and their reflections on the Serenity Prayer wisdom.

Handouts: What & How Skills

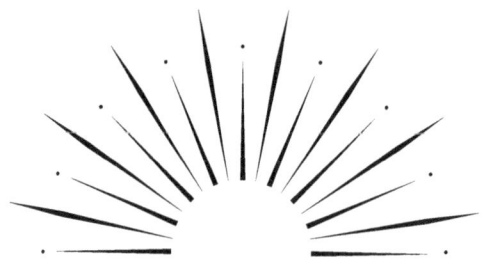

THE LIGHTHOUSE EFFECT
What & How Skills

WHAT SKILLS

In DBT, "what" skills are developed by bringing these three directives into the practice of mindfulness: observe, describe, participate. These directives (which are also basic precepts of other mindfulness practices and beliefs, such as Buddhism) also help us move away from judgmental programming by encouraging us to zoom out or step back and take the perspective of Observer Self.

OBSERVE: Learning to step into Observer Self or the "art of stepping back" is crucial to moving toward wholeness. We might use the analogy of the camera lens, how, when you open the lens to its wide angle option, you have a wider perspective. Observer Self takes that wider perspective. The Theater of Life meditation introduced earlier encourages us to simply observe and notice from different perspectives, as we shift our focus from the perspective we might have on the stage of a theater, to the perspective from the audience, and then, the perspective from above, from the balcony.

DESCRIBE: When we merely describe an event without adding a dramatic story or our own narrative, it diminishes the lure of it and, thus, offers us a wiser perspective. As the story or narrative is dropped, we can see or observe the event for what it is in the present moment. When we describe rather than qualify, we take judgment, analysis, and "good" or "bad" categorizations out of the equation. Ego does not like this practice, but when we remove the dramatic or emotional details, it can decrease stress levels quite effectively.

PARTICIPATE: This means to totally submerge ourselves in the moment with whatever we are doing, to fully "be with" the task at hand. It is to be fully engaged, like when a band musician does a solo and just lets go, as if the instrument is an extension of their whole mind-body-spirit complex. (It can be a spiritual experience to observe this in a live performance!) We can be with whatever we are engaged in, in the same way, in any given moment. Over time, with practice, we increasingly gain confidence and feel more in control of our lives.

IMPACT OF WHAT SKILLS: Practicing the observe/describe/participate skill set helps us with how we move through a challenging moment or circumstance; how to come from a more grounded, centered, and wise perspective, or, in other words, to be in our Wise Mind. From this wise perspective, this place of centeredness, we can take all sides into account, without judgment, and come into vertical alignment with our higher power and Authentic Self. We can shift our perspective or stance, both with external and internal conflicts.

HOW SKILLS

In DBT, "how" skills are also developed by bringing specific directives into the practice of mindfulness: One-Mindfully, Nonjudgmentally, and Effectively: The "how" is in "the now!"

ONE-MINDFULLY: This is about being with the moment and being fully present with whatever we are doing in the moment. We might look at the "wax on/wax off" exercise in the movie *Karate Kid,* the Buddhist teaching "chop wood/carry water," or the AA maxim "one day at a time" or "one moment at a time" as examples of this "how" skill. Another aspect of the practice is to bring into the present moment something that we *want* to experience but are not experiencing in our life. For example: *I want to feel healthy in my mind and physical body. Though I may not be currently feeling well, I can imagine what it would feel like to be mentally and physically well. I can bring this feeling into the present moment.*

NONJUDGMENTAL (JUDGMENTAL STANCE VERSUS NONJUDGEMENTAL STANCE)

JUDGMENTAL STANCE: This tends to be the automatic-response stance where we unconsciously default to negative core beliefs and see our emotions as inseparable from who we are: *My emotions are part of me. When I am sad or angry, I believe that I am bad.*

NONJUDGMENTAL STANCE: This stance comes from a more conscious perspective where we understand that our emotions are simply to be experienced without commentary or judgment: *I learned to associate what I feel with who I am. My feelings are getting me to attend to a need that is not being met. This need is a vulnerable part of who I am, and is worthy of being heard and met with understanding, kindness, and compassion, as we would be with a child.*

Feelings and emotions are neither good nor bad. They are indicator lights pointing to a deeper issue that needs to be explored and understood. Ego/Lower Mind loves to chase "why?" Why did this happen? Why am I like this? The problem with these "why" questions is how they lead to the thinking, I am a problem to be fixed. That, in turn, fuels self-judgment: what is wrong with me? When we chase "why," we race past the emotional need calling out to be heard. "Why" questions are of the intellect and they are worthy of exploration, but they tend to distract us from those vulnerable parts of ourselves that are so in need of recognition. Lower Mind is like a dog chasing a scent, hyper-focused on tracking down information in a physical sense or physical form: in-*form*-ation.

In contrast, Wise Mind takes its cues from the inspirational, nonphysical, or spiritual part of our being and has a more detached perspective. To come into Wise Mind, we need to meet Emotional Mind with radical acceptance, understanding, and compassion. Rational Mind's reflective What & How questions can lead us to the vulnerable places within Emotional Mind, where the hooks of our traumatic early memories are wedged and waiting to be released, and with them, the fears that drive them. When we expand into the wiser viewpoint of Wise Mind, we can better manage whatever challenges we face.

EFFECTIVELY: This "how" skill is about entering a flow state where we are doing what works as opposed to what we think is "right." It is about being rational, not emotional: it has to make sense, while also aligning with or being in the spirit of harmony and balance.

To fully participate in life is to be fully present, to be fully mindful. When you are fully engaged and fully present in life, you are fully you, your Authentic Self. You are the present and you are a gift. You are here, now, in this moment——and that is All!

Group Exercise ~ What & How Skills

Use the What & How Skills handout as a group exercise, using your whiteboard to underscore primary concepts and reflect back participants' comments.

Suggested Closing Meditation ~ Be the Tree Meditation

Get into a comfortable standing or sitting position, and close your eyes or lower your gaze. (Sound chime or toning bowl.) Take a slow, deep breath, and imagine your body as a tree. Feel your feet planted on the ground, and the tendrils of your energetic root system reaching deep down into the earth. Take another slow, deep breath. Imagine your torso as the trunk of the tree, solid and firm. Now, imagine your arms as branches reaching upward towards the sky, and your face as a canopy of leaves turned toward the sun, gazing upward and into the cosmos.

As you continue to breathe slowly and deeply, imagine drawing the earth's energy up through your feet, your torso, and all the way through your spine; feel this life force moving through your heart, arms, and hands. Feel this energy as nourishment for your entire body. Continue to breathe deeply, as you visualize this earth "qi" energy moving through your neck, your head, and up through your crown, then extending further outward and upward, energetically nourishing your auric field and beyond. As you continue to breathe slowly and deeply, feel the alignment between earth and sky. Take one more deep inhalation, and exhalation. (Sound chime.) Slowly open your eyes and return to presence. Feel the strength and stability of being the tree and carry this feeling throughout your day.

Alternatively, you can lead an "eyes open" meditation, where you direct the group to observe the room, without judging and simply describing (silently, to themselves) what they are seeing in the room.

Suggested Homework: In your journal, reflect on what you learned in this session regarding "why" questions. Consider how shifting out of why questions and into "what" or "how" questions shifts the mind away from needing to come up with an intelligent answer. Notice how mindfulness practice invites you to observe and experience the moment instead of projecting into the future. What happens when you move out of your head and into the present, when you stand firm, just like the tree?

"I am the master of my fate: I am the captain of my soul."

--William Ernest Henley, "Invictus"

Module I (Mindful Recovery) Session 9: Attachment to Detachment

Suggested Opening Meditation ~ Be the Mountain Meditation

Get into a comfortable position, and close your eyes or lower your gaze. (Sound chime or toning bowl.) Take three, slow, deep breaths and imagine a majestic mountain. See its grandeur in your mind's eye, and stand at its base. Turn your back to it and lean into it, as if to merge your body with the mountain. Feel the solid physicality of it, extending down into the earth's bedrock; feel the power and strength of it in your entire body. As you continue to breathe deeply, imagine the extreme weather and seasons your mountain endures. Imagine standing firm as snow and ice swirl about you; now, imagine the warmth of the sun melting the ice away. Feel the strength of that ability within yourself, how you can stand firm and in alignment with your environment, in alignment, mind, body, and spirit. (Sound chime.) Slowly open your eyes and return to presence. Carry the sense of strength and power of your inner mountain with you through your day. Remind yourself that change is inevitable. This too, whatever this obstacle is, shall come to pass.

Check-Ins and Q&A: Continue to monitor check-ins, making sure they are kept brief, and encourage participants to focus on skills they've applied or concepts that resonate with what is happening in their lives. A prompt might be: *What detachment skill or concept are you applying or could apply that would help you gain your Wise Mind perspective when you are triggered?*

Handouts: No new handouts. (You might review previous handouts that support group process.)

Detachment/Nonattachment & Attachment

Mindfulness practice is vital for coming into our Authentic Self, and a vital component of mindfulness is to practice detachment. The reaction I often get when I use the word "detachment" is that it sounds cold and somewhat apathetic or uncaring, so I often interchange it with the word "nonattachment." But either way, what I stress to the group is that detachment is actually about *caring*: it is self-care.

Detaching means stepping back and looking at a relationship (whether with another person or a substance) from a distance. It is integral to building our internal lighthouse as it helps us break away from our emotional sea of fears, triggers, and reactions. To practice detachment, we need to take a close look at our *attachment* programming or imprinting. In the first months and years of life, we form attachments to our caregivers. We do this to meet an instinctual and basic survival need, just as we need food, water, and air. Some attachment styles will be healthier than others, but whatever our attachment style, it tends to be repeated throughout our lives in our relationships.

As we transition through the stages of human development, we naturally move through a process of individuation, which gets amplified in our teen years when we undergo hormonal changes. It is by design that it is a time when we are likely to experiment with more intimate relationships and when our early-attachment pattern will emerge. The brain is indiscriminate with attachment wiring, so it can happen not just with another *person*, but with an addictive substance or chemical, as we will explore further in Module IV, "Conscious Interpersonal Communication: The Visible Shine of your Lighthouse ～ Transmitting your Light."

The threat of losing a person or quitting a substance we've become dependent upon for our survival is terrifying to our inner child and triggers fears of abandonment and rejection. I'm speaking to any type of dependency arising out of whatever attachment style we initially form. For example, our attachment encoding might be such that it can trigger huge emotional reactions, such as extreme jealousy in our relationships, or an acute sense of abandonment when a relationship ends or a substance to which we have a chemical dependency is removed. We've looked at Observer Self in earlier sessions, and we touch on it again here in the context of attachment/detachment. In this context, it's about recognizing and detaching from the part of us that is our personality or ego, and moving into the more expanded Observer Self that is of the soul.

Group Exercise ~ Zoom Out

Using your whiteboard and building on the previous group exercise, draw a small round circle in the center of the board and label it "telephoto lens/small self." Draw a larger circle around the small circle and label it "wide-angle lens/Tall Self/Wise Mind." Select a volunteer from the group to share a current challenge they are facing and the emotion or feeling it triggers. Write their answer in the small circle at the center. Then ask them to imagine moving away from that emotion or the feeling and zoom out to the wider angle perspective. Ask them how they feel now, distancing themselves from it, and write their answer in the outer circle. A group discussion will naturally ensue from there. You might ask other participants to chime in and share their reaction to this exercise.

Detachment is a simple micro-intervention for taking pause, to allow a more informative and inspired perspective to be accessed. I might use the phrases "step back," "take a breath," "time out," "let it go," or "take space" interchangeably as encouragement to detach from the moment, captivating or dramatic as that moment might be. When we choose to take pause in this way, a more loving, kind, and healthy path forward becomes possible. Life has a way of increasing the volume of our programming and patterns until we surrender and listen to our inner callings, as if to call attention to what no longer can be ignored. It's about experiencing life on life's terms, which we looked at in an earlier session. In this context, it is about taking responsibility for ourselves, with whatever it is we are facing. We can't control what happens to us, but we can choose how we navigate through it.

It is also about developing our ability to listen attentively and kindly to our inner child, rather than avoiding, repressing, and neglecting their call for supportive help no matter how challenging it might be. Developing a healthy relationship with the most vulnerable part of ourselves is like re-parenting from within to provide the loving care and attention we would a child. It is an "inside job," something only we can do. It also supports us in establishing healthy relationships with others. The goal is to no longer be driven to *survive*, but instead to *thrive* in relationship to people, places, and things. From this place, we can move through life in balanced alignment with our Authentic Self, radiating love rather than internalizing and feeding fear narratives and beliefs.

Urge Surfing ~ Riding the Wave

Another effective DBT skill to learn and incorporate into our Lighthouse Effect Toolkit is "Urge Surfing," to keep with our lighthouse and ocean imagery. Learning how to "ride the wave" of urges and cravings is not an easy feat. It takes practice (with frequent pulls into the undertow of our turbulent emotional sea) to get to a place where we can readily find our center and maintain a sense of presence in any given moment.

Urges and cravings are prompts that occur in the mind-body complex (brain/muscle memory) and that compel us to find short-term relief or fixes for physical or emotional threats, pain, and other stressors. Most of us understand triggering patterns in the context of substance addictions, such as alcohol, nicotine, and other drugs. What is less commonly understood is how they occur with behaviors. For example, obsessive-compulsive urges: cleaning, organizing, working, internet surfing, overusing social media, looking at porn, and so on. These are just as powerful and addictive. As are more covert compulsions, such as obsessing about intrusive thoughts or threatening inner voices.

As noted earlier, Emotional Mind is composed of two opposing experiences within its own sphere. The lower half/lower vibration is powered by fear, and the top half/higher vibration, by love. No matter how pervasive these intrusive thoughts or urges and cravings are, we need to recognize that they come from those lower frequencies within the Emotional Mind. When the sympathetic nervous system kicks in, the brain (limbic system) immediately seeks a dopamine hit to satisfy its need for a release or to gain instantaneous pleasure. This reactive process gets hardwired in the brain and requires serious interventions to cut the circuitry and interrupt the power source. The human experience is essentially a dance between fear and love, as we learn to work with our natural instinct for self-preservation and physical safety, while making conscious choices rather than reactive.

The way to alter our trigger-and-fix pattern is by applying intervention tools and practices, one of which is always available to us: the breath. We can use the breath to "turn the mind," to bring us from a linearly focused stressor or *external* threat or from an emotionally charged stressor or *internal* threat, to a *vertically* centered stance or perspective. We do this by simply taking deep, long, slow breaths, which we can do in pretty much any situation. When we practice refocusing our mind in real time, we start to develop new pathways in the brain that eventually create new circuitry and redirect our reactive-behavior patterns.

Another effective practice for addressing trauma triggers, panic attacks, or any strong emotional reaction is the Emotional Freedom Technique (EFT), which we dive into in detail later in Module III (Emotional Balancing). Reflective Inquiry, which we get into in depth in Module II (Tolerance Building) module, is also highly effective. In terms of mindfulness, the practice of self-reflection helps us to check in on intrusive thoughts or urges and address them with conscious attention. Either of these practices could be introduced and touched on in this module, if it seems appropriate for the group, and then picked up again in the modules where they are more thoroughly addressed.

To urge surf and ride the wave of opposing internal voices is to become skilled at questioning the demanding authoritative voices in our heads, listening to them with discernment, and choosing to act from the higher perspective of Wise Mind. It's about responding from within–

-not from fear, but in vertical alignment with love. When we can identify the part of ourselves that is running the narrative, when we see that it's the voice of our emotional inner child, we can then act from our adult self.

Suggested Closing Meditation ~ Urge Surfing Meditation

Get into a comfortable position, and close your eyes or lower your gaze. (Sound chime or toning bowl.) Take three long, slow, deep breaths; visualize being in the ocean on a surfboard. Feel the board beneath your feet or your stomach as you ride a huge wave; feel the salt-spray and wind; feel how strong and sturdy you are, secure on your surfboard. Now, think of the wave as an urge or craving. Notice how you are skirting above it, just riding along with it, without judgment, without commentary, without running a story about how much you need it. As you slowly inhale, breathe in the strength of your whole being, riding above the urge; as you slowly exhale, release all attachment to the urge. Continue to breathe, deeply, calmly, as you ride the wave all the way to the shore. Now, step off of your surfboard, and observe as the wave recedes, as the urge recedes. (Sound chime.) Slowly open your eyes, and stretch; keep this image of you riding the wave of urges and challenges as you move through your day.

Suggested Homework: Reflect on the concept of Detachment/Nonattachment in your journal and notice what comes up for you. Practice applying the skill in real time. Reflective questions: *How do I feel when I am attached to my urges and thoughts? How do I feel when I practice detaching from my urges and thoughts?*

Module I (Mindful Recovery) Session 10: Movement Meditation

Suggested Opening Meditation ~ LaQi Movement Meditation: This is a movement meditation, and as with any meditation or exercise that involves movement, instruct participants to not do or follow through with anything that feels uncomfortable or causes pain. Advise them to simply remain in their relaxed sitting or standing position and *visualize* the movements. (Interestingly, it has been observed in medicine-less hospitals in China that simply visualizing qigong movements can be as powerful as doing the actual movements!)

Sit or stand comfortably in a relaxed and open body posture. Lower your gaze but keep your eyes open. (Sound chime or toning bowl.) Hold your hands in front of you about sternum level, facing your palms toward one another, about a foot apart. Slowly and mindfully move your hands closer together to almost touch, then move them back to the starting position. Now focus completely on the energy that you feel between your palms as you move them closer together, and then as you move them further apart. Notice any sensations of warmth or tingling from the life-force energy.

Begin to move your hands back and forth slightly, cupping your hands around the energy and playing with it. Now, slowly move this "ball" of energy upward, directing it toward your chest, feeling the healing life-force energy, then move it up to your neck, your face, eyes, ears, and head. Return to the original position and close your palms: *Namaste*. You can use this method for self-healing and self-soothing at any time. Practice the LaQi Movement Meditation on your entire body and auric field, returning to the original position to gather more qi between your palms, as you need it.

Check-Ins and Q&A: Invite participants to reflect on their homework and share how they have used the Urge Surfing and Detachment/Nonattachment concepts in their lives.

Handouts: Qigong Basic Exercises

Body-Movement Practices

Body-movement practices or movement meditations like yoga, stretching, mindful walking, or qigong help to focus the mind in the moment. I have been practicing qigong for many years, so it's my "go-to" and the one I like to share with my group. I take them through some warmup and basic qigong movements (as presented in the handout) so they can experience qi firsthand and get a sense of the healing effect and presence of mind it cultivates. (View my video of me demonstrating the movements on my website, innerfaiththerapy.com.)

Qigong

Qigong is an ancient Chinese healing practice that has its roots in Taoism: "qi" refers to life-force energy and "gong" means to cultivate. Qigong can be a viable relapse prevention practice, especially for those who have a co-occurring anxiety disorder or trauma history, as it aids in grounding our energy and sedating the central nervous system. It is also an effective way to practice mindfulness, which is why I introduce it at this point in the Mindful Recovery Module. (I have also found qigong to be beneficial in learning to tolerate sitting meditations.) Practicing qigong expands our conscious awareness and fosters connection with all creation, thus aiding in mind-body-spirit alignment.

Qigong brings a sense of inner peace, and as a daily practice, can increase overall health and vitality. We are creatures of habit, but we can become skilled at redirecting our default thoughts and focusing our attention. Qigong is a way to align our minds in the present and balance our energy. The body is always in a state of presence, while the mind moves between the past, the present, and projections of the future. The mind can choose to be present, or not, and the body can encourage the mind to attend to "the now." In helping the mind stay focused and present, qigong is an effective intervention tool when we are experiencing urges, cravings, or symptoms of anxiety or depression, as the mind will follow the body movements and rhythmic breathing of the practice.

We have the idea that if we are in physical or emotional pain, it may become chronic. When we cultivate and attach to a narrative that we are in chronic pain, it becomes our experience. This is not to say the pain isn't "real," it's that when we attach to the belief that it's chronic, that it will always be there, we limit our own ability to heal ourselves. Qigong practice has been used to address both physical and emotional pain. When we think of ourselves as an energetic system, as being less dense and not solid matter, as physics teaches us, we empower ourselves to heal. The act of bringing our focused attention to places in our body that need healing or release is the first step, the second is to "move" the energy. Qigong is a movement meditation and practice for moving energy and healing the body-mind-spirit complex.

As I am writing this segment on qigong, I am remembering a time when I was running the Mindful Recovery Group at Keenan House in Pittsfield, Massachusetts. Participants in group therapy who were in residence at Keenan House were mandated to be there, so I had a "captive" audience. I was introducing qigong to the group, and quite a few members were belittling the practice. I was being playful with them, understanding that it might seem weird to them, while continuing to guide them through it. Towards the end of the class, several participants asked what it was they were feeling between their hands. The answer is, they were feeling the energy they had been cultivating by simply doing the movements. One of the members, James, expressed enthusiastic interest as his chronic hip pain had dissipated during the session. (James had sustained multiple injuries in a near-fatal car accident some years earlier.)

I ran into James about a month later and he couldn't thank me enough for introducing him to the practice of qigong. He told me he had been practicing it regularly, that his pain had significantly decreased, and his mood had greatly improved. I was grateful to learn of his firsthand experience of how qigong was benefitting his health and wellbeing. It reinforced for me how we can empower ourselves in our own healing process through the direct experience of learning and practicing new skills.

Group Exercise ~ LaQi Power to Heal

Lead a conversation about participants' experience or felt sense during the opening LaQi meditation. What did they feel? What is the life force? What is qi? Introduce the idea that we each have the power to heal, the power to move pain, to reduce pain, to transcend pain. Reflect on the concept of pain as *energy*, the body as *energy*. Ask them to consider and reflect on the physics of our bodies, how we are more "space" than solid matter. How does that scientific fact help us to see that we can move emotional and physical pain? Pain can feel permanent yet in truth nothing is permanent. Through focused attention and practices like qigong, and with conscious intention, we can reduce, transform, and heal emotional and physical pain.

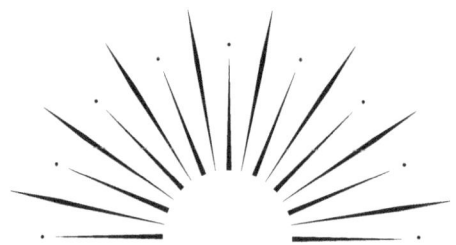

THE LIGHTHOUSE EFFECT
Basic Qigong Exercises for Cultivating Qi

These movements generate qi energy through the entire body and auric field, which naturally relaxes the body to allow the flow of energy to be restored and moving through all of the meridian pathways. (Modify the movements if you have had an injury or are experiencing pain.)

CIRCLE HANDS: Rotate your hands at the wrists in a circular motion, with both hands moving the same way or in alternating directions. Do this for a count of ten. This movement is good for carpal tunnel.

CIRCLE SHOULDERS: Move both shoulders in a circular motion, slowly and mindfully, directing them backward and around for a count of ten, and then alternating to direct them forward and around for a count of ten.

CIRCLE HEAD: Point your chin outward while simultaneously sticking out your "tail" (tailbone). Then reverse the action by tucking your chin towards your chest and your tailbone inward. Circle your head slowly around, left to right, for a count of ten, and then right to left. Come back to center and gently look to the right over your right shoulder for a count of ten, then to your left over your left shoulder for a count of ten.

CIRCLE WAIST, HIPS, PELVIS: Stand in a relaxed position with your upper body fully relaxed. Feel your feet on the floor, and the sense of being rooted in the earth. Allow your arms and hands to be fully relaxed and hanging loosely to the sides of your body. Gently rotate or "swing" from the hips in a half circle from one side to the other and back, allowing your arms to gently hit your body as you move. Continue the swinging movement for a count of ten to twenty.

CIRCLE KNEES: Place your feet together with your hands on your knees, if you can. Rotate your knees gently to the right for a count of ten, and then gently to the left for a count of ten. Notice how this circular rotation gently massages your feet.

CIRCLE ANKLES: You might want to stabilize your body by holding onto a wall or a chair, or if you can, take the challenge of balancing your body. Lift your right knee up and rotate your ankle ten times to the right and ten times to the left, and then do the same with your left knee and ankle for a count of ten.

BOUNCE HEELS: Rise up onto the balls of your feet so that your heels are slightly off of the floor, and then gently drop down, and repeat this gentle bouncing motion for a count of twenty.

Alternative Movement ~ Myofascial Unwinding: You might also introduce Myofascial Unwinding to the group, as an alternative or additional way to move tension out of the body, foster relaxation, and reduce the stress that accumulates in the body. Developed by John F. Barnes, it is another technique for releasing energy knots and blockages in the body. It is a sort of improvised stretching process that is about fully attending to whatever place in the body is calling to be unwound or released. My mentor Lynne Forrest likens it to being tangled up like a telephone cord, then allowing our body to unwind by completely surrendering to the release of energetic tension that has been holding us in lockdown patterns from childhood trauma, to then be set free from those patterns. When Lynne presents Myofascial Unwinding at her Family of Origin workshops, she incorporates expressive, evocative music, which can help to facilitate a vibrational or energetic opening. The energetic release can be felt on a deep cellular level and is powerfully healing.

Suggested Closing Meditation ~ Qi Ball (Playing Ball) Movement Meditation

Sit or stand comfortably in a relaxed and open body posture. Lower your gaze but keep your eyes open. (Sound chime.) Hold your hands in front of you about sternum level, facing your palms toward one another, about a foot apart, as with the LaQi Movement Meditation. Slowly and mindfully move your hands closer together to almost touch, then move them back to the starting position, feeling the qi energy between your hands.

Hold the energy as you would a beach ball, with your right hand on the top of the "ball" and left hand on the bottom. Move from your waist turning slowly to the right as far as you can comfortably go, holding your qi ball in front of you, and then back to center. Switch hands; place your left hand at the top of your qi ball and right hand on the bottom. Move slowly to the left as far as you can comfortably go, and then back to center. Repeat for a count of five. (Sound chime.) Release your qi ball, knowing you can pick it up and "play ball" at any time.

Suggested Homework: Practice qigong, yoga, stretching, mindful (slow) walking, or any mindful movement that resonates with you.

Resources: Myofascial Unwinding (myofascialrelease.com)

"Wholeness is never lost, it is only forgotten. Integrity is more an undoing than a doing, a freeing ourselves from beliefs we have about who we are and ways we have been persuaded to 'fix' ourselves to know who we genuinely are."

--Rachel Naomi Remen, MD, *Kitchen Table Wisdom: Stories That Heal*

Module I (Mindful Recovery) Session 11:
Stages of Change Reflection & Progress

Suggested Opening Meditation ~ Presence Practice: Repeat a presence or mindfulness meditation of your choosing, or simply guide the group to "be with" the silence and stillness, with no other instruction other than to remind them the goal is to still the mind, turn awareness to the breath, and sit in the stillness of the moment.

Check-Ins and Q&A: Invite group participants to share their experiences of qigong and how practicing it affected their stress levels and frame of mind. Ask them to share any progress, insights, and points of awareness that have come to light throughout this module and how they have made an impact in their recovery.

Handouts: Stages of Change Addiction/Recovery Pros & Cons Worksheet

Group Exercise ~ Stages of Change Review, Repeat, & Reflect

This next-to-last session of Module I is dedicated to Stages of Change and the SOC Addiction/Recovery Pros & Cons Worksheet. Review the SOC Model and then have the group complete a new Pros & Cons Worksheet together, showing their responses on your whiteboard. Repeating the exercise spurs the group-reflection process, and also helps participants reflect on their individual processes and progress since the start of the module. Have them review the worksheets they completed individually as homework at the beginning of the module and reflect on notable changes. Invite them to share what they learned and what they continue to be challenged by as they build their toolbox of mindfulness practices, skills, and exercises. The focus is on what they already have and what they might need to cultivate inner strength, resilience, and presence.

Suggested Closing Meditation ~ Lighthouse Effect Theater of Life Meditation

Get into a comfortable position, and close your eyes or lower your gaze. (Sound chime or toning bowl.) Feel your feet on the floor, your back against your chair; relax your shoulders and jaw. Take three long, slow, deep breaths. Each time you exhale, feel your body softening and relaxing more deeply. Now, as you continue to breathe deeply, bring your attention to a conflict that is occurring in your life or a recurring challenge in a close relationship. Imagine you are sitting in a theater, in the front row, watching this scene play out on the stage. Feel yourself sitting there, simply observing the drama as it unfolds in front of you, just a few feet away. Watch how the actor playing you interacts with the person causing you discomfort.

Take another slow, deep breath; as you exhale, imagine you are moving from the front row to the very back of the theater. Notice how you feel as you observe your drama playing out from a greater distance. Continue to breathe, letting go of judgment, negative thoughts, and emotions with each exhalation. Now, imagine yourself moving up into the balcony of this life theater. Notice what it feels like to view the scene from a bird's eye perspective; notice you are more detached from your emotions. Take another slow, deep breath all the way into your back, and slowly exhale, allowing your body to fully relax. (Sound chime.) Slowly open your eyes and begin to move your body, as you return to the present moment. Carry this sense of relaxation with you throughout your day.

Suggested Homework: Complete the SOC Addiction/Recovery Pros & Cons Worksheet on your own and compare it to the one you completed at the start of the module. Continue to practice the skills you've learned throughout the module. Reflect on the major takeaways and write about them in your journal. What were the highlights and what were the challenges? Be prepared to share your reflections with the group at the final session. Consider bringing art, poetry, or other works you created or were inspired by as you moved through the module.

Module I (Mindful Recovery) Session 12: Closing Ceremony & Graduation

Suggested Opening Meditation ~ Attending to the Breath Meditation

Get into a comfortable position, and close your eyes or lower your gaze. (Sound chime or toning bowl.) Take three long, slow, deep breaths. With each inhalation, sense the temperature of the air, feel the sensation of the air as it enters your nostrils, and follow the flow into your lungs. Notice how your chest rises with each "in" breath and relaxes with each "out" breath, as if the process of breathing is gently rocking you. Feel into this subtle rocking motion, noticing your "in" breath and "out" breath as you continue to breathe deeply. Notice how soothing it feels to attend to your breathing. If your mind tries to comment or judge and distract you from the present moment, simply acknowledge that it is what the mind does. Breathe into it and just observe it, without worry, without engaging, and let it go. Just continue to follow the rocking rhythm of your breath. One more deep inhalation; one more full exhalation. (Sound chime.) Slowly open your eyes, and gently begin to move your body. Take your time. Slowly bring your attention back to the group.

Check-Ins and Q&A: Encourage participants to share highlights of the module in terms of both their individual progress and the group process, and to express gratitude towards the group for their courage and participation. Invite the group to do an appreciation round where they express appreciation to their fellow participants for what they brought to the group. Invite them to share artwork, poetry, journal passages, or other such works they've produced or been inspired by as they moved through the module.

Handouts: Module I Completion Certificate

In this last session, go over any unanswered questions participants raised during the check-in or challenges they talked about.

Closing Ceremony & Closing Out the Module

Present completion certificates to the group. Invite them to join you for the next module, "Module II Tolerance Building: The Structure of Your Lighthouse ~ Developing Resilience." Share that you are looking forward to seeing them at the first session and provide the date and time.

Suggested Closing Meditation ~ Grounding Through Sound & Sensation Meditation

Get into a comfortable position, and close your eyes or lower your gaze. (Sound chime or toning bowl.) Take three long, slow breaths, deep into your lungs, abdomen, and all the way into your back. Notice the sounds in the room; notice the sounds outside of the room. Continue to breathe slowly and deeply; notice the subtle sensations on your skin, your feet in your shoes, the weight of your clothes on your body. Breathe in, breathe out; breathe in, breathe out. Notice the temperature of the room. Notice how your breath feels moving into your body through your nose and how it feels as it leaves your body through your mouth. Breathe in, breathe out; breathe in, breathe out. Feel how your breath grounds you in your body; feel how it anchors you to the moment. (Sound chime.) Now, slowly open your eyes and return to presence. Carry that sense of being grounded and rooted with you throughout your day.

Suggested Homework: Reflect in your journal about the takeaways of this module. Continue to practice mindfulness and self-care daily, using the tools in your Lighthouse Effect toolkit.

THE LIGHTHOUSE EFFECT SKILLFUL RECOVERY PROGRAM

Certificate

This certifies that

_____

has successfully completed The Lighthouse Effect Skillful Recovery Program
Module I Mindful Recovery
The Bedrock of Your Lighthouse ∼ Anchoring Awareness

_____   _____
FACILITATOR   DATE

Guiding Principles For Life Beyond Victim Consciousness by Lynne Forrest with Eileen Meagher (lynneforrest.com/store)

"The Three Faces of Victim," by Lynne Forrest (lynneforrest.com)

Loving What Is: Four Questions That Can Change Your Life by Bryon Katie, with Stephen Mitchell (thework.com)

The Power Of Now: A Guide To Spiritual Enlightenment by Eckhart Tolle (eckharttolle.com)

The Earthing Movie (earthingmovie.com)

The Way Of The Peaceful Warrior: A Book That Changes Lives by Dan Millman (peacefulwarrior.com)

Peaceful Warrior, directed by Victor Salva, 2006, DEJ Productions

Spiritual Emergence and Recovery from Addiction by Jacquelyn Small

Myofascial Release/John F. Barnes (myofascialrelease.com)

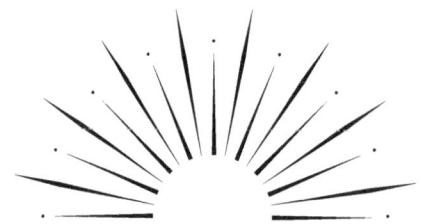

THE LIGHTHOUSE EFFECT MODULE II SYLLABUS
Tolerance Building: The Structure of Your Lighthouse ~ Developing Resilience

Session #1 Welcome & Introduction: Group Rules, Confidentiality, & Building Group Cohesion; Building a Recovery Network; Meeting the Authentic Self; Understanding the Nature of the Ego & the Soul; Group Exercise ~ Safe & Acceptable

Session #2 Stages of Change Review: Group Exercise ~ Stages of Change Review & Repeat with a focus on tolerance (Participants also complete the Pros & Cons worksheet on their own as homework)

Session #3 Identifying Triggers: Origin of Triggers; Identifying & Charting Triggers Group Exercise ~ Lighthouse Effect Determining Your Triggers

Session #4 Radical Acceptance: Accepting Reality (whatever it is); Upgrading & Navigating Patterns of Resistance; Understanding the Inner Critic/Judge; Group Exercise ~ Stepping into Observer Self

Session #5 Opposite Thought/Opposite Action: The "move a muscle/change a thought" concept; Group Exercise ~ Opposite Thought/Opposite Action (how applying the skill in real time in daily lives)

Session #6 Turning the Mind & Half-Smile: Applying tolerance building skills (Turning the Mind, Half-Smile, River Wisdom); Start & Stop Practice; Group Exercise ~ Half-Smile & Turning the Mind (from The Lighthouse Effect Comprehensive Tolerance Building Skills)

Session #7 Resistance versus Receptivity: The function of Resistance; Survival vs. Revival; Practice not Perfection; Comprehensive Tolerance Building Skills continued; Group Exercise ~ What Do I Want?

Session #8 Reflective Inquiry ~ Know Thyself: The Tall Self (adult) and small self (inner child): Group Exercise ~ LHE Serenity Prayer Reflective Inquiry Exercise

Session #9 Deepening Reflective Inquiry ~ Negative Core Beliefs: Our Relationship with the Self; Group Exercise ~ Going Fishing (Changing the Narrative: Is it a Capital-T Truth?)

Session #10 Valued Living ~ A Change of Perspective & Gratitude Journal: Valued Living Model & Worksheet; Group Exercise ~ The Lighthouse Effect Values & Goals Worksheet

Session #11 Stages of Change Reflection & Progress: Charting "tolerance building" progress over the course of the module; Group Exercise ~ Stages of Change Review, Repeat, Reflect

Session #12 Closing Ceremony & Graduation: Certificates of Completion; Appreciation/Gratitude Circle; Invite group to continue on to the next module (Emotional Balancing)

MODULE II TOLERANCE BUILDING:

THE STRUCTURE OF YOUR LIGHTHOUSE ~ DEVELOPING RESILIENCE

My perspective as a trauma and addictions therapist is that the path from addiction into recovery, from survival to revival, is to learn to light our own way through the dark night of the soul. We need to acknowledge and accept the darkness, in order to move out of it. (This is why "hitting bottom" has its merits; from there, the only way out is up.) The dance between fear and love plays an important role in the development of the self: both/and. This program was informed by my own experience. My personal journey started by healing my body through dance and martial arts, which taught me how to focus the mind in the present. Then I slowly found my way to inner work or shadow work through martial arts, presence practice, and learning (and applying) self-care and intervention skills. Along the way, I increased my ability to step back, to take a broader or wide-angle-lens perspective, to get to know all parts of myself and to meet those inner selves with understanding and without judgment, essentially, to learn to align mind, body, and soul and make conscious choices from Wise Mind.

When we commit to a path of recovery, it becomes a way of life. It's not easy; we will have setbacks and it takes courage and perseverance, but we are perfectly unique souls that came into the world and we can find our way home to our Authentic Self. Once we begin to live our lives from the inside out, once we begin to come into alignment with our authentic nature, we can feel the truth of that in real time, in any given moment. Our journey home to full presence is actually our greatest gift; that is why we call it "the present." Learning to accept all parts of ourselves is essential to coming into alignment, mind, body, and soul, which is why Radical Acceptance is the core concept of Module II. We build tolerance by developing the art of acceptance.

Module II (Tolerance Building) Session 1:
Developing the Art of Acceptance ~ A Radical Stretch

Review Protocol: Review logistics and group rules; distribute Repeat Handouts and ask group members if there is anything that can be done to ensure group safety. Begin and end each session with a mindfulness meditation to reinforce and integrate the importance of being in the present.

Repeat Handouts: Group Rules, Stages of Change Model, Stages of Change Addiction/Recovery Pros & Cons Worksheet, Stages of Change: Metamorphosis from Survival to Revival Lifestyle, The Role of an Accountability Partner & How to Give Constructive Feedback Relapse Prevention Plan Worksheet.

Gentle Reminder: Provide new members with the PAWS Self-Assessment Worksheet and How to Manage Emotional Denial handout. Keep in mind that you might want to provide participants who've already received them with another copy, as needed, based on your assessment. (It is always beneficial to provide the Relapse Prevention Plan Worksheet, for example, for participants to update as they move through the program.)

Suggested Opening Meditation ~ The Art of Acceptance Meditation

Sit comfortably in a relaxed and open body posture. Lower your gaze or close your eyes. (Sound chime or toning bowl.) Take three long, slow, deep breaths. Bring to mind a current challenge you are facing. What is the story your mind is running? Just be with that "story" for a moment, as you continue to inhale and exhale, slowly and deeply. Notice how this challenging life situation makes you feel. Take a slow, full inhalation, and as you exhale, zoom out to your Observer Self position. Take another deep breath. As you inhale, ask yourself, *Is there something I can change or is it entirely out of my control*? As you exhale, let Observer

Self answer.

Now breathe in; give your attention to the thing you can change, or if there is nothing, simply acknowledge that truth. As you breathe out, focus on releasing what you cannot change; simply accept that it is what it is. Breathe in acceptance; breathe out resistance. Notice changes to your stress level as you come into acceptance; notice how your physical body and emotional body soften. Take one more slow, deep inhalation and then slowly, fully exhale. (Sound chime.) Slowly open your eyes and return to presence. Carry this sense of acceptance, of allowing yourself to navigate life on life's terms, through your day.

Check-Ins and Q&A: Facilitate the introductory check-in round, and then allow time for group members to ask questions, express concerns, and/or share reflections regarding handouts and any lingering questions from the previous module. Focus on group rules and building a safe container. Ask if there is anything more that can be done to support participants in maintaining confidentiality and creating boundaries. We develop resilience through repeated application of skills, meditations, exercises, and techniques, and it's also good to remind them again of the importance of practicing in real time.

Handouts: Module II Syllabus

The Art of Acceptance ~ A Radical Stretch

As noted above, the core concept of this module is Radical Acceptance--radical acceptance of *what is*, which I also think of and refer to as "the art of acceptance." In this module, participants are introduced to skills and practices to develop and foster tolerance, with great emphasis on developing their ability to breathe through feelings of resistance when they come up and/or when survival instincts kick in. The key is to understand that such instincts arise whether the danger or threat is real, imagined, or remembered. When we are mindful of that and can *accept* our responses as natural reflexes, we are better able to redirect the energy by applying skills that build strength, agility, and resilience: hence, the art of acceptance.

We get into the tolerance building skill of Willfulness versus Willingness or Resistance versus Receptivity a little further along, but I mention it here in the context of our early development. Resistance versus Receptivity is the exploration of an inner conflict where the intellect *believes* it is receptive and willing but the emotional system is resistant or willful. That resistance is a hallmark of the programming we get in our first years of the human experience and stems from the instinctual survival responses of the ego.

We learn to protect our physical form in childhood and develop our ability to maneuver these vessels (our bodies) that move us through life so that we don't get hurt. And of course, we do get hurt, to some extent. We have mishaps when we are learning to walk, to swim, to ride a bike, and so on. Such natural consequences are essential to our development, but even those "hurts" can create roadblocks by the ego and emotional system. The brain remembers our early experiences and has a tendency to lock in fear reactions, which can keep us from advancing or growing in life. To move the emotional system out of resistance, we need to see things as they really are--radical acceptance--instead of relying on what we *feel*, what happened in the past, or what we project might happen in the future. The goal is to learn to *trust what happens*.

Understanding the Nature of the Ego & the Soul

In order to come into acceptance and to come into alignment, mind, body, and soul, we need to understand the nature of the ego and the soul. Ego needs a guru/teacher, has to see it to believe it, is indoctrinated into the shame/blame game from birth, believes it is separate from God/Spirit/Higher Power, and is naturally ruled by fear. Soul knows that it is its own guru/teacher, that wisdom is found within, that it is an integral part of and one with God/Spirit/Higher Power; it is aligned with love--our very essence.

Ego is motivated by fear as a survival instinct, and is therefore easily threatened and constantly seeking safety or shelter. Ego carries expectations and it judges, compares, and is easily victimized. When we encounter emotional and physical stressors in our early life, they get stored in our memory and encoded through our five senses. We learn to compare our life situations and experiences with others, and we experience being separate from others. As we are essentially pack animals, we develop attachments with our caregivers and family of origin. We attach to our early social circumstances and create narratives around them and then carry those narratives into adulthood. We were all born into this reality of polarizing opposites and indoctrinated into our family of origin and the cultural dogma of what is unacceptable, unsafe, and "bad," and what is acceptable, safe, and "good."

As children, we are naturally egocentric, so the "bad" thing we did or witnessed gets emotionally imprinted and internalized as being about us, about the self. Like a fish swallowing a hook, we latch on to that negative core belief and it becomes a mantra of identity: *I am bad*, or *I am not good enough*. Even our natural curiosity can be unconsciously encoded as dangerous, as in the old adage, *curiosity killed the cat*. We get fear-based lessons throughout childhood. For example, *look both ways before crossing the street or you'll get hit by a car*. Of course, such guidance is meant to teach us and protect us from the dangers of life, and every child will interpret these early lessons differently. For some, an unintended result is that the child becomes overly cautious and afraid to take risks of any sort.

We also learn to perceive love as conditional and/or dependent on our behavior: *good girl; good boy*. While we do need to teach children how to navigate the grading system that underlies our Western culture (in school systems, in our work lives, even in social dynamics), we need to be conscious about how we teach them and what we might be conveying with our own behaviors. Parents who have not healed their own childhood wounds and trauma unconsciously raise their children in the same dysfunctional way they grew up.

Group Exercise ~ Safe & Acceptable

Engage the group in a whiteboard exercise with the title "Safe & Acceptable." Ask participants to share examples of childhood memories where they were taught what was safe and acceptable using the qualifying words "good" and "bad." Create a "Safe & Acceptable" column on the left side of the board and "Dangerous & Bad" on the right. Ask them for examples of when their caregivers' feedback was favorable and unfavorable, and how they felt with each. Share with the group that we will circle back to the emotional impact of our childhood programming in Module III, the Emotional Balancing module.

A Perfect Seed ~ The Authentic Self

I liken our human experience to the journey of a seed, how a seed gets planted in the dirt and grows against all odds, with much of its success depending on whether or not it got a good start, whether it was planted (or naturally seeded) in such a way that it takes root. The terrain in which the seed gets established also determines its level of resilience. While the seed itself came into being already perfect, it is quickly influenced or shaped by its environment--as are all beings. We are very much influenced and shaped by our "environment" (people/places/things), including how others react or respond to us; our responses and reactions to those outside influences become patterns that reinforce our own false, negative narratives. Thus, understanding our early experiences and programming is essential to healing into wholeness.

We might think of the soul as the spark of light in the seed that we carry into this world. Though the terrain and environment in which we are raised is beyond our control, it is our responsibility as adults to come back to our Authentic Self. If we focus only on the imprinting that we received--how we performed up against the grading system, for example--we reinforce the false narratives we adopted in childhood, but we can reclaim our authenticity and come into our sacred purpose. If the soul is the light or essence of the seed, then returning to or stepping into our Authentic Self comes through the integration of the ego and the emotional system within the soul.

We need to embrace our vulnerability and meet our fragile child-self with compassion and understanding to emerge out of the matrix of our early programming and come into who we truly are as our unique expression of Spirit (God of our understanding). We need to listen to all parts of ourselves without judging them, including the most fearful parts of ourselves, and every emotion (energy in motion). It is challenging for all of us, and especially for those "seeds" whose terrain and environments were not optimal. The bottom line is, we are the only ones who can do it: It is up to us to choose the path of recovery, the path of integration into wholeness. The good news is, we don't have to do it alone. We can engage a support network, and we can choose to walk each other home.

Suggested Closing Meditation ~ Observer Self Meditation

Get into a comfortable position, and close your eyes or lower your gaze. (Sound chime or toning bowl.) Sit up straight with your feet flat on the floor and your shoulders and jaw relaxed and open. Take three long, slow, deep breaths, exhaling longer with each breath. Take another deep breath; as you inhale, zoom in on a current challenge or conflict. See it in your mind's eye; notice how your body feels, notice where you might have tension. Now, slowly exhale and zoom out; breathe your way out to a safe distance and simply observe, without judgment.

Continue to observe from this broader perspective as you take another long, slow, deep inhalation. As you exhale, notice any changes in your emotional body or your physical body. Notice the softening of your muscles. Feel the power of your Observer Self and how it supports and protects your nervous system. One more deep inhalation, one more slow exhalation; feel the sense of security and stabilization throughout your body and mind. (Sound chime.) Now, slowly open your eyes and bring yourself back to the present. Know that you always have the ability to zoom out to a broader perspective.

Suggested Homework: Reflect on the handouts distributed at the beginning of this session and complete the Relapse Prevention Worksheet. Bring any questions or reflections you might have to share during the check-in or Q&A at the next session.

Sometimes suddenly, sometimes slowly, a veil lifts and we glimpse the true scope of the being that we already are. Nature reveals her handiwork – a being unbound by time or space and yet focused in a specific time and place. The work has already been done; there is nothing to add or take away. There is only the harvest."

--Christopher Bache, *Dark Night, Early Dawn: Steps to a Deep Ecology of Mind*

Module II (Tolerance Building) Session 2: Stages of Change Review

Suggested Opening Meditation ~ Presence Meditation

Get into a comfortable position, and close your eyes or lower your gaze. (Sound chime or toning bowl.) Take three long, slow, deep breaths. As you inhale, feel the breath move all the way down into the base of your abdomen and all the way into the back. As you exhale, completely empty your lungs, extending the length of the exhalation each time. Breathe in; feel the support of the chair beneath you. Breathe out; allow your body to soften. Breathe in; feel how you are supported in this moment. Breathe out, softening even more with each breath. Feel deeply into the calm sense of simply being present. Breathe into Wise Mind: Breathe in the mantra, *I am supported, I am completely supported*. Breathe out the knowing, *I am safe, here, now, in this moment*. (Sound chime.) Slowly open your eyes and bring your awareness to the group. Carry this sense of calm presence with you throughout your day.

Check-Ins and Q&A: Remind the group to keep check-ins to two minutes. Have them reflect on the first session and be sure to answer any logistical questions and/or questions about any of the handouts. Encourage participants to write in their daily journals throughout the module to inform their progress and capture any insights along the way.

Handouts: Stages of Change Pros & Cons Worksheet

As noted in the Introduction, we review Stages of Change in the first or second session of each new module, revisiting the SOC Model and doing the Stages of Change Addiction/Recovery Pros & Cons worksheet again. In this module, we look at Stages of Change in terms of building resilience, focusing on changing intolerances that lead to triggers.

Group Exercise ~ Stages of Change Review & Repeat

Review the SOC Model in the context of building tolerance, and have participants complete the Pros & Cons Worksheet as a group exercise, using your whiteboard. Ask them to share ways they resist and how they might become less resistant and more accepting of change in terms of their relationships to people, places, and life situations. The group exercise helps participants get started and inspired to do the worksheet on their own as homework because, ultimately, it is self-work and self-care.

Suggested Closing Meditation ~ Both/And Meditation

Get into a comfortable position, and close your eyes or lower your gaze. (Sound chime or toning bowl.) Take three long, slow, deep breaths, filling your lungs and expanding into your abdomen. Imagine a challenge you currently face. Notice what happens to your body when you bring this conflict to mind. What stress level does it carry? Now, take another long, slow, deep breath to clear the mind, and zoom out to observe the same conflict from a distance. Notice the stress level of your body now. Notice how it is the same conflict, but looks different from another perspective. Continue to breathe deeply, as you consider the change in perspective. Neither perspective is wrong, you are just seeing things in two different ways: both/and. Maybe you see details in the closer perspective that you don't see in the broader perspective; maybe you can detach from your emotions from the broader perspective.

Continue to breathe deeply, allowing the "both/and" concept to settle in. Instead of looking for an either/or resolution, consider a compromise where you are stepping back enough to be the mediator of your own conflict. Consider both points of view. Notice what happens to your stress level when you allow and integrate the best of both perspectives. Take one more deep inhalation through the nose, and one more exhalation through the mouth. (Sound the chime) Now slowly open your eyes and stretch your body returning to your day with a sense of ease. Practice this both/and concept with any conflict that presents itself.

Suggested Homework: Complete the SOC Addiction/Recovery Pros & Cons Worksheet again, focusing on what you would need to change in order to become more tolerant or resilient in challenging circumstances. For example, you might reflect on the ways you are willful and/or in resistance when you are triggered or come up against a situation you find intolerable, and list them in the Addiction Pros & Cons columns. Then consider how you might apply skills and concepts you've learned, and list those thoughts in the Recovery Pros & Cons columns.

Suggested Opening Meditation ~ River Wisdom Meditation

Get into a comfortable position and close your eyes or lower your gaze. (Sound chime or toning bowl.) Take three long, deep breaths and bring your attention inward. Visualize a winding river and watch as it flows downstream. Now, imagine you are the water, flowing smoothly and peacefully along, completely in harmony with your environment. Imagine you see an enormous rock up ahead, in the middle of the river. Continue to breathe gently and naturally as you observe the approaching obstacle. Notice how you intuitively flow around the rock; it does not stop you from moving forward. Think of a current challenge in your life; visualize it as another rock in the river. Simply notice that it is there, and then continue to breathe gently as you flow around it. Breathe in, slowly and deeply, letting this feeling of being river water move all the way through you. Breathe out, allowing your body to fully soften and relax. (Sound chime.) Slowly open your eyes and return to the group. Know that you can be as powerful, agile, and resilient as river water whenever you need to be; know that you can skillfully move past obstacles in your path.

Check-Ins and Q&A: Invite group participants to check in (briefly) and share insights based on last week's homework, specifically on their individual Pros & Cons Worksheet.

Handouts: The Lighthouse Effect Determining Your Triggers Worksheet

Origin of Triggers

Before we can learn how to radically accept anything, we have to know what we are accepting, so it's essential to both identify our triggers *and* where they originated. The first place we experience fear is in childhood. I believe it is universal that we all have a trauma history, though for some, they are more intense than others. The birthing process itself is to some extent a traumatizing event. Whether it is a vaginal birth or surgical birth, the infant experiences contractions and some degree of trauma, and with a vaginal birth, it includes being squeezed through a very small tunnel, often for hours. Even with a home birth, where the environment might be more inviting than a hospital setting, we experience some level of trauma during our entry into this world. Because, with all forms of delivery, we leave an aquatic environment that is warm and completely contained, and enter a cold environment with many unknowns.

So, our "trauma programming" began as early as when we were in utero, and continued throughout our infancy and childhood. Early childhood is when we first encountered physically and emotionally challenging experiences that got encoded into our instinctual survival center, wired into both the brain (limbic system) and the energy body (central nervous system and muscle memory). Our trauma memories might not be just from this lifetime or from our own singular experiences, but could include transgenerational trauma transferred through DNA. In other words, trauma memory can be inherited from our ancestors. Whatever the origin, it is critical that we identify our emotional triggers so that we can deprogram imprinted memories.

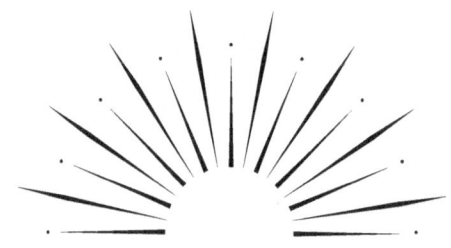

THE LIGHTHOUSE EFFECT
Determining Your Triggers Worksheet

Reflective Inquiry and inner work are essential for unpacking our triggers, coming into awareness, and implementing skills to rewire our negative programming. We need to divert the ego from looking for someone or something else to blame. When we see our challenges as outside of our control, we thwart our own ability to make conscious choices and deny ourselves the opportunity to reach our goals and live our dreams. Moving from survival to revival really is an "inside job!"

Positive Thought or Idea:

Consider an idea you had recently about something you wanted or desired, but did not follow through on. Or one that you have now that you are not likely to follow through on. Write down what thoughts and feelings first came/come to mind? Did it/does it first send a surge of joy or optimism through you?

_____

_____

_____

_____

Negative Thoughts, Judgments, Narratives:

What were/are the default "yeah, buts" that maybe cause you to feel defeated or deflated, and to not follow through? List them below. Example: *Not enough money; not enough time.*

_____

_____

_____

_____

Those default negative responses are essentially an internal "emergency alert system." Once we become aware of them, we can then get to the negative core beliefs they stem from. Look deeper to see if you can find the negative core belief.

Imprinted Trauma Memory:

_____

What early trauma memories or events are you carrying? What jugdments by a caregiver, family member classmate, or others have you internalized? List them below. Example: *My teacher was always telling me, "you just don't try hard enough."*

_____

_____

_____

_____

Negative Core Beliefs:

What are the negative core beliefs that are tied to that early trauma memory? Examples: *I am not good enough; I am bad; I am a loser; I am a failure, so why even try?*

How are the Negative Core Beliefs working for you? Example: *If I identify as a loser, I don't have to be responsible for my choices.*

_____

_____

_____

_____

Rewiring Default Programming:

By uncovering the underlying negative core beliefs, we can take steps to rewire our programmed thinking and self-judgments, and make conscious choices for moving forward. Willingness is a key factor. What strategies have you used in the past to move past default programming?

_____

_____

_____

_____

What new strategies or tools might you use now and in the future? Example: Observer Self, Opposite Thought/Opposite Action.

_____

_____

_____

_____

Practice identifying your triggers whenever you notice negative narratives or mind chatter and begin to weave skills, interventions, and techniques for rewiring that programming into your daily practice.

Group Exercise ~ Lighthouse Effect Determining Your Triggers

The inquiries in the Lighthouse Effect Determining Your Triggers Worksheet help to determine personal triggers and where they originated from. Doing the worksheet as a group exercise also helps to ground the concept of victim consciousness, as in the Victim (Inverted) Triangle.

Victim Consciousness

We touched on victim consciousness in Module I, and go into it in more depth here, in this session of Module II. I was first introduced to victim consciousness by Lynne Forrest, in the context of her Family of Origin workshops. Lynne worked with a modified version of Stephen Karpman's Drama Triangle, which is in the form of an inverted triangle, as presented in Module I. Refer back to that handout, and have your group take a closer look at it now.

As mentioned in Module I, victim consciousness is about roles we take on as unconscious defense mechanisms or coping strategies for surviving our family of origin. As the model shows, there are three "victim" roles: Persecutor or "Abuser," as I call it, Rescuer, and Victim. The role we take on informs how we receive approval and criticism, what sort of self-preservation habits we develop, how we are in relationship with others, and so on. Though we tend to predominantly take on one role, the roles are not static; we might shift from one to the other, depending on who we are interacting with and the power dynamics of that relationship.

While Abuser and Rescuer may appear to be more powerful and confident, they are also victim roles; they are just more covert, whereas Victim's victimhood is more overt. Those who tend toward the classic Victim role might be the youngest, "the baby" of the family, or the sibling who has chronic health challenges, whether physical or mental. Identifying and understanding the role we predominantly played in our family of origin is instrumental in helping to understand our behavior as adults; we need to accept it in order to begin to change it.

TIP: The victim consciousness concept can be tricky to convey in the context of mental health and addiction. (It is not to be confused with being the victim of chronic illness, and accident, or catastrophic event.) It might be correlated or confused with the phrase "blaming the victim." You might want to clarify the concept with your group if it seems there is some confusion. Assure them that it's is not about blame and shame, it's the very opposite. It is about coming into awareness about how we attach to and continue to identify with the role or roles we took on in childhood, and how those roles present obstacles in moving toward wholeness.

Suggestion Closing Meditation ~ The Balloon Meditation (Detaching from Negative Core Beliefs)

Get into a comfortable position, and close your eyes or lower your gaze. (Sound chime or toning bowl.) Take three long, slow, deep breaths, focusing your awareness on the present moment. Bring to mind a negative self-judgment that keeps coming up; recognize that it is a negative core belief. Imagine writing that negative core belief on a balloon, whatever it might be, "I am not good enough" or "I can never follow through." Now take that balloon with the belief you've held, and release it to the sky. Continue to breathe gently and deeply as you watch it slowly drift up and away; watch it getting smaller and smaller; watch it fading out of sight and disappearing into the vastness of the sky, your higher power. Breathe into the sense of release, of letting go of that belief. Feel the lightness of being in your mind, in your body. Take another full inhalation, and slow, gentle exhalation. (Sound chime.) Open your eyes and return to presence. Know that you can practice this in the moment, whenever you catch yourself making self-judgments that come from a negative core belief. There is an endless supply of balloons!

Suggested Homework: Over the coming week, reflect on the Victim Triangle Model and concept of victim consciousness. Write in your journal about any triggers and insights that come up. Contemplate the roles and how you resonate with them under various conditions or within different relationship dynamics. Be prepared to share your observations and/or ask questions at the next session.

"Life is ten percent what happens to you and ninety percent how you respond to it."

-- Charles R. Swindoll

Module II (Tolerance Building) Session 4: Radical Acceptance

Suggested Opening Meditation ~ Riding the Horse Meditation

Sit comfortably in your chair and position your body to receive openly. Close your eyes or lower your gaze. (Sound chime or toning bowl.) Take three long, slow, deep breaths. Imagine you are sitting on a horse. Imagine a challenging life situation that has you feeling defeated and victimized. Notice how it feels in your body. Imagine that situation as a fence in front of you; imagine that you are beginning to slide off of the horse. That fence seems impossibly high. Now pause, take a slow, full breath and ask yourself, *Can I make the choice to feel confident and skillful, to not be in victim consciousness?* As you exhale, imagine you are righting yourself in the saddle. Look at the fence. Imagine you and your horse flying over it. Take another full, deep breath, allowing a sense of calm confidence to move through you. Think: *I've got this!* (Sound chime.) Slowly open your eyes and return to the group. With daily practice and self-discipline, you can choose to get back in the saddle and ride the horse of recovery in any moment, no matter how intense the trigger.

Check-Ins and Q&A: Invite group participants to keep check-ins brief and focused on how the material relates to their daily lives. They might reflect on the Victim Triangle Model again, Identifying Triggers handout, and what last week's session brought to light during the week.

Handouts: How to Wisely Upgrade Negative Patterns of Resistance

Coming Into Radical Acceptance

Earlier in the module, we looked at the Art of Acceptance, which is a variation of or lead-in to the DBT concept of Radical Acceptance. Resistance is a protective function of the ego and needs to be met with understanding and acceptance. Radical Acceptance is about taking pause to check in on what we find intolerant in ourselves. It's not about minimizing our experience of being hurt, nor condoning the thing that led to it; rather, it's about riding the wave of life on life's terms, as the AA adage goes. Resistance can be a catalyst for change, and in that sense, it can serve us. If we simply notice and "attend to it" without judging, it can be the tipping point from which we transcend our current perspective and move out of automatic, default reactions.

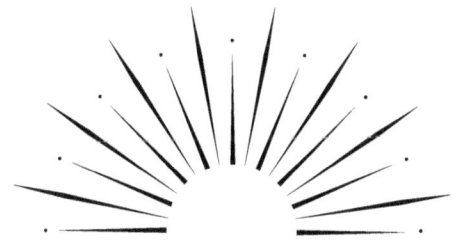

THE LIGHTHOUSE EFFECT
How to Wisely Upgrade & Navigate Patterns of Resistance

To come into "radical acceptance of what is," we need to understand our default strategies for coping and our patterns of resistance.

Default Coping Strategies

Denial
Avoidance (pushing away)
Wanting (grasping)
Boredom
Restlessness (doubt)

Practices for "Upgrading" & Moving Out of Resistance

Observer Self

A powerful way to upgrade or change a negative coping strategy is to make the experience of the coping strategy itself the focus of your mindfulness practice. To do that, we want to step into Observer Self and acknowledge what is happening without fighting it or judging it. Simply place your attention on the negative strategy or strategies: denial, avoidance, wanting, boredom, or doubt. Notice the energy they carry. Now, take a step back and observe from a more detached perspective of Observer Self. See denial for what it is: a strategy for coping. By naming it and acknowledging it, you can now detach from it; you can choose to release its hold on you. You can choose to step into Observer Self at any time. From this perspective, you can begin to skillfully manage default coping strategies, trains of thought, trauma memories, childhood programming, the emotional system, and symptoms (anxiety, depression, mood swings) in real-time.

Opposite Thought/Opposite Action: Apply Opposite Thought/Opposite Action to each coping strategy.

For Denial: An opposite thought to denial would be "truth," and the opposite action would be to be completely honest with yourself. Being in denial or keeping secrets from ourselves, even unconsciously, takes an enormous amount of energy that weighs down the body and mind. Continuous denial leads to further resistance and deeper attachment to the old coping strategy. Notice what being truthful with yourself feels like, how it has the opposite effect to denial. Does your body open, soften, and relax when you acknowledge what is true? Do you have a sense of relief? When you acknowledge "truth," you can consciously choose a healthy alternative to the addictive substance or behavior that was the coping strategy.

For Avoidance: An opposite thought to avoidance would be "confront," and the opposite action would be to face your fears. Instead of thinking, how is this against me? Think: how is this for me? Learn how to advocate for yourself, how to be assertive, how to embrace obstacles and aversions instead of avoiding dealing with them.

For Wanting: An opposite thought to wanting would be "let go," and the opposite action would be to pause, step into Observe Self, and detach. When you find yourself wanting/grasping, use focus breathing to help you pause and move into the observer stance. Notice the "narrative" that comes with the want: I can have just one, I've been doing so good not (drinking/eating sugar/overspending/rescuing someone). Is it a Capital T Truth or a Small t Truth, a convenient narrative. Is this narrative or advice coming from Wise Mind, or Emotional Mind? Be nonjudgmental and gentle, yet firm; feel the power of choice and resist the temptation of desire. Choose to act from your "Tall Self," from Wise Mind; the choices you make from Wise Mind are fully empowered choices.

For Boredom: An opposite thought to boredom is "focused interest," and the opposite action is focusing your mind to "zoom in" on your own morals and values. What is important to you in your life? Focus on the benefits of choosing healthy alternatives. This too helps you step into the Wise Mind perspective; notice how it feels when you become "interested" in what works for you and your wellbeing.

For Doubt (restlessness): An opposite thought to doubt is "faith," and the opposite action is to choose to believe in yourself—your right to be here and your own self-worth—and invest in yourself. Invest in yourself by taking time for you; read (or listen to) inspirational books; watch self-empowerment or mindfulness practice videos; whatever activities help to shift your focus toward what uplifts you.

~

Choose You: Once you choose to mindfully focus on changing default negative coping strategies and learn to observe them without judgement, you will increasingly feel the change in your mind/body/spirit complex. Remind yourself that you learned your resistance patterns and ways of coping when you were a child; you could not possibly have known the long-term impact, and how they might follow you into adulthood. When you come to see that those negative core beliefs and patterns of behavior don't define you, you can begin to detach from them, un-identify from them, and free yourself to choose alternatives that support you on your journey to wholeness, to your Authentic Self: the truth will set you free!

Daily Practice: Meet your old ways of coping with compassion, kindness, and radical acceptance; focus with intention on a life worth living as you integrate skills and choose new behaviors that support your wellbeing. Upgrade your life by navigating from Wise Mind consciousness; from surviving (resistance) to thriving (embracing the whole self).

Group Exercise ~ Stepping into Observer Self

Though we covered Observer Self extensively in the first module, it is applicable here too, as a tool for coming into radical acceptance and addressing patterns of resistance. (And it's always beneficial to repeat and review any intervention skill, to help integrate it into our daily practices and lives.) Work with the group using your whiteboard to engage them in a conversation about Observer Self in this context.

A key point to introduce is that when we come from a more detached or neutral Zen stance, we are better able to accept "what is," and to then explore our internal landscape, unpack the causes of our triggers, and implement interventions. Almost anything we do can be done with mindfulness, which means we can step into Observer Self at any time. Cravings and compulsions ebb and flow; when we can step back and observe them, we can make a conscious choice to *not* follow them.

Suggested Closing Meditation ~ The Art of Acceptance Meditation

Sit comfortably in a relaxed and open body posture. Lower your gaze or close your eyes. (Sound chime or toning bowl.) Take three long, slow, deep breaths. Bring to mind a current challenge you are facing. What is the story your mind is running? Just be with that "story" for a moment, as you continue to inhale and exhale, slowly and deeply. Notice how this challenging life situation makes you feel. Take a slow, full inhalation, and as you exhale, zoom out to your Observer Self position. Take another deep breath. As you inhale, ask yourself, *Is there something I can change or is it entirely out of my control*? As you exhale, let Observer Self answer.

Now breathe in; give your attention to the thing you can change, or if there is nothing, simply acknowledge that truth. As you breathe out, focus on releasing what you cannot change; simply accept that it is what it is. Breathe in acceptance; breathe out resistance. Notice changes to your stress level as you come into acceptance; notice how your physical body and emotional body soften. Take one more slow, deep inhalation and then slowly, fully exhale. (Sound chime.) Slowly open your eyes and return to presence. Carry this sense of acceptance, of allowing yourself to navigate life on life's terms, through your day.

Suggested Homework: Reflect on the concept of acceptance and write in your journal about the challenges and benefits of practicing "radical acceptance of what is."

Additional Practice: Mindfully eat a piece of fruit, gaze at the stars, or play with a pet. Mindfully prepare a meal or drive your car. Mindfully listen to a friend. The more we practice, the more reflexive it becomes, and the less likely we are to default to old programmed behaviors.

Module II (Tolerance Building) Session 5: Opposite Thought/Opposite Action

Suggested Opening Meditation ～ Swimming with the Current Meditation

Sit comfortably in a relaxed and open position and close your eyes or lower your gaze. (Sound chime or toning bowl.) Take three, slow, deep breaths to bring yourself to the present moment. Consider a current challenging life situation or a feeling of resistance in your body or mind. Now, imagine being in a river, feeling the pull of the current. Imagine the current is a challenge you are currently facing. Imagine you begin to swim against that current; imagine how hard it feels to keep going, how much energy it takes. Now, as you continue to breathe deeply, imagine that you stop swimming, and turn over onto your back. Imagine yourself being gently carried along, flowing downstream. Feel the sense of peace that going with the flow brings, feel the release of tension as you let go of the struggle and accept that you will be cared for. Allow yourself to think, *I don't have to fight so hard to be safe, to cope with challenges; I have faith that I will be cared for.* Take another long, slow, deep breath, allowing the feeling of going with the flow to move all the way through your mind-body complex. (Sound chime.) Slowly open your eyes and return to the present moment. Practice going with the flow as you move through your day.

Check-Ins and Q&A: Invite group participants to reflect on how resistance shows up in their daily lives and how applying the skills and exercises have impacted their experiences.

Handouts: No new handouts. Continue to work with How To Wisely Upgrade & Navigate Patterns of Resistance, focusing on the Opposite Thought/Opposite Action tool.

Doing a One-Eighty: Opposite Thought/Opposite Action

The mechanism of a trigger response is that it takes us back in a nanosecond to a childhood event, whether mild or severe, that became encoded in the brain as a trauma memory. Triggers can come through any of the five senses associated with the encoded (trauma) memory, and we can be transported back in time so fast that we experience nausea or a racing heart or any symptom associated with a surprise threat or attack. One of the best skills to apply when we are triggered is Opposite Thought/Opposite Action, which is where we do the opposite thing from what our emotions or Emotional Mind wants to do. Opposite Thought/Opposite Action is an effective intervention for substance addiction, codependent relationships, or other maladaptive behavioral patterns. Instead of being on autopilot and defaulting to emotionally driven narratives that do not serve us, we can choose narratives that are true for us and consciously think of a healthy alternative when we have an urge for an addictive substance or habitual behavior.

For example, you have an urge to go to a bar and have a drink, but you take a pause and tell yourself something along these lines: *Alcohol is a deceptive trap that leaves me physically, mentally, and emotionally sick. It is like poison to me. I am not going to give into this neurological biochemical reaction. Instead, I am going to breathe through the urge and consider it from the Observer Self perspective. I see through the deception. I see it for what it is, an unhealthy dependency that has become hardwired in my brain.* Then, instead of following through with the urge to go to a bar, you do a "one-eighty." You go to the gym, go on a hike, or visit a friend in your recovery network.

Group Exercise ~ Opposite Thought/Opposite Action

Have participants come up with examples of situations when they applied Opposite Thought/Opposite Action and/or potential future scenarios when they could.

Recovery from addiction is a matter of will; it's about choosing to be in control rather than being controlled by the substance or habit. It is to experience sovereignty and self-empowerment in a moment, using skills to bring the mind-body-spirit complex into alignment: the "lighthouse effect" in practice. Encourage participants to be patient and forgiving with themselves. Many times, clients share how they knew the skill but didn't think of applying it at the time the trigger happened. Given the emotional impact in the moment, it makes sense that we might not immediately think of it. The more we practice, the more aware and conscious of our body's response mechanisms we become and the better we get at detecting an emotional trigger before it gets fully activated; thus, the more easily we can come back to a place of balance. It takes practice and patience to be able to readily access any of the skills we add to our Lighthouse Effect Toolkit.

Mindfulness Tasks & Looking Within

In any experiential training, basic skills are learned and practiced repetitively. When I was training in Tae Kwon Do, much of the focus was on basic movements, techniques, and forms. This practice of focusing the mind while doing mundane tasks is what I think of as *mindfulness in action*. Wax on/wax off, chop wood/carry water, and "one moment at a time" are mindfulness in action practices that encourage us to be fully aware and conscious of our actions in the moment. Such repetitive work might seem contrary to the recovery adage that "insanity is doing the same thing over and over again and expecting different results," but the adage speaks to maladaptive addictive patterns and behaviors, where the thing we might do over and over is to resort to our "quick fix" substance or behavior and expect to feel better. And of course, while we might feel better momentarily, in the long run we are compromising all aspects of our being. In contrast, doing repetitive tasks or chores in a mindful way is highly beneficial and transformational in reframing negative core beliefs, especially when we are also applying interventions (techniques, skills, and exercises) to move out of surviving and into thriving.

The "expecting different results" adage also speaks to the futility of trying over and over to change *someone else*, for whatever reason. Maybe the other person is unable to hear our wisdom or truth, or not ready to receive our perspective because of their own intrinsic fears and resistance. The point is, it's not personal to us, it's about them. We can *request* a behavioral change from someone, but to keep putting energy into trying to change them and *expecting* them to change will inevitably backfire and cause us to feel defeated and unacknowledged. We can't change them, but we can change our own behavior.

When we find ourselves wanting to change someone else, we can choose to see it as an opportunity for Reflective Inquiry. As the maxim goes, when we point a finger of shame and blame at someone else, we are pointing three fingers back at ourselves. More often than not, when we judge someone's behavior, action, or idea, it's because we are intolerant or afraid of that thing or potential for it in ourselves. Upon deeper inquiry, we might discover, for example, that we are afraid to allow ourselves to do what they are doing and we might be secretly wishing we could do it and get away with it.

Another example would be where a person in recovery might judge someone else in recovery who goes to an event where alcohol is served. Their rationale is that the other person is too vulnerable and putting themselves at risk of relapsing; but they are really concerned about their *own* potential to relapse under the same circumstances. Through Reflective Inquiry, we can use our judgments of others as a way to turn that judgment back to ourselves and resolve to change our own behavior.

Alternative/Additional Group Exercise ~ Reflective Inquiry

Use the above example and pose questions to the group along these lines: *What happens to you when you see someone else in recovery acting out old behaviors and/or relapsing? What is the first thought or judgment that arises?* (We will be doing a deeper exploration of Reflective Inquiry further along in this module.)

Suggested Closing Meditation ~ Opposite Thought/Opposite Action Meditation

Get into a comfortable position, and close your eyes or lower your gaze. (Sound chime or toning bowl.) Take three slow, deep, breaths, allowing your body to relax into this moment. Now, focus your attention on a situation or relationship dynamic that feels out of your control, that might be challenging you to the point where you might consider resorting to your old behavior or quick fix. Notice what happens to your body, your nervous system, your stress level. Take a full deep inhalation, and think instead, *I've got this*, as you imagine the opposite scenario to the one playing out in your mind's eye. Slowly exhale, allowing your body to soften. Breathe in, *I've got this*; now, slowly exhale, feeling the release of tension, the release of resistance, as your body softens even more. One more full inhalation, feeling all the way into the positive thought, *I've got this*; one more full exhalation, feeling the full release of resistance. (Sound chime.) Slowly open your eyes and return to the present moment. Carry this sense of self-empowerment through your day. Know that you can choose Opposite Thought/Opposite Action in real time whenever you feel the pull of your old coping mechanism. Think in the moment: *I choose the long-term benefits of recovery; I choose to thrive, not just survive.*

Suggested Homework: Practice applying the Opposite Thought/Opposite Action skill in real time during the week. Reflect in your journal on what happens when you apply this skill, and be prepared to share your insights with the group next week.

Module II (Tolerance Building) Session 6: Turning the Mind & Half-Smile

Suggested Opening Meditation ~ Thought Train Meditation

Get into a comfortable position, and close your eyes or lower your gaze. (Sound chime or toning bowl.) Take three long, slow, deep breaths. Allow your body to relax; feel the softening in every muscle. Continue to breathe in a natural rhythm. Begin to notice any thoughts that drop into your mind. Notice what these thought streams are promoting, like they are news headlines; notice from a place of an observer. Now imagine these thought headlines as cars on a passing train. Simply watch them go by without any need to engage with them; without jumping on the thought train. Watch the train as it moves further away into the distance. What does it feel like in your body to detach from these thoughts and narratives and just let them pass by. Now, take a deep, full breath, and as you exhale, feel into the release of this letting go. Feel into the sense of peace. (Sound chime.) Open your eyes and return to presence. Practice this new way to detach from intrusive thoughts by watching the thought train pass as you move through your day.

Check-Ins and Q&A: Remind group participants to keep check-ins brief. Encourage them to focus on the skills they have been applying in their daily lives and any challenges that might have come up. And as this is the halfway point in the module, invite them to share homework, journal reflections, or insights they've gained over the past six weeks of the module.

Handouts: The Lighthouse Effect Comprehensive Tolerance Building Skills, The Lighthouse Effect Start & Stop Practice

Half-Smile: Half-smile is a Buddhist technique that we can use to signal the brain that everything is copacetic. It has the opposite effect of a frown, which signals the brain that something is wrong or that there is some sort of confusion or threat. The facial muscles can hold muscle memory of a previous, similar experience where there was a threat. When we make a half-smile (or Mona Lisa smile, as I've heard it called) we directly communicate to the Central Nervous System that there are no worries here: all is well. It is highly effective, but in the same way that calling up our Opposite Thought/Opposite Action skill can be difficult in the moment, we might not be inclined to smile in the midst of a challenge or uncomfortable experience. But here, too, we become more adept with practice.

Turning the Mind: This skill is quite literally what it says: it is intentionally turning our mind away from whatever story it is running because that narrative is not serving us. I use "the breath" to help me turn my mind, and I believe we all do this instinctively on some level--how you suddenly take a deep breath to clear your mind as you try to deal with whatever is unfolding in front of you at that moment. It is a skill we can develop further and implement as an intervention tool when our thoughts get out of hand. I practice by taking three deep, diaphragmatic breaths as I consciously shift my perspective from horizontal or linear to vertical. I call it "going vertical to the level of Higher Mind." In other words, the Lighthouse Effect.

River Wisdom: The goal with mindfulness practice is to be like river water, to learn how to move around the obstacles in our lives, whether people, places, things, or life situations. It's what I think of as "River Wisdom," which is about going with the flow and being pragmatic about dealing with what is in front of us. It is easier to move ourselves around the rocks and boulders of life's obstacles and challenges than it is to convince (or try to convince) anyone else to change course, or move things out of our way, or do things our way.

Practice meeting victim consciousness (lower vibrational energy) with patience, understanding, and acceptance (higher vibrational energy). Be open to other perspectives, practice discernment, detach from fear, and align with love.

Group Exercise ~ Half-Smile & Turning the Mind

Given how comprehensive the list of skills is on this handout, focus on the practices of Half-Smile and Turning the Mind in this session. Reinforce and ground the concepts by making them experiential, as a group exercise, using your whiteboard to convey the group's feedback and insights. A prompt might be: *Some examples of turning the mind are washing dishes or folding laundry; what are other examples?*

As long as you are willing, the door is wide open. Choose wisely by choosing you!

--Faith Burrington Jones

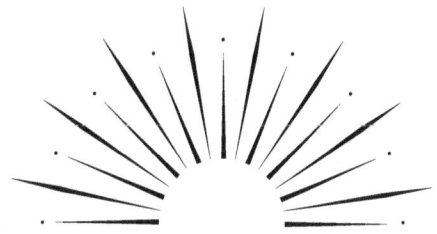

THE LIGHTHOUSE EFFECT
Comprehensive Tolerance Building Skills

This list of skills has been modified from various sources and strongly influenced by DBT. These skills are not meant to prevent you from feeling and experiencing your emotions. Rather, they help to reduce stress and support you in moving out of an emotional reaction or trigger response. Meeting yourself with understanding and compassion is key to healing old wounds and changing reactive patterns.

STABILIZE THE MIND

ACTIVITIES: Do errands or chores, such as cooking, cleaning, collecting the mail from the mailbox; Engage in a hobby; Call or visit a friend; Play a game (crossword, puzzle, board game).

ACTS OF KINDNESS: Do something for someone else and/or engage in acts of service, especially if you customarily don't; shovel snow for a neighbor, volunteer at a soup kitchen, pick up groceries for someone who doesn't drive.

RESPECT DIFFERENCES: There will be times when you perceive someone as having either a more challenging life situation or a less challenging situation; avoid such comparisons. There will be times when others have different views; take pause and allow for both perspectives. Treat each life situation as unique, and respect the differences.

EMOTIONAL SHIFT: Listen to music, watch a movie, or read a book that will evoke the opposite emotion to what you are experiencing, something inspirational, comical, upbeat.

SELF-PROTECT DELAY: Mentally choose to leave a situation that is triggering; build an imaginary bubble around it and circle back to it when you feel more confident and grounded. Censor negative thoughts in the moment, and reflect on the situation in your journal later, before going to bed.

DISTRACT: Move your mind away from narratives and anxious thoughts to decrease your stress level; take several slow, deep, breaths; focus on your environment, whether outdoors or indoors, and observe and describe it in detail in your mind.

SENSORY STIMULATION: Run cold water on your wrists, splash cold water on your face, place a cold cloth on the back of your neck, take a hot or cold shower, squeeze a stress ball, listen or dance to loud music, snap an elastic band on your wrist.

SELF-COMFORT

FOCUS ON VISUALS: Look at natural landscapes; watch animal-antics videos; light a candle and watch the flame; stargaze; look at pictures that make you smile; be present and observe without commentary or judgment; move your gaze without lingering on any specific object.

SOUND IMMERSION: Listen to music that calms your nervous system; listen to nature sounds; sing, or hum, or play an instrument; listen to a video of a spiritual teacher that you enjoy; be mindful of sounds.

AROMATHERAPY: Take a bath and infuse it with essential oils; light non-toxic scented candles, incense, or potpourri; smell flowers; walk in the woods and breathe in the natural aromas.

STIMULATE TASTE: Bake a healthy treat or make a healthy meal and chew mindfully, savoring the tastes; make a healthy and refreshing drink, hot or cold, and add spices or herbs; chew gum; savor a piece of dark chocolate or mint.

MINDFUL TOUCH: Take a bubble bath or immerse yourself in a shower; get a massage; put fresh linens on your bed; pet a dog or cat; walk on the grass or beach barefoot; brush or braid your hair or someone else's; hug someone; practice mindfully touching with your partner or yourself. Notice how touch has a sedating effect; practice "havening."

CHOOSE TO IMPROVE THE MOMENT

IMAGINATION/IMAGINING: Imagine a relaxing scene (your happy place) and yourself in it; Imagine a secret room/safe haven within, go in, close the door, and visualize all of the details. Imagine everything going smoothly; see yourself coping well and effectively applying skills. Think of the stressful life situation you are experiencing and the negative beliefs as rocks in the river, and imagine you are river water moving past them.

FIND PURPOSE: Find meaning in pain or challenges: *How is this for me*? *What am I learning*? Read (or listen to) spiritual works; focus on the positive; find the silver-lining; make lemonade out of lemons.

CONNECT TO SPIRIT: Open your heart to Spirit (God of your understanding), nonphysical reality, or Higher Power. Know that you and your Higher Power are one when you align with higher consciousness: thy will is your will when it is in alignment with love.

RELEASE & RELAX EXERCISE: Do a simple tense and release exercise/meditation, where you tense muscle groups as you breathe in and relax them as you exhale. Start with your hands and arms, then your face, neck, and shoulders, then move slowly down to your chest, abdomen, and hips, and finally, your legs and feet. Listen to a guided meditation; take a walk in nature; get a massage or self-massage.

PRESENCE PRACTICE: Focus your attention on this moment, on *now*. Practice *being* instead of *doing*. Mindfulness is about observing and being present without judging or problem-solving. Practice yoga or qi-gong; dance playfully; do the dishes, feeling the warmth of the water on your hands.

TIME OUT/MOCK VACATION: Take a twenty-minute nap; get cozy and snuggle up with a good book or listen to music; make yourself a cup of tea or soothing non-alcoholic beverage. Unplug social media, the TV, your phone, and just rest and breathe. Go on a hike, and do some expressive writing or artwork or just gaze at the view. Simply be present, be mindful, where you are, whatever you are doing.

SELF-MENTORING: Cheerlead yourself (be your own best friend) with self-affirming mantras: *I've got this! This too shall pass. I'm doing the best I can, considering the circumstances. The only way out is through! One day, one moment at a time. Seize the day! Just breathe!*

SOC PROS & CONS: Complete the Stages of Change Pros & Cons worksheet, focusing on whatever it is you want to change. Consider how the coping strategy/addiction/belief has never worked for you and only caused you shame and lack of respect for yourself; look at alternative, healthy ways for coping.

Notice the difference between short-term "pros" (quick fixes) and long-term "cons" (negative impact over time) compared to short-term cons (what may be more challenging in the moment) and long-term pros (what is sustainable and beneficial). Know that you can choose to move from survival to revival: *I choose recovery; I choose to practice my skills.*

ENGAGE IN FOCUSED BREATHING

DIAPHRAGMATIC BREATHING: Lie on your back, place one hand on your chest and the other on your stomach; take a full, deep breath into your abdomen and all the way into the back, then slowly exhale, feeling the release all the way through your body; continue for ten to twenty breaths, with longer exhalations each time.

BREATH COUNTING: Sit comfortably, and bring all of your attention to your breathing; Take a slow, deep breath and think, *inhalation*; then slowly, fully release, and think, *exhalation*. Repeat for a count of ten, elongating the exhalation each time.

BREATH SWINGING: Imagine you are on a swing; take a deep mindful inhalation, all the way into your abdomen as you swing back, then exhale fully as you swing forward. Notice that moment where you are suspended in the air, just before you begin to swing back. Breathe deeply filling your lungs again as you swing all the way back, and exhale as you swing forward, noticing again that moment of suspension. Keep "swing breathing" mindfully for ten minutes, noticing that moment of suspension each time.

BREATHING MANTRA: Sit comfortably, close your eyes, relax your body, and focus on your breath. As you breathe in, slowly and deeply, think the mantra, *I breathe in peace*; as you slowly exhale, think the mantra, *I breathe out tension*. On the next inhale, think, *I breathe in love*, and with the exhale, *I breathe out fear*. Continue to breathe deeply, repeating your mantras. Make up other mantras that reflect where you are at that moment. For example, *I breathe in compassion; I breathe out self-harm*.

APPLY INTERVENTION PRACTICES

HALF-SMILE: This simple practice actually changes brain chemistry and is similar to "move a muscle/change a thought."

Close your eyes, take a slow, deep breath, and mindfully releasing tension in your face, neck, and shoulders, and then "half-smile" (think: Mona Lisa) with lips slightly upturned, teeth slightly apart, jaw softened, and a serene facial expression.

PRESENCE THROUGH MOVEMENT: Come into presence through the movement of the body. Practice qigong or yoga or another movement meditation. Be mindful of the movement and position of your body as you breathe.

RADICAL ACCEPTANCE OF WHAT IS: What you resist, persists! Coming into acceptance means not judging things as good or bad, and simply acknowledging that which cannot be changed. Read or recite the Serenity Prayer or use lines from it as mantras: *I accept the things I cannot change; I have the courage to change the things I can.*

OPPOSITE THOUGHT/OPPOSITE ACTION ~ DOING A ONE-EIGHTY: This is a powerful, effective intervention for substance addiction, codependent relationships, or other maladaptive behavioral patterns. Instead of being on autopilot and defaulting to emotionally driven narratives that do not serve us, we can choose narratives that are true for us and consciously think of a healthy alternative when we feel the urge to default to our addictive substance or behavior.

For example, you have an urge to go to a bar and have a drink, where your thought is, *I can go and just have one drink.* But you take a pause and tell yourself the opposite: *I cannot go and have just one drink. I am not going to give into this neurological biochemical reaction. Instead, I am going to breathe through the urge and take my Observer Self perspective.*

Then you take the thought further: *Drinking is a deceptive trap that leaves me physically, mentally, and emotionally sick. Alcohol is like poison to me. I see through the deception. I see it for what it is, an unhealthy dependency that has become hardwired in my brain.* Then, instead of following through with the urge to go to a bar, you do a "one-eighty." You go to the gym, go on a hike, or visit a friend in your recovery network.

TURNING THE MIND (REFOCUSING): When your mind obsesses about a situation you cannot change or attaches to a narrative that does not serve you, choose to consciously move your attention to the opposite of your complaint; focus on what you *can* do or how you can look at it in a different way, one that doesn't feel so restricted, sort of like unkinking a hose so the water can flow more freely.

RESISTANCE VERSUS RECEPTIVITY (WILLFULNESS VS WILLINGNESS IN DBT): The invitation here is to move out of acting from a place of contraction, like a tight-fisted hand ready to fight, and act instead from a place of openness, like an upturned hand with palm open, ready to receive. If you are experiencing resistance to any extent, try this exercise to move from contraction to openness:

Take a deep breath and tighten your hand into a fist, as tight as you can, as you breathe in, and then release your hand as you exhale completely. Keep doing this until you can sustain a soft and open, receptive palm. Facing a conflict from an open stance doesn't mean you like it, it just means that the probability of effecting a more positive change or making a better connection is higher than facing a conflict with a negative or fighting stance.

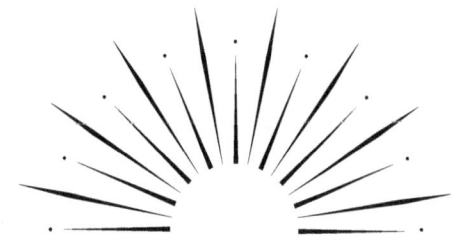

THE LIGHTHOUSE EFFECT "START" AND "STOP" PRACTICE

The practice of using "start" and "stop" statements is a simple way of course correcting. It's a cognitive repositioning that we can practice at any time, with the statements serving as buoys that lead us to the shore. It is similar to the Both/And concept or tool in how using the opposing words "start" and "stop" help us to understand and accept the dualistic experience of being human, and help us to navigate our physical reality and inner worlds. Recite start and stop statements as part of your morning routine and use them like mantras throughout your day. Add your own to the statements provided below.

START STATEMENTS open the mind, expand perspectives, and foster receptivity and willingness.

I will START visualizing the reality I want to experience in my life.

I will START relaxing into my Authentic Self.

I will START to think vertically AND step into my Tall Self, Wise Mind, Higher Power.

I will START reflecting on what is true for me.

I will START believing in myself, the way I see things, and aligning to the teachings and principles that resonate with me.

_____

_____

_____

STOP STATEMENTS serve to open the mind and provide a deep sense of rootedness for managing survival instincts and establishing healthy boundaries from a stance of anchored confidence.

I will STOP being afraid; I will fear not.

I will STOP swimming against the tide; I will go with the flow.

I will STOP allowing my small self/inner child to manage my life and will allow my Tall Self to lead.

I will STOP believing that I need approval from outside sources; I am self-empowered.

_____

_____

_____

CREATE A MANTRA and say it as you go about your day. For example, when you're driving and come to a stop sign, you might say, "Stop being afraid; Start being courageous!" Have fun with it.

Suggested Closing Meditation ~ Half-Smile Meditation

Sit comfortably with a relaxed and open body posture, and close your eyes or lower your gaze. (Sound chime or toning bowl.) Take three, long, slow deep breaths and feel your entire being come into this present moment. Scan your mind and notice if there are any distracting narratives running unchecked. Now, smile slightly with a "half-smile," even if it doesn't feel natural. Notice if you feel any subtle changes in your thoughts. Continue to slowly inhale and exhale as you scan your body; if there is any discomfort, tension, or pain, half-smile at the place in your body where you experience discomfort, noticing how this facial expression releases endorphins. Notice how this gentle smile sends a message of reassurance and comfort through your mind, physical body, and emotional body. Continue to scan your mind and body, and half-smile at any other thoughts or sensations that bring discomfort. One more deep inhalation; and one more full exhalation. (Sound chime.) Slowly open your eyes, carry the sense of calm your half-smile brings and apply it throughout your day to bring comfort and kind reassurance to your being.

Suggested Homework: Reflect in your journal what you learned in this session, and practice Turning the Mind, Half-Smile, and River Wisdom in real time throughout the week. Be prepared to share what you experienced with the group.

Module II (Tolerance Building) Session 7: Resistance versus Receptivity

Suggested Opening Meditation ~ Turning the Mind Meditation

Sit comfortably and close your eyes or lower your gaze. (Sound chime or toning bowl.) Take three long, slow, deep breaths and follow the sound of the chime inward. When random thoughts drop into your mind, turn your mind away from the thought, to the rhythm of your breath. Focus on or "attend to" the breath. Breathe in, breathe out; breathe in, breathe out; breathe in, breathe out. Notice how focusing on the breath keeps you in the present, in the here and now. Take one more slow, deep inhalation, and now, a slow, full exhalation. (Sound chime.) Slowly open your eyes and return to the room. Keep applying this simple yet effective skill as you move through your day. Continue to be aware of any thoughts that try to seduce you, and consciously turn your mind away from them by attending to your breath.

Check-Ins and Q&A: Invite group participants to focus their check-ins on their current life situations and how the previous session's skills (Half-Smile/Turning the Mind/River Wisdom) or the Start and Stop practice have supported them in building tolerance and accepting life on life's terms.

Handouts: No new handouts. Continue to work with the Comprehensive Tolerance Building Skills handout, focusing on the Resistance versus Receptivity concept. It helps to reinforce how these skills are only beneficial if we actually use them in real time, and it takes practice, practice, practice for them to become second nature.

Practice Not Perfection

We touched on Resistance versus Receptivity or Willfulness versus Willingness, which is the DBT language for the concept, in the first session of this module in the context of the Art of

Acceptance. It also applies here, as self-sabotage is an example of resistance, and often it comes from setting our standards too high: perfection. The higher the standards we set for ourselves or others, the higher the magnitude of effort it takes to try to obtain them. Thus, the more unstable and anxious we might become when we can't meet those unrealistic standards, which then has the adverse effect of us giving up and relying on or reverting to unhealthy coping behaviors. However, if we look at the saboteur as a teacher, we can see that our inner saboteur is showing us where and why we are resisting.

Again, it goes back to our early-childhood caregivers and authority figures and the standards we learned to measure ourselves up against. Over time, it became our default way, and often we ended up raising the bar and setting ever higher standards for ourselves. Setting high standards can be beneficial and healthy, in that doing so can help us to challenge ourselves to learn a skill or motivate us to take other positive steps in our lives. But setting standards that are too high and unsustainable leads to an inner conflict where our sense of self presses up against a negative core belief that we are not good enough, which often becomes a self-fulfilling prophecy that reinforces victim consciousness.

Resistance versus Receptivity

This powerful internal conflict is worth diving into and processing with the group. As the example of sabotage/perfection shows us, we can *think* we are completely willing to do inner work, while another part of us is resisting and thwarting our intentions and efforts, leading to inertia, procrastination, or avoidance--which are learned coping mechanisms and strategies that become habitual. It is not uncommon to have a great idea and then experience an influx of "yeah, buts" from our internal naysayer, a younger version of the self that resides within the Emotional Mind. This younger self is afraid of change, thus, it protectively holds a mindset of resistance. Our inner child simply needs us to listen to their worry, fear, or complaint without judgment, so that our adult self can step in and take the lead. To do that, we need to meet them where they are broadcasting from. (I think of these voices as my inner newscasters--

overzealous and dramatic so they will get my attention and have me take them seriously.)

When exploring internal conflicts, there naturally seems to be a part that wants to experience life with greater ease and confidence yet another part will argue against it. When these inner conflicts arise, it is a powerful practice to go within to seek a connection to our Higher Power to tune into our own intuition to understand what it is that we really want or need.

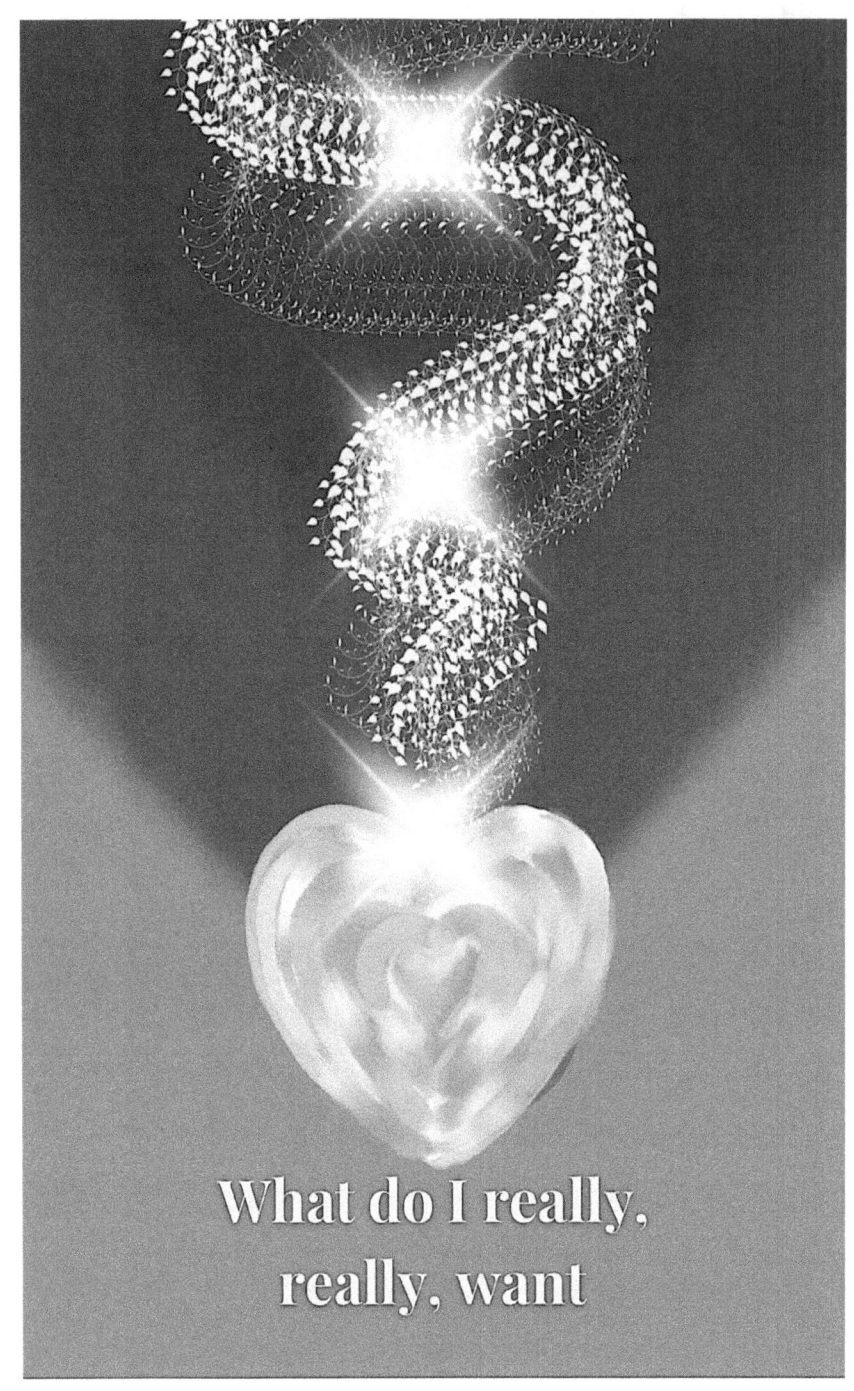

What do I really, really, want

Group Exercise ~ What Do I Want?

I have found it helpful to use oracle cards to support our Reflective Inquiry process. One of my favorite oracle decks is "Ask Your Soul…The Soul Knows" by Karen Paolino Correia, a dear friend, colleague, and spiritual teacher. I use her cards to facilitate group exercises, where I pull a card and use it as the prompt for the exercise. You might do the same, but you don't need to have the deck to do this exercise. You can use the questions below as prompts for the group to explore where resistance lies. They emphasize the power of focusing on the part of us that wants to find our purpose or passion, to understand what we actually want.

What do I want?
What do I *really* want?
What do I *really, really* want?

I have found that this exercise helps participants to build a relationship with their spirituality and develop a spiritual practice, which is such a vital part of recovery.

Suggested Closing Meditation ~ What do I Really Want? This meditation is verbatim from Karen's oracle deck:

This card has a message for you today to reflect on what you really want to feel and experience. Whether it is in a specific situation that has created feelings of confusion and uncertainty, or it is throughout every aspect of your life.

Meditation: Take a moment and bring a life situation to the forefront and ask your soul for clarity. Take a long slow deep breath and ask yourself, What do I want? *Let that go. Take another long slow deep breath into the belly and ask yourself,* What do I really want? *Go with the first thought. Take another long slow deep breath and let that go. Then ask,* What do I really, really, want? *Go with the first thought.*

If all three answers are the same, you know what you want; go for it. If they shifted as you went deeper, pay attention to your last answer. This is your soul's wisdom. Many times, when you get caught up in the thinking mind, your ego influences your perception of what you "think" you want and often it's focused on exterior desires. The gift of this card and this meditation is to reveal the "feeling" of what you really, really, want on the level of your soul.

Suggested Homework: Record in your journal what you really, really want. Write down how it feels to be receptive rather than resistant. Notice any "yeah, buts" that may arise. Ask the reflective question, *What does this part of me that is in resistance need for me to be fully receptive to what I really want?*

Module II (Tolerance Building) Session 8: Reflective Inquiry ~ Know Thyself

Suggested Opening Meditation ~ The Art of Allowing Meditation

Get into a comfortable position, and close your eyes or lower your gaze. (Sound chime or toning bowl.) Take three long, slow, deep breaths to bring yourself to this present moment. Imagine opening up your body and mind to the warmth of the sun. Turn your face upward, like a flower receiving the sun's rays. Allow the comforting warmth to move all the way through you, as you continue to breathe gently and naturally. Focus your mind on the word "allow" and feel into what it means to you. How does it feel in your physical body? How does it feel in your emotional body? How does it feel in your mind? Breathe in, *allow*; breathe out, *release*. Breathe in, *allow*; breathe out, *release*. Feel the sense of warmth that pours into every cell and every muscle of your body. Feel the sense of relaxation radiating from your core. (Sound chime.) Slowly open your eyes and return to presence. Allow this deep sense of peace to comfort you as you move through your day.

Check-Ins and Q&A: Invite group participants to focus their check-ins on sharing their own personal experiences with resistance and how it plays a big role in self-sabotaging behaviors.

Handouts: The Lighthouse Effect Serenity Prayer Reflective Inquiry Worksheet

Reflective Inquiry

I mentioned Byron Katie's The Work® (thework.com) in Module I. The Reflective Inquiry component of my program is an adaptation of The Work's self-inquiry practice. It's a process for taking us inward, to attend to the inner child and heal unresolved wounds, instead of focusing on people, events, or things outside of ourselves. It's a journey toward self-realization. One of the questions The Work® poses is, *Is it true*? "It" being the thought that I'm thinking, the urge that I'm having, the powerful command in my mind. Self-inquiry, as Katie presents it, is a journaling meditation that encourages us to *notice* how a judgment, narrative, or belief negatively impacts our body and stress level.

Reflective Inquiry helps bring to light where our resistance lies and how it holds us back from experiencing what we really want in this life. It encourages us to consider how our judgments impact our nervous system. I see it as both a writing meditation or practice *and* an intervention tool that can be applied in real time when we are triggered or spiraling. Thus, I've modified reflective questions to be applied in either way. For example, *Is this narrative that I'm running true and based in reality*? Then the follow-up question would be, *Is this narrative a small-t truth or Capital-T Truth?* Meaning, is it *actually* true, as in a Capital-T Truth; or is it simply a *belief* that I've been carrying or story that I am running, thus, a small-t truth? I equate the small-t truth with the inner child or small self, and the Capital-T Truth with the adult self or Tall Self. As we practice applying Reflective Inquiry in our daily lives, the Capital-T Truths become more evident and more easily integrated. Just like anything that we learn, it takes practice and focused discipline to become more skilled and gain mastery.

Asking ourselves reflective questions helps us to notice how the mind fixates on storylines that are scary, dramatic, or worrisome, and how these narratives are compelling, seductive, and addictive. It's about recognizing that these fixations are the function of a psyche that has experienced trauma––and we have *all* experienced trauma to varying degrees. The details of our traumatizing experiences may not be as important as the ego makes them out to be; what is significant is the way we interpreted or made meaning out of them. The process is one that simply asks us to *experience* the impact that a judgment or belief has on our nervous system, and to notice how we feel in our bodies when we let go of it. A longtime client and graduate of The Lighthouse Effect Skillful Recovery Program shares how Reflective Inquiry has been a beneficial tool for her. And for "Tiger," considering whether it's a little-t (small-t) truth or Tall-T (Capital-T) truth when she is triggered is especially helpful.

I learned how to calm my tongue and not always say what's on my mind, because what's on my mind doesn't necessarily mean that it's one hundred percent true. … Is it a little-t truth or Capital-T Truth? I love that. Because even these minimal strategies, like Capital-T and little-t, sound basic, but you know what? That inner part of me gets it. When we're in our adult mind, we don't need to hear the little-t and the Capital-T story, because we know it. But not when we're in that childlike fear of "I can't do this, I'm afraid to do this."

This is my take on how it is for me. I'll give you a scenario. Like maybe two people gave me a dirty look when I walked into a room, and my first thought is, nobody likes me. And I'm with my friend, and I'll say, "I don't want to be here, nobody likes me." Then I'll check myself, Is that the truth, the Capital -T Truth? Most likely not. There are other people in this room besides those two people you thought gave you a dirty look. And really, maybe they just have gas. And the fact is, somebody likes you: the person you're with likes you.

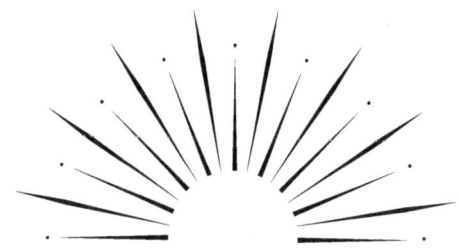

THE LIGHTHOUSE EFFECT
The Serenity Prayer Reflective Inquiry Exercise

Reflective Inquiry is an essential skill to develop, as it encourages us to consider how deeply we are attached to a particular narrative and whether we want to take a different course. It's about acceptance of what is, and acknowledging that the thing we can change is how we respond to whatever we are facing that is outside or in front of us. In other words, it's an "inside" job. The wisdom of knowing what we can change and what we cannot change is a staple in the addiction and recovery field, as expressed in The Serenity Prayer. We can apply it as an experiential exercise for practicing Reflective Inquiry.

Practicing this intervention exercise develops inner strength, self-confidence, and overall resilience as it discloses our internal resistance and our fear of change. Reflect on the questions below mindfully as a meditative inquiry. They are based on a default narrative about being judged and assuming someone is judging you, with the example being that someone is giving you a "dirty look." You can substitute it with any narrative you are running.

Exercise Prompts:

Is it true? Can I really know that it is true (that the person who gave me a dirty look meant it for me)?

_____

_____

_____

_____

Is it a Capital-T Truth? (Was it really even a dirty look or could something be going on with them that has nothing to do with me?) How could I really know?

_____

_____

_____

_____

How does it feel to run a story negatively judging that person and assuming they are judging me? How does it feel emotionally? How does it feel in my body?

___

_____

_____

_____

What happens when I look at them and drop the story? What do I see? How do I feel? Does my stress level change?

_____

_____

_____

What part of me insists that the story is true? Is it my small self (child self) or Tall Self (adult self)?

_____

_____

_____

As I zoom out and move from the small self to Tall Self perspective, what happens to my stress level?

_____

_____

_____

Make a commitment to yourself right now, in this moment: _I will observe my self-talk and practice Reflective Inquiry so that I can become more skilled at coming up with alternative, supportive narratives._ Now, ask yourself: How does it feel to make a positive statement instead of a negative statement when I am triggered? How does it feel to have a plan of action for addressing triggers that is supportive and proactive?

_____

_____

_____

How will the practice of Reflective Inquiry positively impact my life and the way I interpret life situations and circumstances that challenge me?

_____

_____

_____

Group Exercise ~ The Lighthouse Effect Serenity Prayer Reflective Inquiry Exercise

Walk the group through the exercise, using your whiteboard.

Suggested Closing Meditation ~ Tall Self Meditation

Sit comfortably in your chair and position your body to receive openly. Close your eyes or lower your gaze. (Sound chime or toning bowl.) Take three long, slow, deep breaths. Recall an experience when you were a child where you felt scared about something that wouldn't seem scary now. Maybe it was learning to ride a bike, or diving into a pool for the first time. Remember the feeling of fear you had about taking the risk to try something you had no experience in, and how *true* it felt that you couldn't possibly do it. Now, take another long, slow, deep breath, and step into your Tall Self; feel yourself getting taller, aligning vertically.

Breathe into this Tall Self version of you, the one who has had years or decades of experience taking risks, falling and getting up again, carrying on, developing the skills you need to ride a bike, drive a car, or dive into a pool, the one who is developing the skills you need to move from survival to revival. Now, take the hand of that small self, that child self, and reassure them: *We've got this*. Take another full inhalation, and full exhalation. (Sound chime.) Know that you can take the hand of the small self within you who is afraid, uncertain, or confused at any time. You always have the capacity to take three long, slow, deep breaths and align yourself with your Tall Self, the one who carries the wisdom of years and decades of experience. You have what it takes to listen to that tallest, wisest, and most resilient part of yourself no matter what challenges cross your path.

Suggested Homework: Reflect in your journal about what came up for you regarding Reflective Inquiry. Complete Byron Katie's Judge-Your-Neighbor Worksheet, which is about judging something outside of yourself and then making a deeper inquiry. Bring it to the next session to share with the group. Practice Reflective Inquiry on a daily basis, both as a written exercise and in real time as things come up.

Resources: Byron Katie's Judge-Your-Neighbor Worksheet (thework.com)

Self-mastery is an inside job.

When we do our inner work and deal with our inner conflicts,

we are better able to deal with external conflicts with skill and grace.

--Faith Burrington Jones

Module II (Tolerance Building) Session 9:
Deepening Reflective Inquiry ~ Negative Core Beliefs

Suggested Opening Meditation ~ The Mirror Meditation

Get into a comfortable position, and close your eyes or lower your gaze. (Sound chime or toning bowl.) Take three slow, deep breaths to come fully into presence. Think about all the times you are considerate, forgiving, and kind to others. Now, imagine you are looking in the mirror at yourself. Being perfectly honest, how do you treat yourself? Are you considerate, forgiving, and kind? How might it feel if you treated yourself the way you treat others? Continue to breathe gently and naturally, as you imagine telling yourself, *I will be considerate, I will be forgiving, I will be kind to me*. Notice how it feels in your body to give yourself permission to care for *you*. Let the feeling move through you. Take one more full deep inhalation and exhalation. (Sound chime.) Slowly open your eyes and return to the room. Self-care is a process. Make a habit of looking in the mirror and committing to being considerate, forgiving, and kind to yourself no matter what is happening in your life. Afterall, it is a house of mirrors out there. Take care of your own reflection, it will serve you well!

Check-Ins and Q&A: Invite group participants to reflect on the previous session and focus their check-ins on how the concepts can be applied in their daily lives.

Handouts: Going Fishing Exercise

Our Relationship with the Self ~ The Core Beliefs We Hold Deep Within

The best relationship to invest in to find inner peace is our relationship with ourselves--and the multiple cast of characters within. Reflective Inquiry allows for a deeper exploration of the programming we received in childhood, which is often opposite to the truth of who we are.

The hierarchical system in families, the grading system in schools, and, now, the culture of social media all play a role in shaping and defining who we think we are and who we come to *believe* we are. We looked at the impact of the rubric of these standards in sessions four and five, and we pick it up again here in the context of how it creates a sense of separation, and look at what we can do to come back to oneness.

A primary focus in The Lighthouse Effect program is on the "not good enough" core belief that so many of us hold. As children, the world in front of our eyes is captivating and holds our attention, like a dramatic movie, yet we take it literally and accept it without question. It creates an internal and external divide, a sense of separateness (me against them) in our life experiences, and initiates a pattern of comparing ourselves to others. Pick up on the work from the previous session about our own beliefs and how they arise in our judging of others, and do a deeper exploration. I liken this exploration to fishing, where the judgment of others or the things outside of ourselves are the "hooks" or triggers calling us to look at our internalized beliefs: We are the ones working the pole and targeting the fish of our negative beliefs. Through deeper Reflective Inquiry, we can "unhook" from that internalized negative core belief; More often than not, we will see that the judgment we projected outward is a judgment we hold about ourselves. That is the mirror or reflective aspect of the inquiry process. When we accept that we have an inner critic judging us for the thing we judge others for, we can make peace within.

Here, too, we can look at the Serenity Prayer, how it encourages us to look within to understand the difference between what we can and cannot change. We cannot change the small-t part of us, the small self; we can change our perspectives and our actions. We can choose to acknowledge, listen without judgment, and then make a decision and act from our adult self, Tall Self. Reflective Inquiry takes us out of shame/blame narratives where we project our issues onto others; it is a journey of self-realization, of returning home to the Authentic Self.

We are born into a form of bondage, not having agency over our family of origin and the environment within which we experience in our formative years, but we can find liberation and sovereignty through this experiential inner work. Ego tends to avoid doing inner work because it likes to believe it is autonomous and it doesn't like to be challenged, humiliated, or held accountable. So just by making the choice to practice inner work, we begin to deprogram and free the mind to explore our own truth. Even if we were unaware that we were doing so, Reflective Inquiry can bring to light how we are projecting onto someone else a judgment we have about ourselves.

Another Reflective Inquiry experiential exercise for group work would be to have participants provide examples of "following the internalized hook," using a whiteboard to convey their responses. For example, I'm having a conversation with my friend Sara and I might be thinking, *I am angry at Sara because she never listens to me.* When I follow the internalized hook, I can see that it might be about me: *I am angry with* myself *because I never listen to me, this part of me--especially when I'm angry with Sara.* When we are busy being in someone else's business, we neglect ourselves. As a result, neither person is listening to the other. In this example, I wasn't listening to myself, I wasn't listening to Sara, and I was blaming it on Sara: the blame/shame game. The next question in that moment with Sara would be, *Who would I be, or how would I be feeling if I dropped the story that Sara is the one who needs to listen to me?* In recognizing that Sara is merely doing what Sara does, I can see that it would behoove me to listen to myself.

In such moments, we might pause, step away, take a walk, whatever we need to do to come back to the conversation in a better place to apply effective communication skills. The Going Fishing Exercise demonstrates how we all project and cast self-judgments. It is Ego's way of protecting us and part of being human. We can use Reflective Inquiry to take our fear-based narrative to our own inner council to better understand how we feed our fears and how we judge and project our fears onto others.

THE LIGHTHOUSE EFFECT GOING FISHING EXERCISE
Change the Narrative/Change the Belief

CAPITAL-T TRUTH

What is truer: small-t "I am not good enough" or Capital-T "I am enough"?

I hold the pole! I can choose to throw back the small-t truth and keep the Capital-T Truth

my child self is worthy; I am worthy; I am enough!

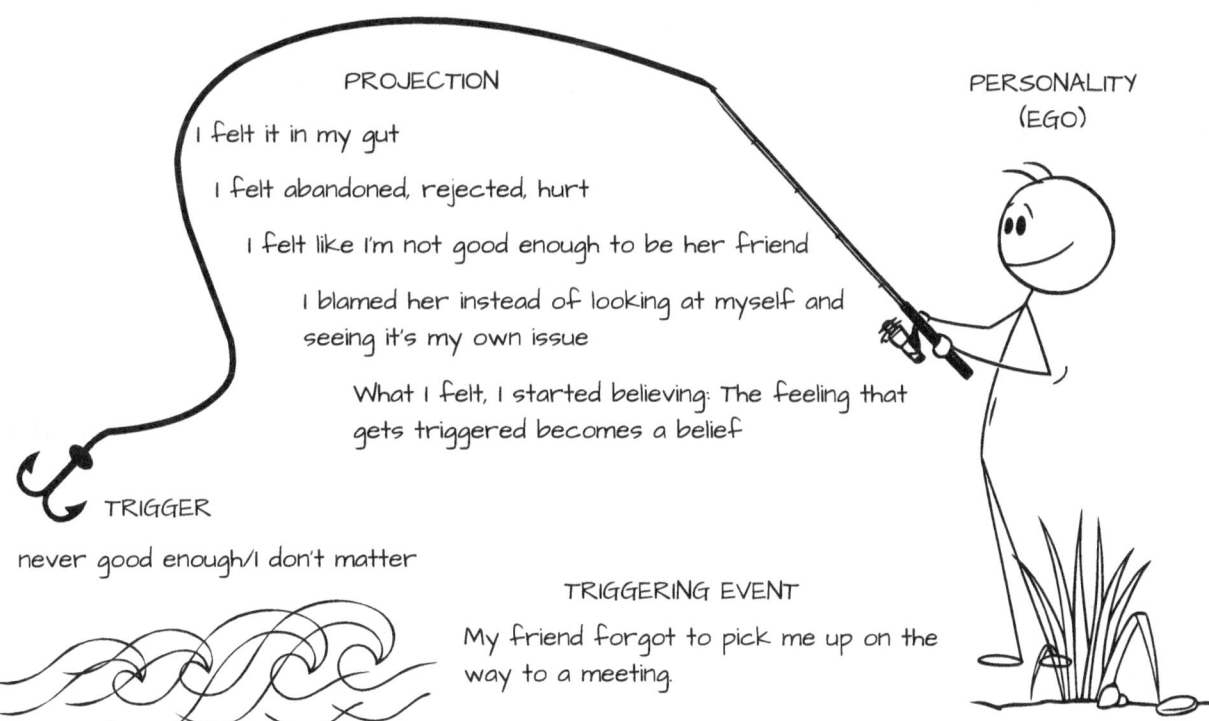

PROJECTION

I felt it in my gut

I felt abandoned, rejected, hurt

I felt like I'm not good enough to be her friend

I blamed her instead of looking at myself and seeing it's my own issue

What I felt, I started believing: The feeling that gets triggered becomes a belief

PERSONALITY (EGO)

TRIGGER

never good enough/I don't matter

TRIGGERING EVENT

My friend forgot to pick me up on the way to a meeting.

Group Exercise ~ Going Fishing

On the right side of your whiteboard, draw a stick-figure of a fisherman holding a pole on the seashore (you don't have to be an artist!) and on the left side of the board, draw waves to represent the sea. Draw a fishing line from the fisherman's pole toward the left side of the whiteboard above the "sea" and draw a hook dangling down from the line into the sea. Label the fisherman as Personality (Ego), the hook as Trigger, and the fishing line as Projection. Ask for a volunteer from the group to do this Reflective Inquiry exercise based on a current trigger.

Ask the other group members to observe, while reflecting on triggers in their lives and how "going fishing" might benefit them. Ask the volunteer to write the name of the trigger on the whiteboard, and then follow the fishing line (projection) back to themselves by asking, *Where do you hold this fear-based core belief in your body? How does it make you feel? How does it impact your life? What is the story you are telling yourself that triggers the emotion?* Engage in a conversation about how these "hooks" live inside of us, how they energetically and psychologically impact us, and how we can willingly unhook ourselves when we detach and step back from them.

Referring back to the Victim Triangle and human conditioning, it is in our nature to try to find someone or something outside of ourselves to blame. The process of Reflective Inquiry shows us that it is not so much about what happens to us, as it is about how we react that makes all of the difference in terms of self-acceptance and self-empowerment. The powerful practices of self-inquiry and self-reflection help us understand the responsibility (ability to respond) for how we engage in relationships (with ourselves and others) is in our hands. When we attend to our own emotions, instead of looking to someone or something outside of ourselves to do it for us, we learn to self-comfort and self-regulate, and are better able to manage our emotional triggers. Whereas, if we are dependent on someone else to manage our emotional system, what do we do when something happens to them? Disregarding or not attending to our own emotions is how codependent relationships form. It is healthy to invite our partner into supporting our process, but it is *our* process, and therefore we need to fully attend to it as our own responsibility.

As noted earlier, how we are in our relationships also goes back to our experiences as children. As a child, our needs were predominately met by our caregivers and once we were old enough to engage in relationships of our own, we would default to our particular experience of being cared for and how we received love and attention. Thus, what came of our early experiences is the expectation that someone else was responsible for meeting our emotional needs, and rightly so at that time in our young lives. But that baseline programming impacts how we are in relationships as adults, and it is up to us to establish healthy beliefs and behaviors.

Unfortunately, many of us were not taught healthy ways to self-regulate and soothe our emotions; rather, what was modeled for us was to avoid, repress, or blame our emotional reactions on someone or something else. There may also be transgenerational trauma, with the pattern of unmet emotional needs passed down from our parents, and theirs from their parents, and so on. Through the practice of Reflective Inquiry, we can cut the cord of that outdated programming and reset our attention back to ourselves, to where our locus of control is found--not with another, but *within*. Socrates's maxim "know thyself" speaks to an extremely important personal quest that we can undertake to obtain self-mastery of the mind-body-spirit complex and become adept at meeting our negative emotions with radical acceptance, respect, and kindness. Questioning the narratives and, ultimately, the underlying beliefs about ourselves, others, and the world is what transforms us and brings us home to our Authentic Self.

Suggested Closing Meditation ~ The Balloon Meditation (Detaching from Negative Core Beliefs)

Get into a comfortable position, and close your eyes or lower your gaze. (Sound chime or toning bowl.) Take three long, slow, deep breaths, focusing your awareness on the present moment. Bring to mind a negative self-judgment that keeps coming up; recognize that it is a negative core belief. Imagine writing that negative core belief on a balloon, whatever it might be, "I am not good enough" or "I can never follow through." Now take that balloon with the belief you've held, and release it to the sky. Continue to breathe gently and deeply as you watch it slowly drift up and away; watch it getting smaller and smaller; watch it fading out of sight and disappearing into the vastness of the sky, your higher power. Breathe into the sense of release, of letting go of that belief. Feel the lightness of being in your mind, in your body. Take another full inhalation, and slow, gentle exhalation. (Sound chime.) Open your eyes and return to presence. Know that you can practice this in the moment, whenever you catch yourself making self-judgments that come from a negative core belief. There is an endless supply of balloons!

Resources: Byron Katie's One-Belief-At-a-Time Worksheet (thework.com)

Suggested Homework: Complete Byron Katie's One Belief At a Time Worksheet. Focus on self-judgment, negative core belief patterns, and the self-talk that holds you back from self-realization and healing into wholeness. Review the Comprehensive Tolerance Building Worksheet. Be prepared to share your insights and reflections at the next session.

Module II (Tolerance Building) Session 10:
Valued Living ~ A Change of Perspective and Gratitude Journal

Suggested Opening Meditation ~ Following the Sound Meditation

Get into a comfortable position, and close your eyes or lower your gaze. (Sound chime or toning bowl.) Take a long, slow, deep inhalation and exhalation as you follow the sound of the chime, listening intentionally and intently until it fades completely. (Sound chime.) Take another full, deep, inhalation through the nose as you focus on the sound: feel the air moving through your nose, down into your lungs, expanding into your abdomen, and all the way into the back. Slowly exhale through the mouth, completely emptying your lungs as you continue to listen intentionally. (Sound chime.) Follow the sound as you breathe in through the nose, all the way down through your lungs and into your back. Now slowly exhale, releasing through your mouth, following the sound as it fades. (Sound chime again.) Slowly open your eyes and mindfully return to the present moment.

Check-Ins and Q&A: Invite group participants to share how the practice of Reflective Inquiry has helped them become more aware of what they can do to increase their tolerance. Encourage them to focus on Reflective Inquiry as they share about their current life situations.

Handouts: Valued Living Model, The Lighthouse Effect Valued Living Worksheet, The Lighthouse Effect Values & Goals Worksheet

What is Valued Living?

Focusing on what we value most in life helps us to see all that life has to offer and to better appreciate it. It often seems easier to complain about the challenges we face and to focus on the negative aspects of our personal journey, but the Capital-T Truth is that it isn't easier. It simply leads to a loss of confidence and decreases our motivation. Choosing to invest time and energy into creating a list of values and then making it a priority to uphold those values in our daily lives is one of the most valuable investments we could make.

For example, in listing healthy relationships as a value, you would put energy into upholding that value by setting goals and practicing skills to help support healthy relationships. For instance, a goal might be to make a *conscious choice* to communicate your love and appreciation to your friends, family, coworkers, and so on.

The notion of "valued living" has become a core component in therapy, with the Valued Living Questionnaire (VLQ) having been introduced in an article in *The Psychological Record* journal in 2010: "The Valued Living Questionnaire: Defining and Measuring Valued Action within a Behavioral Framework" by Kelly G. Wilson, Emily K. Sandoz, Jennifer Kitchens, and Miguel Roberts.

THE LIGHTHOUSE EFFECT
Valued Living Model

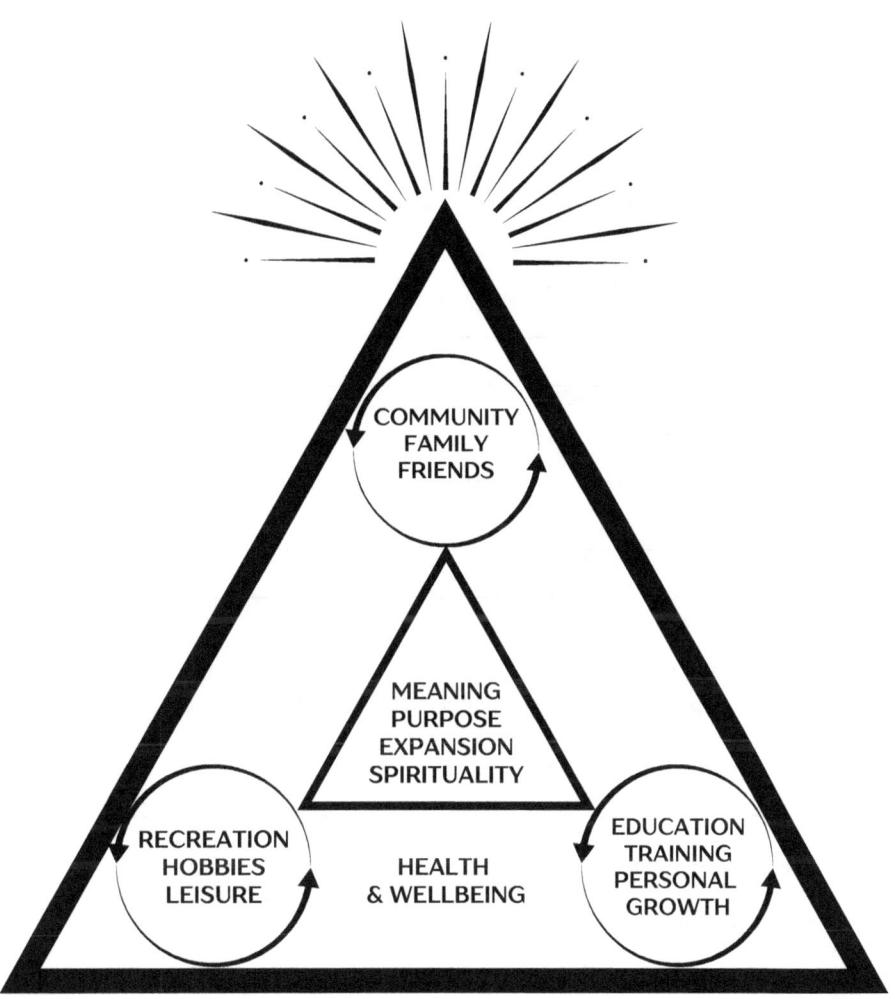

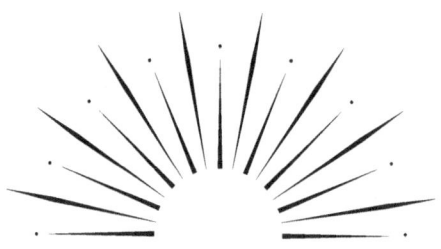

THE LIGHTHOUSE EFFECT
Valued Living Worksheet

What do you get excited or passionate about?

_____

_____

_____

What would you love to do that would create or contribute to a healthy work life?

_____

_____

_____

What could you do to become more educated or skilled in your field of employment?

_____

_____

_____

What do you do for recreation? What are your hobbies?

_____

_____

_____

What is your understanding of spirituality and/or connection to the nonphysical realms?

_____

_____

_____

How do you invest in your health and wellbeing?

_____

_____

_____

How do you care for your whole self, your mind, body, and spirit? Do you take as good care of yourself as you do others?

_____

_____

_____

How do you contribute to your community?

_____

_____

_____

How do you show appreciation to your family, friends, partner (if you are in a relationship)?

_____

_____

_____

What are you doing to invest in your relationships?

_____

_____

_____

What else is important to you that you would like to manifest in your life?

_____

_____

_____

Use your Valued Living Worksheet to create your Valued Living Goals. Share both with your recovery support person.

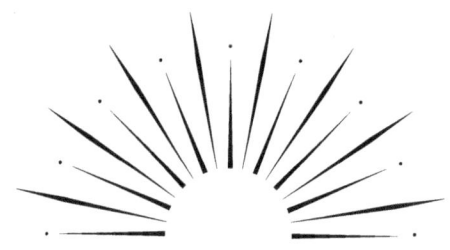

THE LIGHTHOUSE EFFECT
Values & Goals Worksheet

Values & Goals: Refer to your Valued Living Worksheet and list three values you hold that you want to manifest (set as goals) in your life.

1) _____

2) _____

3) _____

Mind States & Actions: Consider how Emotional Mind has two spheres, one with higher vibration emotions (love, joy, gratitude) and the other, lower vibration emotions (fear, self-doubt, blame). Rational Mind meeting Emotional Mind with acceptance fosters your ability to act from higher vibration emotions and access Wise Mind. List skills from your Lighthouse Effect toolbox that can help you maintain mind, body, spirit alignment.

Example: Movement Meditation/Mindful Walking. *When I practice mindfulness by walking in nature, I raise my Emotional Mind vibrations; no matter how I am feeling, I will feel better, and will be better able to follow through on my goals.*

_____

_____

_____

Self-Talk & Reflective Inquiry: On days when it's challenging to take actions to achieve your goals, what is happening with your thoughts/emotions (interference/blocks) compared to days when you can follow through? What have you observed about your own narratives? Notice the difference in energy/frequency between negative self-talk and positive self-talk: How does a positive, self-supportive narrative feel in contrast to a negative, self-judgmental narrative?

_____

_____

_____

Recharging your Internal Battery: When your thoughts are positive it's easier to follow through and take action; your emotional frequency is higher and lighter and your internal battery is fully charged. When your thoughts are negative, your emotional frequency is lower and heavier; your internal battery needs to be recharged. List self-care practices for recharging your internal battery.

Example: Spiritual Practice. *When I listen to uplifting, spiritual music, I feel both calmer and motivated.*

_____

_____

_____

Reframing: What reframing exercise could I do to support my ability to follow through when I feel like I am not able to?

Example: Half-Smile. *When I practice Half-Smile, it sometimes feels silly but I actually end up feeling better and I'm in a better state of mind.*

_____

_____

_____

Meeting Needs: What do I need to encourage myself to follow through? What needs are not being met? How can I gain the support that I need so I am better able to follow through? For example:

Sleep Deprived: *I am not getting enough sleep because I can't keep up with household stuff, but if I ask my partner/friend/family to help by taking on some of the daily chores, I know I will sleep better.*

_____

_____

_____

Rational Mind meets Emotional Mind: Our "needs" are within/arise from Emotional Mind. We can manage our life from Wise Mind when Emotional Mind and Rational Mind are in balance, where Rational Mind meets Emotional Mind with understanding and compassion. (Think: Radical Acceptance.) In this balanced state, we can implement the self-discipline (skills, exercises, practices) of Rational Mind to support us in our healing process. How might you improve your ability to follow through (action) while also restoring your internal battery (energy) in order to meet your desired goals?

Example: *Even though I don't want to do it (small self/inner child), I know I will feel better if I take action toward my stated value and goal (Tall Self/adult self). I know it will raise my emotional vibration to a higher frequency and improve my state of mind.*

_____

_____

_____

There may be times when your perspective is, *It's really hard to turn things around when I feel so depleted and defeated inside.* Apply Reflective Inquiry and ask yourself, "Isn't it getting harder to *not* make a change?" Focus on what you can be grateful for despite the challenges you face. Meet yourself and life with acceptance, understanding, and compassion.

Group Exercise ~ The Lighthouse Effect Valued Living Worksheet

Move through the Valued Living Worksheet with the group, and then introduce the Values & Goals Worksheet to encourage participants to present their values as goals. (These worksheets are my adaptations of the industry-standard VLQ.)

As I've noted before, the modules build on each other, and skills become more deeply woven into the recovery process through repetition and practice. At this point in the group process, it's beneficial to circle back to Second Stage Recovery, and you might also refer back to the Cycles of Addiction & Recovery Model.

Remind the group that second stage recovery is essentially a process of *uncovering* and *discovering*, of getting to the root of why we became vulnerable to addiction, dependency, or attachment. Our repressed core beliefs and trauma memories are screaming for an outlet, to be seen and expressed, instead of neglected and denied their day in court. Second stage recovery is about creating a safe space where these core beliefs or secrets can be aired and integrated or released in the presence of love. In my view, as I've conveyed before, we are *all* on a path of healing into wholeness and self-realization.

Raising your Tolerance: Gratitude Journal

Encourage participants to make a "gratitude" entry in their daily journal at the end of each day or in a separate gratitude journal. Keeping a gratitude journal helps to build tolerance and develop resilience because it is a daily reminder about what we already have and enjoy in our lives. When we focus on loving what we already have, we raise our ability to endure challenges. It doesn't remove the stressful circumstance or dynamic that comes up, it turns our focus to what is already working for us. That simple change in perspective can reduce the intensity of whatever it is we are facing.

When I was an intern at the Brien Center in Pittsfield, Massachusetts, my first client was "Rick." I still work with Rick; he is a peer leader in my current (at the time of this writing) skillful recovery group. I provide an excerpt from an interview with Rick further along, in Module IV, where he speaks more to this and other experiences. Rick wholeheartedly supports a daily gratitude/reflection practice. He will often convey to the group how he would not have come as far as he has in his recovery journey nor gained the level of mastery that he has of these skills if he didn't focus on what he is grateful for on a daily basis. His daily practice also helps to keep his stress levels down and spirits up.

Suggested Closing Meditation ~ I Am Worthy Meditation

Get into a comfortable position, and close your eyes or lower your gaze. (Sound chime or toning bowl.) Take three slow, deep breaths and allow a sense of stillness to penetrate your entire body. Feel this stillness clearing your mind. Tell yourself, *I am worthy*, as you take another slow, deep breath all the way into your belly; breathe out even more than before. Again, breathe in, *I am worthy*. Allow this sense of self-worth and self-value to penetrate every cell of your body; breathe out. Breathe in, *I am worthy*. Allow this deep sense of tranquility to penetrate your mind; breathe out even more than before. Breathe in, *I am grateful to know that I am worthy*. Allow gratitude to fill your body and clear your mind; breathe out slowly and completely. (Sound chime.) Slowly open your eyes, and return to the circle. Now carry this energy of worthiness with you and within you as you move through your day.

Suggested Homework: Practice moving through your daily life modeling your own morals and values, and reflect on them in your journal. Write a list of what you are grateful for in your life, and what you are grateful for about your recovery group. Reflect on what was shared about Rick's process and how gratitude has been a significant part of his recovery. Be prepared to share your reflections with the group at the next session.

Module II (Tolerance Building) Session 11:
Stages of Change Reflection & Progress

Suggested Opening Meditation ~ Self-Value Meditation

Sit comfortably in a receptive, open position with your eyes closed or lowered. (Sound chime or toning bowl.) Take three slow, deep breaths to bring yourself into this present moment. As you continue to breathe slowly and deeply, feel yourself softening even more with each successive in-breath and each elongated out-breath. Now, bring your attention to your third chakra, the area between your chest and your belly, and place a hand there. It is the chakra of self-worth and self-value. Allow yourself to feel the energy of your third chakra, the essence of your own unique value and worth. Continue to breathe gently and naturally. Now, see the color yellow in your mind's eye; see it as a yellow flower. Imagine that vibrant color of yellow resonating in your belly, under your hand, and flowering and radiating out. Take another full in-breath, and full out-breath. (Sound chime.) Slowly open your eyes and return to presence. Carry this golden light and sense of self-worth with you throughout your day.

Check-Ins and Q&A: Invite participants to focus their check-ins on a current life situation where it would benefit them to come from a place of self-value and self-worth.

Handouts: No new handouts. (You might review previous handouts that support group process.)

The Tolerance Building module underscores Mindfulness Practice and development of Observer Self as strong foundations for becoming more proficient, confident, and resilient. This session provides an opportunity for participants to reflect on the progression of the modules and skills they are learning, and how they all weave together.

Group Exercise ~ Stages of Change Review, Repeat, & Reflect

As in the eleventh session in Module I, this next-to-last session of Module II focuses on the Stages of Change. Review the SOC Model, and then have participants complete a new worksheet together as a group exercise, this time with the focus on building tolerance. Have them review the worksheets they completed individually as homework at the beginning of the module and reflect on notable changes, and then share with the group what they learned and what they continue to be challenged by. Invite them to also share what concepts, skills, and exercises from the module most resonate with them and those they find challenging.

Suggested Closing Meditation ~ Metamorphosis Meditation

Sit comfortably with your eyes closed and your body completely open and relaxed. (Sound chime or toning bowl.) Take three slow, deep breaths to breathe your way into this present moment. Imagine the process of transformation from a caterpillar into a butterfly, the magic and wonder of it all. Now consider the perspective of a caterpillar compared to the perspective of a butterfly. The caterpillar is unaware of the process of change that it is soon to experience, while the butterfly is the outcome of that change. Continue to breathe deeply, as you turn your mind's eye to the butterfly emerging from its cocoon and taking flight; imagine you are the butterfly. Breathe in; breathe out. Imagine the wisdom you carry now, having completely changed your form and having shed your old self. Breathe in; breathe out. Imagine what advice your butterfly-self could offer the caterpillar from this "higher" perspective.

Ponder what advice you might offer to comfort and encourage that caterpillar-self. Take another deep breath, and as you inhale, breathe in the courage and faith to face whatever changes are before you and view them from this higher perspective. As you exhale, release any resistance to change you might be holding. Take one more long, slow inhalation, and one more long, slow, exhalation. (Sound chime.) Slowly open your eyes and come back to the present moment. Allow yourself to be open and trust your personal journey of transformation and expansion. Consider how your butterfly-self feels, the power of your wings, and the liberty to fly free. Carry that feeling with you through your day.

Suggested Homework: Complete the SOC Addiction/Recovery Pros & Cons Worksheet, focusing on building tolerance. Continue to practice the skills you've learned throughout the module. Reflect on the major takeaways from the module and write about them in your journal. What were the highlights and what were the challenges? Be prepared to share your reflections with the group at the final session. Consider bringing art, poetry, or other works you created or were inspired by as you moved through the module.

Module II (Tolerance Building) Session 12: Closing Ceremony & Graduation

Suggested Opening Meditation ~ Gratitude Meditation

Get into a comfortable, receptive position and close your eyes or lower your gaze. (Sound chime or toning bowl.) Take three slow, deep breaths as you feel yourself come fully into this moment. Focus on the gentle lull of your breathing. Feel your body softening more and more with each exhalation. Now, using your creative imagination, breathe in the felt sense of the word "gratitude." What color is it, what does it feel like in your body as it flows through you? Continue to breathe gently and naturally. Now, think of the people, places, and things you are grateful for. See them in your mind's eye. Take another full, deep breath as you reflect on simple daily pleasures that bring a sense of appreciation and gratitude into your life. Take another full, deep breath and turn your attention to *you*. Reflect on the positive aspects of your personality and your unique way of being in the world. Take one more full, deep inhalation, breathing gratitude all the way into your being; one more full exhalation, as you fully relax your body. (Sound chime.) Slowly open your eyes and return to the present moment.

I invite you to commit to a daily practice of gratitude, not just for others and what is outside of you, but for you. Reflect in your Gratitude Journal on all the ways you are grateful for yourself. Acknowledge your willingness to practice, your willingness to forgive yourself for being human, your willingness to let go of the past and allow the energy of gratitude to heal you. Carry this high-frequency practice throughout your day and shine your light, best as you can.

Check-Ins and Q&A: Review questions or challenges participants might have, and then invite them to do a gratitude round where they express appreciation to other members for what they brought to the group. Invite them to share their takeaways from the three-month process and encourage them to share artwork, poetry, journal passages, or other such works they produced or were inspired by as they moved through the module.

Handouts: Module II Completion Certificate

Closing Ceremony & Closing Out the Module

Present completion certificates to the group. Invite them to join you for the next module, "Module III Emotional Balancing: The Power Source of Your Lighthouse ~ Authentic Power." Share that you are looking forward to seeing them at the first session and provide the date and time.

Suggested Homework: Reflect on takeaways from the three-month Tolerance Building Module and record them in your journal. Think about the group experience, and reflect on the insights and wisdom that you've gained and given.

Suggested Closing Meditation ~ Attending to the Breath Meditation

Get into a comfortable position, and close your eyes or lower your gaze. (Sound chime or toning bowl.) Take three long, slow, deep breaths. With each inhalation, sense the temperature of the air, feel the sensation of the air as it enters your nostrils, and follow the flow into your lungs. Notice how your chest rises with each "in" breath and relaxes with each "out" breath, as if the process of breathing is gently rocking you. Feel into this subtle rocking motion, noticing your "in" breath and "out" breath as you continue to breathe deeply. Notice how soothing it feels to attend to your breathing. If your mind tries to comment or judge and distract you from the present moment, simply acknowledge, that is what the mind does. Breathe into it and observe it, without worry, without engaging, and let it go. Just continue to follow the rocking rhythm of your breath. One more deep inhalation; one more full exhalation. (Sound chime.) Slowly open your eyes, and gently begin to move your body. Take your time. Slowly bring your attention back to the group.

THE LIGHTHOUSE EFFECT SKILLFUL RECOVERY PROGRAM

Certificate

This certifies that

_____

has successfully completed The Lighthouse Effect Skillful Recovery Program
Module II Tolerance Building
The Structure of Your Lighthouse ~ Developing Resilience

_____   _____
FACILITATOR   **DATE**

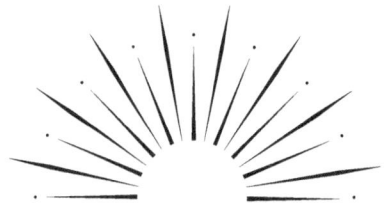

THE LIGHTHOUSE EFFECT MODULE III SYLLABUS
Emotional Balancing: The Power Source of Your Light ~ Authentic Power

Session #1 Welcome & Introduction (Navigating our Emotional Sea): Group Rules, Confidentiality, & Building Group Cohesion; (Review Mindfulness and Tolerance Building Skills); Cognitive Distortions in Depression with Interventions; Emotional Mind Model; Group Exercise ~ Deep Dive on Emotional Mind

Session #2 Stages of Change Review ~ Making Changes at the Emotional Level: Group Exercise ~ Stages of Change Review & Repeat (Participants also do a Pros & Cons worksheet as homework)

Session #3 Understanding the Function of Emotions: Understanding the function and value of the emotional system; Group Exercise ~ Challenging Ten Common Myths about Emotions

Session #4 Charting Emotional Triggers: Understanding Primary and Secondary Emotions; Decreasing Emotional Vulnerability; Group Exercise ~ Capital-T Truth Telling

Session #5 The Emotional Spectrum: Impact of Self-Labeling (Shame & Guilt); Emotional Spectrum Model; Group Exercise ~ Breaking the Cycle of Reinforcing Negative Core Beliefs

Session #6 The Power of "I Am": Anchoring the Mind in The Eye of the Hurricane (alignment, stabilizing, and resiliency); Group Exercise ~ I Am (NOT) Bad worksheet; I AM Mantra.

Session #7 Emotional Freedom Technique: Introduction to EFT; Experiencing & Learning to "Be With" Emotions; Group Exercise ~ Proactive Shifting to Change Negative Core Beliefs

Session #8 Self-Regulating The Nervous System ~ Vagus Nerve Reset: How to Reset & Tone the Vagus Nerve; Qigong to Address the Vagus Nerve; Group Exercise ~ Vagus Nerve Reset

Session #9 Impact of Chemical Imbalances on Mental Health and Recovery ~ Hierarchy of Needs: Maslow's Hierarchy of Needs (comparison); Group Exercise ~ Lighthouse Effect Addiction & Trauma Hierarchy of Needs

Session #10 Integration of Rational Mind and Emotional Mind: Integration of Emotional Mind via Daily Application of Skills (Rational Mind); Group Exercise ~ Reviewing Concepts & Practicing Interventions

Session #11 Stages of Change Reflection & Progress: Charting "emotional balancing" progress over the course of the module; Move a Muscle/Change a Thought; Group Exercise ~ Stages of Change Review, Repeat, Reflect

Session #12 Closing Ceremony & Graduation: Certificates of Completion; Appreciation/Gratitude Circle; Invite group to continue on to the next module (Conscious Communication); Group Exercise ~ Was it Really Rock Bottom?

MODULE III EMOTIONAL BALANCING:

THE POWER SOURCE OF YOUR LIGHTHOUSE ~ AUTHENTIC POWER

In this Emotional Balancing Module, we take a deeper dive into one of the three mind states introduced in the first module, that of Emotional Mind. (Refer back to The Lighthouse Effect Mind States Model.) Learning to accept the emotional system and to manage it with kindness, understanding, and compassion is essential to emotional self-regulation and for the discovery or *recovery* of our Authentic Self. (Think of the Authentic Self as the unprogrammed self.) Our emotions need to be respected, accepted, and allowed to be fully expressed rather than avoided, abused, or neglected. Our emotions provide the voltage for our lighthouse and are a direct link to Spirit.

Module III (Emotional Balancing) Session 1: Navigating our Emotional Sea

Review Protocol: Logistics, group rules, confidentiality. Distribute Repeat Handouts and ask group members if there is anything that can be done to ensure group safety. Begin and end each session with a mindfulness meditation to reinforce and integrate the importance of being present and "in the now."

Repeat Handouts: Group Rules, Stages of Change Model, Stages of Change Addiction/Recovery Pros & Cons Worksheet, Stages of Change: Metamorphosis from Survival to Revival Lifestyle, The Role of an Accountability Partner & How to Give Constructive Feedback Relapse Prevention Plan Worksheet.

Gentle Reminder: Provide new members with the PAWS Self-Assessment Worksheet and How to Manage Emotional Denial Worksheet. Keep in mind that you might want to provide participants who've already received them with another copy, as needed, based on your assessment.

Suggested Opening Meditation ~ Tense and Release Meditation

Get into a comfortable, receptive position and close your eyes or lower your gaze. (Sound chime or toning bowl.) Take a slow, deep breath, filling your lungs, your abdomen, and bringing it all the way through to your back; exhale slowly, completely emptying your lungs. Take another slow, deep breath while pushing your feet into the floor and tensing up your feet, knees, and legs; hold it for a slow count of three: one, two, three. Now, completely relax and release the tension as you exhale. Slowly inhale again as you tense up your glutes, stomach, and back; hold for a slow count of three: one, two, three. Now, release as you exhale; feel the softening and calming effect.

Inhale again, slow and deep, as you make fists with both hands, tensing your arms and your shoulders, and feeling the tension through your chest. Hold for a slow count of three: one, two, three. Now exhale slowly, releasing all of that tension out of the body. Inhale again, scrunching up your face and gritting your teeth and jaw, tighter and tighter, and then hold for a slow count of three: one, two, three. Now slowly exhale, releasing all of the tension. Once more, inhale slowly, tensing your entire body, tightening every muscle, from head to toes. Hold for a slow count of three: one, two, three. Exhale slowly and completely, while shaking your hands; feel the full-body release. Slowly open your eyes, and return to presence. Carry that sense of release and calm with you.

Check-Ins and Q&A: Facilitate the introductory check-in round, and then allow time for group members to ask questions, express concerns, and share reflections regarding handouts and from the previous module. Focus on group rules and building a safe container. Ask again if there is anything more that can be done to support them in maintaining confidentiality and creating boundaries. We develop resilience through repeated application of skills, meditations, exercises, and techniques, so it's good to also remind the group again of the importance of practicing in real time.

Handouts: Module III Syllabus, Emotional Mind Model, Cognitive Distortions in Depression

TIP: View the "Deep Dive on the Emotional Mind" video on my website ahead of this session. (innerfaiththerapy.com)

Navigating the Emotions

Children need to express their emotions in order to get their needs met, and they need to learn healthy boundaries. But so many of us did not learn how to effectively manage our emotional selves and were taught to avoid negative feelings. Many of us were even taught that expressing our emotions is a weakness and something to be ashamed of. Common condemnations such as "you're so emotional" or "don't be so dramatic" are judgments that shame a natural human experience. What we learn is that our emotions are not welcome, valued, or allowed, which leads to us internalizing and repressing them. Those repressed feelings accumulate over time, causing *dis-ease*, instability, and disempowerment.

We might wear a mask of confidence, while underneath, our repressed, vulnerable inner child yearns to be acknowledged. To be truly rooted in our authentic power, the Authentic Self, we need to mindfully attend to that inner child. Otherwise, the mask of confidence is just that, a superficial mask, a facade that does not come from heart-mind coherence. Committing to an exploration of the emotional landscape and developing the skills necessary to maintain a sense of balance and inner peace are essential to coming into alignment. It is an ongoing Reflective Inquiry process that takes courage, forgiveness, patience, and practice. This alignment of the mind, body, and spirit is the foundation of The Lighthouse Effect Skillful Recovery Program.

Our emotional system is made up of the central nervous system and the hormonal or endocrine system. Our thoughts, judgments, and narratives--including our belief systems--dictate our feelings and emotions and, thus, the moods we experience. We need to understand that the mind is the command center and has dominion over the body in the mind-body complex. Thus, we are highly vulnerable to being controlled and overtaken by negative core beliefs or past trauma, in other words, by Emotional Mind or Child Mind. We continue to be triggered as adults when these repressed emotions have not been faced, heard, and accepted. Rather like food in our refrigerator, if we don't keep attending to what is in there and just keep pushing old food to the back and out of sight, the smell will eventually become so overpowering it gets our full attention and we finally are compelled to give it a good cleaning. This is true for our emotional triggers; our emotional system has ways of letting us know when something is out of whack, and it is up to us to notice.

Zooming In on Emotional Mind

As we looked at earlier, the emotional system (Emotional Mind) resides in the right brain. In its higher vibration state, it is childlike and purely innocent, vulnerable, and uninhibited, and in complete alignment with the nonphysical (Spirit, Higher Power, or God of your understanding). It is where we connect directly to the world of imagination, creativity, and total wonderment. We fully integrate mind, body, and spirit by connecting the emotional system and the intellect (Rational Mind) through the heart: heart-mind coherence. Learning to self-regulate our emotions is how we find and experience true wisdom. *Conversations with God* author Neale Donald Walsch sums it up perfectly with his *"wisdom is knowledge experienced"* maxim, as I noted earlier, in the first module. We are here to learn how to navigate this life, fully present and experiencing our senses, emotions, and feelings, and thereby unifying all parts of the self in our physical body and physical reality; to me, this is the very definition of *living* and, as the popular AA adage encourages, it is how we *create a life worth living*.

As you can see, moving through these modules is like putting together puzzle pieces or weaving a tapestry of the human condition; it is a process for healing into wholeness. Let's look at Rational Mind for a moment. We experience Rational Mind as black and white, rather than the gray of Emotional Mind. Rational Mind is concrete, limited, and structured, which works well in some dynamics, as within the medical establishment. It helps us focus, in the way that blinders on draft horses help to not distract them and keep them focused on the road in front of them. Yet, it can be too self-contained, rigid, and limiting. Rational Mind needs to connect to Emotional Mind in order to come into vertical alignment (Wise Mind), which allows the self to be both rooted and in a creative flow-state. This integration is not easy because Rational Mind sees Emotional Mind as foolish or crazy, and thinks that Emotional Mind makes it look bad sometimes, but with daily practice Rational Mind can learn to understand, accept, and come into balance with Emotional Mind.

Emotional Mind, in turn, needs Rational Mind to provide it with a sense of grounding and containment, especially when it becomes fearful. Emotional Mind carries a boundless perspective, which can make it more difficult to focus. Emotional Mind is taking in so much information, it can get overwhelmed and overstimulated, as can occur with people diagnosed with Attention Deficit Hyperactivity Disorder (ADHD). (Though I don't see it as "attention deficit," but rather, "hyper-attentiveness" or "attention without borders.") Within the full spectrum of emotional experience, it can be difficult to feel grounded, stable, and confident. Understanding and accepting the way our emotional system works is essential to coming into alignment, and for those in addiction recovery, for maintaining sobriety.

It is much easier to map out Rational Mind than it is to map out Emotional Mind because you can't box in emotions. While they are not meant to be boxed, they can be regulated. Radical Acceptance is one of the most significant skills or concepts to master. If we were to put "skills" in a mind state, we would put them in Rational Mind. Skills are a form of healthy programming that help to regulate the emotional system by anchoring us in our foundation: it is self-regulation, but also, from Emotional Mind's perspective, *containment*. Reflecting back to the mind states discussion in Module I, Emotional Mind rejects being controlled and wants to be free from being regulated, and this is where radical acceptance comes in. Rational Mind and Emotional Mind need to be more understanding and accepting of each other, to radically accept "what is" in order to enhance the whole.

Now let's really zoom in on the Emotional Mind as its own system within the human experience. Remember that Emotional Mind is composed of two opposing experiences within its own sphere. The top half of the Emotional Mind circle is where love and joy reside. It resonates at a higher frequency, which we experience as feeling lighter and more free. The lower half is where fear and resentment reside. It resonates at a lower frequency, which we experience as heavier, denser; it tends to cause symptoms like anxiety and/or depression.

The heavier the emotion, the more weight it bears on the mind and the greater the suffering it causes. For example, when someone is exhibiting feelings of anger, it might be that they are experiencing some sort of underlying fear or insecurity (defense reaction); they are in a triggered state. On the other hand, the lighter the emotion, the more likely we are to be loving and compassionate with ourselves and others. Some personality types experience the spectrum of emotional frequencies more intensely and rapidly than others, depending on their wiring and trauma history.

In a sense, we are being called to fully step into our adulthood, to no longer allow our inner child-selves to manage our lives, and to move away from thinking that someone outside of us will come to save us: it is up to us to save ourselves, which we do by living with intention and presence. This is not to suggest we should refrain from reaching out for help when we need guidance, a sounding board, or assistance, quite the contrary. It is about discerning what we need and arranging to the best of our ability for it to happen. With practice, we can learn how to walk gracefully between the tension of opposites as a sovereign being, in the midst of opposing views and conflicts. We can have the broad, zoomed out Observer Self perspective, where we witness the interplay of all of our relationships (with friends, family, money, work, and so on) without being tempted by the drama; we can maintain a center in the eye of the storm. We can intentionally enter into whatever is at play, fully awake and prepared to navigate effectively.

THE LIGHTHOUSE EFFECT EMOTIONAL MIND MODEL

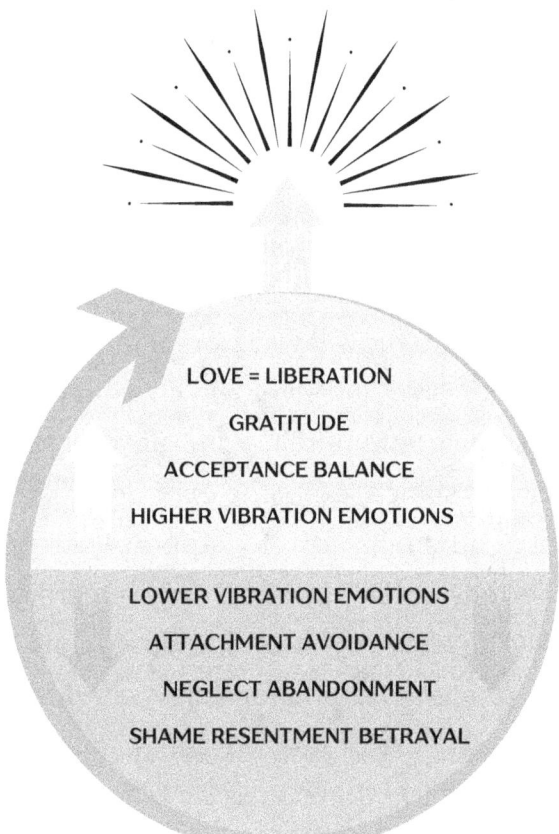

LOVE = LIBERATION

GRATITUDE

ACCEPTANCE BALANCE

HIGHER VIBRATION EMOTIONS

LOWER VIBRATION EMOTIONS

ATTACHMENT AVOIDANCE

NEGLECT ABANDONMENT

SHAME RESENTMENT BETRAYAL

In Western cultures, the intellect (IQ) is revered, and emotional intelligence (EQ) undervalued. In our journey toward wholeness, we need to give EQ its day. Looking at Emotional Mind in terms of energetic frequency, it has two halves. The upper half is love-based and resonates at a higher frequency; the lower half is fear-based and resonates at a lower frequency. The "love" frequency is the highest emotional state of mind we can experience. In this state of Emotional Mind, we are thriving and in alignment, mind, body, and spirit. Whereas the "fear" frequency is the lowest emotional frequency we can experience. We might think of both our lower vibration and higher vibration emotions as indicator lights. When we experience lower vibration emotions, they are flagging us that there are issues that need to be addressed, whereas our higher vibration emotions convey that we are connected to our spiritual essence.

When we are in the lower realm of Emotional Mind, we are in survival mode; our fear-based reactions are tied to early, negative childhood experiences encoded as cellular memory. (Even as early as when we were in the womb.) As our cognitive abilities to think and reason develop, usually around the age of seven, we begin to interpret our cellular memories and often suppress them as a safety mechanism to protect ourselves. As adults, we need to meet those default fear-based emotions as we would a child, with patience, compassion, and understanding, so that we can take agency over our emotional system. As we become more skilled at managing our emotions and resonating from the upper half of Emotional Mind, we gain emotional resilience and inner peace.

Group Exercise ~ A Deep Dive on the Emotional Mind

Do a "deep dive" with the group using the Emotional Mind Model, presenting it on your whiteboard to underscore key points, as demonstrated in the Emotional Mind Model video.

Suggested Closing Meditation ~ Presence Meditation

Get into a comfortable position, and close your eyes or lower your gaze. (Sound chime or toning bowl.) Take three long, slow, deep breaths. As you inhale, feel the breath move all the way down into the base of your abdomen and all the way into the back. As you exhale, completely empty your lungs, extending the length of the exhalation each time. Breathe in; feel the support of the chair beneath you. Breathe out; allow your body to soften. Breathe in; feel how you are supported in this moment. Breathe out, softening even more with each breath. Feel deeply into the calm sense of simply being present. Breathe into Wise Mind. Breathe in the mantra, *I am supported, I am completely supported*. Breathe out the knowing, *I am safe, here, now, in this moment*. (Sound chime.) Slowly open your eyes and bring your awareness to the group. Carry this sense of calm presence with you throughout your day.

Suggested Homework: Reflect in your journal on your understanding of the Emotional Mind. How might you change your perspective, judgments, or emotional vibration? Review the Cognitive Distortions in Depression handout. Bring your reflections to the next session to share with the group and stimulate further discussion.

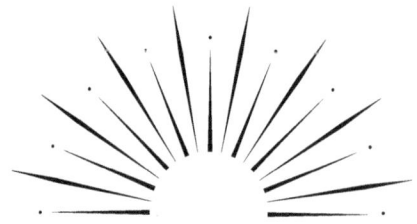

THE LIGHTHOUSE EFFECT
Common Cognitive Distortions in Depression with Intervention Suggestions

The concept that there are common cognitive distortions that people in depression experience was introduced in 1989 in *The Feeling Good Handbook* by David T. Burns. It is now broadly accepted in psychiatry, therapy, and wellness fields. This adaptation of these common cognitive distortions (negative patterns of thinking) include suggested interventions, as it is a core premise of The Lighthouse Effect Skillful Recovery Program that we can change negative patterns, programming, and default behaviors by applying intervention skills in real time.

1) All-or-Nothing: This is extreme black-and-white thinking. You are unable to apply the Both/And concept or a more dialectical way of thinking, believing, and speaking. This extreme thinking comes from the lower vibrations of Emotional Mind (Child Mind), is fear-based, and often dramatically expressed, whether internally (self-talk) or out loud (socially): I *always* or I *never*. For example, *I can never win; You always look good; I always look terrible*. It is distorted from reality and what is true, as in a Capital-T Truth.

All-or-Nothing Interventions: Practice restating the thought from a Both/And perspective: *Even though I feel like things never work out for me, the truth is, sometimes they do; that's my inner child talking; I can see that it's an old belief that no longer serves me*. Ask a trusted friend/accountability partner to flag the all-or-nothing thinking when you convey it in conversations. For example, they might say, *I'm not sure about what you said, could you say it again another way*? It gives you the opportunity to rephrase the thought in a self-supportive way.

2) Overgeneralization: This is another form of extreme thinking, where you fixate on a mistake you made in the past and believe that it is fated to keep repeating. It's a self-fulfilling prophecy: *This always happens to me; I am cursed*. Again, the distortion is in seeing only the negative and giving up all of your power and agency to the belief; it is not dialectical. The ego is relentlessly looking for someone to blame, the self or another; it is wired for survival.

Overgeneralization Intervention: Practice catching yourself mid-sentence and then reframe the thinking: *Even though I have a pattern of making the same mistake, I will commit to being present and try to see this in a more positive way; I am learning; I will keep trying; I am actually getting better even though it doesn't feel like it sometimes*. Notice that these statements are more accurate/true and they allow for a more balanced and tolerable outcome.

3) Labeling: Whether it's spoken out loud in conversation or to yourself in your own mind (self-talk), labeling is a form of judgment and self-identification. It is emotion-based and inaccurate (not a Capital-T Truth) and can be abusive: *I'm stupid; I'm bad*. When the judgment/label is about someone else, it's most often a projection about something you feel or believe about yourself: *They are stupid; they are bad*.

Labeling Intervention: Practice shifting the narrative to not identify the behavior with the person, whether yourself or someone else: *I might feel like I'm stupid, but it's really a lack of confidence; it might take me longer, but with practice I can learn and get better at things; I feel stupid/broken/bad right now, but I have felt this way before, and it will pass; this feeling is not the truth of who I am*.

4) Denying Compliments and Positive Experiences: You have difficulty allowing for or acknowledging positive experiences, as if they have no value. You feel uncomfortable with compliments, ignore your own positive attributes, and downplay/deny when others celebrate and encourage you. When they say, *I really appreciate your kindness,* you say, *Anyone would do the same.* You also have difficulty saying "thank you."

Denying Positive Experiences Interventions: Practice being present. Take a pause when someone compliments you (step into Observer Self) and allow yourself to receive it, to feel it in your body, and say "thank you." Avoid firing a compliment right back at them to deflect the positive energy intended for you. When something good happens, practice being present and simply allow it to be; don't default to negative thinking based on past experiences. When something challenging happens, remind yourself that it is not everything, it's just the moment and it will pass. Just keep practicing: Look for the light, the silver lining, and focus on what is true, and eventually, it will become your way to accept yourself and life as it is.

5) Making Assumptions (Predictions & Mind Reading). Predictions: Projecting worst-case scenarios into the future. This anticipatory anxiety is also extreme thinking and preemptively denies the possibility of positive outcomes. **Mind Reading**: Assuming you know what others are thinking, feeling, and doing––and *why*. Both are absent of critical thinking and Reflective Inquiry.

Making-Assumptions Interventions: When you find yourself projecting, step into presence and apply Reflective Inquiry. Allow yourself to present with the unknown and face your fear with compassion and acceptance. Ask yourself, *Is it a Capital T Truth?* And then answer yourself: *The truth is, I don't have proof/I need more information; I can't really know what the future holds; I can't really know what someone else is thinking. Therefore, I'm going to allow for positive outcomes, at least as much as negative ones. I am not going to let my inaccurate/delusional thinking lead.* (Consider that sometimes what we see as negative experiences or negative outcomes can be catalysts for change and opportunities to learn, build resilience, and gain wisdom.)

6) Amplification/Catastrophizing: Overly dramatic, theatrical, disproportionate reactions; you lead from the lower vibrations of Emotional Mind. You focus on the most negative outcome, almost compulsively. *I woke up in the middle of the night with a shooting pain in my head; I must have a brain tumor or aneurysm. The judge doesn't like me; my appeal will be rejected.*

Catastrophizing Interventions: Notice when you have disproportionate thoughts or reactions, and then apply self-care and self-soothing practices, such as Emotional Freedom Technique (EFT). Talk to yourself (whether out loud or in your mind) in a reassuring tone and remind yourself there is more than one potential outcome. Apply the "opposite thought" part of the Opposite Thought/Opposite Action skill and ask yourself, *What is the opposite outcome; What other outcomes might there be*?

7) Emotional Reasoning: Using your emotions to manage your thinking and to come to conclusions; essentially, you let your emotions lead and manage your life from Emotional Mind: *I feel like I'm going to die, so I probably will. I feel uneasy, so I know something bad is about to happen. My heart is racing and I feel like I might pass out; I am probably having a heart attack.*

Emotional-Reasoning Interventions: Practice soothing yourself instead of exaggerating symptoms and projecting outcomes. Use "the breath" (take slow, deep breaths) to step back from your emotions and step into Observer Self so that you can separate what you *feel* from what *is*. Try meeting Emotional Mind from a rational perspective (Rational Mind) and apply Reflective Inquiry: *Is it a Capital-T Truth; Am I really having a heart attack, or did I maybe drink too much caffeine*?

8) Fixated Thinking: A contracted, inflexible, and fear-based way of thinking where you are walled off and extremely guarded, protecting feelings of insecurity and vulnerability.

It is a Rational Mind trait that is rigid, rule-based, and follows strict guidelines: *I should; I can't; I have to*. It is fixated thinking that leads to internal conflict, procrastination, and agitation. It comes from default "authority" or "scolding parent" programming: *What if I lose/fail/never get it right?*

Fixated-Thinking Interventions: Step into Observer Self and from this larger perspective, consider whether you are coming from your Tall Self (Wise Mind) or your Small Self (Child Mind). The Tall Self is more mature, wiser, and can act from a calmer or neutral state, whereas the Small Self acts from an emotionally triggered fear-based state. Take several slow, deep breaths to help shift your thinking and, once again, apply Opposite Thought. Instead of thinking, *What if I lose?*, ask yourself, *What if I succeed?* Allow yourself to imagine what success looks like. Instead of thinking, *I shouldn't, I can't, I have to*, think, *I can decide if I should, if I can, and it's up to me whether I do, or not.*

9) Mental Filtering: Mental filtering is informed by fear-based, emotional, trauma memory. It is another form of fixated thinking, combined with and reinforced by default reactive patterns that are predominantly negative. The thinking becomes a belief as it is reinforced over time, and any positive thoughts are automatically filtered out: *Nothing positive ever happens to me; I can never win; Nobody cares what happens to me; I am forever cursed.*

Mental-Filtering Intervention: Once again, when you find yourself defaulting to mental filtering, apply Reflective Inquiry: *Is it really true, a Capital T Truth, that nothing positive has ever happened to me?* Step back (zoom out) and think again.

10) Personalization: You unconsciously believe that you are responsible for other's feelings, reactions, and negative behaviors. You do not consider that the other person may be reacting to something that has nothing to do with you. You take it personally: *They're angry; I must have done something wrong.*

Personalization Intervention: Be curious about another person's negative behavior and ask them directly what is happening instead of assuming it is about you or your fault. Practice Reflective Inquiry by asking clarifying questions: *Can I really know that they are angry because of something I did? Can I absolutely know it to be true? It might feel true, but I can't be sure that it is true because I don't know what is in their mind; I don't know what their experience is.*

11) Blaming: The shame/blame game is the opposite of personalization. You accuse the other person of committing the "crime" and take the stance that you are innocent, that you had nothing to do with whatever it is that is a problem. It is a lack of accountability: *It's all your fault; I didn't have anything to do with it.* It is a defensive stance and ego's way of protecting itself.

Blaming Intervention: Pause and take several deep breaths to come into Radical Acceptance. Look at the situation without judging it, you, or the other person. Meet it with understanding and compassion and hold yourself accountable for any part you might have played. There may be occasions when you did not play a part. In that case, be empathetic and consider when you might have been or could be in a similar situation.

Module III (Emotional Balancing) Session 2:
Stages of Change ~ Making Changes at the Emotional Level

Suggested Opening Meditation ~ Grounding Through Sound & Sensation Meditation

Get into a comfortable position, and close your eyes or lower your gaze. (Sound chime or toning bowl.) Take three long, slow breaths, deep into your lungs, abdomen, and all the way into your back. Notice the sounds in the room; notice the sounds outside of the room. Continue to breathe slowly and deeply; notice the subtle sensations on your skin, your feet in your shoes, the weight of your clothes on your body. Breathe in, breathe out; breathe in, breathe out. Notice the temperature of the room. Notice how your breath feels moving into your body through your nose and how it feels as it leaves your body through your mouth. Breathe in, breathe out; breathe in, breathe out. Feel how your breath grounds you in your body; feel how it anchors you to the moment. (Sound chime.) Now, slowly open your eyes and return to presence. Carry that sense of being grounded and rooted with you throughout your day.

Check-Ins and Q&A: Take questions or reflections on the Cognitive Distortions handout from the previous session's homework and consider it in the context of valuing emotions.

Handouts: No new handouts. (You might review previous handouts that support group process.)

Group Exercise ~ Stages of Change Review & Repeat

Review the SOC Model in the context of managing Emotional Mind, and have participants complete the SOC Addiction/Recovery Pros & Cons Worksheet as a group exercise, using your whiteboard. Focus on addictive, instinctual, or reactive emotional patterns that participants know are unhealthy, and what changes they would like to make--setting an intention for the module--to manage their emotional system in a healthier way. For example: A "pro" for a maladaptive way to manage emotions might be, *I avoid dealing with my feelings*. The "con" would be, *I avoid or numb my feelings, but end up neglecting myself and not choosing self-care*.

Suggested Closing Meditation ~ Urge Surfing Meditation

Get into a comfortable position, and close your eyes or lower your gaze. (Sound chime or toning bowl.) Take three long, slow, deep breaths; visualize being in the ocean on a surfboard. Feel the board beneath your feet or your stomach as you ride a huge wave; feel the salt-spray and wind; feel how strong and sturdy you are, secure on your surfboard. Now, think of the wave as an urge or craving. Notice how you are skirting above it, just riding along with it, without judgment, without commentary, without running a story about how much you need it. As you slowly inhale, breathe in the strength of your whole being, riding above the urge; as you slowly exhale, release all attachment to the urge. Continue to breathe, deeply, calmly, as you ride the wave all the way to the shore. Now, step off of your surfboard, and observe as the wave recedes, as the urge recedes. (Sound chime.) Slowly open your eyes, and stretch; keep this image of you riding the wave of urges and challenges as you move through your day.

Suggested Homework: Complete the SOC Addiction/Recovery Pros & Cons Worksheet, focusing on your emotional-management goals and what changes you intend to make. Reflect on emotional management in your journal, and be prepared to share insights and questions at the next session. Continue your mindfulness practice each and every day.

Module III (Emotional Balancing) Session 3:
Understanding the Function of Emotions

Suggested Opening Meditation ~ Anchoring Awareness (Here/Now/This Moment) Meditation

Get into a comfortable position, and close your eyes or lower your gaze. (Sound chime or toning bowl.) Take three long, slow, deep breaths, allowing your entire respiratory system to gently fill and then slowly and fully empty. Take another deep breath; focus your attention on the question, *Where are you*? As you exhale, consider the answer: *here*. Inhale, breathing the felt sense of the word *here* all the way through your body. Exhale, allowing yourself to be here, fully present. Take another deep breath; focus your attention on the question, *What time is it*? Don't look for the answer from a place outside of you. As you exhale, consider the answer: *now*. Breathe deeply into the felt sense of the word *now*. Allow yourself to be here, now, fully present. Feel the emerging awareness from within. Take another deep inhalation; focus your attention on the question, *What are you*? As you exhale, consider the answer: *this moment*. Breathe fully into the felt sense of you as *this moment*. Allow yourself to be *here, now, this moment*, fully present. Take one more full inhalation as you anchor yourself fully in this gift of presence that is you, and slowly exhale, releasing all resistance. (Sound chime.) Slowly open your eyes. Carry this feeling of being anchored *here, now, this moment* throughout your day.

Check-Ins and Q&A: Remind your group to keep check-ins brief. Invite them to focus on insights they gained from the previous session's homework regarding cognitive distortions or their personal SOC Pros & Cons Worksheet.

Handouts: Challenging Ten Common Myths About Emotions

The Function of Emotions

Emotions in and of themselves help us to express how life is interfacing or impacting us at any given moment; they can also inform how we are seen. Where some people appear to have a handle on their emotions, it might be that they are more introverted in their coping style; thus, they convey the energy of being unaffected by life or of having a Zen quality. Others might outwardly express their emotions; they might be more extroverted, tending to freely express themselves, unaware of how they might be affecting those around them. It bears mentioning that most people fall somewhere between introvert or extrovert on the spectrum. (We cover different communication styles more in the next module.) Regardless, our personality style and the way we engage socially becomes the way people see us, judging our behavior as being who we are. No matter our style of emotional expression, it is essential that we understand that our emotions are predominantly governed by internalized programming--imprinting from our family of origin, lived experiences from childhood, trauma, even transgenerational genetics. All of these are hardwired in the command center of the brain and encoded in the body as cellular memory.

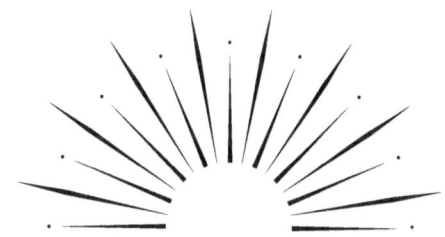

THE LIGHTHOUSE EFFECT
Challenging Ten Common Myths About Emotions

This exercise is along the lines of the Opposite Thought/Opposite Action practice and has a component of "Capital T Truth" as well. Reflect on these common myths about emotions, and challenge them. *Is it true*? (Hint: it's not.) *What is true*?

(1) **Myth**: There is a right way to feel in every situation.
Challenge: _____

(2) **Myth**: Letting others know that I am feeling bad is a weakness.
Challenge: _____

(3) **Myth**: Negative feelings are bad and destructive.
Challenge: _____

(4) **Myth**: Being emotional means being out of control.
Challenge: _____

(5) **Myth**: Emotions can just happen for no reason.
Challenge: _____

(6) **Myth**: Some emotions are really stupid and useless.
Challenge: _____

(7) **Myth**: Painful emotions are the result of a bad attitude, so, my fault.
Challenge: _____

(8) **Myth**: If others don't approve of my feelings, I obviously shouldn't feel the way I do.
Challenge: _____

(9) **Myth**: Other people are the best judges of how I'm feeling.
Challenge: _____

(10) **Myth**: Painful emotions are not really important and should be ignored or denied.
Challenge: _____

Another Myth? **Myth**: _____
Challenge: _____

Group Exercise ~ Challenging Myths

Use the handout to do a group exercise, using your whiteboard to convey your group's responses.

Emotions and Body Memory

In *How the Body Keeps the Score*, Dr. Bessel van der Kolk makes the crucial point that talk therapy, while incredibly healing in terms of establishing a safe place to process painful life transitions, doesn't reach the deeper roots of trauma. With talk therapy, there is more likely to be resistance because the ego is on high alert to try to protect us by keeping painful experiences hidden away. The mind is constantly sizing up its environment to protect itself from harm, comparable to how our bodies try to protect our organs by creating a tumor or cyst to encapsulate abnormal cells that are assessed to be invading organisms.

Likewise, our emotional system is wired to work in concert with the central nervous system (limbic center of the brain) to protect us from anything that might be *perceived* as a threat. The brain doesn't know the difference between a real threat and a remembered threat or trauma memory. Furthermore, repeated experiences of being harmed reinforce the original trauma memory, so it gets even more deeply encoded or embedded in the mind-body complex. This is precisely why body-centered and/or experiential therapies work with the *subconscious* and can get to the covert places where the body has stored those painful memories on a cellular level. When we accept our emotions and respect that they are doing their job as protectors, we can see they are not something to get rid of or avoid. We can then learn to meet them with understanding and gratitude for their valuable function. Once we understand our attachment style--the ways we learned to manage fears and handle threats to protect ourselves in our childhood and teen years--we can begin to establish healthy boundaries and practice healthier ways to self-regulate and self-soothe; we can upgrade the emotional system and work with it to grow into more confident, centered, and integrated human beings. We can reset our reactive patterns and attachment styles by practicing self-regulation and self-soothing techniques and skills.

Suggested Closing Meditation ～ Tall Self Meditation

Sit comfortably in your chair and position your body to receive openly. Close your eyes or lower your gaze. (Sound chime or toning bowl.) Take three long, slow, deep breaths. Recall an experience when you were a child where you felt scared about something that wouldn't seem scary now. Maybe it was learning to ride a bike, or diving into a pool for the first time. Remember the feeling of fear you had about taking the risk to try something you had no experience in, and how *true* it felt that you couldn't possibly do it. Now, take another long, slow, deep breath, and step into your Tall Self; feel yourself getting taller, aligning vertically.

Breathe into this Tall Self version of you, the one who has had years or decades of experience taking risks, falling and getting up again, carrying on, developing the skills you need to ride a bike, drive a car, or dive into a pool, the one who is developing the skills you need to move from survival to revival. Now, take the hand of that small self, that child self, and reassure them: *We've got this*. Take another full inhalation, and full exhalation. (Sound chime.) Know that you can take the hand of the small self within you who is afraid, uncertain, or confused at any time. You always have the capacity to take three long, slow, deep breaths and align yourself with your Tall Self, the one who carries the wisdom of years and decades of experience. You have what it takes to listen to that tallest, wisest, and most resilient part of yourself no matter what challenges cross your path.

Suggested Homework: In your journal, reflect on takeaways on the function of emotions: How did it land with you? What insights are you gaining as you learn about the power and function of your emotional system? Be prepared to share your insights at the next session.

Module III (Emotional Balancing) Session 4: Charting Emotional Triggers

Suggested Opening Meditation ~ Body Scan & Sensory Meditation

Position your body to be comfortable, relaxed, and open. Close your eyes or lower your gaze. (Sound chime or toning bowl.) Take a slow, deep breath, utilizing your entire lung capacity, moving the breath down into the belly and all the way into the back. Now, slowly exhale. Continue to breathe deeply, allowing your entire body to soften a little more with each exhalation. Notice how you are completely supported. Notice how your body naturally rises and falls with each breath, as if the breath is rocking you ever so gently and consistently.

Now, as you continue to breathe deeply, slowly scan your body, beginning at the crown of your head and moving all the through to the tips of your toes. Simply notice each area of your body without judgment or commentary. If you notice any tension or tightness, bring your attention to that area and breathe into it to help open and release it. If there are thoughts trying to distract you, move your attention back to the breath. Feel the coolness of the breath as you inhale and warmth as you exhale. Move your attention to any sounds that you hear and simply notice them as you continue to breathe deeply. Now bring your attention to what you see behind your eyelids, whatever colors, shapes, or patterns appear; just notice as they appear and fade away. Continue to breathe deeply. Turn your awareness to your sense of taste, and simply notice any taste sensations, however faint. Now, move your focus to your sense of smell, as you breathe in, slowly and fully. Simply notice with curiosity and openness, as you slowly exhale.

Move your attention to the sensations you are feeling on your skin. Notice the movement and temperature of the air; notice clothing or textures against your skin. Sense your feet in your shoes, and the floor beneath you. Now, slowly move your attention back to your breath as you step into Observer Self. Observe the process of breathing as you take one more full, deep inhalation all the way down through your lungs and into your back. Breathe in awareness and gratitude. As you exhale, feel your body release and relax fully. (Sound chime.) Slowly open your eyes and return to the room. Offer gratitude to your breath and your mind-body-spirit complex. Send yourself a blessing of full acceptance for you, just as you are!

Check-Ins and Q&A: Invite group participants to focus on their homework from the previous session on the function of the emotional system. The prompt might be: *Share how these concepts are increasing your awareness about what sets off your emotional system and how feelings and emotions serve as indicator lights.*

Remind participants that this is about building tolerance by learning to respect and accept our emotional system; it is not about judging our emotions and feelings. When we can see that our emotions are essentially a navigational system that points us toward what needs to be addressed, we are better able to manage or regulate our emotions. We looked at identifying emotional triggers in the Tolerance Building Module and expound on the concept in this module with a focus on *charting* triggers. (You might have participants refer back to the Determining your Triggers Worksheet they filled out in the previous module.) In order to chart our emotional triggers, we need to distinguish between "primary" and "secondary" emotions.

Handouts: Primary and Secondary Emotions & Tips for Managing Emotions, Decreasing Emotional Vulnerability

Primary & Secondary Emotions

Primary emotions are those that first come up when we are triggered in any relational interaction, whether in relation to a person, our environment, or an event, while secondary emotions are the underlying emotions that follow and that point to the core fear or trauma memory that was triggered.

So, for example, if you are in a recovery group and you hear that one of your group members has relapsed, your initial emotion might be anger or frustration because the person didn't reach out to you for help when they felt the urge. The secondary emotion might arise from a deeper fear that someone within your circle relapsed so the possibility of you relapsing seems more likely: *It's closer to me, so it's more of a threat to me.*

In managing our emotions, it's helpful to understand that emotions come in waves and have many layers, and to know, as the saying goes, "this, too, shall pass." We also need to understand that they predominantly come from fear/contraction or love/expansion. As physical beings, we are naturally wired to protect our physical form. On a psychological level, we are also wired to protect our character, to protect against humiliation and embarrassment, because Ego's worst fear is how others might negatively evaluate or judge us.

One of the best practices for emotional balancing is to not take anything personally. Don Miguel Ruiz speaks to that principle in his books, *The Four Agreements: A Practical Guide to Personal Freedom*, and *The Fifth Agreement: A Practical Guide to Self-Mastery*. I wholeheartedly recommend both books. I appreciate how Ruiz's guiding principles are applicable to the recovery process and how we manage our emotions. The five principles (spoiler alert!) are listed below, with my interpretation in the context of emotional balancing presented in italics.

1. Be impeccable with your word. *Tell the truth and be respectful with yourself and others.*
2. Don't take anything personally. *Protect your heart.*
3. Don't make assumptions. *Speculate with pause.*
4. Always do your best. *Come from Wise Mind or Tall Self.*
5. Be skeptical, but learn to listen. *Engage in conscious listening to learn others' perspectives.*

Group Exercise ~ Capital-T Truth Telling

In the same way that we might apply the Serenity Prayer as a Reflective Inquiry tool, we can use Ruiz's principles or other wisdoms we come across that resonate with us as tools. Do your group exercise for this session based on that premise, using your whiteboard. Turn each principle into a question. For example, the first might be: *Am I being impeccable with my word*? *Is what I'm thinking or saying accurate and true*? It is not unlike asking, *Is what I am saying about myself or someone else a Capital-T Truth*?

We reduce our physical, mental, and emotional vulnerability by stepping fully into our tallest, most mature and developed Self, i.e., Wise Mind. Acknowledging our emotions and having awareness and appreciation for their function as indicator lights is essential. This inner detection system is directly connected to our brain via the nervous and endocrine systems. In learning to manage our emotional system, we foster our connection to the nonphysical aspect of the self and bring our mind, body, and spirit into alignment as the multidimensional beings that we are.

Opposite Thought/Opposite Action ~ A Remedy When We Are Triggered

We looked at Opposite Thought/Opposite Action as a technique for building tolerance. It can be applied to emotional balancing too, as an intervention for when we find ourselves going into auto mode and having reactive behaviors to a trigger. We can simply *notice* when we are emotionally triggered and then change our thought or perspective so that we can respond and act more effectively. So, for example, if you find yourself getting stressed because you are comparing yourself to someone who has easily achieved a goal that you aspire to, just pause and take notice that you are being triggered. You can change your reaction if you are aware of it. Practice catching yourself in automatic-projection mode, and then use Opposite Thought/Opposite Action to change the thought and respond in a mindful way.

Suggested Closing Meditation ~ Tuning In "Radio Frequency" Meditation

Get into a comfortable, receptive position and close your eyes or lower your gaze. (Sound chime or toning bowl.) Take three slow, deep breaths to bring yourself to this present moment. Now, as you continue to breathe deeply, imagine that your mind is a radio, giving and receiving signals. Imagine that your emotions are the radio frequencies or channels. Set your radio to the frequency you desire. Set it to love, or acceptance, or gratitude, whatever you desire in this moment, keep adjusting the dial until you get the frequency to where the energy flows freely without static and distorted electronic sounds. Continue to breathe deeply. Notice how it feels in your physical body, your mind, your emotional body to be tuned in. Do you feel energized? Do you feel relaxed. Feel into your experience of being tuned in. One more deep inhalation, and one more full exhalation. (Sound chime.) Slowly open your eyes, and return to presence. Know that you can tune in to the frequency you want anytime!

Suggested Homework: Reflect in your journal on how this session inspired you and/or how it challenged you. Complete the Decreasing Emotional Vulnerability handout, focusing on how it relates to you and your life experience. Be prepared to share your insights at the next session.

Resources:

The Four Agreements: A Practical Guide to Personal Freedom and *The Fifth Agreement: A Practical Guide to Self-Mastery* by Don Miguel Ruiz (miguelruiz.com)

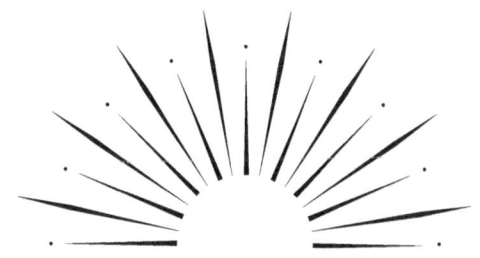

THE LIGHTHOUSE EFFECT
Primary & Secondary Emotions

Emotions are mutable, everchanging, and episodic. Learning how our emotional system works helps us to understand and "radically accept" that our emotions are part of the human condition. When we attach to our emotions and identify with them as being who we are, we get caught in a negative emotional feedback loop.

PRIMARY EMOTIONS are our initial reactions or triggers in the moment. They are unconscious, defensive interpretations and perceptions that come directly from trauma memory and negative core beliefs. For example, *I'm so angry you relapsed after being abstinent for so long!*

SECONDARY EMOTIONS are the underlying emotions that emerge after the initial or primary emotions erupt. They are more likely to be true or closer to the truth. For example: *After I wrote in my journal and faced my feelings of anger, I discovered that I was actually scared and sad that you were tempted after all this time and I then made up a story that if it happened to you, it could happen to me.*

In learning to manage our emotional system, we need to understand that primary emotions have a protective function, while our secondary emotions point to a core issue that needs to be addressed. When we recognize that the function of primary emotions is to "protect" us from having the secondary emotions surface, we can allow them to be expressed without fear or judgment, and can then allow secondary emotions to express themselves. When secondary emotions are repressed and neglected, our self-sabotaging patterns prevent us from experiencing self-empowerment, healthy relationships, and inner peace. We can deepen our understanding of the function of our emotions through a daily self-care practice of Reflective Inquiry journaling. As with all efforts in moving toward wholeness, the first step is awareness. We can apply the skill of Assertive Listening to our own inner process, which helps us to be present, accepting, and compassionate; it is the way to inner contentment. By tuning inward and turning toward our emotional pain, we are better able to see that it stems from negative core beliefs and can then begin to manage our emotions.

Tips for Managing Emotions

- Face your emotions. (Simply observe.)
- Apply mindfulness skills to meet your emotions with patience and understanding.
- Build self-confidence by allowing Tall Self (adult self) to manage the emotional system.
- Focus your mind on what you can change, not what is out of your control.
- Choose positive or high-vibration emotions to override low-vibration emotions.
- Be with your emotions without judgement and with an accepting presence.
- Feel through your emotions and allow them to move through you: energy in motion.
- Practice Opposite Thought/Opposite Action to turn your mind away from negative narratives that cause emotional upheaval; choose a healthy alternative or behavior.
- Reach out to trusted professionals, family, friends, and others in your recovery network for support with your emotional management.

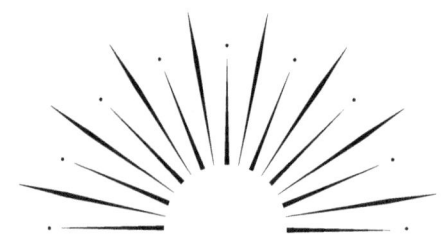

THE LIGHTHOUSE EFFECT
Decreasing Emotional Vulnerability by Increasing Emotional Power

MIND: Decrease mental vulnerability by increasing mental stability.

Mental vulnerability is tied to emotional instability (being fearful and worried); it's a state of mind where we run narratives (self-talk) that are not true. These narratives are like ticker tapes that run along the bottom of the news channel, bombarding us with "breaking headlines." But the headlines are not fact-checked. We need to rewrite the narratives by zooming out and distancing ourselves from the story, focusing on the present moment, and imagining or visioning the life we want to experience. Detaching and distancing ourselves from the narrative and our emotions brings clarity of mind and stabilizes our mind and emotional system, even amidst chaos.

List some intervention skills for zooming back to reframe narratives and stabilize the mind:

_____

_____

_____

_____

BODY: Decrease physical vulnerability by increasing physical activity.

Physical vulnerability happens when we neglect our physical self-care. We want to fully experience and nurture our five senses by caring for our physical bodies: taste, smell, sight, sound, touch. What are you doing to support your body? How do you talk about your body in the privacy of your own mind? Are you kind, supportive, accepting, and forgiving? Are you relating to and caring for your body with the same care that you give in your relationships, to your friends, family, romantic partners? By increasing our physical strength, endurance, and vitality, we also support our mental and emotional wellbeing.

Think about what prevents you from taking the best care of yourself, and then list the ways you do care for your physical health and wellbeing and/or things you think could work for you:

_____

_____

_____

_____

SPIRIT: Decrease spiritual vulnerability by engaging with the nonphysical and/or Spirit, Higher Power, God of your understanding.

We do this through ceremony; by reciting mantras, prayers, and blessings; by meditating, toning, practicing qigong or yoga; by listening to devotional music, being in nature, and participating in celebrations or religious holidays; and so on. Fostering a conscious connection with our spirituality as part of our daily practice brings us into alignment, mind, body, and spirit. High-vibration emotions (love, joy, gratitude) are activated when we listen to uplifting music, watch a movie with a great love story, or observe a touching moment, and when that happens, our hearts are more open and our consciousness expands. Our emotional system makes it possible to connect with Spirit. Whereas addictive substances and behaviors cause us to check-out and to get stuck in lower vibration emotions (fear, self-doubt, blame).

List practices that work for you or that you think could work for you to connect more deeply with the nonphysical and/or Spirit, Higher Power, God of your understanding:

_____

_____

_____

_____

_____

_____

Module III (Emotional Balancing) Session 5:
Shame and Guilt ~ The Emotional Spectrum

Suggested Opening Meditation ~ The Balloon Meditation (Detaching from Negative Core Beliefs)

Get into a comfortable position, and close your eyes or lower your gaze. (Sound chime or toning bowl.) Take three long, slow, deep breaths, focusing your awareness on the present moment. Bring to mind a negative self-judgment that keeps coming up; recognize that it is a negative core belief. Imagine writing that negative core belief on a balloon, whatever it might be, "I am not good enough" or "I can never follow through." Now take that balloon with the belief you've held, and release it to the sky. Continue to breathe gently and deeply as you watch it slowly drift up and away; watch it getting smaller and smaller; watch it fading out of sight and disappearing into the vastness of the sky, your higher power. Breathe into the sense of release, of letting go of that belief. Feel the lightness of being in your mind, in your body. Take another full inhalation, and slow, gentle exhalation. (Sound chime.) Open your eyes and return to presence. Know that you can practice this in the moment, whenever you catch yourself making self-judgments that come from a negative core belief. There is an endless supply of balloons!

Check-Ins and Q&A: Invite group participants to focus their check-ins on how their homework, insights, and growing awareness is impacting their lives. Encourage them to practice the program material by applying the skills and insights in real time in their daily lives as an ongoing discipline.

Handouts: The Emotional Spectrum Model, Breaking the Cycle Models, Breaking the Cycle of Reinforcing Negative Core Beliefs

---

The Impact on the Self of Labeling

Research professor and author Brené Brown delves deeply into the concepts of shame and guilt. As Brown wisely points out, the difference between guilt and shame is the difference between I *did* something bad and I *am* bad! Using an "I am" statement is extremely powerful, whether it is a positive claim or negative claim. It is vital that we understand when we make such pronouncements, we are energetically declaring them as a truth and linking them to our personal identity: *I am bad, I am unlovable, I am forever damaged*. The "I am" claim is almost like a spell, with its powerful intention. Whereas, when we make a claim that we *did* something bad, we are pointing to a *behavior* and the label gets attached to *it*, rather than *us*. Brown suggests that we can't do anything with *shame*, because it arises from absolute labels. *Guilt*, on the other hand, can be worked with because it is about a behavior, not the person, and with practice, behaviors can be changed. The goal is to bring full attention and awareness to what we are doing and ask ourselves whether that is what we want to manifest or invest in.

It's about how we interpret a label and attach to it as the truth, without applying critical thinking. And that applies to more than the statements we make; it applies to what we read or hear in other contexts and from other sources. When we accept someone else's labeling of themselves or others or our own about ourselves, it is more likely to manifest; it gets locked in. There's also the element of how, when someone identifies as bad with absolute conviction, they are perpetuating the programming; thus, they are giving themselves permission to step into that role or identity and act accordingly.

I apply Brown's teaching here, in the context of emotional balancing, as it ties to how our labels about ourselves impact our central nervous system and emotional system and can trip encoded trauma memories. I offer a slightly different perspective--that we *can* change the label, even one that seems absolute, such as shame. Shame is a feeling and not an entity or being, so we can *feel* shame but we are not shame itself. An effective remedy for addressing shame and our claims about it is the Reflective Inquiry skill that was covered on the module

II: *Is it really true? Is it a Capital-T Truth? What is the truth?*

When we recognize that we are not the label, the feeling, shame, in this case, loses its power and we can begin to detach from the internalized identification. This is true with any feeling that we might have identified with: guilt, humiliation, embarrassment. Once we identify the feeling, we can find the belief we've attached to it. For example, I identify what I am feeling as shame, and I can see the belief I've attached to is that I must be bad. Energy frequency charts show that shame carries the lowest energetic frequency within the emotional spectrum; it is extremely dense. The more powerful the conviction, the more powerful the release when we acknowledge the truth and detach from identifying with a false belief. Practicing experiential reflective inquiry is liberating and empowering. The key is to keep addressing the feeling of shame each time it arises and to continue to meet it with radical acceptance, understanding, and compassion; make it an ongoing practice.

THE LIGHTHOUSE EFFECT EMOTIONAL SPECTRUM MODEL

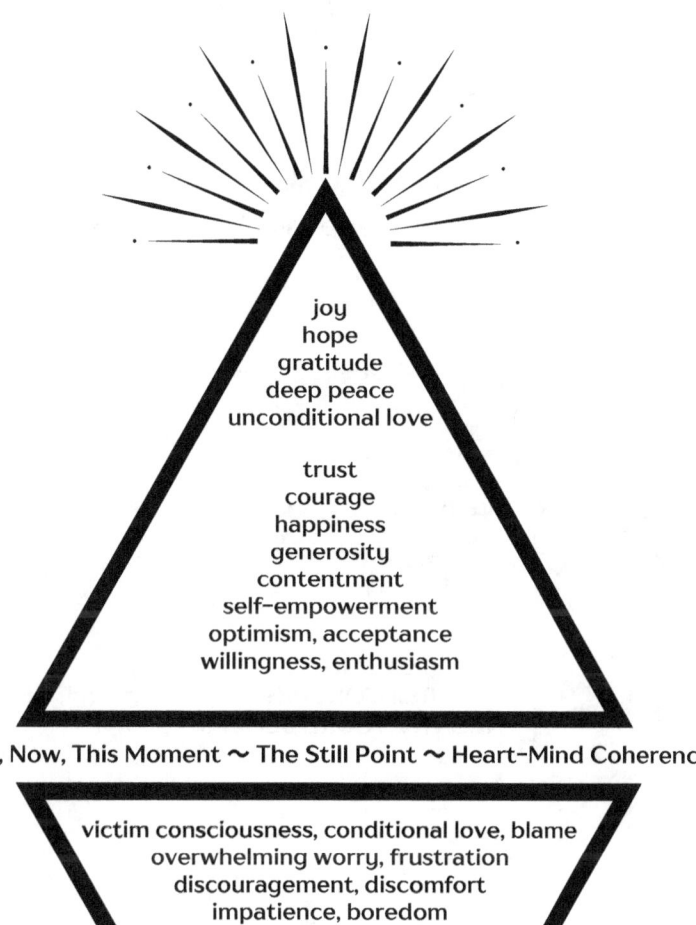

joy
hope
gratitude
deep peace
unconditional love

trust
courage
happiness
generosity
contentment
self-empowerment
optimism, acceptance
willingness, enthusiasm

Here, Now, This Moment ∼ The Still Point ∼ Heart-Mind Coherence

victim consciousness, conditional love, blame
overwhelming worry, frustration
discouragement, discomfort
impatience, boredom
pessimism, doubt

Anger, hate, rage, resentment
jealousy, betrayal, greed
revenge, pride
grief, despair

fear, unworthiness
powerlessness
shame
guilt

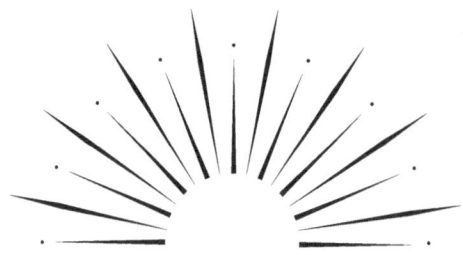

THE LIGHTHOUSE EFFECT
Breaking the Cycle of Negative Core Beliefs Model

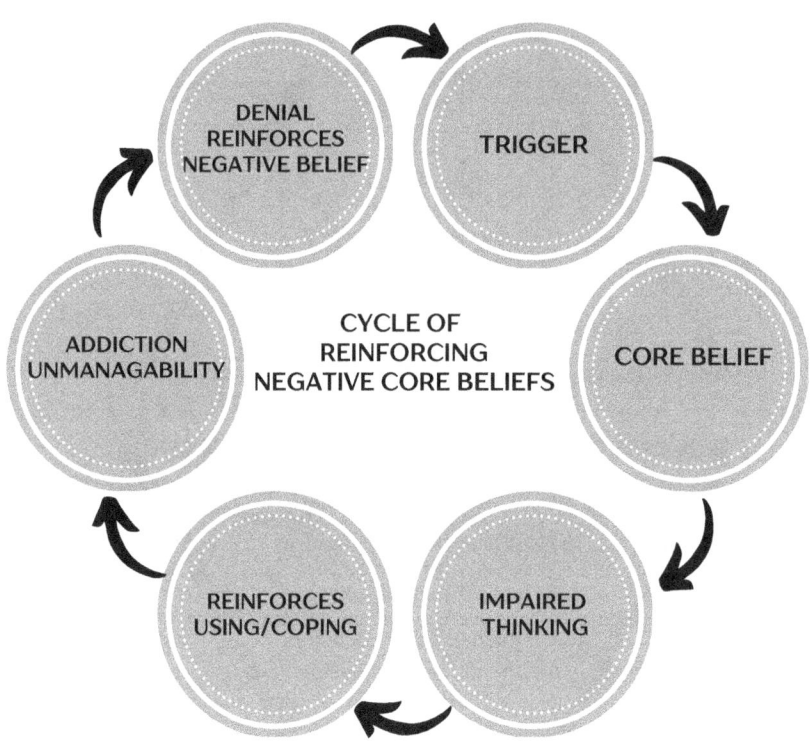

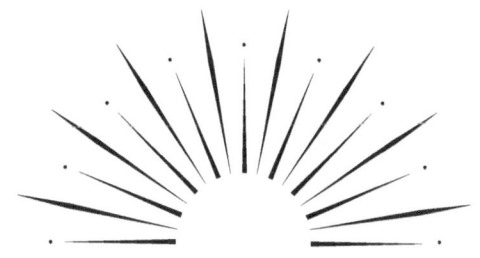

THE LIGHTHOUSE EFFECT
Breaking the Cycle of Negative Core Beliefs Model

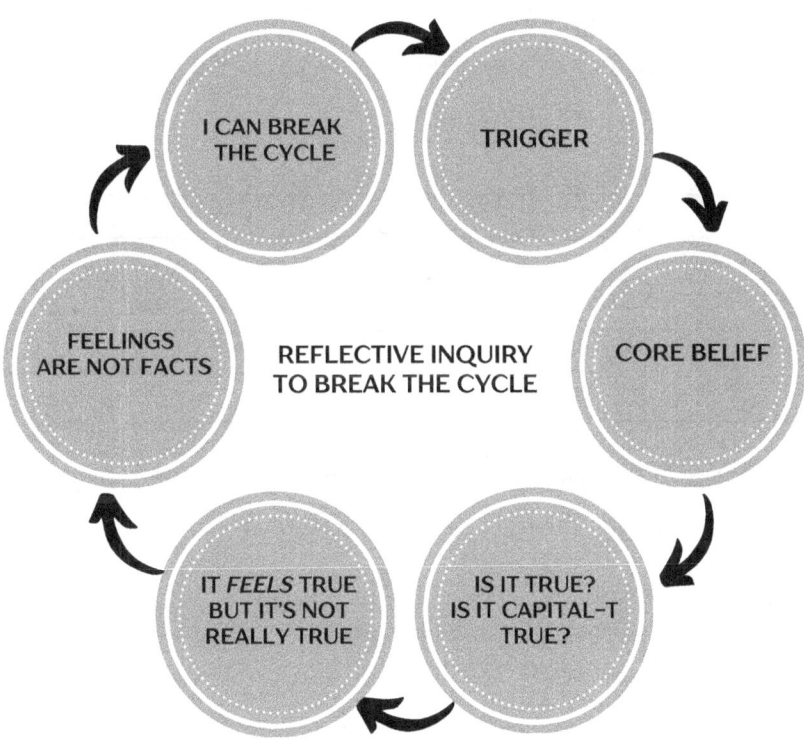

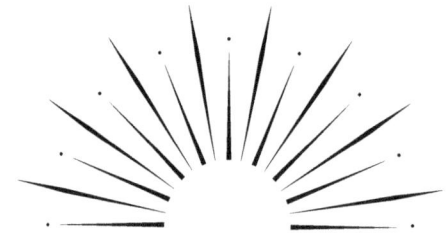

THE LIGHTHOUSE EFFECT
Breaking the Cycle of Reinforcing Old Beliefs

1. WHAT IS THE BELIEF? What is your reasoning for your need for your addictive substance or behavior? What is the negative core belief behind it?

Example Reasoning: *Having a drink helps me cope with my stress over not being able to pay my bills and care for my family. I wouldn't have to "use" if I had a better paying job. I'm just trying to make ends meet.*

Example Negative Core Belief: *I am a failure. I am failing my family.* [Impaired thinking gets reinforced.]

Write down your reasoning and the core belief behind it:

My Reasoning: _____
_____
_____

My Negative Core Belief: _____
_____
_____

2. REFLECTIVE INQUIRY: IS THIS BELIEF TRUE? Ask yourself if it's really true: Is it a Capital-T Truth?

Example Inquiry: *Have I really failed my family? Can I absolutely know that I have failed them? What is the evidence?*

Example Capital-T Truth: *If I look at the facts, I have a budget and I work full time, and that shows that I am making every effort to take care of my family. It just is really hard to keep ahead of my expenses.*

My Inquiry: _____
_____
_____

The Capital-T Truth: _____
_____
_____

3. DIFFERENTIATE FEELINGS FROM FACTS: What are you feeling? What are the facts?

Example Feeling: *I feel like I'm failing my family when I can't cover my expenses. I feel bad when I overspend on my budget, and it causes me to think or believe that I am a failure.*

Example Fact: *The fact is, the truth is, I am a good parent and I am not a failure.*

What I'm Feeling:
_____
_____
_____

The Facts:
_____
_____
_____

4. HONEST PERSPECTIVE: It's "costly" on many levels to reinforce self-lies and negative core beliefs. It "pays" to tell the truth! Choose to shift your perspective based on the facts and benefits that would come with telling the truth.

Honest Perspective Example: *If I didn't spend money on my coping habits, which only support my negative core beliefs (lies), then I could meet my expenses and have some money left over for a family outing or start a savings account. If I tried a different strategy of reducing my stress levels and dealing with my triggers, my family and I would all benefit: fewer expenses, more money for my family, I'd be more present and available. The coping and intervention skills I'm learning are free.*

Honest Perspective:
_____
_____
_____
_____

Group Exercise ~ Breaking the Cycle

Refer to the Emotional Spectrum Chart and use the Breaking Cycle of Reinforcing Negative Core Beliefs handout. You might use the universal example of the "not good enough" core belief as the basis for the exercise, or ask for a volunteer and focus the exercise on one of their core beliefs.

Breaking the Cycle as a Practice

As you move through the program, continue to reinforce with your group how recovery is an iterative process and the goal is to incorporate the skills and tools they learn into a daily practice. The key word here is practice. The more they apply these tools in real time in their daily lives, the stronger the foundation they build. We introduce "Breaking the Cycle" here, but it draws on content covered in earlier sessions, such as session 4, where we looked at charting emotional triggers.

Suggested Closing Meditation ~ Warm Golden Light Meditation

Get into a comfortable, receptive position, and close your eyes or lower your gaze. (Sound chime or toning bowl.) Take three slow, deep breaths and with every exhalation breathe out more fully and longer than before. Imagine a soft, warm, golden light shining down upon you. Imagine this light beginning to flow through you, starting at the top of your head, the crown chakra. Continue to breathe gently and naturally, as you imagine this golden light moving through you, through your face, neck, and shoulders; through your arms and hands and torso; your hips and legs; all the way down to your toes, filling every aspect of your being. Imagine every cell in your body is absorbing this warm golden light. Notice how every muscle in your body is softening and becoming more flexible; allow yourself to be completely relaxed. Allow this healing light to fill your being and clear your mind. (Sound chime.) Slowly open your eyes and return to the present moment. Carry this sense of being embraced and filled with warm, golden light with you throughout your day.

Suggested Homework: Reflect in your journal how this session landed with you. How did it resonate or how did it challenge you? Complete the Emotional Balancing: Breaking the Cycle of Old Beliefs handout on your own. Consider what skills you could apply as interventions to break the cycle. Bring your insights to share at the next session.

"Where the mind goes, energy flows."

--Ernest Holmes

Module III (Emotional Balancing) Session 6: The Power of "I Am"

Suggested Opening Meditation ~ Stillness Meditation

Sit comfortably in a receptive, open position with your eyes closed or lowered. (Sound chime or toning bowl.) Take three long, slow, deep breaths, inhaling all the way into your lungs, your abdomen, your back, releasing even more fully and completely with each sequential exhalation. Let your body rest; let your mind rest; let your emotions rest. Imagine this energy of rest, of sublime stillness, filling you. Breathe in the simple radiant energy of stillness; breathe out full relaxation. Feel into this sublime, radiant energy of stillness. Breathe in stillness; *be* in stillness. One more deep inhalation, one more full exhalation. (Sound chime.) Slowly open your eyes and return to presence. Carry this exquisite state of being throughout your day.

Check-Ins and Q&A: Remind group participants to keep check-ins brief. Encourage them to focus their check-ins on challenges that are coming up and insights skills that have come to light as they practice tolerance-building skills in their daily lives. As it's the halfway point in the module, encourage them to reflect on the benefits and challenges of working with the emotional system, and to share any homework, journal reflections, or insights they've gained over the past six weeks.

Handouts: Anchoring the Mind in The Eye of The Hurricane, I Am (NOT) Bad Worksheet

Moving out of Entrenched Narratives

"I am" statements are powerful because we are claiming a personal identification with what comes after "I am:" I am bad, I am tired, I am cursed, I am messed up, I am done, I am broke, I am crazy.

When we don't explore our negative "I am" thinking and don't allow ourselves to meet it with acceptance, we create a feedback loop that becomes a self-fulfilling prophecy. Mindfulness practice is essential to coming into awareness of how the mind talks *at us*, often on autopilot and sometimes incessantly. In being mindful, we can shift out of our entrenched narratives and learn to identify in the positive: *I am wise, I am patient, I am courageous, I am resourceful*.

When I introduce the I Am (NOT) Bad exercise to the group, I encourage them to be open to how they might resist letting go of negative "I am" statements, along these lines:

You might resist letting go of your negative "I am" statements, and that is not uncommon; it's even to be expected. Though we might understand that such statements are unhealthy and ultimately untrue, they are familiar, and in that sense, comfortable. When we begin to question the validity, it can be destabilizing. It takes courage and willingness, but we can let old familiar ways of identifying ourselves go so our Authentic Self can fully emerge--like a butterfly from its chrysalis.

TIP: Prior to this session, you might watch the "Power of I Am" video on my website (innerfaiththerapy.com), where I demonstrate the I Am (NOT) Bad work with someone who holds an internalized belief that they are bad.

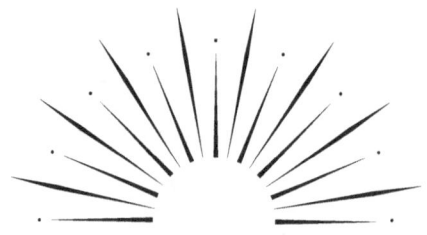

THE LIGHTHOUSE EFFECT
Anchoring your Mind in the Eye of the Hurricane

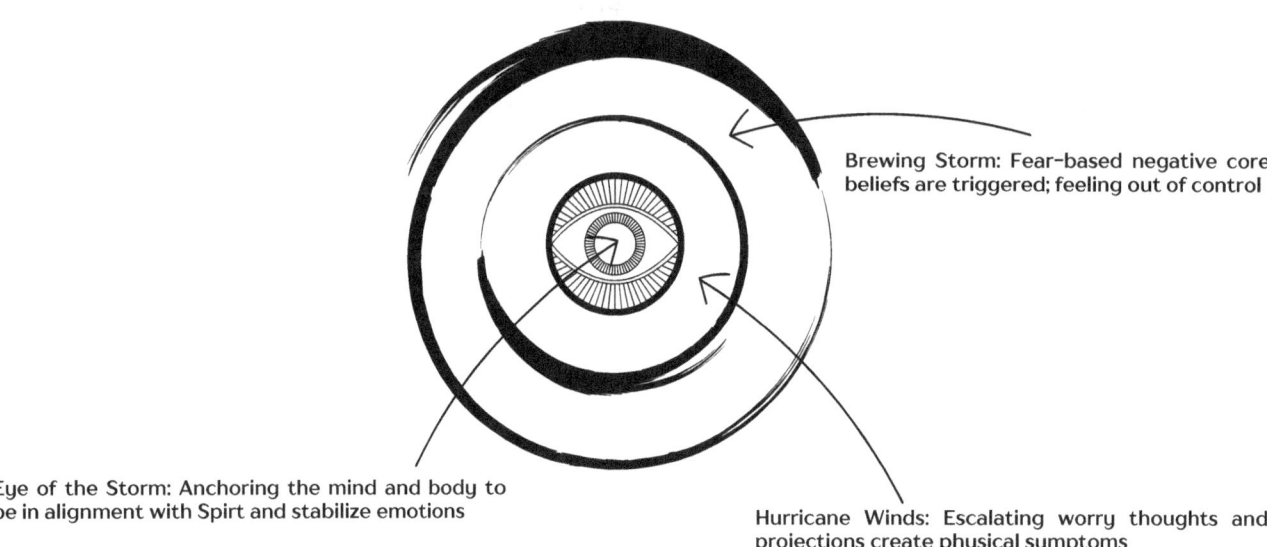

Brewing Storm: Fear-based negative core beliefs are triggered; feeling out of control

Eye of the Storm: Anchoring the mind and body to be in alignment with Spirt and stabilize emotions

Hurricane Winds: Escalating worry thoughts and projections create physical symptoms

Using analogies, images, and symbols helps us to view a challenging or potentially retraumatizing event from a more detached perspective. It helps us to move out of Emotional Mind (right brain) thinking and instead come from a more grounded perspective when we are triggered. We might think of our emotional landscape when we are triggered as a brewing hurricane. The negative core beliefs and untrue stories that are fueling our emotions are like hurricane winds that trip the limbic system and send us into survival mode. The entire process happens in a nanosecond, where we are suddenly caught in the gale force winds of fear.

We can learn to navigate these moments by centering and grounding ourselves in the eye of the storm, and we do that by applying intervention skills such as DBT, EFT, Reflective Inquiry, and so on to move out of horizontal or linear thinking and into vertical thinking. Even the simple intervention of attending to the breath can instantly bring us into vertical alignment, mind, body, and spirit, and ground us in the moment amidst the hurricane-force winds of our emotions. Finding our center in the eye of the hurricane stabilizes the emotions, provides a sense of strength and safety, and anchors us: we become the lighthouse, standing tall, radiating our light through the storm with a clear and focused mind.

Think: *Even though the storm is all around me, I am completely centered and aligned between earth and sky. I am the lighthouse radiating my unique light in alignment with my Higher Self, Spirit, God of my understanding.*

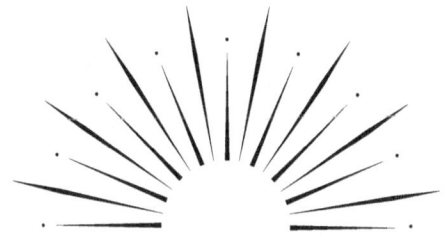

THE LIGHTHOUSE EFFECT
I Am (NOT) Bad Worksheet ~ An Exercise for Revealing the Truth

This exercise is about giving mindful attention to how you use "I am," so that you can learn to move away from identifying with the negative, and instead see the positive of who you are.

Take a deep breath and contemplate the identifying statement, *I am bad*, or *I am crazy*, or whatever self-identifying statement you want to release.

In the space below write down how this message impacts your body and mind. How does it make you feel? Where is it located in your body? Where do you have tension?

_____

_____

_____

_____

Take another deep breath, and as you exhale, release the negative thinking. Imagine it drifting further away with each breath until you clear it fully out of your mind.

Now, think of an opposite statement, and write it down. For example: *I am good*; *I am human*; *I am resourceful*; *I am kind*.

_____

_____

_____

_____

Continue to breathe deeply. Breathe into how your new, opposite-thought mantra impacts your body and mind. How does it make you feel? Where do you feel this in your body? Practice simply staying present as you breathe into the mantra, with no commentary, just giving it space to be. Notice if you are more contracted and stressed, or more open and relaxed, and write down how you feel.

_____

_____

_____

The narratives that hold our negative core beliefs are what re-traumatize and trigger the nervous system, thus creating a cycle of reinforcing those negative beliefs. Some people are actually more triggered by the positive statement. If that is your experience, it might be that shame or whatever other negative label you've identified with is so entrenched, you are not accustomed to or comfortable with positive statements applying to you. You align more with what isn't working instead of what is working; the negative is known, the positive is suspect.

There's no right or wrong. It's about understanding the impact of "I am" statements, and if a positive statement is more triggering for you, that tells you something significant. Take a moment and repeat each statement, and assess which is most triggering for you. Whichever one it is, breathe into it, without commentary, until you see or feel a shift of perspective. Whether you are triggered by the negative statement or positive statement, just observe it. Write down how it feels as you simply allow it to be, without attaching to it.

_____

_____

_____

_____

_____

Take slow deep breaths, at least twenty breaths. Notice how the triggered feeling increasingly loses its punch when you are simply present with it, without running a story; it's just a statement.

Breathe into the present moment; focus your mind on the here and now. Now practice "turning your mind" in the direction of the positive statement, towards what brings a sense of calmness, reduced stress, and openness. You may experience resistance, and that's okay. Just continue to breathe into the moment, and practice turning toward your feelings as they arise. Treat them with acceptance and loving kindness, just as a grandmother, guiding angel, or power animal might do.

Keep practicing, regardless of your critical judgments; keep bringing yourself back to the here and now, without any commentary or analysis. Over time, the negative narrative will carry less and less weight. Write down a few positive "I am" mantras you can carry through your day.

_____

_____

_____

_____

_____

Take a moment now, and thank yourself for taking time for yourself, for attending to yourself with care and kindness.

Group Exercise ~ I Am (NOT) Bad

Go through the I Am (NOT) Bad Worksheet as a group exercise, using your whiteboard to underscore primary concepts and reflect back participants' comments.

Encourage the group to practice Reflective Inquiry in their daily lives, specifically to notice when and how they've internalized negative childhood experiences and identified with them as being who they are. Encourage them to practice shifting their "I am" narratives in real time, so when a situation arises where they fear they are being judged by someone, they can look within and engage in the process of self-reflection.

For example, the thought in a given moment might be, *They think I'm bad.* When that happens, we can take a pause, look within, and adjust our thinking to consider, *Maybe I think I'm bad*, and then ourselves directly, *Am I bad?* Go deeper and apply the Capital-T Truth Reflective Inquiry tool. *Is it a Capital-T Truth? Am I really bad, one hundred percent bad?* It is essential that we be honest with ourselves in terms of our own morals and values--the same morals and values we apply to other people. Is "bad" who we are? Do we really want to identify ourselves as bad? Or is it that we *feel* bad sometimes? It's vital to make the distinction between feelings and truth. When we come to see that it's not a Capital-T Truth, we can begin to shift out of the negative "I am bad" thinking.

It's not just our own "I am" statements that we identify with, it's the opinions of others. I have observed in my personal and professional life that what so many of us fear most is what others think of us, how others judge us. We seem to be okay with judging ourselves, but if someone else judges us and even if they make the same judgment we've made of ourselves (whether direct, assumed, or imagined) we are devastated, hurt, or angry. This dynamic is a setup for disempowerment; we default to thinking our value or worthiness is determined by someone outside of us and, thus, outside of our control.

If we fear being judged by others, we will be in fear in any social or relationship dynamic. Worrying about how we are being perceived by others keeps us focused on what is outside of our control. That fear of judgment can even develop into a social phobia where we avoid engaging socially. When we take ownership for the negative thinking and see that it is us, not others, who are attached to whatever negative critical judgment we have, then we can change the narrative. We can work mindfully with our negative "I am" statement and see it for what it is--a fabrication--and start detaching from and deidentifying with it.

To be freed from this programming or belief and become a sovereign being, we have to *consciously* disallow others (family, friends, authority figures, and so on) from having the power to determine who we are. Essentially, we want to cut energetic ties to outside judgments, opinions, and condemnations. No one is less than or better than any one of us, nor in any better position to determine who we are, which is why I encourage *vertical* thinking in terms of mind-body-spirit alignment. When we claim alignment with our benevolent, loving, wise Higher Power or God of our understanding, we gain back our free will to explore our lives to their fullest.

The "I AM" Mantra

A favorite mantra of mine is the "I AM mantra." It is a simple but powerful higher-frequency affirmation. When I first began to practice the mantra, it was easier for me to use the word "of" and then eventually I was able to drop "of" and embrace the full power of the mantra. (If participants or groups are not comfortable with the language of "Light" or "Love," use the word "Good.")

I Am of Light; I Am of Love; I Am of Truth; I Am!
I Am Light; I Am Love; I Am Truth; I Am!

Encourage your participants to practice this powerful mantra to replace the programmed belief "I Am Bad." It's an essential software upgrade.

Suggested Closing Meditation ~ I Am of Light Meditation

Get into a comfortable, receptive position, and close your eyes or lower your gaze. (Sound chime or toning bowl.) Take three slow, deep breaths to bring yourself to the present moment. Now, take a deep breath and as you inhale, think, *I am of Light.* Breathe the thought all the way through you, and as you slowly exhale, allow your body to soften. Breathe in, *I am of Light, I am of Love.* Allow yourself to feel the energy of light and love flowing through your physical body, your emotional body, your mind. As you exhale, allow your body to soften even more. One more time. Breathe in, *I am of Light, I am of Love*, letting it seep into your core. Now exhale slowly, and allow your body to soften even more. (Sound chime.) Slowly open your eyes and return to the room and this present moment. Know that you can use the breath and "I Am" mantra at any time. Just breathe and really feel into it; feel the energy of the words permeating every cell of your body, every room in your mind. Allow your whole being to resonate with the energetic frequency that the words carry.

Suggested Homework: Reflect on how this session felt to you. What did it bring up? What was revealing? What was reinforcing? What was challenging? Journal about your experience every time you practice turning your mind, giving careful attention to your thoughts and noticing how it feels in your body when you shift them. Notice the holes in your "I am bad" and other negative "I am" beliefs and reconstruct the truth of who you are, from the inside out, using this powerful process of self-reflection as a daily practice. Bring your insights to the next session to share with the group to inspire group discussion and connection.

Module III (Emotional Balancing) Session 7: Emotional Freedom Technique

Suggested Opening Meditation ~ Havening Meditation: This opening meditation introduces the Emotional Freedom Technique. It is a simple way to self-regulate and self-soothe, and a powerful "Breaking the Cycle" technique.

Get into a comfortable, receptive position and close your eyes or lower your gaze. (Sound chime or toning bowl.) Cross your arms in front of your chest, placing your hands around each shoulder. Take a slow deep breath, and as you inhale, squeeze your shoulders inward as if giving yourself a hug. As you slowly exhale, move your hands downward toward your elbows and relax your shoulders, then silently tell yourself, *I'm here, I'm okay,* as you continue moving your hands gently all the way down to your wrists. Take another deep inhalation, and hug yourself again, squeezing your shoulders with your arms crisscrossed over your chest. Now, exhale, as you slowly move your hands down your arms again. Think, *I'm safe, I'm here, I'm okay*, as you continue to move your hands down to your wrists. Let's repeat one more time. Take a slow, full inhalation and hug yourself. Now, as you slowly exhale, move your hands gently down your arms past your elbows to your wrists, thinking, *I'm safe; I'm here; I'm okay*. (Sound chime.) Slowly open your eyes and return to presence. Know that you can self-soothe using this havening method and meditation at any time, in real time.

Check-Ins and Q&A: Invite the group to share about about how they are applying emotional balancing skills and concepts in their daily live to help support their recovery and self-care.

Handouts: Proactive Shifting Practice, Experiencing & Learning to "Be With" Emotions

Emotional Freedom Technique (EFT)

EFT is a highly successful intervention for any kind of emotional trigger, the ultimate self-regulating, self-treating technique for deprogramming trauma memory and healing physical and emotional pain. It can be accessed anytime and anywhere, at no cost, and with great holistic-health benefits. You literally take your wellbeing into your own hands, as you use your fingers to tap on certain pressure points in your body. EFT provides two different emotional-healing modalities in one, as there are two components: 1) tapping on sedation points; and 2) speaking a dialectical narrative, which is a form of neurolinguistic reprogramming that addresses the emotions, fosters acceptance, and leads to the desired outcome(s). It is the combination of these two highly effective modalities, each incredibly cathartic on its own, that make this "dynamic duo" of a self-administered intervention so powerful and deeply healing.

Tapping activates the sedation points that acupuncture and acupressure practitioners stimulate to release emotional trauma held in the body (cellular memory) while simultaneously sending an energetic sedative or calming signal to the central nervous system. On a national and even global scale, EFT teams are often mobilized to large-scale traumatic events, where they treat people of all ages who have experienced natural disasters and mass violence, such as earthquakes, tsunamis, and school shootings. To the latter, tapping teams work with students and teachers to teach them this self-soothing technique in order to sedate the central nervous system and help to integrate traumatic experiences.

Over my three decades of experience as an Integrative Acupressure practitioner, it naturally flowed that I brought EFT and havening into my work with victims of trauma and addiction. Havening is a variation of tapping that I find to be soothing, simple, and easy to remember. Havening is a great way to ease into tapping, especially for those who are highly sensitive to the tapping action on their body. (Havening is a good practice to introduce to children, to teach them how to self-soothe in a healthy way.) In the midst of a trigger, urge, or panic attack, we can choose it as a healthy replacement for our go-to fix, whether an addictive substance or maladaptive behavior. EFT can immediately and directly soothe the trauma memory held in the mind-body complex and decrease stress levels, with no negative side effects.

The narrative component of EFT is what you say to yourself as you are tapping or self-soothing. The goal is to unwind your fear-based narrative and tape over it with a soothing and reassuring narrative that will instill a calming effect. For example: *Even though I feel scared, abandoned, and rejected, I accept my feelings as normal reactions that come from fear and trauma memory. I choose to meet these feelings with understanding and acceptance to invite a more healing experience.* EFT addresses all parts of our being, including our feelings and emotions (and our judgments about them) and embraces the entirety of our human experience.

EFT can be integrated with other tools for self-regulating and managing mind states. When Rational Mind meets Emotional Mind with respect, love, and understanding, we naturally come into Wise Mind. It is beneficial to have a supportive witness to our triggers, emotions, and memories and EFT is a great ally in that process. We become our own witness by engaging in EFT to self-calm and create a supportive narrative. For example: *I deeply and completely accept myself and all of my emotions, without reinforcing my original trauma. Today I'm safer than I've ever been and I have a solid support network around me; I accept myself just as I am in this and any given moment.*

I can't say enough about the power of combining the modalities we are covering in this module, some of which were introduced in previous modules. Using skills together can be all the more transformative in repatterning the neural networks formulated by the brain when the original trauma or negative experience occurred. When we bring ourselves out of the past and into the present, we can safely acknowledge the trauma memory, deprogram it, and replace the narrative. The effect of practicing such skills daily, and over and over, is that we eventually let go of the fearful, survival-based stories we've been carrying, and in the process, we override our neural pathways with supportive narratives that allow us to thrive. We are our own best advocates to support and empower our mind-body-spirit complex.

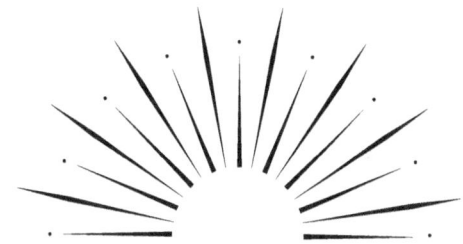

THE LIGHTHOUSE EFFECT
Proactive Shifting to Change Negative Core Beliefs

We have the power to change and reprogram our negative core beliefs. It is essentially a search for the truth. We can be proactive and choose to move out of self-judgment to align with what is true and change our self-talk and old narratives. There are five steps: Desire, Identify Negative Core Belief, Shift the Narrative, Reach Higher/Apply Skills, Conclusion/Reflection.

DESIRE: *I want to learn how to manage my emotional reactions.*

IDENTIFY NEGATIVE CORE BELIEF:

I always jump on the "thought train" and get caught up ruminating about all the things that are wrong in my life.

SHIFT THE NARRATIVE (REFLECTIVE INQUIRY: IS IT TRUE?):

It only feels like I am always jumping on the "thought train," yet the truth is sometimes I do catch myself and shift to a more balanced assessment, so I have evidence that it's not a Capital-T Truth.

REACH HIGHER/APPLY SKILLS:

I am learning to differentiate between feelings and facts: I am not my feelings. I can apply interventions like EFT or Opposite Thought/Opposite Action to change my thinking. I am getting better at managing my moods and not sticking to or identifying with outdated, untrue core beliefs. When I do, I feel more in charge and grounded in my body and mind.

CONCLUSION/REFLECTION:

The Capital-T Truth is that I'm doing better than I used to at managing my emotions. I have evidence that the trick is to keep practicing taking control of my self-talk to express what is truer about my process and progress. The truth is, I can choose to get off the thought-train anytime; I can choose to not identify with childhood wounds. I am choosing to let my Tall Self (adult self) lead, to meet my Small Self (child self) with patience and kindness, to move out of victim consciousness, and to correct my distorted thinking and untrue narratives.

CREATE "TRUE STATEMENT" MANTRA:

The more I practice proactively shifting my thinking and focusing on what I can do, the more confident I am and the better able to manage my emotions: I am more in control and more skillful.

PROACTIVE SHIFTING EXERCISE

DESIRE:

_____

_____

_____

_____

IDENTIFY NEGATIVE CORE BELIEF:

_____

_____

_____

_____

SHIFT THE NARRATIVE (REFLECTIVE INQUIRY: IS IT TRUE?):

_____

_____

_____

_____

_____

REACH HIGHER/APPLY SKILLS:

_____

_____

_____

CONCLUSION/REFLECTION:

_____

_____

_____

_____

CREATE "TRUE STATEMENT" MANTRA:

_____

_____

_____

Bring your mantra into your daily practice. Examples:

I am getting more skilled everyday.
I am balanced; I am centered.
I am skillfully managing my thoughts and calming my emotions.

Group Exercise ~ Proactive Shifting

Use the Proactive Shifting handout to do a group EFT exercise. (If you don't have experience with EFT, view the video on my website or visit one of the sites noted in the Resources section, below.) You might refer back to the Emotional Spectrum Model and the Emotional Balancing: Breaking the Cycle of Old Beliefs Worksheet to inform the EFT work.

Suggested Closing Meditation ~ Presence Meditation

Get into a comfortable position, and close your eyes or lower your gaze. (Sound chime or toning bowl.) Take three long, slow, deep breaths. As you inhale, feel the breath move all the way down into the base of your abdomen and all the way into your back. As you exhale, completely empty your lungs, extending the length of the exhalation each time. Breathe in; feel the support of the chair beneath you. Breathe out; allow your body to soften. Breathe in; feel how you are supported in this moment. Breathe out, softening even more with each breath. Feel deeply into the calm sense of simply being present. Breathe into Wise Mind: Breathe in the mantra, *I am supported, I am completely supported*. Breathe out the knowing, *I am safe, here, now, in this moment*. (Sound chime.) Slowly open your eyes and bring your awareness to the group. Carry this sense of calm presence with you throughout your day.

Suggested Homework: Reflect in your journal what came up for you during this session about EFT. Practice EFT during the week so you can do it without looking at the handout. Practice it until it becomes second nature. This technique is one of the most effective exercises that you can incorporate into your life to support the repatterning of the brain, especially with trauma memory. Complete the Experiencing & Learning to "Be With" Emotions Worksheet, and be prepared to share your insights at the next session. You can use it to inform your tapping exercise and get more in touch with your own emotional spectrum. Havening is a variation of EFT that may be more appropriate in certain situations. Both are powerful self-regulation techniques that can, with practice, change trauma memories.

Resources:

EFT Tapping Training Institute/Gary Craig (efttappingtraining.com)
The Tapping Solution (thetappingsolution.com)

Knowledge is for the mind; experience is for the body.

Align your mind with your heart (heart-mind coherence) and your creativity will flourish!

You can then walk between the tension of opposites (Yin/Yang, dark/light) with grace.

-- Faith Burrington Jones

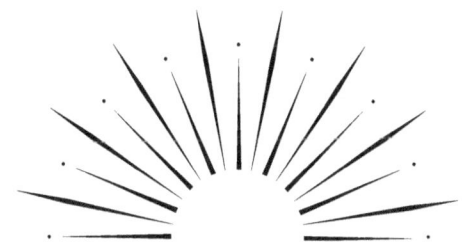

THE LIGHTHOUSE EFFECT
Experiencing & Learning to "Be With" Emotions

To move out of survival mode and into revival, we need to learn to "be with" our emotions, without analyzing them and without judging them or judging ourselves for experiencing them. Let's look at these primary emotions: Love, Joy, Anger, Sadness, Fear, Shame.

1) NAMING/DESCRIBING EMOTIONS: List words that describe, are synonymous, or are similar to each:

LOVE: _____

JOY: _____

ANGER: _____

SADNESS: _____

FEAR: _____

SHAME: _____

2) IDENTIFYING TRIGGERS: What events or dynamics prompt or trigger these emotions?

LOVE: _____

_____

JOY: _____

_____

ANGER: _____

_____

SADNESS: _____

_____

FEAR: _____

_____

SHAME: _____

_____

3) SELF-TALK: What are your interpretations, the narrative you tell yourself (self-talk) when you feel each of these emotions?

LOVE: _____

_____

JOY: _____

_____

ANGER: _____

_____

SADNESS: _____

_____

FEAR: _____

_____

SHAME: _____

_____

4) PHYSICAL EXPERIENCE: What do you experience with each emotion? How do they impact your body? What symptoms or changes occur?

LOVE: _____

_____

JOY: _____

_____

ANGER: _____

_____

SADNESS: _____

_____

FEAR: _____

_____

SHAME: _____

_____

5. IMPACT: What is the aftereffect when you express or act on these emotions? What are the judgments by others or consequences?

LOVE: _____

_____

JOY: _____

_____

ANGER: _____

_____

SADNESS: _____

_____

FEAR: _____

_____

SHAME: _____

_____

Module III (Emotional Balancing) Session 8:
Self-Regulating The Nervous System ~ Vagus Nerve Reset

Suggested Opening Meditation ~ River Wisdom Meditation

Get into a comfortable position and close your eyes or lower your gaze. (Sound chime or toning bowl.) Take three long, deep breaths and bring your attention inward. Visualize a winding river and watch it flow along. Now, imagine you are the water, flowing smoothly and peacefully along, completely in harmony with your environment. Imagine you see an enormous rock up ahead, in the middle of the river. Continue to breathe gently and naturally as you observe the approaching obstacle. Notice how you intuitively flow around the rock; it does not stop you from moving forward. Think of a current challenge in your life; visualize it as another rock in the river. Simply notice that it is there, and then continue to breathe gently as you flow around it. Breathe in, slowly and deeply, letting this feeling of being river water move all the way through you. Breathe out, allowing your body to fully soften and relax. (Sound chime.) Slowly open your eyes and return to the group. Know that you can be as powerful, agile, and resilient as river water whenever you need to be; know that you can skillfully move past obstacles in your path.

Check-Ins and Q&A: Invite group participants to keep check-ins brief and focused on emotional self-regulation techniques and concepts as they experience them in their daily lives, and to share insights they've logged in their journals.

Handout: How to Reset & Tone the Vagus Nerve

Self-Regulation of the Nervous System

The vagus nerve is the main part of the parasympathetic nervous system, and it is the primary bioelectrical messenger connecting the body with the mind. Allopathic medicine separates the body from the mind in its texts, teachings, and treatment, but my experience is that they are not separate, especially when it comes to healing trauma. With my background in integrative acupressure, my understanding and approach is more holistic. The mind and body are intricately connected as the mind-body complex. The vagus nerve is an electrical wiring that allows the brain and body to communicate automatically or instinctively. It is a direct link from the brain to the gut, essentially, the facilitator for gut instinct. So when we experience trauma, the body encodes it on a cellular level and alerts the brain to act accordingly when any of the five senses trigger the encoded emotional memory. The time it takes us to return to our center when we are triggered becomes less and less as we develop our skill for self-regulating; the more we practice, the more adept we become. Our tolerance, resilience, and wiring also comes into play.

Empathic people, for example, are overly sensitive to outside stimuli. We experience it as a felt sense; we *feel* it in our body, and our body's nervous system responds accordingly. My nervous system has always been hypersensitive to everything in my environment. No matter how many skills I learn, teach, and store in my Rational Mind, I have a tendency for an exaggerated reflex response. For example, if there is a loud unexpected bang in earshot, my body will overreact and I will automatically jump a foot in the air.

My heightened startle reflex has to do with the wiring of my Emotional Mind. In that instant, my vagus nerve signals my autonomic nervous system, which instantly dumps a load of hormones into my body, causing increased heart rate, weakness, shaking, and other such symptoms. Once my brain has a chance to assess and establish that there is no immediate physical danger, which occurs in a nanosecond, the symptoms dissipate and my body is able to recenter. It recognizes that it was just a car backfiring, all clear/all safe. It's been an ongoing process for me, learning how to manage my highly sensitive nervous system and to accept how I am wired, rather than resisting and judging my sensitivity as a bad thing or a curse. On occasions where I don't naturally recenter immediately, I will implement EFT until I am calmer.

It is crucial to our wellbeing that we support the way we are, right now, in this moment, by stepping into Radical Acceptance. From that stance, we can deepen our understanding of our own wiring, trauma memories, and childhood programming, and can then take steps to forgive ourselves and others so we can begin to heal. Once we let go of the weight of those burdens, we can reset our nervous system and take back our power. To learn how to overcome negative beliefs about ourselves, we need to look at our early story, as we did in Module I in the context of mindfulness.

On my own path of healing, I studied early development, including conception and the birthing process. I came to see how our first traumatic experience is whatever our mother was experiencing emotionally during pregnancy, as that energy is transmitted to us in our fetal state; the next is the experience of being born, which is naturally traumatic. Two fears that infants are born with are fear of falling and fear of loud noises. I was born hypersensitive to both. I still jump and overreact to loud noises, as I noted above, and I also have a fear of heights. I have no memory of any trauma, but my nervous system has a low tolerance to my environment generally, and especially to unexpected changes or shifts. What I share in this book and what I present in the program came from my own need to learn how to be fully in my body.

When we are in a triggered state, our body chemistry (adrenaline) floods the mind, which instantaneously activates or trips our survival instinct. In order to develop the ability to access Rational Mind and apply the necessary skills to ground ourselves, we need to develop and tone the vagus nerve. I equate this to how, in martial arts training, we learn how to defend ourselves against multiple attackers, and in doing so, we first deprogram and then reprogram our muscle memory; rather than going into flight mode, freezing, or overreacting, our default response becomes to skillfully protect and defend.

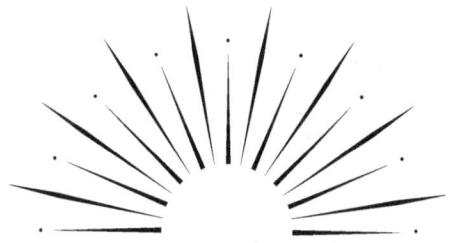

THE LIGHTHOUSE EFFECT
How to Reset & Tone the Vagus Nerve

BREATHING: We have a tendency to hold our breath or take short breaths that don't use our full lung capacity. When we take short breaths, we send a message to the nervous system that there may be danger and all systems need to be on alert. Our nervous system doesn't know the difference between remembered danger and danger in "real time." Keeping our lungs exercised and toned by "attending to the breath" helps to reset our vagus nerve.

Take the opportunity during the day to focus on your breathing. Try to do this at least three times per day; it can be during everyday activities, like washing dishes or when you are in your car, stopped at a traffic light. Simply take several slow, deep breaths, filling your lungs and expanding into your belly and all the way into your back. Drop your jaw and shoulders as you exhale, slowly and fully. Notice how your whole body relaxes and how "attending to the breath" shifts your mindset. Exhale a little longer each time. It sends a message to your nervous system that everything is okay.

MEDITATION: Meditation is a mindfulness practice that helps us to be in the present moment, rather than projecting into the future or ruminating about the past. Try to meditate, even for a few minutes, every day. You may notice your mind attempting to take you out of the present and back to running its narratives. When that happens, simply observe it without judgment and turn your mind back to the present moment. With daily meditation practice and mindfulness practice we become more grounded and focused in our daily lives, and are better able to navigate challenges.

COLD WATER: Include some form of cold-water immersion in your morning ritual: splash cold water on your face, take a brief cold shower (or end your shower with cold water), or, if you can, take a plunge into cool water, all while holding your breath. What is called the "mammalian dive reflex" kicks in, where the vagus nerve is activated and directed to channel energy to the vital organs. It decreases the heart rate, which in turn, creates a calming effect. It relaxes the muscles and fires up our metabolism. Even stepping into the cold can reset vagus nerve pathways.

EARTH WALKING: Our bodies are biomagnetic, and so is the earth. The earth's magnetic field regenerates any other being with a magnetic field. The simple practice of walking barefoot on the earth is one of the most powerful ways to calm and heal our bodies. Earth walking or "earthing" stimulates the nerve endings in the soles of our feet and then our entire autonomic nervous system—including the vagus nerve, which regulates and calms the body. (There's a great documentary about earthwalking called *The Earthing Movie:* www.earthingmovie.com.)

SINGING, CHANTING, TONING: Singing helps to focus the mind in the moment, exercises the lungs, lifts the mood, and soothes the soul. Chanting helps to connect energetically with the nonphysical or spiritual realm and helps us understand ourselves as being an integral part of the whole. Toning sounds such as "Om" or other vowel sounds also stimulate the vagus nerve.

PLAYING OR LISTENING TO MUSIC: We are vibrational beings with our own frequencies, and our frequency attunes to the music we are listening to or playing. Have you noticed that some genres of music you resonate with and others, not so much? Have you noticed that sometimes different kinds of music get you moving and other types slow you down? When choosing music to stimulate the vagus nerve, select the tones that cause you to feel softer and more open. When the vagus nerve is stimulated you naturally feel more open and relaxed in your body and mind.

LAUGHTER: There are few things that can so quickly and powerfully send a message to the nervous system that everything is good as laughter. When we laugh, we send positive energetic waves throughout the entire body, which releases stress and resets the vagus nerve. Laughter elevates our energetic frequency as it is in alignment with love. Take or create opportunities to laugh with abandon: watch cute animal antics, watch a funny movie, spend time with a light-hearted friend. Practice "Half-Smile," where you simply smile slightly, which sends a message to your nervous system that all is well.

MOVEMENT & EXERCISE: Moving the body grounds us and supports the nervous system. Make a point of exercising every day, even something as simple as taking a walk or hike. Yoga; Qi-gong; Tai Chi; martial arts; dance; athletics of any kind. Your body was designed to move! Engage in a new practice: try yoga, qigong, tai chi or another martial art, dance, athletics of any sort. Investing in ways to strengthen and tone your body is one of the best investments you can make; the benefits outweigh all of the reasons your mind will tell you not to. There is wisdom in the maxim, "Move a muscle, change a thought."

NATURE: We increase our tolerance for accepting life on life's terms by simply engaging with nature. Make it a habit to be in nature every day, even if it is to take a walk and observe the foliage, or walk your dog. If you don't have a dog, dog-sit or become a dog walker; it is a great way to lift your mood, invest in your recovery, and feel more connected to the thriving energy of life. If work or other commitments keep you indoors, make a conscious effort to take a break, step outside, and "smell the flowers."

GARGLING: Similar to singing, the vibrations in our throat when we gargle stimulate the vagus nerve, which runs between the sternum and the brain on either side of the larynx. Even the simple act of chewing your food thoroughly activates your vagus nerve, with the grinding action of your teeth and jaw. (It also improves digestion.)

MASSAGE: Receiving a massage or doing self-massage sends a message to your brain that all is well as the gentle rubbing motion engages the parasympathetic nervous system and resets the vagus nerve. It also improves digestion and aids in restful sleep.

GRATITUDE JOURNAL: Keeping a gratitude journal is a Reflective Inquiry exercise that helps to focus the mind and stimulate endorphins or "feel good" chemicals in the brain. This healthy brain exercise raises your frequency, helps you to feel lighter and more open, and signals the nervous system that all is well.

Group Exercise ~ Vagus Nerve Reset

Walk the group through the handout, while underscoring key points.

Qigong to Address the Vagus Nerve

Refer back to Module I where we explored qigong and convey to participants that we can reset the vagus nerve by directing energy to it. For example, doing LaQi, we would direct qi into the area between the sternum and brain where the vagus nerve network resides.

Suggested Closing Meditation ~ Vagus Nerve Reset Meditation

Sit comfortably in a receptive position. Close or lower your eyes to bring your attention within and to this present moment. Take three long, slow, deep breaths. With each exhalation feel your entire body softening even more; notice the tension leaving your jaw, shoulders, torso, and legs. Bring your attention to your breath. Place your hand on your lower abdomen and inhale, slowly and deeply, and feel the breath expanding into your belly as we count to five: one, two, three, four, five--and hold it. Now, slowly and completely exhale, feeling your belly deflate as we count to five: one, two, three, four, five. And again, inhale slowly, feeling your belly expand under your hand, as we count to five: one, two, three, four, five--and hold it. Now exhale slowly, feeling your belly deflate as we count to five: one, two, three, four, five. One more time. Inhale to the count of five, allowing the breath to fill your lungs and belly: one, two, three, four, five--and hold it. Now exhale slowly to the count of five: one, two, three, four, five. (Sound chime.) Slowly open your eyes and return to presence. Know you can reset your vagus nerve using the breath anytime, anywhere.

Suggested Homework: Write in your journal about what you gained from this session, from the content covered and through doing the exercises and meditations. Bring your insights and experiences to share with the group for the next session.

Module III (Emotional Balancing) Session 9: The Impact of Chemical Imbalances on Mental Health and Recovery ~ Hierarchy of Needs

Suggested Opening Meditation ~ Serenity Prayer Meditation

Close or lower your eyes and get comfortable in your body. (Sound chime.) Take three long, slow, deep breaths to bring yourself fully into presence. Focus your mind on the Serenity Prayer concept: *I will accept the things I cannot change, and I will change the things I can.* Take another slow, deep inhalation, feeling the breath move all the way through your lungs and into your back, breathing the truth of this wisdom into your being. Now slowly exhale, releasing tension and resistance. Take another slow, full inhalation, breathing in the energy of "acceptance;" feel the serenity of *acceptance* flowing through you. Now slowly exhale, releasing resistance. One more time, inhale deeply, breathing in "courage;" notice how it feels in your body, the energy of *courage*. Now slowly exhale, releasing all remaining resistance. (Sound chime.) Slowly open your eyes and return to presence. Allow yourself to feel the serenity of this energy and truth of acceptance as you move through your day.

Check-Ins and Q&A: Invite group participants to focus on how their current life situations are being supported by the concepts and application of skills, techniques, and exercises they've learned thus far in this module.

Handouts: Maslow's Hierarchy of Needs Model, Lighthouse Effect Addiction & Trauma Hierarchy of Needs Model

The Impact of Chemical Imbalances (Addiction/Trauma/Attachment)

Uncontrollable mood swings can be a sign that there is an imbalance in the mind-body complex, perhaps due to illness, intoxication, dependencies, dehydration, or other stressors or deficiencies. Our ability to think clearly and carry out daily tasks gets distorted, which can be disabling to varying degrees. It is extremely important that we consider each of these possibilities when working with trauma and addictions of any kind, and crucial that we team with other healthcare professionals who have a background in natural medicine.

As an Advanced Integrative Acupressure practitioner, I recommend a protocol that focuses on maintaining a healthy microbiome in the digestive system; nutrients from a well-balanced diet are better absorbed through the small intestines and can make their way into the circulatory system. Depending on how long a person has been living with repressed trauma and self-medicating through whatever addictive substance or behavior, it can take years to fully recover from the imbalances and damage to vital organs that have occurred--especially with alcohol dependence.

As we move through these modules it becomes increasingly clear how interconnected the mind-body complex actually is, and how crucial it is that we learn to self-regulate our nervous system and nourish our bodies as best we can in order to heal on all levels of our being. We need to remember that it's a process, that when we are vulnerable we might still default to the lower levels of awareness and energetic frequencies, and lose strength or run out of fuel. When that happens, we might numb out and disconnect from Wise Mind, or Higher Mind.

Circling back to mind states discussions in previous chapters, Emotional Mind has lower and higher frequencies within its own sphere. In the Lower Mind state, we are in fear-based *survival* mode, while in Higher Mind, we are in heart-based *thriving* mode. We need to work with our emotional system rather than fight it. When our alert system goes off, it is a call for us to identify where we are on the emotional spectrum, and to then self-regulate our emotions. In applying and practicing self-regulation techniques, we more easily access the higher frequency of Emotional Mind, which naturally upgrades Rational Mind's 'software', and then through this integration, we radiate from Wise Mind.

Refer to Maslow's Hierarchy of Needs pyramid to help the group understand "needs" in the context of moving from addiction into recovery, from surviving to thriving. It is an oldie but goodie and has evolved over time, as most of these models have.

You are not a problem to be fixed, you are a complex human being.
It is your birthright to know that you were born worthy and of precious value,
no matter what you have experienced.

--Faith Burrington Jones

MASLOW'S EVOLVED HIERARCHY OF NEEDS MODEL

SELF-TRANSCENDENCE
Meaning & Fulfillment

SELF-ACTUALIZATION
Creativity, Growth, Joy
Achieving Personal Potential

ESTEEM
Respect, Self-esteem, Recognition
Achievement, Confidence

LOVE & BELONGING
Family, Friendship, Intimacy, Community

SAFETY NEEDS
Health & Wellbeing, Personal Security, Financial Security
Access to Resources

PHYSIOLOGICAL NEEDS
Air, Water, Food, Shelter, Clothing, Sleep, Reproduction

Maslow's Hierarchy Of Needs

Abraham Maslow introduced the Hierarchy of Needs Model in his 1943 paper, "A Theory of Human Motivation." Maslow presented needs as either "deficit" or "growth" and placed deficit needs at the lower levels of the pyramid and growth needs at higher levels. Maslow's paper suggested a linear progression, how our lower-level deficit needs must be met before we can move up to higher-level growth needs, but he later clarified that it wasn't strictly linear, that there may be movement between levels.

Maslow's original pyramid had five levels, with self-actualization at the top, but as you can see in the diagram above, he later added a sixth, self-transcendence, as the pinnacle. Lower-level deficit needs are both things we need to survive (food, water) and physiological needs (sex, safe harbor, shelter). When we lack such things, we are highly motivated or driven to get them. Higher-level growth needs are those that we have energy for once our lower-level needs are met, like finding our mate, exploring or finding our purpose, thinking about what we want or desire in life.

Once we satisfy lower-level deficit needs and move out of survival mentality, we have more bandwidth for meeting higher-level growth needs and accessing higher mind states. But Maslow's later clarification is significant, in underscoring that there can be a more fluid interaction or movement between levels. For example, someone might have met all lower-level growth needs, but then they lose their job and they are back in survival mode. This more elastic progression pattern is also seen in the grieving process, where we move through stages of emotion, while also potentially relapsing.

Addiction expert, speaker, and bestselling author Dr. Gabor Mate proposes that for people with addictions, their dependency is hardwired into their brains on the same level as the physiological needs for oxygen, water, and food. This is why it is so difficult to break the addiction, and why I endorse the concept of tapering off any addiction to allow the body/mind to adjust to the change--rather than the "cold turkey" approach. Recovering from addiction is a process that is to be respected and supported as much as any other physical and psychological healing process. Mate's perspective resonates with mine, in that addictions can be so powerful that not meeting them can feel like not being able to breathe.

THE LIGHTHOUSE EFFECT
ADDICTION & TRAUMA HIERARCHY OF NEEDS MODEL

SELF-TRANSCENDENCE
Mind/Body/Spirit
Alignment

**SELF-ACTUALIZATION:
FREEDOM**
Experiencing the benefits of recovery:
from surviving, to reviving, to thriving

ESTEEM: DETACHMENT
Detaching from addiction & applying skills
to maintain abstinence and build confidence

LOVE & BELONGING: SUPPORT SYSTEM
Choosing abstinence & developing a support system

SAFETY NEEDS: AWARENESS & HITTING ROCK BOTTOM
Hitting rock bottom brings awareness.
It was a survival coping mechanism; there are healthier ways to cope.

PHYSIOLOGICAL NEEDS
Chemical addiction feels as strong as the need for air, food, water

Group Exercise ~ The Lighthouse Effect Addictions & Trauma Hierarchy of Needs

Refer to the model and use it to create a group exercise. The key here is that while, ultimately, we *do* have a choice to not drink, not smoke, etc., it doesn't *feel* like a choice. The stress we might experience from not meeting what feels like a "need" can greatly and negatively impact individuals moving from addiction and/or trauma into recovery. We need to be patient with ourselves as we learn skills to help us overcome these powerful drives to satisfy that "need." Understanding addiction in this way also helps to address shame, and to then apply skills (such as EFT and Havening) to detach from and rewire those entrenched narratives.

What is especially relevant in the context of recovery is how meeting or not meeting needs *at any level* might affect our process of moving from addiction to recovery, and how it is universal in the human condition. This underscores the importance of practicing Radical Acceptance and taking a nonjudgmental stance with ourselves, and others. We can see this in the Stages of Change Model, how there can be a lapse back into old patterns when stressors are elevated because needs are not being met. Of course, people experience varying degrees of intensity and for how challenging it might be to move out of an addiction, habit, or behavioral pattern. A person's trauma history, duration of dependency, overall health, and level of resilience all come into play, which, again, is why Maslow's Hierarchy of Needs is so relevant here. It illustrates how essential it is to our growth and recovery to be meeting our needs *as we go*, and how learning new ways to cope can support us in our efforts.

That fluidity of movement also comes into play in how or when we access higher mind states, which I believe can happen from a lower-level deficit position. For instance, we might hit rock bottom so hard that a spiritual awakening spontaneously occurs. In that sense, hitting bottom can actually be a blessing in disguise, and our unmet deficit needs might just be catalysts. Over the years, working through my own process and with others suffering from trauma, trauma memory, and addiction, I have certainly seen this bear out, where our highly painful experiences can be a direct portal into nonphysical reality.

It was that sort of experience that changed a client's life, and actually saved his life, as he describes it. This is an excerpt from my interview with "Rene" in *The Lighthouse Effect: Practicing Your Way From Survival to Revival.*

I got on my bike. I took off down the road. I didn't know where I was going. I didn't know what I was doing. It was St. Patrick's Day, March 17, and I remember it vividly. I was drunk, depressed, could hardly keep my balance on the bike, that's how wasted I was. Needless to say, I had given up. I went down to the canal by the power plant, to the walking path between the power plant and the river. There's an incline between the path and the river, an eighty foot drop, maybe, but an incline, not a cliff; you can walk down it. I went over the side and just laid down in the snowbank. I was hoping I'd have a peaceful end, that I would get hypothermic. You know, they say at the end, it's really warm, you don't really feel it. I was waiting for death to come.

And then, I got struck. *It wasn't a bolt of lightning, but it was a profound sense of,* I don't want to do this. *So I got up off that bank, I got back on my bike, and I rode to the variety store. I must have been quite a sight. It was early in the morning, two or three in the morning. I said, "Please, call an ambulance. I'm not good. I think I've got hypothermia. I need to go to the hospital." They called an ambulance. The ambulance came, took me to the emergency room, and called my wife. And that's what got me started on this journey.*

Rene talks about how he'd been through recovery programs and had been going to AA on and off over the years, but up until now, it was almost a sort of game: *Go through the program, get my driver's license back, get my wife back on my side. I had to perform these things. Even with all that recovery education, it didn't take. Until that snowbank. That was it. The snowbank literally saved my life. It was instantaneous. Just, snap! Just, now! I'd never had that feeling. Not until that moment.*

Rene's "awakening" led him to The Lighthouse Effect Skillful Recovery Program. He says what resonated mostly with him in the early days of moving through the program was the concept of mind states and coming into vertical alignment to Wise Mind. Rene says the idea of zooming out to change perspective or take what I call the "Butterfly View" also really resonated with him.

I guess it was the spiritual side of it, the focus of it. When you started getting into Wise Mind and Butterfly View, those concepts, those ways of thinking--thinking vertically. ... Initially, in the program, that's what kept me going. I was much calmer; I was much more tolerant. ... After the snow bank, after the [proverbial] lighthouse became the [inner guiding] lighthouse, it taught me about those few seconds that you need to have before you do something stupid. It's taught me a lot. I know my life now is one hundred percent better than it was before.

Having these sorts of awakenings can also occur through dissociative states and spontaneous spiritual emergencies such as severe trauma events, near-death experiences, and psychic breaks. We might be diagnosed as having a disorder and it might be accurate clinically (and be a challenging way to move through life) but it might also be a gift in how it catapults us into altered or higher mind states--in an instant, from any state of need. So when we pathologize or see these conditions strictly in a clinical sense, we might be denying ourselves profound experiences that cannot be explained from a linear, evidence-based perspective. When we see the mind-body-spirit complex as a whole, as a team, we can appreciate that we really are "spiritual beings having a human experience," and that all levels of our experience are interconnected. We have the physical, five-sensory experience of the mind-body complex and the intuitive sixth-sense experience of the nonphysical or Spirit.

In terms of addiction, when our dependency on a substance, person, or behavior gets wired into the brain, it becomes programmed in the mind-body complex as urges or triggers. But the mind-body-spirit complex is both an electromagnetic system and an *energetic* system and the two systems are powerfully connected. Where the electromagnetic system (central nervous system) is more physical and part of our animal-survival nature, the energy system, our life force or qi energy, is more auric or metaphysical. It is connected to our spiritual self, to the soul or spirit, and is less dense; it knows that, ultimately, there is no death and nothing to fear. Reflecting back to the Mindful Recovery Module we can see the wisdom of living in the moment in order to free ourselves of past and future, and to open ourselves to our own internal higher frequency and healing energy--to be our own lighthouse.

From the wise perspective of "now," we can see that we do not need anything or anyone outside of ourselves to validate our experiences or to heal. We need to trust ourselves and to appreciate that there is much more to life than what we see and feel in physical reality. We can use our own internal guidance system, our lighthouse within, to move from stormy seas to the safety of the shore and integrate Ego (physical) into Soul (nonphysical).

Suggested Closing Meditation ~ Turning the Mind Meditation

Sit comfortably and close your eyes or lower your gaze. (Sound chime or toning bowl.) Take three long, slow, deep breaths and follow the sound of the chime inward. When random thoughts drop into your mind, turn your mind away from the thought, to the rhythm of your breath. Focus on or "attend to" the breath. Breathe in, breathe out; breathe in, breathe out; breathe in, breathe out. Notice how focusing on the breath keeps you in the present, in the here and now. Take one more slow, deep inhalation, and a slow, full exhalation. (Sound chime.) Slowly open your eyes and return to the room. Keep applying this simple yet effective skill as you move through your day. Continue to be aware of any thoughts that try to seduce you, and consciously turn your mind away from them by attending to your breath.

Suggested Homework: Reflect in your journal about how this session resonated with or challenged you. Review Maslow's Hierarchy of Needs and The Lighthouse Effect Addiction & Trauma Model and bring your insights to share with the group at the next session.

Module III (Emotional Balancing) Session 10: Integration of Rational Mind & Emotional Mind ~ Projecting into the Future and Ruminating about the Past

Suggested Opening Meditation ~ Butterfly View Meditation

Get into a comfortable position, and close your eyes or lower your gaze. (Sound chime or toning bowl.) Take a long, slow, deep breath. As you inhale, in your mind's eye, take the caterpillar view and zoom in on a current life challenge; now, as you slowly exhale, zoom out, like a butterfly rising above the conflict. Continue to take long, slow, deep breaths and observe from this higher perspective; simply observe, without judgment or resistance. Notice changes in your emotional body and your physical body; notice any softening or lightening sensations. Take one more deep inhalation, and slow exhalation. (Sound chime.) Now, slowly open your eyes and bring yourself back to the present. Know that you always have the ability to zoom out to the butterfly view to gain a higher and more expanded perspective at any given moment. Practice this skill throughout your day and make it a daily practice.

Check-Ins and Q&A: Invite group participants to keep check-ins brief. Encourage them to focus on how they are being supported in their daily lives by ongoing application of skills, techniques, and concepts that have been covered thus far, including Rene's personal sharing of his recovery story and "hitting bottom" experience.

Handouts: No new handouts. (You might review previous handouts that support group process.)

Integration of Emotional Mind through Daily Application of Skills (Rational Mind)

When we project into the future, we are telling a story that imagines a negative or positive outcome. Negative projections tend to be fear-based (survival) and often tie to earlier experiences and ways of coping. When we ruminate about the past and rehash hurtful events or experiences, even if they only occurred once, by mulling over them, we give them more energy and they become more deeply embedded in our mind-body complex as a negative feedback loop. Projecting into the future and ruminating about the past are both mechanisms of Ego in its fear or fight-or-flight survival mode.

Ego is obsessed with quickly sizing up situations and being alert to whatever may be lurking around the corner; it has a tendency to jump to conclusions, imagine future scary outcomes, and/or attach to negative past events that are stored in memory. When we focus, ground, and stabilize the mind by aligning with the present moment, we can apply skills and techniques to override the fear chatter and default mechanisms of Ego. Over time, with practice, we gain self-mastery in emotional management. Importantly, the skills and tools we learn are stored and drawn from Rational Mind and the more we use them, the more they become second nature and the more skilled we become at self-regulation.

A key point to convey to your group is that it is through the practice of mindfulness and the application of emotional balancing skills that we can most effectively intervene when Ego gets lost in fear, to be better able to then bring our attention back to the present moment. This is how we override and rewrite the brain's neural network and the outdated wiring that has kept us locked in automatic emotional responses. The more we practice these interventions, the more skilled, resilient, and tolerant we become.

As you near the end of this module, remind participants that it is an iterative process, moving through the modules and building our toolkit of skills. Each set of skills builds on the other, and weaves together as a whole: from the Mindful Recovery module and skills for anchoring awareness, to the Tolerance Building module and skills for building resilience (the art of acceptance), to this Emotional Balancing module and skills for self-mastery of the emotional system, to the upcoming Conscious Communications module and skills we will learn for navigating relationships. We can be like master martial artists, rooted in the center of our being and in the present moment, to navigate our lives with grace and confidence and a level of resilience that transcends fear.

We each need to radically accept our unique personality, temperament, and wiring, and meet Ego and Emotional Mind (scared, innocent child) with understanding and compassion. Once we accept and make peace with our past, we can proactively take steps to heal the wounds and trauma we have experienced in our lives. This healing journey reconnects us to our Authentic Self.

Group Exercise ~ Reviewing Concepts

Check in with the group to see how they are progressing with integrating concepts, skills, and interventions, and do a deeper dive around a skill that might need further exploration. (Refer to and reinforce specific skills such as EFT and havening to reset the brain and move out of old narratives and default responses.)

Suggested Closing Meditation ~ I Am Worthy Meditation

Get into a comfortable position, and close your eyes or lower your gaze. (Sound chime or toning bowl.) Take three slow, deep breaths and allow a sense of stillness to penetrate your entire body. Feel this sense of stillness clearing your mind. Tell yourself, *I am worthy*, as you take another slow, deep breath all the way into your belly; breathe out even more than before. Again, breathe in, *I am worthy*. Allow this sense of self-worth and self-value to penetrate every cell of your body; breathe out. Breathe in, *I am worthy*. Allow this deep sense of tranquility to penetrate your mind; breathe out even more than before. Breathe in, *I am grateful to know that I am worthy*. Allow gratitude to fill your body and clear your mind; breathe out slowly and completely. (Sound chime.) Slowly open your eyes, and return to the circle. Now carry this energy of worthiness with you and within you as you move through your day.

Suggested Homework: Reflect in your journal how this session resonated with or challenged you. Keep practicing mindfulness, EFT, havening, and vagus nerve exercises throughout the week to manage and care for your emotional system. Remember to meet all emotions with acceptance, understanding, and compassion; your emotional self is the most vulnerable part of your being. What we might label as negative emotions are indicator lights leading us inward to where we need to heal.

Module III (Emotional Balancing) Session 11:
Stages of Change Reflection & Progress

Suggested Opening Meditation ~ Energy of Self-Care Meditation

Sit comfortably in a receptive, open position with your eyes closed or lowered. (Sound chime or toning bowl.) Take three slow, deep breaths, following the breath all the way to the base of your lungs and into the back as you inhale, fully relaxing your body as you exhale. Now, consider what the "energy of care" feels like; is it warm and comforting like the rays of the sun? Is it cool and refreshing like a summer breeze? Whatever it is, let it fill you. As you inhale, breathe this energy of care into every part of your body; as you exhale, let your body fully relax. Breathe in this energy of care; breathe out full-body relaxation. Now breathe the energy of care into your emotional body; imagine it permeating every thought in your mind. Notice the gentle, soothing energy as it flows through you. Take another full deep breath, filling your whole mind/body/spirit with this compassionate energy of self-care, fully relaxing as you exhale. Take one more breath, slow and deep: As you exhale, imagine the energy of care radiating out to everyone in this room, to all of your loved ones, to all beings. (Sound chime.) Slowly open your eyes and return to presence. Know that the energy of self-care extends to others. This is the Lighthouse Effect! Radiate it throughout the day.

Check-Ins and Q&A: Invite group participants to focus their check-ins on their current life situations and how they are applying the various skills, concepts, and practices to support their personal growth and recovery.

Handouts: No new handouts. (You might review previous handouts that support group process.)

This Emotional Balancing Module is the heart of the program, as understanding the function of the emotional system and learning how to skillfully self-regulate is essential to repatterning trauma memory and negative core beliefs. The more we practice these skills, the more our default programming reverses, until it is recalibrated at the cellular and energetic level.

Group Exercise ~ Stages of Change Review, Repeat, & Reflect

As with previous modules, review the SOC Model, and then have participants complete a new SOC Addiction/Recovery Pros & Cons Worksheet together as a group exercise, this time with the focus on emotional balancing. Have them review the worksheets they completed individually (as homework) at the beginning of the module, reflect on notable changes, and share what progress they've made and what challenges they might still be facing. Through this group-reflection process and looking back at the skills they've learned, participants become more aware of the progression of the modules and how they weave together.

Move a Muscle/Change a Thought

The body itself is physical and exists in physical reality. It is an electromagnetic vessel, electrically and energetically programmed to follow orders from the mind. At the same time, as we've learned, there is a negative feedback loop that occurs when the body holds a memory that the brain has flagged and that it is programmed to respond to when that memory is triggered. Our central nervous system is responsible for receiving stimulus or messages through the five senses, and, as we talked about earlier, it doesn't know the difference between danger in real time and remembered danger. Negative experiences are encoded in the body as cellular memory and muscle memory, in the brain (amygdala) and limbic system (hippocampus). The brain and the body are electrically and energetically wired together; the amygdala is the alarm mechanism of the limbic system, and the hippocampus, where memory is stored.

When our mind falls out of alignment, which happens when Emotional Mind is in a lower vibrational state, we become vulnerable to relapsing to old behaviors. When we put our body into action--walking, hiking, weight training, martial arts, yoga, qigong, biking, swimming, to name a few--we naturally reset the mind. One method for resetting the mind is the AA-based Move a Muscle/Change a Thought tool.

Additional Group Exercise ~ Move a Muscle/Change a Thought

Demonstrate the intervention tool, using your whiteboard. A sample prompt would be: *Have you ever had an experience where you were really troubled and in a negative, obsessive thought process, and you decided,* I just can't do this. *So you did something else, something physical? What other physical activities might you do to take you out of the loop?*

Follow the exercise with a reminder of other skills that can be used to interrupt negative thought loops, such as EFT. Another technique that is quite effective for decoding and deprogramming our stored negative memories is Eye Movement Desensitization and Reprocessing (EMDR). I find EMDR to be particularly effective with people who have experienced physical and emotional trauma, in how the cross-stimulation of the brain's hemispheres works on the amygdala. The method of moving the eyes back and forth from left to right (or holding probes in the hands that vibrate from left to right) as the event is being recounted decreases the intensity of the trauma memory.

I've mentioned Dr. Bessel van der Kolk, who is one of the world's foremost experts on trauma and an experienced practitioner in healing trauma, and how his concepts resonate with me. What makes him stand out from most other psychiatrists for me is that he fully understands the mind-body connection and the importance of treating the whole person, especially in how trauma gets encoded in both the brain, as memory, and the body, on a cellular level.

Having a background in energy medicine and bodywork, I was delighted to meet him and that I could use his findings to validate my work and years of experience as a bodyworker. I remember attending one of his seminars where he shared a bar graph of a twenty-year study showing that medication had the least impact on the healing of trauma over the long term. Dialectical Behavioral Therapy was more effective than medication. EMDR and EFT were greater in effectiveness than applying DBT alone, but most impressive was that yoga was indicated as the most effective of all therapies. That applying such skills is proven to be effective is why I bring DBT, EFT, havening, qigong, yoga, and various other movement practices into The Lighthouse Effect program; all are practices that stimulate the vagus nerve and, in turn, sedate the central nervous system and work to heal the brain.

Suggested Closing Meditation ~ Riding the Horse Meditation

Sit comfortably in your chair and position your body to receive openly. Close your eyes or lower your gaze. (Sound chime or toning bowl.) Take three long, slow, deep breaths. Imagine you are sitting on a horse. Imagine a challenging life situation that has you feeling defeated and victimized. Notice how it feels in your body. Imagine that situation as a fence in front of you; imagine that you are beginning to slide off of the horse. That fence seems impossibly high. Now pause, take a slow, full breath and ask yourself, *Can I make the choice to feel confident and skillful, to not be in victim consciousness*? As you exhale, imagine you are righting yourself in the saddle. Look at the fence. Imagine you and your horse flying over it. Take another full, deep breath, allowing a sense of calm confidence to move through you. Think: *I've got this!* (Sound chime.) Slowly open your eyes and return to the group. With daily practice and self-discipline, you can choose to get back in the saddle and ride the horse of recovery in any moment, no matter how intense the trigger.

Suggested Homework: Reflect in your journal on what resonated with you or challenged you. Practice the skill of Move a Muscle/Change a Thought. Bring your insights and questions to the next session to inspire the group and stimulate group discussion. Complete your SOC Addiction/Recovery Pros & Cons Worksheet and compare it with the one you filled out at the beginning of the module.

Module III (Emotional Balancing) Session 12:
Hitting Bottom, Gratitude Practice, and Closing Ceremony

Suggested Opening Meditation ~ Gratitude Meditation

Get into a comfortable, receptive position and close your eyes or lower your gaze. (Sound chime or toning bowl.) Take three slow, deep breaths as you feel yourself come fully into this moment. Focus on the gentle lull of your breathing. Feel your body softening more and more with each exhalation. Now, using your creative imagination, breathe in the felt sense of the word "gratitude." What color is it? What does it feel like in your body as it flows through you? Continue to breathe gently and naturally. Now, think of the people, places, and things you are grateful for. See them in your mind's eye. Take another full, deep breath as you reflect on simple daily pleasures that bring a sense of appreciation and gratitude into your life. Take another full, deep breath and turn your attention to *you*. Reflect on the positive aspects of your personality and your unique way of being in the world. Take one more full, deep inhalation, breathing gratitude all the way into your being; one more full exhalation, as you fully relax your body. (Sound chime.) Slowly open your eyes and come back to presence.

I invite you to commit to a daily practice of gratitude, not just for others and what is outside of you, but for you. Reflect in your Gratitude Journal all the ways you are grateful for yourself; acknowledge your willingness to practice, your willingness to forgive yourself for being human; your willingness to let go of the past and allow the energy of gratitude to heal you. Carry this high frequency energy throughout your day and shine your light, best as you can.

Check-Ins and Q&A: Invite group participants to focus their check-ins on their personal progress and any reflections they feel are significant in their personal growth and recovery.

Handout: Module III Completion Certificate

Gratitude Practice for Our Emotional System

I often hear from clients, friends, and family members that it was only when they started to attend to their mental, emotional, and physical pain that they began to heal. One of the ways we attend to our emotional system is to be in gratitude, to thank it for doing its job, and to thank our indicator lights--our symptoms, urges, and triggers--for letting us know there was something we needed to attend to. Being grateful to our symptoms or painful experiences might seem contrary, but truly, it is a call to love. We can use our self-care toolkit and practices such as Reflective Inquiry on our pathway to becoming our own best friend, which we do with compassion, understanding, and patience.

Group Exercise ~ Was it Really Rock Bottom?

To wrap up this Emotional Balancing Module, explore what it means to hit rock bottom. Invite the group to take a Wise Mind perspective on experiences of hitting bottom, where lessons were learned or insights gained, which they would not have found otherwise, and which helped them to develop resilience and create inner peace.

Suggested Prompt: Reflect on an experience that might be considered hitting rock bottom, yet in which you felt strangely comforted or guided and had a sense that everything was or would be okay: *What did you do differently or how did your life change because of this event, that you wouldn't have done or wouldn't have happened otherwise? Did you seek help or reach out in a way that is outside of your comfort zone? What can you say that you are grateful for--despite the tragic or challenging part of the experience?*

Emotional Balancing Takeaways

When we're in our Emotional Mind, we need to remember we are not our feelings, and feelings are not facts--though they can certainly *feel* real and true. They are wired into our nervous system and vital to our health and wellbeing. We can allow ourselves to feel our feelings (Emotional Mind) and then make a conscious choice to self-regulate (Rational Mind). We can center ourselves and come into balance with our more rational perspective using our intervention skills, which are stored in Rational Mind. Ask participants what they see as the takeaways from the module, and add these three key points. 1) Avoid writing the story before it happens or ruminating on a narrative you're running. 2) Get the facts: Is what I'm feeling the truth? Am I my feeling? (Spoiler alert; the answer is no!) 3) Pause and take a step back, just *observe*, and then describe what is *actually* going on.

Closing Ceremony & Closing Out the Module

Present completion certificates to the group. Invite them to join you for the next module, "Module IV Conscious Communication: The Visible Shine of your Lighthouse ~ Transmitting your Light." Share that you are looking forward to seeing them at the first session and provide the date and time.

Suggested Closing Meditation ~ Group Appreciation Meditation

Consider creating your own "group appreciation" meditation where you express and honor participants' courage and willingness for showing up for the work and one another. You might express what a privilege it is to witness the power of group work, how each person has become an integral member and together you've created this strong recovery community! If you are not comfortable creating your own meditation, use the Gratitude Meditation.

Module III Additional Resources

EFT Tapping Training Institute/Gary Craig (efttappingtraining.com)
The Four Agreements: A Practical Guide to Personal Freedom, and *The Fifth Agreement: A Practical Guide to Self-Mastery* by Don Miguel Ruiz (thefouragreements.com)

THE LIGHTHOUSE EFFECT SKILLFUL RECOVERY PROGRAM

Certificate

This certifies that

_____

has successfully completed The Lighthouse Effect Skillful Recovery Program
Module III Emotional Balancing
The Power Source of Your Lighthouse ~ Authentic Power

FACILITATOR   **DATE**

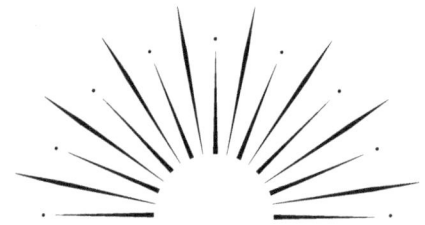

THE LIGHTHOUSE EFFECT MODULE IV SYLLABUS

Conscious Communication in Relationships:
The Visible Shine of Your Lighthouse ～ Transmitting Your Light

Session #1 Welcome & Introduction (Healing Relationships with Ourselves & Others): Group Rules, Confidentiality, & Building Group Cohesion; Codependency/Interdependency Model; Group Exercise ～ Stages of Change Review & Repeat

Session #2 Mindful Attention in Conscious Relationships ～ Passive vs Aggressive Communication Styles: Mindful Attention in Relationships; Determining Your Communications Style; Group Exercise ～ Returning to the Conversation

Session #3 Codependency & Addictive Relationships ～ Getting Clear about your Desires: Love and Lust and the Wisdom to Know the Difference; Group Exercise ～ Reflective Inquiry in Relationships

Session #4 Identifying Relationship Values & Getting Clear about your Rights and Desires: Identifying Values; Your Authentic Rights; Group Exercise ～ Identifying your Relationship Values

Session #5 Effective Communication & Assertive Listening: How to Negotiate: The "Lighthouse Seven" Key Communication Skills; Group Exercise ～ Skill Building for Conscious Communication

Session #6 Skillful Recovery ～ Coping with Resistance & Conflict: Moving toward Resolution and establishing Mutual Respect; Group Exercise ～ Coping with Resistance & Conflict

Session #7 How to Say No Skillfully & Gracefully: Applying Assertiveness Scripts; Integrating the Components; ALIGN Guide for Conscious Communications; Group Exercise ～ Assertiveness Scripts

Session #8 Group Mirror Work ～ Bringing Attention & Intention into Relationships: Introducing The Clearing Protocol; Group Exercise ～ Understanding the Clearing Protocol

Session #9 Role-Playing & Clearing Protocol: Group Exercise ～ Clearing Protocol & Mirror Work

Session #10 Higher Power Alignment ～ Building a Relationship with Your Higher Power: Higher Power Activities & Practices; Group Exercise ～ Connecting with Your Higher Power

Session #11 Stages of Change Reflection & Progress: Charting "conscious communication" progress over the course of the module; Group Exercise ～ Stages of Change ～ Review, Repeat, Reflect

Session #12 Closing Ceremony & Graduation: Certificates of Completion; Putting It All Together (PAT) Packet; Appreciation/Gratitude Circle; Commit to the "Bookending Your Day" Practice!

MODULE IV CONSCIOUS COMMUNICATION:

THE VISIBLE SHINE OF YOUR LIGHTHOUSE ~ TRANSMITTING YOUR LIGHT

This entire program is essentially about learning to integrate the opposite mind states of Emotional Mind and Rational Mind through daily practice. It is about coming into acceptance that we are emotional beings; we need structure and grounding to feel aligned and stable. Learning to respect opposing views or experiences, whether internally or with others, both challenges us and helps us to accept our unique selves--with our inherited trauma, DNA, wiring, the environment we landed in, and our childhood experiences. When we accept ourselves, we have the capacity to accept others and their unique selves and we can live in harmony within ourselves and with others. Learning to navigate this life from the inside out is a process of self-mastery: the "lighthouse effect."

To reiterate, the program is designed for the modules to feed into each other and weave together. This final module integrates the first three modules in how we learn to present ourselves consciously in any form of interpersonal relationship: Module I, being present and anchoring our awareness in the context of any conversation or social interaction; Module II, coming from a place of acceptance of differences of opinion and freely expressing oneself from our truth, with integrity; Module III, meeting other people's emotional expressions with understanding and compassion, as we would want them to do for us. Learning to be in conscious communication with another draws from all the previous modules we have covered. In a sense, this module is where we practice recovery in real time, where we get to model what we have learned through role-playing and daily practice to become skilled in creating *interdependent* relationships instead of *codependent* relationships.

This module also will circle back to how the Victim (Inverted) Triangle dynamic can show up in relationships based on the roles that we default to in that particular relationship: caretaker, parent, employer, employee, sponsor, sponsoree, partner, and so on. In this Conscious

Communications module, we begin to weave everything we have learned throughout the program towards cultivating conscious relationships. Our goal is to communicate from a position of alignment *within*, in order to radiate out and into every relationship we have, with people, animals, plants, planet Earth, and all sentient beings.

Be curious and mindful when connecting with others.

--Faith Burrington Jones

Module IV (Conscious Communication) Session 1:
Healing Relationships with Ourselves and Others

Suggested Opening Meditation ~ Stillness Meditation

Sit comfortably in a receptive, open position with your eyes closed or lowered. (Sound chime or toning bowl.) Take three long, slow, deep breaths, inhaling all the way into your lungs, your abdomen, your back, releasing more fully and completely with each sequential exhalation. Let your body rest; let your mind rest; let your emotions rest. Imagine this energy of rest, of sublime stillness, filling you. Breathe in the simple radiant energy of stillness; breathe out full relaxation. Feel into this sublime, radiant energy of stillness. Breathe in stillness; *be* in stillness. One more deep inhalation, one more full exhalation. (Sound chime.) Slowly open your eyes and return to presence. Carry this exquisite state of being throughout your day.

Review Protocol: Review logistics, group rules, and confidentiality. Distribute Repeat Handouts and ask group members if there is anything that can be done to ensure group safety. Begin and end each session with a mindfulness meditation to reinforce and integrate the importance of being in the present.

Check-Ins and Q&A: Facilitate the introductory check-in round, and then allow time for group members to ask questions, express concerns, and/or share reflections regarding handouts and any lingering questions from the previous module. Focus on group rules and building a safe container. Ask again if there is anything more that can be done to support participants in maintaining confidentiality and creating boundaries. We develop resilience through repeated application of skills, meditations, exercises, and techniques, so it's also good to remind them again of the importance of practicing in real time.

Repeat Handouts: Group Rules, Stages of Change Model, Stages of Change

Addiction/Recovery Pros & Cons Worksheet, Stages of Change: Metamorphosis from Survival to Revival Lifestyle, The Role of an Accountability Partner & How to Give Constructive Feedback Relapse Prevention Plan Worksheet.

Gentle Reminder: Provide new members with the PAWS Self-Assessment Worksheets and How to Manage Emotional Denial Worksheet. Keep in mind that you might want to provide participants who've already received them with another copy, as needed, based on your assessment.

New Handouts: Module IV Syllabus, Codependency/Interdependency Model

How We Are with Ourselves is How We Are With Others

Relationships require our full presence. It is part of the human experience to have emotional responses and reactions in relationship dynamics; the goal is to be able to self-regulate them. Whether it's a lover, friend, coworker, or carpool companion, to create and maintain a good relationship, it is essential to notice the other person's feelings and reactions, to be an observer of the dynamics between you. How we are with others is impacted by the relationship we have with ourselves, and that relationship is an ongoing process of forgiveness and acceptance of all parts of the Self. As we make peace with internal conflicts, we naturally come from a place of presence and can move forward from that place in our engagements with others, rather than think about what happened in the past or about what we want to say next. With mindful attention, we can address potential conflicts before they erupt and obtain the presence of mind to ask questions that might help to clarify misconceptions.

In the same way that we can breathe, walk, or even do the dishes mindfully, we can also *relate* with mindfulness. To give mindful attention means to be present with what we see, hear, and intuit emotionally in the moment. By observing facial expressions, body language, tone of voice, and choice of words, we are better able to assess the mood and state of the relationship, understand the other person's perspective, and come into acceptance of it—even if we don't necessarily agree. We are also better able to observe our own behavior in relation to the other person by coming from Observer Self and applying the tool of Reflective Inquiry in the context of the moment.

It is important to take the time to address these deeper questions as a process of getting to know and understand ourselves better in how we relate with other people: Again, *know thyself*! It is why I encourage group participants to keep a journal as a way of deepening their relationship with themselves from the place of Observer Self. When we are not paying attention or staying in the moment with others, we are more inclined to react in negative ways. We might miss vital cues about the other person's needs and reactions because we are so distracted by our own unexplored internal defensiveness. If this is the case, we might unconsciously project our fears and feelings onto the other person or we might blow up, act out, or run away when we are surprised by a negative response we didn't see coming.

Provide the Codependency/Interdependency Model to the group and consider it in the context of how important it is to understand the impact of codependency on relationships.

THE LIGHTHOUSE EFFECT
Codependency/Interdependency Model

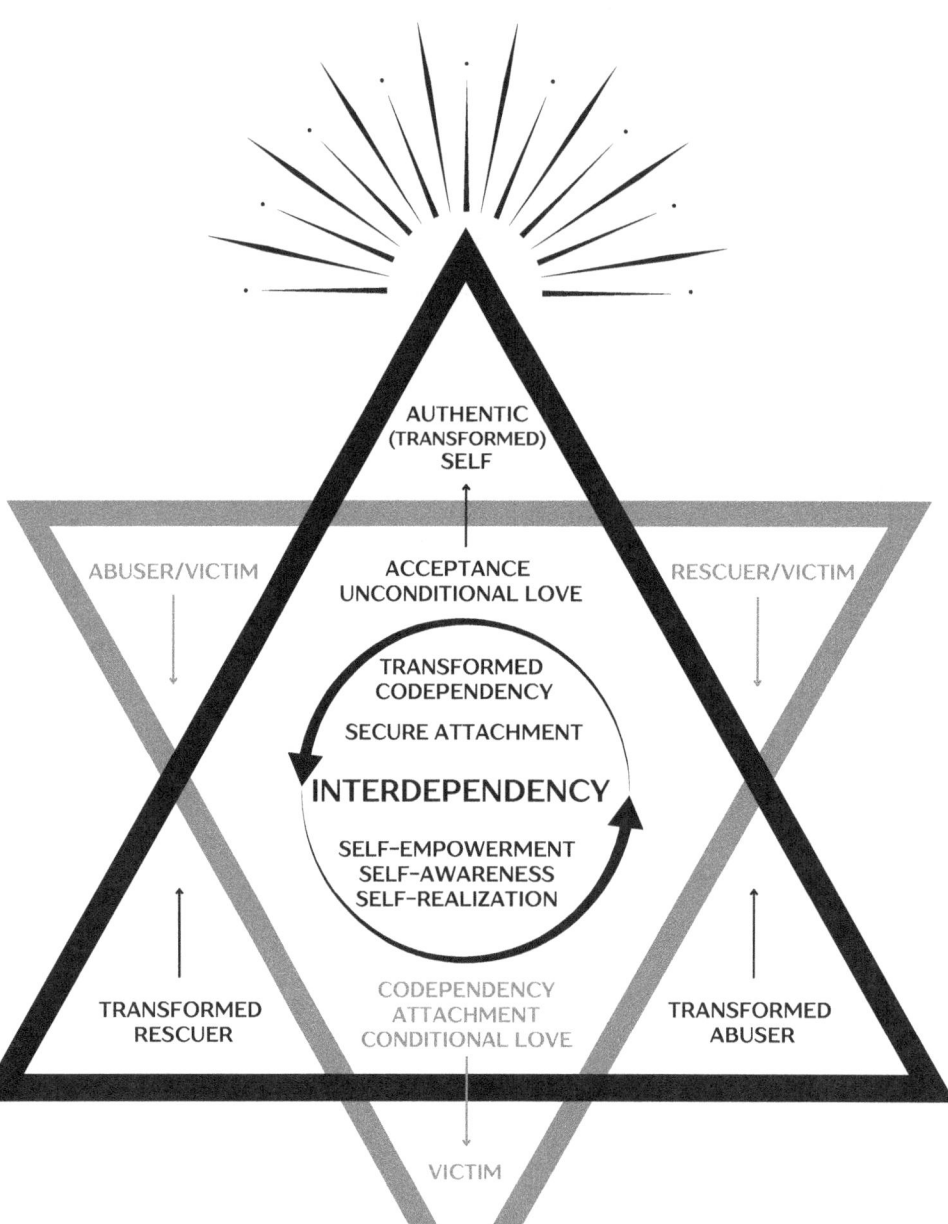

AUTHENTIC
(TRANSFORMED)
SELF

ABUSER/VICTIM

RESCUER/VICTIM

ACCEPTANCE
UNCONDITIONAL LOVE

TRANSFORMED
CODEPENDENCY

SECURE ATTACHMENT

INTERDEPENDENCY

SELF-EMPOWERMENT
SELF-AWARENESS
SELF-REALIZATION

TRANSFORMED
RESCUER

CODEPENDENCY
ATTACHMENT
CONDITIONAL LOVE

TRANSFORMED
ABUSER

VICTIM

Group Exercise ~ Stages of Change Review & Repeat

Review the SOC Model in the context of interpersonal communications and have participants complete the SOC Addiction/ Recovery Pros & Cons Worksheet as a group exercise, using your whiteboard. Focus on addictive, instinctual, and reactive communication patterns they want to change. What changes do they need to make to build communication skills that will help them relate to others in a healthier way?

For example, a "pro" for a maladaptive way to communicate a need or to set a boundary might be to assume that the other person should know what we need or want, so then we don't have to be accountable. The "con" would be when we assume or project onto the other person, we disrespect them, we disrespect and disempower ourselves, and we lapse in our self-care.

Suggested Closing Meditation ~ Be The Tree Meditation

Get into a comfortable standing or sitting position, and close your eyes or lower your gaze. (Sound chime or toning bowl.) Take a slow, deep breath, and imagine your body as a tree. Feel your feet planted on the ground, and the tendrils of your energetic root system reaching deep down into the earth. Take another slow, deep breath. Imagine your torso as the trunk of the tree, solid and firm. Now, imagine your arms as branches reaching upward towards the sky, and your face as a canopy of leaves turned toward the sun, gazing upward and into the cosmos.

As you continue to breathe slowly and deeply, imagine drawing the earth's energy up through your feet, your torso, and all the way through your spine; feel this life force moving through your heart, arms, and hands. Feel this energy as nourishment for your entire body. Continue to breathe deeply, as you visualize this earth "qi" energy moving through your neck, your head, and up through your crown, then extending further outward and upward, energetically nourishing your auric field and beyond. As you continue to breathe slowly and deeply, feel the alignment between earth and sky. Take one more deep inhalation, and exhalation. (Sound chime.) Slowly open your eyes and return to presence. Feel the strength and stability of being the tree and carry this feeling throughout your day.

Suggested Homework: Complete the Stages of Changes Addiction/Recovery Pros & Cons Worksheet based on what you want to change and how you want to improve your communication skills in your relationships. Read the Codependency and Addictive Relationships handout and be prepared to share your insights at the next session.

Module IV (Conscious Communication) Session 2: Mindful Attention in Conscious Relationships ~ Passive versus Aggressive Communication Styles

Suggested Opening Meditation ~ Be The Mountain Meditation

Get into a comfortable position, and close your eyes or lower your gaze. (Sound chime or toning bowl.) Take three, slow, deep breaths and imagine a majestic mountain. See its grandeur in your mind's eye, and stand at its base. Turn your back to it and lean into it, as if to merge your body with the mountain. Feel the solid physicality of it, extending down into the earth's bedrock; feel the power and strength of it in your entire body. As you continue to breathe deeply, imagine the extreme weather and seasons your mountain endures. Imagine standing firm as snow and ice swirl about you; now, imagine the warmth of the sun melting the ice away. Feel the strength of that ability within yourself, how you can stand firm and in alignment with your environment, in alignment, mind, body, and spirit. (Sound chime.) Slowly open your eyes and return to presence. Carry the sense of strength and power of your inner mountain with you through your day. Remind yourself that change is inevitable. This too, whatever this obstacle is, shall come to pass.

Check-Ins and Q&A: After taking any questions about the individual SOC Pros & Cons Worksheet participants did for homework, have a group discussion about the handout on Codependency from the previous session. Codependency is a significant theme within family systems in general, but even more so within families where parents suffered from mental health challenges or addictions of any kind.

Handouts: Conscious Relationships & Determining your Style: Passive versus Aggressive

Mindful Attention in Conscious Relationships

Every relationship, whether romantic, familial, friend, colleague, or even a casual encounter, requires attention. Practicing assertive (attentive) listening and being aware of the other person's feelings, body language, and reactions without making assumptions is paramount to fostering conscious relationships, especially romantic, intimate relationships. To apply assertive listening is to take the Observer Self perspective, to observe facial expressions and hand gestures, and to pick up on the tone of voice to get a take on the health of the connection during a conversation.

By being present in interpersonal exchanges (instead of thinking about what we are going to say next or replaying a memory) we acknowledge and give consideration to the other person. Unfortunately, for many of us, our caregivers' communications style--and thus, our early programming--didn't necessarily model conscious communication in relationships. Practicing being present in the here and now as we are conversing with another person is the greatest gift we can offer to ourselves as the listener and the person being listened to. In meeting the other person's emotional need (to be heard), we build mutual trust and respect. In this alert state, we can sense when something is off, and instead of making assumptions and casting judgement, we can ask the other person clarifying questions to understand where they are coming from. Whereas, when we are not attending to the moment and not being attentive to the other person, we often inadvertently misread the conversation, miss the social cues and mood changes, and fall into the default mode of unconsciously projecting our own fears onto the other person, acting out, or exiting the conversation.

Mindful attention in conscious relationships is also about observing our own responses and reactions to the other person. From this Observer Self perspective, using Reflective Inquiry, we might ask questions of ourselves in the moment:

What is my motivation or intention in asking this question or making this comment?

What is it that I need or want from this person?

Am I feeling defensive or am I feeling supported and welcome in the interaction?

What are my emotions telling me? What are they flagging that I need to pay attention to? (Anxiety, sadness, resentment, attraction, validation, whatever might be coming up.)

Taking note of how and what we are feeling during a conversation can guide us to a response that can help to clarify a misunderstanding or set a boundary, if one is needed. When we do not include ourselves in our field of attention, it is more likely that the conversation will take a negative turn and a reaction, exit, or blow up will occur. The good news is, the story doesn't need to end there. We can circle back to the conversation at a later time and apply assertive listening, with the goal of mutually exploring what was missed and what skill or intervention we might use, should it happen again.

Group Exercise ~ Returning to the Conversation

Explore the dynamic of returning to a conversation that took an off-turn, using your whiteboard. Provide some examples and ask the group to offer their own. For example:

The other day when you walked out on me, it left me feeling abandoned, scared, and rejected. What could I have done differently to prevent you from leaving so abruptly?

It seems like we both are looking to maintain a sense of love and connection in our relationship, what are we willing to do to strengthen our commitment? What are we not willing to do?

Mindful Attention Practice

Every interpersonal interaction is an opportunity to practice mindful attention. Each time you interact, practice observing the other person's social cues and behaviors. Notice eye contact, tone of voice, physical distance, facial expressions, word choices, and so on. Be curious and ask clarifying questions if you are confused or find it hard to read where they are coming from.

Are you doing okay? You seem a bit down, do I have that right?
How are we doing?
How can I support you?
What is it that you need? Is everything ok with you? With us?
I am getting that you are not on the same page as I am. Do I have that right?
I'm making up that you don't believe that what I am saying is true? Is that right?

Sometimes it is helpful to ask for feedback regarding the way you are communicating. You might ask:

How could I communicate my feelings with you in a way that you could accept?
I want to connect with you in a way that helps you to feel comfortable and open with me. What would you suggest for how I might do that?

Keep clarifying that your intention is to build a mutually trusting and conscious relationship and cultivate a loving connection.

Example: John had a history of being excluded from social gatherings, going back decades to high school. Early in his relationship with Susan, she told him that she had gone to a friend's party the previous week but she hadn't let him know she was going. John was triggered and started to become withdrawn. Rather than get upset, Susan applied assertive listening and got curious about John's reaction. Susan asked him if he was feeling okay, noting that he was quieter than usual. John replied that he was somewhat embarrassed to admit it, but that he felt left out that she went to a party without inviting him. Susan let him know she was sorry to have hurt his feelings and explained that she didn't think he would want to go to a fashion accessories party, and she can see now that she could have asked rather than assuming he would not want to go. They agreed they would both talk about such things beforehand.

Mindful attention and assertive listening are *practices*. We have to keep trying them out and applying them in our daily lives as an ongoing process for cultivating nourishing and nurturing relationships with others and ourselves: practice, not perfection.

Suggested Closing Meditation ~ Observer Self Meditation

Get into a comfortable position, and close your eyes or lower your gaze. (Sound chime or toning bowl.) Sit up straight with your feet flat on the floor and your shoulders and jaw relaxed and open. Take three long, slow, deep breaths, exhaling longer with each breath. Take another deep breath; as you inhale, zoom in on a current challenge or conflict. See it in your mind's eye; notice how your body feels, notice where you might have tension. Now, slowly exhale and zoom out; breathe your way out to a safe distance and simply observe, without judgment.

Continue to observe from this broader perspective as you take another long, slow, deep inhalation. As you exhale, notice any changes in your emotional body or your physical body. Notice the softening of your muscles. Feel the power of your Observer Self and how it supports and protects your nervous system. One more deep inhalation, one more slow exhalation; feel the sense of security and stabilization throughout your body and mind. (Sound chime.) Now, slowly open your eyes and bring yourself back to the present. Know that you always have the ability to zoom out to a broader perspective.

Suggested Homework: Reflect in your journal on your takeaways from the session's group exercise. Complete the Passive versus Aggressive Communication Styles Worksheet, and review the Codependency & Addictive Relationships handout. Be prepared to share your answers and reflections with the group at the next session.

Personal Exercise: Recall a relationship interaction where the other person reacted in a triggered or unexpected way and explain how you resolved the issue.

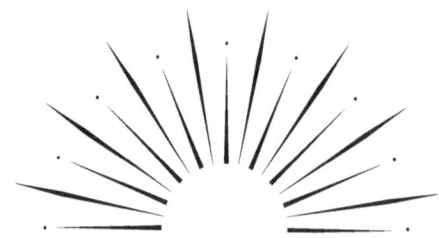

THE LIGHTHOUSE EFFECT
Conscious Relationships & Determining Your Style: Passive versus Aggressive

A core component of conscious relationships is the ability to communicate our needs and desires, and mindfully advocate for them. To do that, we need to understand our communication style. The way we communicate (our communication style) is informed by temperament, level of confidence (personality), and behavioral patterns that arise from the roles/coping strategies we took on in our family of origin, and mostly, the latter.

Passive Communication Style: Passive communicators tend to be introverts; they find it easier and more comfortable to "go along to get along." When we go along with something we don't want and don't express our feelings, we discount our own needs, which creates internal conflict and builds resentment. It's a telltale sign of codependency. Bottling our feelings and denying our own needs can lead to passive aggressive behaviors, to quietly "acting out." For example, you promise that you will follow through on a request or an agreement when you have no intention of carrying it out. Eventually, this unhealthy way of being in a relationship can lead to depression, anxiety, intestinal distress, headaches, body aches, chronic fatigue, and so on. As with any addiction or addictive behavior, being passive/not advocating for our own needs is a short-term solution: we don't have to deal with any blowback/confrontation we think might come from expressing ourselves in the moment. But it is detrimental in the long term as it deepens the unhealthy (for both people) dynamics, and often leads to the demise of a relationship.

Aggressive Communication Style: Aggressive communicators tend to be extroverts and have high expectations or standards about how people should behave. When others behave in ways that are in conflict with their own sense of morals and values, they may feel an urge to correct them or try to persuade them to see their perspective. They may even feel compelled to reprimand the other person for not measuring up to their standards or beliefs. These behaviors can escalate the more stressed and insecure the person feels, especially if they feel like they are losing control within the relationship. In stark contrast to the introvert, the extrovert can be flat-out aggressive and has a tendency to express their feelings openly. This communication style at its extreme is that of the bully.

Both communication styles can destroy relationships, and neither is healthy for us or for the other person/people. But we can change these default styles and become more conscious in our relationships by applying assertiveness skills that allow us to advocate for our needs and desires, understand the other's needs and desires, and be kinder and more supportive to one another; more dialectical in nature. It's about establishing healthy boundaries, and learning how to negotiate potential conflicts. Especially in dynamics where there are opposite communication styles. Interestingly, people who have a passive communication style will often attract a person with an aggressive communication style, and vice versa.

Identify Your Communication Style

Reflect on interactions in significant relationships. Check the statements that resonate most with your behavior.

1 ☐ I feel more comfortable letting someone else be the leader.

2 ☐ I encourage people to do what's right, even if there's a conflict.

3 ☐ I try to please and just get along.

4 ☐ I tell people what I think when I believe they should know the truth.

5 ☐ I always try to be sensitive to the needs of others, even if my own needs aren't met.

6 ☐ I know what I want and make sure I get it, even if it means I have to speak up or raise my voice.

7 ☐ When there is a conflict, I tend to give in and let the other person have their way.

8 ☐ When people don't do the right thing, I don't let them get away with it.

9 ☐ I'll avoid a conflict in a new relationship rather than say anything that might disappoint them.

10 ☐ You can't allow people to be selfish or stupid; you have to correct them and set them straight.

11 ☐ I leave people alone; I allow them to be whatever they are.

12 ☐ If people ignore my needs and force their ideas on me, I get really upset and tend to raise my voice.

If you checked more odd numbers your predominant communication style is passive. If you checked more even numbers, it's aggressive. It's not unusual to have some of both; we might step out of our predominant style under certain conditions.

For example, you might be predominantly passive/an introvert, but can be aggressive with people who are younger than you. Or you are predominantly aggressive/an extrovert, but become more passive with authority figures.

Module IV (Conscious Communication) Session 3: Codependency & Addictive Relationships ~ Getting Clear About your Desires

Suggested Opening Meditation ~ Attending to the Breath Meditation

Get into a comfortable position, and close your eyes or lower your gaze. (Sound chime or toning bowl.) Take three long, slow, deep breaths. With each inhalation, sense the temperature of the air, feel the sensation of the air as it enters your nostrils, and follow the flow into your lungs. Notice how your chest rises with each "in" breath and relaxes with each "out" breath, as if the process of breathing is gently rocking you. Feel into this subtle rocking motion, noticing your "in" breath and "out" breath as you continue to breathe deeply. Notice how soothing it feels to attend to your breathing. If your mind tries to comment or judge and distract you from the present moment, simply acknowledge that is what the mind does. Breathe into it and observe it, without worry, without engaging, and let it go. Just continue to follow the rocking rhythm of your breath. One more deep inhalation; one more full exhalation. (Sound chime.) Slowly open your eyes, and gently begin to move your body. Take your time. Slowly bring your attention back to the group.

Check-Ins and Q&A: Ask participants if they have any questions or comments about last week's concepts, homework, or handouts. Encourage them to base their check-ins on current content, relative to what is going on in their daily lives.

Handouts: Addictive Relationships & Codependency Guideposts

Codependency & Addictive Love Relationships ~
Love and Lust and the Wisdom to Know the Difference

Despite how painful unhealthy relationships are, we might be resistant to leaving one because our fear narratives (worry thoughts) talk us into staying.

What is the difference between a conscious, healthy love relationship and an unconscious, addictive love relationship? As we delve into this rather broad topic, we might want to define love. We might think of love as the opposite of fear, although love is of course much more than that. In this context, addictive love isn't really love, it is fear masking as love or fear wearing love's clothing. A healthy, mature love relationship is one where each person allows the other to be their own unique expression of self and where each supports the other in their growth and wellbeing without the need or desire to control them. In contrast, an addictive, immature love relationship is one in which one or both partners are dependent on the other in a way that holds their partner captive and suffocates, limits, and controls them in order to feel safe and secure themselves.

We adopt the societal norms of the culture, family system, and religious belief system in which we are raised, including how we view love relationships and what expectations we might have within them. Most of us were raised with "conditional" love, in the sense that we learn what behaviors are rewarded and encouraged and what behaviors are not. Because humans have egos that are focused on the physical and fundamentally wired for survival, we have to allow for a both/and definition of love, where we are indoctrinated into conditional love while at the same time, we aspire to give and receive unconditional love. We can radically accept the likelihood that anyone with whom we might engage in an intimate relationship will have programmed behaviors that will come into play, just as we do. To expect anyone, even ourselves, to come from a purely unconditional loving place is illusory and unreasonable.

Rather than entering a relationship fantasizing that it will be the perfect love, we want to be present with what is actually happening in the dynamic and recognize the conditional aspects, while allowing for unconditional love to emerge too. Because love in its purest or authentic form *is* unconditional, and we can tap into its flow, as it is always there--always, and in all ways. We can practice being present in the mystery of love, allowing the soul to guide the relationship instead of the ego. The desire to experience a healthy conscious relationship that is mutually supportive and loving is a common human need: everyone thrives on love and connection. It is essential that the mature part of us learns that love has to be grounded in reality.

What we learned from parents or caregivers is often not what they set out to teach us, but what we picked up through their actions and reactions to our behaviors, for example, what actions we interpreted as deserving of their love and acceptance. Though unintentional, this leads to us developing a "not good enough" core belief as children. We can even see conditional love in common societal maxims like, "my child is my pride and joy."

We learn through observation what a love relationship is by witnessing how our parents or caregivers relate to one another and to us. We also learn to compare and compete for attention, especially when we have siblings. We make observations and absorb information without questioning the validity; it's just the way to behave in relationships. As young adults, we take these childhood experiences into our peer groups and romantic relationships, and then we get triggered when the dynamic doesn't meet with our understanding of what the relationship should be like. Hurtful experiences, both those we witnessed and those we directly experienced, have been encoded in our brain and central nervous system.

In adulthood, this can lead to trauma bonding, where we instinctively seem to be attracted to relationships that mirror our negative core beliefs and experiences, such as those of abuse or neglect. These early experiences are chemically and hormonally wired into the brain and tied to our survival instincts, and whether it be healthy or abusive, the brain sees whatever our relief mechanism is as safety; it puts the emphasis on relief. As a result, in order to feel safe, whole, and "normal," that emotional part of us that was neglected or abused is constantly seeking reassurance, approval, and validation from others (with varying degrees of intensity) in an addictive, obsessive way. Ultimately, to move out of codependency, we need to get to the root of our dependency and come into our own wisdom: It is up to us to validate, approve, and accept ourselves, and then we can begin to create and maintain a healthy relationship with someone else. This is the premise of The Lighthouse Effect. Healing into wholeness (or holiness) is an inside job; we heal from the inside out.

Love or Lust?

The behaviors we learned that would make us "well-behaved" and respected citizens are also often what we rebel against as we mature and individuate from our caregivers and authority figures. We yearn to explore new horizons and concepts. While this process of development and becoming a sovereign being is healthy, it may or may not be encouraged. Fearful, overprotective parents or caregivers can unintentionally thwart healthy development and unconsciously create a codependent relationship. The need to escape the social norms and constraints of society and family systems can be quite compelling. Experiencing hormonal urges and desires for sexual explorations while also being introduced to mind-altering substances can be profoundly expansive and exciting. While they can be healthy, these coming-of-age adventurous and risky experiences can also be a setup for addictive behavior. Ego is seduced into equating these exhilarating experiences with love, when they are more likely lust or "love lust."

Such experiences can create a downward spiral that leads to addiction and/or dependency, which is why teenagers are at such high risk of developing addiction, contracting sexually transmitted diseases, having unplanned pregnancies, being in tragic car accidents, and committing suicide. Circling back to caregivers who might unintentionally create codependency by being overprotective of their children, we can see why they might become especially fearful when their children learn how to drive and start to date. What we can do as parents or caregivers is to model healthy behaviors--stand in our own morals and values and make healthy, conscious choices ourselves--and allow our children to have their own experience with the hope that our example will support them and not hinder them.

Coming from a spiritual perspective, addictive love has a low vibrational frequency, one of density or confinement and darkness or lack of light. Addictive love leads to emotional and physiological enslavement of both partners, is fear-based, and ultimately destructive. In contrast, conscious love is psychologically, physiologically, and emotionally liberating, expansive, and freeing. It carries an extremely high vibrational frequency of light and spaciousness. It is the purest expression of the divine; it cannot be controlled or contained because it is pure consciousness.

Self-exploration and a willingness to know thyself is not just a worthwhile investment in our overall wellness, it is the pathway to loving, healthy relationships. Part of that exploration is to notice how we operate within various relationships, and then to simply follow the thread of whatever triggers us back to the source of where and when it occurred and how it informed our core beliefs.

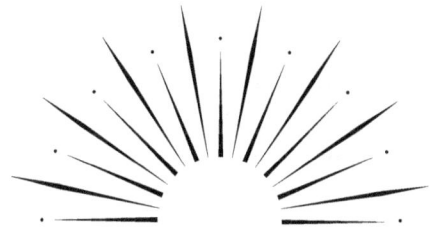

THE LIGHTHOUSE EFFECT
Addictive Relationships & Codependency Guideposts

To overcome codependency and create a healthy love relationship, we need to understand the differences between an addictive, toxic relationship and a conscious, nourishing relationship. We can then use behaviors we identify as "addictive" as guideposts for navigating our relationships in healthier ways. Importantly, our self-inquiry can also help us in moving through relationships that are not necessarily toxic, but where we may simply have grown apart and become incompatible. So, let's take a close look at those codependency guideposts.

A toxic relationship will make us feel like we are in a constant state of frustration or on a roller coaster of emotional intensity. There is often a noncommittal or unattainability aspect to the relationship that keeps us in a state of chaos and instability. We focus on the other person instead of ourselves, and therein lies a key challenge to overcome: self-neglect. If we are lacking in our self-care and believe we are only okay when our partner is under our control or we are under their control, the relationship is conditional and codependent. The experience of constantly not getting our needs met leads to resentment and mental, emotional, and physical dis-ease, as it lowers our immune system. It can destroy our self-esteem to the point that it becomes difficult to focus on work and daily life and we experience anxiety and depression, in the same way that substance addiction and dependency lead us on a downward spiral. We are chasing or reaching for the "high" of love, but we never get it because we are seeking love that is outside of ourselves rather than the conscious love of self, which is what we actually need in order to fully love and be loved by another.

Importantly, there are varying degrees of intensity in addictive and toxic relationships, ranging from passive-aggressive to openly aggressive, which can escalate to domestic violence. Oftentimes, it is the quieter, more covert toxic relationships that are the hardest to leave. In a toxic relationship we keep ourselves in a state of denial in order to fool ourselves into accepting that all is good. And even when we see that we've been in a state of denial and despite how painful the unhealthy relationship is, we might be resistant to leaving the person because the familiar pain is less scary than the unknown. Thus, coming into radical acceptance of the reality of the relationship dynamic is the first step toward changing it. Though it may not seem like it, we always have a choice. Even if it is just to step away and allow ourselves time to process and gain insight.

The Justification and Entrapment of Addictive Relationships

There are multiple reasons why we might stay in unhealthy toxic relationships, including economic entanglement, shared living or other practical/logistical considerations, emotional stability for children, consideration for pets, feelings of failure, fear of being alone, fear of being judged by others. How we were socialized (what we witnessed and experienced as children) informs the negative core beliefs we carry into adulthood and our expectations about what a love relationship "should" be like.

It can lead to negative reasoning for why we "should" stay in a relationship that isn't measuring up: *It's too painful to be alone; If you leave you're being selfish; If you leave, you didn't work hard enough.* It's not just within our family of origin that we learn what to expect of love. We are greatly influenced by direct and subtle messages that get repeated in our social circles, on social media, in love songs, in movies, and so on.

For example: *Someday you will find your princess/knight-in-shining armor; Love is forever; Your soulmate is out there.* All of these influences lead to insecurities, self-doubt, and fear-based rationales for staying in unhealthy relationships: *What if I never find someone else? What if this is the best I could do? I should be grateful for what I have. I'm not pretty enough or smart enough to find someone else.*

These fears can keep us hooked and only deepen our despair and sense of hopelessness. Humans need love, connection, and nurturance; we thrive when we are encouraged to be our unique selves as creative, sovereign, and independent beings. Unfortunately, it isn't the way most of us grew up. Whether unintentional or intentional, most of us witnessed and experienced things that led to negative core beliefs that make us vulnerable to some extent to addictive/toxic relationships.

Are you addicted?

Consider whether any of the following signs resonate with you:

1) Even though you know the relationship is toxic, you don't take active steps to change or end the relationship. (The "contemplation" stage in the Stages of Change).

2) You keep coming up with excuses for why it isn't a good time to end the relationship or to take steps to establish healthy boundaries to meet your needs. (Lack of self-care and self-responsibility.)

3) When you think about leaving the relationship, you feel overwhelmed with the thought of being alone and your projection of abandonment reinforces that it would be worse if you leave the relationship. (Fear-based "futurizing" or projecting.)

4) You are taking action to end a toxic relationship, but you begin to experience symptoms similar to substance withdrawal and convince yourself they can only be relieved by reconnecting with or going back to your partner. (Getting a 'fix.")

5) Friends and family members offer feedback that this relationship isn't healthy for you and encourage you to take action, and you either sheepishly agree but don't follow through or you become resentful of their advice. Over time, your relationship with them suffers to the extent they no longer invite you and your partner to gatherings.

If these signs seem familiar to you, chances are you are caught in an addictive, codependent relationship and it has most likely left you feeling unhappy and out of balance. It is vital that you seek support in taking steps toward recovery. The first step is awareness, the second is making an action plan and following through with an accountability partner (trusted friend, therapist, support group) that will support you in moving out of the addictive relationship. Without help, you are more likely to stay in the "small-t truth" perspective of fear and locked in the codependency cycle. With professional and peer support, you can develop skills and learn to manage your love relationships from your Tall Self, your mature, wise, loving Higher Self. From the stance of Tall Self, you develop the inner strength to cultivate healthy relationships and move toward wholeness.

A healthy relationship requires mutual trust, where each partner encourages the other's freedom for creative expression and spiritual growth. It is to wake up every morning and choose to be in a mutually loving relationship. To experience the love that we are longing for is to turn inward with the intention, perseverance, and patience to love and accept all parts of ourselves: the good, the bad, and the ugly. When we choose to commit to inner work, reflect honestly on how we behave within relationships, and effort to notice what our patterns are, we will gradually expand our consciousness. From this state of enhanced awareness, we gain a larger perspective and can see how we might have had unattainable and even unfair expectations in our relationships, thinking that the other person is responsible for meeting our emotional needs. Once again, we begin to see the wisdom of turning inward to learn how to unconditionally love and accept ourselves.

When we do the inner work, the experience of a toxic, dependent, addictive relationship can serve a purpose in how it shows us what does not work and does not serve our (or the other person's) wellbeing; it gives us clarity on what we do want (and actually need) to be in a healthy, loving relationship. In that sense, we might consider that the path of addiction can be a spiritual path: When we do the work, we can see that the toxic relationship is what catapulted us into making healthier choices for our growth and wellbeing. Committing to a daily practice is the key to fully attending to our mind, body, and spiritual needs. It is our responsibility to connect to this higher love within ourselves. When we love ourselves from a place of acceptance, without conditions, we can love another in the same way.

Pros & Cons Exercise: Complete the Stages of Change Addiction/Recovery Pros & Cons Worksheet, focusing on the pros and cons of staying in an unhealthy relationship versus the pros and cons of leaving one. The goal is to gain clarity on why you might be in resistance to leaving or changing the dynamics of an unhealthy, unsupportive, or harmful relationship.

Strategies for Overcoming Relationship Addictions

These strategies were inspired by Robin Norwood, author of *Women Who Love Too Much,* and adapted to not be gender specific and to express and align with The Lighthouse Effect language and recovery concepts.

1) Align fully and totally with your own morals and values to move from survival to revival: make recovery and the right to thrive priorities in your life.

2) Commit to self-care and a daily practice that supports mind, body, and spirit integration and wellness. Think of it as being "soulish," not "selfish."

3) Be courageous and sovereign by doing your inner work: strive for self-mastery to move from victim consciousness to being fully conscious and in charge of your whole self, mind, body, and spirit.

4) Co-create what you want to experience in your life. Be the change you want to experience; don't wait for someone else to do it for you. Choose to live the life you desire, and if your needs are not being met, choose to change course.

5) Practice staying in your own lane. Focus on your own needs and being secure within yourself. Establish healthy boundaries with others and learn how to be assertive and use discernment, while allowing others to be themselves.

6) Engage in a spiritual practice that helps you gain inner peace and experience (be in) higher vibration emotions (gratitude, oneness, compassion, empathy, kindness). You might make a daily practice of reading or meditating on the Serenity Prayer. You might consider *Bookending Your Day: The Lighthouse Effect Self-Care 30-Day Challenge* to create the daily practice that works for you.

7) Take opportunities to apply Observer Self in your relationships. Notice when you fall into a Victim Triangle role, whether rescuer, abuser/persecutor, or victim. Notice when you get triggered and practice stepping back and applying Reflective Inquiry in the moment.

8) Join a support group of peers who have a common focus, who are nonjudgmental, understanding, and committed to holding each other accountable to your personal relapse prevention plan, who share similar challenges and are doing inner work to overcome them.

9) Respectfully share with others using "I" statements to convey your experiences and perspectives, and do so with humility, integrity, and presence.

10) Consider seeking professional help from a therapist, recovery coach, or sponsor/mentor; ask for help from trusted family members and/or friends who will help you be accountable in your recovery journey.

For many of us, it is not obvious that we are in a codependent, addictive relationship because it is simply how we experienced relationship dynamics as children. To move out of codependency, we need to gain a deeper knowing and understanding of our patterns of behavior, both positive and negative, and to do that, it is essential that we explore our childhood experiences.

Group Exercise ~ Reflective Inquiry in Relationship

Invite a volunteer from the group to answer questions and prompts as you move the group through the handout.

Suggested Prompt: Think of a challenging conversation or dynamic you've had recently. Now imagine stepping into Observer Self, and from that calm, nonjudgmental perspective, apply Reflective Inquiry.

What did I need from this person? What were my intentions?
Is it their approval, attention, or help that I wanted?
What made me uncomfortable?
Do I need to change how I receive critical comments, demands, and intrusive questions from them?
Did I internalize their judgments as my own?
What negative core belief was triggered by their comment or judgment?
Are these triggered feelings (hurt, sadness, loss, shame, anxiety) signaling a deeper issue?
How did I get recognition in my childhood? How did I get love?
Have I mistaken love for approval?

If there is time, you might also have your group complete the SOC Addiction/Recovery Pros & Cons Worksheet, where the categories might be the pros and cons of addictive, codependent relationships versus the pros and cons of supportive, interdependent relationships.

Suggested Closing Meditation ~ Anchoring Awareness (Here/Now/This Moment) Meditation

Get into a comfortable position, and close your eyes or lower your gaze. (Sound chime or toning bowl.) Take three long, slow, deep breaths, allowing your entire respiratory system to gently fill, and then slowly and fully empty. Take another deep breath; focus your attention on the question, *Where are you*? As you exhale, consider the answer: *here*. Inhale, breathing the felt sense of the word *here* all the way through your body. Exhale, allowing yourself to be here, fully present. Take another deep breath; focus your attention on the question, *What time is it*? Don't look for the answer from a place outside of you. As you exhale, consider the answer: *now*. Breathe deeply into the felt sense of the word *now*. Allow yourself to be here, now, fully present. Feel the emerging awareness from within. Take another deep inhalation; focus your attention on the question, *What are you*? As you exhale, consider the answer: *this moment*. Breathe fully into the felt sense of you as *this moment*. Allow yourself to be *here, now, this moment*, fully present. Take one more full inhalation as you anchor yourself fully in this gift of presence that is you, and slowly exhale, releasing all resistance. (Sound chime.) Slowly open your eyes. Carry this feeling of being anchored *here, now, this moment* throughout your day.

Suggested Homework: Reflect in your journal on your insights about codependency and where it shows up in your relationships. Review the Addictive Relationships & Codependency handout and complete the SOC Addiction/Recovery Pros & Cons Worksheet the way it is presented in the handout--focusing on moving away from addictive behavior patterns. Bring your insights to the next session to inspire group discussion and connection.

Module IV (Conscious Communication) Session 4: Identifying Relationship Values & Gaining More Clarity About your Rights and Desires

Suggested Opening Meditation ~ Body Scan & Sensory Meditation

Position your body to be comfortable, relaxed, and open. Close your eyes or lower your gaze. (Sound chime or toning bowl.) Take a slow, deep breath, utilizing your entire lung capacity, moving the breath down into the belly and all the way into the back. Now, slowly exhale. Continue to breathe deeply, allowing your entire body to soften a little more with each exhalation. Notice how you are completely supported. Notice how your body naturally rises and falls with each breath, as if the breath is rocking you ever so gently and consistently.

Now, as you continue to breathe deeply, slowly scan your body, beginning at the crown of your head and moving all the way through to the tips of your toes. Simply notice each area of your body without judgment or commentary. If you notice any tension or tightness, bring your attention to that area and breathe into it to help open and release it. If there are thoughts trying to distract you, move your attention back to the breath. Feel the coolness of the breath as you inhale and warmth of the breath as you exhale. Move your attention to any sounds that you hear and simply notice them as you continue to breathe deeply. Now bring your attention to what you see behind your eyelids, whatever colors, shapes, or patterns appear; just notice as they appear and fade away. Continue to breathe deeply. Turn your awareness to your sense of taste, and simply notice any taste sensations, however faint. Now, move your focus to your sense of smell, as you breathe in, slowly and fully. Simply notice with curiosity and openness, as you slowly exhale.

Move your attention to the sensations you are feeling on your skin. Notice the movement and temperature of the air; notice clothing or textures against your skin. Sense your feet in your shoes, and the floor beneath you. Now, slowly move your attention back to your breath as you step into Observer Self. Observe the process of breathing as you take one more full, deep inhalation all the way down through your lungs and into your back. Breathe in awareness and gratitude. As you exhale, feel your body release and relax fully. (Sound chime.) Slowly open your eyes and return to the room. Offer gratitude to your breath and your mind-body-spirit complex. Send yourself a blessing of full acceptance for you, just as you are!

Check-Ins and Q&A: Encourage the group to reflect on their own issues with codependency and challenges they might have when it comes to getting clear about values, rights, and desires.

Handouts: Identifying Relationship Values, Gaining Clarity about your Rights & Desires

In this session you will be introducing the group to the importance of gaining clarity about their relationship morals and values. Each participant will learn to identify what their values are and practice communicating them to someone they would enjoy developing a conscious relationship with. The goal is for participants to carry forward all of the skills they have learned in previous modules, in order to come from a place of alignment and confidence in communicating and expressing themselves as a sovereign being, mind, body, and spirit.

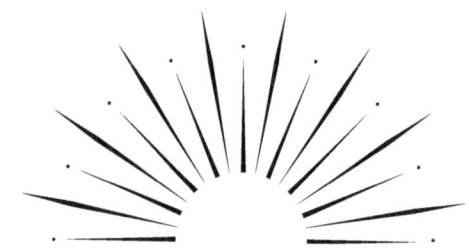

THE LIGHTHOUSE EFFECT
Identifying Relationship Values

What are Relationship Values?

Relationship values are the personal standards of behavior or conduct that are most important to us and that we want to experience in our relationships. For example:

I expect my partner, friend, or family member to be supportive and considerate.
I prefer a partner or friend who has integrity and is conscientious and sincere.
I admire a person who holds themselves accountable when they make a mistake.
Socially, I like to be included, considered, and acknowledged by my partner or friend that I am out with. When I get neglected or ignored, I feel invisible and I get triggered.

While it is our responsibility to comfort ourselves when we are triggered, we can also be proactive by sharing with our partner, friend, or family member what triggers us, so they can be aware and offer a healing (corrective) experience as often as possible. For example:

I like to be acknowledged for my generosity of spirit and the effort that I put into my relationships. I enjoy when you acknowledge my gestures with sincerity and eye contact. I do get triggered when you don't acknowledge me.

Use the following prompts to consider what you value most in a relationship, and write a list: How do you want to be treated? How do you expect a partner or a friend to behave? What are the characteristics that you are looking for that reflect your values?

_____
_____
_____
_____
_____
_____

Relationship Value Violations & Assertive Responses

We need to be clear about our relationship values in order to gain clarity on what does not work for us. For example:

I don't like when I feel that my partner, friend, or family member is being insensitive or criticizes the way I speak, the way I behave, or the way I live, and I get defensive.

When we feel that a relationship value is being violated, it is our responsibility to share our experience and ask for what we need in an assertive (firm/not aggressive) and respectful way. For example:

Can you say that in a different way? I'm experiencing the tone of your voice in a way that it feels patronizing and makes me feel subservient or diminished. I want us to feel like equals and to be mutually respectful.

List some assertive responses you might use in your own relationships:

_____
_____
_____
_____
_____
_____

What is your Love Language?

Our language of love is what we expect our partner, friend, or family member to do in order to feel loved and valued by them. For example:

I like to be appreciated verbally and physically; I like eye contact, hugs, kisses, and physical touch.
I like to be shown that I am loved and valued through acts of service (for example, running a bath or making me a cup of tea).
I like to receive thoughtful gifts that show you are thinking of me and valuing me.
I like to have quality time with you.

Consider what your love language is, and list what you want or need in your relationships to feel loved, valued, and respected:

_____
_____
_____
_____
_____

Create your own "love creed" to live by and commit to a daily practice to hold to your vow and to share it with your loved ones, especially your love partner. It is an act of loving grace to be open and clear with your partner about your values, to be aware of and accept their values, and to radically accept theirs if they differ from yours. You can agree to disagree and respect those differences.

_____
_____
_____
_____

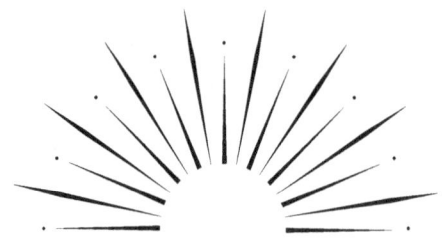

THE LIGHTHOUSE EFFECT
Gaining Clarity About Your Rights & Desires ∼ Reclaiming your Power

In order to cultivate healthy relationships, we need to be clear and specific about what we want and desire. Unfortunately, many of us did not learn how to express our needs in our family of origin and expressing our needs was maybe even discouraged, whether intentionally or just by the behaviors of our caregivers. So it might seem a simple thing to ask ourselves to get clear about what we need, but not if we've spent our lives being afraid to ask for what we need and believing our own narrative that we are undeserving, that our feelings are not important. We all have emotional needs and we all experience what we might label as "negative" emotions, but they are as valid as our "positive" emotions. We all feel, and yearn, and hurt, and we have the right to express our emotions and be heard. Spoiler alert, the answer to each of the following questions is, "yes."

Even if you think you are burdening others, is it okay to express your needs? Do you deserve to have your needs acknowledged? Are you allowed to let someone down or cause disappointment to make a case on your own behalf?

Your Authentic Rights

1) You have a right to express your needs in your relationships.

2) You have a right to prioritize yourself sometimes.

3) You have a right to experience and express painful feelings and emotions.

4) You have a right to your personal morals and values.

5) You have a right to your perspective, perceptions, and world views.

6) You have the right to your unique experiences, even if they are outside of social norms.

7) You have a right to disapprove of treatment or criticism that feels unjust to you.

8) You have a right to advocate for positive change.

9) You have a right to ask for emotional support, even though you may not get it right away or at all.

10) You have a right to say no; saying no does not make you selfish.

11) You have a right to not explain yourself or apologize, at times.

12) You have a right to not accept or be responsible for other people's problems.

13) You have a right to set healthy boundaries in your relationships.

14) You have a right to disappoint someone and not offer help when you do not have the capacity.

Group Exercise ~ Identifying your Relationships Values

Move the group through the handout, and have participants share their own examples.

Follow-up Group Exercise ~ Gaining Clarity About Your Desires

Use the handout to engage the group in a "call and response," where you read each right on the list and they respond. For example, you read the first right, *"You have a right to express your needs in your relationships,"* and they respond, *"I have a right to express my needs in my relationships."*

Suggested Closing Meditation ~ Self-Value Meditation

Sit comfortably in a receptive, open position with your eyes closed or lowered. (Sound chime or toning bowl.) Take three slow deep breaths to bring yourself into this present moment. As you continue to breathe slowly and deeply, feel yourself softening even more with each successive in-breath and each elongated out-breath. Now, bring your attention to your third chakra, the area between your chest and your belly, and place a hand there. It is the chakra of self-worth and self-value. Allow yourself to feel the energy of your third chakra, the essence of your own unique value and worth. Continue to breathe gently and naturally. Now, see the color yellow in your mind's eye; see it as a yellow flower. Imagine that vibrant color of yellow resonating in your belly, under your hand, and flowering and radiating out. Take another full in-breath, and full out-breath. (Sound chime.) Slowly open your eyes and return to presence. Carry this golden light and sense of self-worth with you throughout your day.

Suggested Homework: Reflect in your journal on your takeaways from the exercise(s) and complete the handouts from your own personal perspective to get clear about your rights and desires. Be prepared to share your insights with the group at the next session.

Module IV (Conscious Communication) Session 5:
Effective Communication & Assertive Listening

Suggested Opening Meditation ~ Both/And Meditation

Get into a comfortable position, and close your eyes or lower your gaze. (Sound chime or toning bowl.) Take three long, slow, deep breaths, filling your lungs and expanding into your abdomen. Imagine a challenge you currently face. Notice what happens to your body when you bring this conflict to mind. What stress level does it carry? Now, take another long, slow, deep breath to clear the mind, and zoom out to observe the same conflict from a distance. Notice the stress level of your body now. Notice how it is the same conflict, but it looks different from another perspective. Continue to breathe deeply, as you consider the change in perspective. Neither perspective is wrong, you are just seeing things in two different ways: both/and. Maybe you see details in the closer perspective that you don't see in the broader perspective; maybe you can detach from your emotions from the broader perspective.

Continue to breathe deeply, allowing the "both/and" concept to settle in. Instead of looking for an either/or resolution, consider a compromise where you are stepping back enough to be the mediator of your own conflict. Consider both points of view. Notice what happens to your stress level when you allow and integrate the best of both perspectives. Take one more deep inhalation through the nose, and one more exhalation through the mouth. (Sound the chime.) Now slowly open your eyes and stretch your body returning to your day with a sense of ease. Practice this both/and concept with any conflict that presents itself.

Check-Ins and Q&A: Encourage the group to share how they are increasing their awareness of how they present themselves in their relationships, and how they are practicing expressing their values and desires.

Handouts: Skill Building for Conscious Communication, The Lighthouse Seven: Key Communication Skills

Effective Communication

As a therapist, coach, or group facilitator, you are probably well aware of a common exercise in halfway houses and early-treatment facilities, where participants are asked to write a letter to their drug of choice. It's a process for exploring the emotional attachment the substance supposedly provided for them. In my experience, letter writing is profoundly effective for bringing awareness to the phenomenon of dependency and attachment. It brings to light our deeply entrenched patterns, which come to make perfect sense to us once our early-attachment style is revealed. It helps people in the process of *recovery* to *uncover* the painful emotional experiences that drove them to find ways to numb the pain, rather than expressing, allowing, and airing those internalized fears. In this Conscious Interpersonal Communications module, I sometimes ask participants to write a letter to themselves or to others, with the similar goal of uncovering entrenched patterns in the context of relationship dynamics. Here's an excerpt from my interview with Rick (my first client, who I mentioned in Module II) talking about how letter writing helped him.

I remember writing, I don't know, half a dozen letters. And rewriting them, and admitting blame, and not making excuses for what I did. Eventually, over time, I started getting invited back to my sister's for Thanksgiving. … Now I'm the official turkey-carver at Thanksgiving.

Rick also talks about how The Lighthouse Skillful Recovery Program helped him to understand how deeply his early childhood experiences had informed his addictive patterns and behaviors. His childhood trauma included several concussive head injuries and sexual abuse by an older cousin. He also came to see how his identity or role in his family played into his self-image and self-identification as an adult.

My older brother gave me a nickname when I was probably single digits in age. He called me "the Demon." He had nicknames for everybody, like my younger sister was "Princess." I was the only one with a connotation like that; tells you what I was like as a kid. … It went into adulthood too. My two sisters-in-law, my two brothers' wives, they kept it going even longer. They did not want me around their kids, or even around them.

His practice of such skills as mindfulness, meditation, detachment, and stepping into Observer Self helped Rick to step back and see the whole picture, move beyond the trauma, and deprogram default behaviors.

I've been doing quite a bit more meditation, and that certainly has helped, along with tapping. Just everything in the program that I've been taught has helped me deal with my life now. I guess the drugs made me more of an extrovert. I managed many restaurants over the years, and the drugs just helped me stay normal. And now, I'm leading a totally different life. I'm really calm, I don't go out a whole lot. I mean, I walk every day, and do meetings, and such.

And now they're all back in my life, my family, and very accepting, and the time that's gone by has healed. Of course, my behavior and my lack of drinking and drugs has certainly helped. … Now, it's always, "I love you," with all my brothers and sisters. I'm just so full of gratitude.

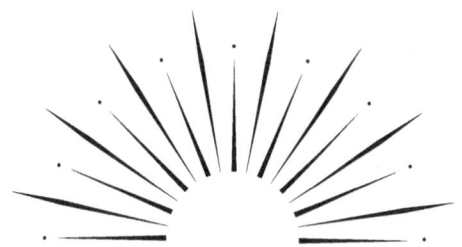

THE LIGHTHOUSE EFFECT
Skill Building for Conscious Communication

It is our responsibility (response-ability) to know what we want and to advocate for ourselves in our relationships with clarity and care. How do we achieve that? Developing conscious interpersonal communication skills takes willingness, practice, and patience. As it is with trying to change any habit, it is beneficial to have a support network to keep us on task when we are developing healthier and more effective communications skills. As we develop our ability to be present and mindful in our relationship dynamics, we will move away from default survival reactions, such as projecting what is really an internal issue onto the other person, blaming them, trying to fix them, or trying to resolve a conflict without understanding our own needs or theirs.

There are two crucial components to moving toward wholeness in our relationships. The first is about establishing a supportive dynamic, which we do by being clear with ourselves about what we want in the relationship or around any issue that comes up, and by being fully present for the other person to express what they want. The second is about conflicts and learning how to negotiate through them, which requires self-awareness and development of our ability to adapt in the moment. We humans are mutable and ever-changing, especially with regard to our emotional system, so it is to our benefit to approach any conflict or potential conflict with curiosity, to ask questions, and to avoid jumping to conclusions.

Adapting in the moment also means being flexible about outcomes, for example, being willing to come to a new understanding that would allow us to enter back into an agreement or repair a relationship we thought was broken. As with most default behaviors, how we function in our relationships was firmly established via the learned behaviors in our early programming. I try to underscore with the group that it takes time to change those behaviors and develop our communications skills, and we might very well default to those old, reactive behaviors, so we need to make an agreement with ourselves to be kind and patient with ourselves and the other person or people, no matter what transpires.

Benefits of Practicing Conscious Communication

Confidence: As we experience the positive impact of conscious communication, we build confidence and inner strength.

Self-Advocacy: When we practice advocating for what we need in all of our relationships (familial, work, romantic, friendships), we are better able to self-advocate during conflicts.

Supportive Dynamic: As we develop effective negotiation skills, we cultivate and preserve a supportive and respectful dynamic for meeting our own and others' needs with understanding.

Self-Respect: In practicing and modeling self-respect, we build mutual respect, as we are cultivating kinder ways to communicate and move out of ineffective reactive patterns.

Reduces Stress: When we are mindful and conscious with our communications, we embody an ease of being and naturally reduce stress levels.

Group Exercise ~ Skill Building for Conscious Communication

Move through the two handouts with the group, using your whiteboard to underscore the concepts and with volunteers role-playing some of the example dialogues.

Suggested Closing Meditation ~ Butterfly View Meditation

Get into a comfortable position, and close your eyes or lower your gaze. (Sound chime or toning bowl.) Take a long, slow, deep breath. As you inhale, in your mind's eye, take the caterpillar view and zoom in on a current life challenge; now, as you slowly exhale, zoom out, like a butterfly rising above the conflict. Continue to take long, slow, deep breaths and observe from this higher perspective; simply observe, without judgment or resistance. Notice changes in your emotional body and your physical body; notice any softening or lightening sensations. Take one more deep inhalation, and slow exhalation. (Sound chime.) Now, slowly open your eyes and bring yourself back to the present. Know that you always have the ability to zoom out to the butterfly view to gain a higher and more expanded perspective at any given moment. Practice this skill throughout your day and make it a daily practice.

Suggested Homework: Reflect on the session and record any insights or challenges that come to mind. Review the group exercise and read over the handout on Skill Building for Conscious Communication. Bring your insights and questions to the next session to stimulate group discussion and connection.

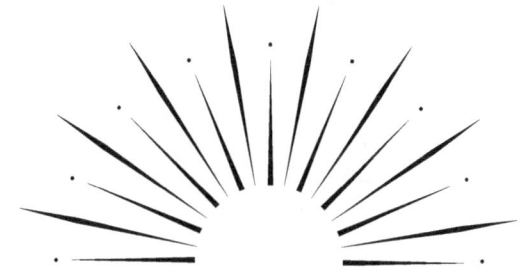

THE LIGHTHOUSE "SEVEN" KEY COMMUNICATIONS SKILLS
Seven core interpersonal skills that will positively change the dynamic in your relationships!

1) SELF-CLARITY: It is your responsibility to advocate for yourself clearly and confidently. To do that, you need to know what you want; you need to be clear with yourself. To get self-clarity, apply self-inquiry. Practice writing in your journal and/or sharing with a trusted friend, your therapist, or someone in your support network. Consider the barriers, including emotions and feelings, that might prevent you from expressing yourself and advocating for yourself.

What do I want to experience in this relationship?
What am I feeling in my body right now?
Am I feeling discomfort or other emotions that might prevent me from advocating for what I need?

2) CONSCIOUS ASKING: Develop your ability to make conscious, mindful requests for what you want, so from a place of presence and groundedness. Use any of your mindfulness practices to detach from the lower vibration of Emotional Mind, that being the child self or small-t self, and step into Emotional Mind's higher vibration of Tall-T Self. Notice that when you step into the higher vibration of Emotional Mind, you naturally align with Rational Mind, and by doing so, Wise Mind comes to the forefront. Notice how you feel when you come from this place of mind-body-spirit alignment. Make a list (whether on paper, or mentally, if you are practicing in real time) of what you would like to experience in the relationship or want to see as an outcome of a conflict; be clear and concise. Then frame your desires into questions.

Desire: I would like to experience an emotional connection with the other person about this issue, and be in my truth at the same time. For example:

I am trying to understand your position for not seeking medical attention for your condition, and I am also wanting you to know how it affects me. Can you see how I feel like I am held hostage by sharing the weight of the consequences if you don't seek medical attention? I care about you, and I am asking that you take responsibility for your health and your physical self-care.

3) HEALTHY CURIOSITY: One of the most beneficial of all conscious-relationship skills is a healthy curiosity. Be curious and ask mindful questions about the other person's needs, concerns, fears, desires, and so on. Gather information that will help you understand the other person's perspective so that you can make conscious choices about your own behavior.

Common blocks that can get in the way are making assumptions about the other person's needs, projecting your fears and feelings onto the other person, letting the fear that you are being intrusive run the show, letting the fear of being rejected run the show, feeling a lack of confidence for picking up on social cues. If you experience a block, observe it with curiosity and turn your mind away from it; turn your focus and your curiosity to the other person. Ask them questions about what they are experiencing or what their desired outcome might be.

4) SKILLFUL NEGOTIATION: Developing your ability to negotiate through a conflict requires a willingness to engage in a resolution process. Coming from a dialectical perspective, you want to enter into the conversation with a clear commitment and understanding that both perspectives are valid. Think "Both/And" and apply Radical Acceptance to accept that the other person's perspective is different from yours. The intention is to compromise, meet in the middle, and come up with a win/win understanding or agreement where both individuals benefit. There are no winners and no losers.

5) THE ART OF SAYING NO: Learning to effectively say no without invalidating, hurting, or offending the other person is an art. How we say no impacts the power dynamic. For example, if we lack confidence, our communication style might be that of a passive communicator; we say no in a low tone, perhaps looking down or away to avoid eye contact. Lack of confidence can also translate to us being a more aggressive communicator; we might say no quickly, in a high volume, while looking sternly into the other person's face and maybe even too closely. Both of these communication styles prevent us from creating a healthy, supportive alliance and connection with the other person. Whereas, when we say no with quiet, calm confidence, our behavior is neither passive nor aggressive.

The art of saying no is about self-confidence and self-care. It's about developing our ability to be an assertive communicator, meaning, we can calmly assert or advocate for our own needs while validating the other person's needs and desires. We are able to set healthy boundaries and communicate them, which gives us the best chance for a positive outcome.

6) THE LIGHTHOUSE STANCE: Taking the lighthouse stance is to be in alignment with your own morals and values. It's about fully stepping into our Authentic Self or Wise Mind, to be aligned vertically, mind, body, and spirit. (Refer to The Lighthouse Effect Mind States Model.) Draw on your mindfulness practice toolkit to come into alignment before you enter into any conversation, discussion, or negotiation. Be prepared and clear with yourself about your desired outcomes so that you can engage with calm confidence. When you are in tune with your own morals and values, you are best able to be in acceptance, no matter the outcome.

7) DAILY SELF-CARE: Develop and commit to a daily practice of self-care to ensure you are engaging in your relationships with a clear and focused mind, nourished and grounded body, forgiving heart and mindset of acceptance and understanding. Bookending Your Day: The Lighthouse Effect Self-Care 30-Day Challenge provides a way to practice self-care for all levels of your being––mind, body, and spirit.

Module IV (Conscious Communication) Session 6:
Skillful Recovery ~ Coping with Resistance & Conflict

Suggested Opening Meditation ~ Basic Mindfulness Meditation

Get into a comfortable position, and close your eyes or lower your gaze. (Sound chime or toning bowl.) Take three long, slow, deep breaths. With each inhalation, follow the cool air up through your nostrils and down into your lungs. Feel your breath expanding fully into the abdomen, and all the way through to your back. Now, slowly exhale through your mouth, completely emptying your lungs; notice the muscles softening in your shoulders, jaw, face, and back. With each exhalation, follow the softening of each muscle group down through your entire body. Continue to inhale and exhale, extending the breath each time, noticing how your body softens even more with each elongated exhalation. Notice how the movement of the breath gently rocks your body. Breathe in, breathe out; breathe in, breathe out; breathe in, breathe out. (Sound chime to bring the group to presence.) Slowly open your eyes and come back into presence. Allow yourself to carry this deep relaxation of your body through your day.

Check-Ins and Q&A: Ask your group to share how hearing about Rick's recovery experiences last week affected them; what resonated? And once again, as this is the halfway point in the module, invite group participants to share homework, journal reflections, or insights they've gained over the past six weeks of the module.

Handouts: Coping with Resistance & Conflict

Assertive Listening

Assertive listening is one of the most conscious and constructive of skills to apply when engaging in communications with another person. Assertive listening is about actively and respectfully *listening* while conversing and *expressing* our own thoughts and feelings with calm clarity. It balances attuning to and being present for the other person's perspectives with establishing boundaries and maintaining our own. That doesn't mean it's always smooth sailing; in some dynamics, we might find the other person is in resistance. There are multiple ways we can effectively respond to someone who is resisting what we are trying to say. Role-playing is a great way to practice how we might address resistance and conflict when they come up in interpersonal interactions. I find it to be one of the most effective ways of grounding concepts. (Encourage participants to continue to practice on their own with someone in their recovery network--their accountability partner, recovery coach, trusted friend, therapist, or another participant in their Lighthouse Effect Skillful Recovery group.)

TIP: Review the How to Wisely Upgrade handout from Module II before going through the Coping with Resistance & Conflict handout with the group.

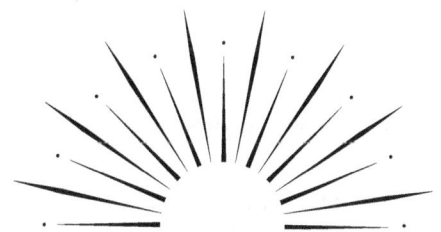

THE LIGHTHOUSE EFFECT
Coping with Resistance & Conflict

What do you do when someone is not listening to you? Even when we apply the skill of Assertive Listening in our communications with others, it is not always smooth sailing; in some dynamics, we might find the other person is in resistance. There are effective strategies we can use in concert with Assertive Listening to effectively respond to someone who is resisting or unable to hear what we are saying.

Role-playing is a great way to practice addressing resistance and conflict in interpersonal interactions. Practice with someone in your recovery network, another group member, your accountability partner, recovery coach, trusted friend, or therapist. These well established DBT precepts have been modified to align with The Lighthouse Effect core premise of moving from survival to revival through mind, body, spirit integration.

Resistance & Conflict Strategies

Mutual Validation
Broken Record
Probing
Clouding (Assertive Agreement)
Assertive Delay

Mutual Validation: This strategy acknowledges and demonstrates appreciation for the other person's experience, needs, and desires. You are putting yourself in the other person's shoes, while at the same time, asserting your own experience with confidence and from a place of presence. You are grounded and in vertical alignment with your Higher Self.

I understand that you think you are being supportive when you offer unsolicited advice about my personal affairs. I can appreciate your good intentions. On my end, you aren't checking in with me to see if it is what I need or want, and your repetitive advising triggers me. I feel like you don't believe I have ideas and possible solutions.

I wonder if you can show your support in a different way? Maybe by asking questions and being curious about what it is that I need from you, instead of jumping to the conclusion that I need your advice.

It makes sense that you would want to drive, since you travel this route so often and have more experience driving it than I do; I am in agreement with you. However, I think you should know the reason I prefer to be the driver on long trips is because I am less likely to get vertigo when I'm keeping my eyes focused on the road, especially on winding roads. With the intention of meeting both of our needs and desires, how about we share the driving? You drive for the first part of the trip since the roads are straighter, and I'll take over for the second half, when the roads become more curvy.

Broken Record: It is what it sounds like, a strategy where you repeat yourself in different ways when the other person is not receiving what you are trying to convey in the way that you are intending. You repeat yourself until the person can "hear" you. It's about stepping into the higher vibrations of Emotional Mind to come into balance with Rational Mind and align with Wise Mind, where you can think and speak with clarity and emotional calmness.

Make a clear statement about what you want, using simple language, a calm voice, and a matter-of-fact delivery. Vary the language to repeat essentially the same statement. Avoid engaging in an argument or trying to enforce your position. Don't take it personally. Don't over-explain yourself or offer additional evidence, as it can distract from your assertive stance and lead you astray. Use language such as, "I just prefer it that way," or "that's how I feel about it."

YOU: *I've noticed you keep parking your car very close to mine. I'm uncomfortable with how close it is to my car. I'm afraid you might inadvertently hit my car with your door when you're getting in and out, or that I might hit yours. I'm wondering if you could park about a foot farther away?*

THEM: *I've been parking that way for months and you never said anything about it before. I think you are being paranoid.*

YOU: *I am saying it now. I think it's too close for comfort and I'd appreciate it if you would simply park farther away to allow for more room for both of us.*

THEM: *Relax! I'm a good driver and I haven't hit your car yet.*

YOU: *I'm concerned about it. I'm asking you to make a minor adjustment to park a bit further away from my car. It will feel more spacious and I will be less likely to accidentally hit your car.*

THEM: *Why have you gotten so nervous about it all of a sudden?*

YOU: *I am asking you, could you kindly park your car farther away?*

Probing: This is a strategy for getting to the core of the issue, using "what" questions. The idea is to keep asking questions, deeply listen, and consciously weigh the other person's responses until you both have clarity and understand each other's perspectives.

THEM: *You're not following the format that I'm used to with your new program approach.*

YOU: *What is it about this format that doesn't land well with you?*

THEM: *We are used to having it set up a certain way, and the new way doesn't work for us because it is different and confusing.*

YOU: *Could you say more about what is causing the confusion?*

THEM: *When you started this recovery program, we thought it was going to be similar to how other facilitators ran the program. Because you have rearranged certain topics, used different terms, and added new material that we are not familiar with, it is causing us to feel misunderstood, disrespected, and not considered.*

YOU: *I really appreciate you bringing this to my attention and explaining your concern further. I will do my best to work this out with you and the rest of the participants. It is my intention to create an environment of learning where everyone feels safe, understood, and respected.*

Clouding: This strategy is also about being in vertical alignment, rather than linear. It also has a "Both/And" element, as it's about agreeing in part with the other person's perspective. It's not about swaying them to your point of view, or accepting all of what they are saying.

You can acknowledge that some of what they are saying rings true with you, while also calmly conveying your own experience, which serves to de-escalate a potential conflict and allow you to move toward a resolution.

THEM: *You can be so defensive when I point out things you are not getting done.*

YOU: *It's true, I do try to stand up for myself if I think someone is negatively judging me, especially considering what I am going through in my life. I can take it personally and be reactive instead of mindfully responding.*

THEM: *You never give me as much attention as you give to your work; you don't even call me back.*

YOU: *It's true, there were several times when I didn't return your calls as quickly as I had in the past.*

Notice how clouding actually clears the way for healthy conversation, as it indicates you are hearing the other person and want to work it out with them. Acknowledging the truth of part of their statement from a centered, self-reflective position provides stable ground for negotiating a resolution that benefits both of you.

Assertive Delay: This strategy is essentially about taking a timeout, whether for a moment, an hour, a day, or an even longer stretch of time. A key element is to be clear about the time frame and come to an agreement about when you will re-engage in the conversation; ideally, that would be when both of you are prepared to apply assertive listening. It's about stepping back in order to contemplate what was said, reflect on your role in the triggered exchange (Reflective Inquiry), and be prepared to mindfully respond, rather than react. It is an especially beneficial strategy when things begin to emotionally escalate and give rise to anger and threats, in which case, neither person is present or centered.

You've told me a lot, and I need time to sift through and see what I think. Can we come back to this after work tonight?

Give me a few hours to regroup. This is important, and I want to reflect on what you've said and think carefully about it, so I can respond in a way that's respectful to both of us.

Group Exercise ~ Coping with Resistance & Conflict

Walk the group through the handout, addressing each of the five skills and using your whiteboard to underscore the concepts and reflect the group's insights.

It goes without saying that when communication turns conflictual and resistance arises, it isn't pleasant for anyone, which is why we tend to avoid having a conversation that has potential for a conflict to arise over differences of opinion, morals, or values. But in the long term, avoidance does not serve us or the other person. When we learn to convey what we most value and enjoy in our relationships and express ourselves from a place of common ground, we set the stage for a healthy relationship. From a foundation of mind-body-spirit alignment, we practice and model self-awareness, self-respect, and self-confidence, and cultivate healthy dynamics where we can negotiate through conflicts in ways that benefit both or all. Essentially the core to any healthy relationship requires us to take a deep look within.

Suggested Closing Meditation ~ Observer Self Meditation

Get into a comfortable position, and close your eyes or lower your gaze. (Sound chime or toning bowl.) Sit up straight with your feet flat on the floor and your shoulders and jaw relaxed and open. Take three long, slow, deep breaths, exhaling longer with each breath. Take another deep breath; as you inhale, zoom in on a current challenge or conflict. See it in your mind's eye; notice how your body feels, notice where you might have tension. Now, slowly exhale and zoom out; breathe your way out to a safe distance and simply observe, without judgment.

Continue to observe from this broader perspective as you take another long, slow, deep inhalation. As you exhale, notice any changes in your emotional body or your physical body. Notice the softening of your muscles. Feel the power of your Observer Self and how it supports and protects your nervous system. One more deep inhalation, one more slow exhalation; feel the sense of security and stabilization throughout your body and mind. (Sound chime.) Now, slowly open your eyes and bring yourself back to the present. Know that you always have the ability to zoom out to a broader perspective.

Suggested Homework: Reflect in your journal on what you gained from the session, and practice role-playing during the week to use the skills in real time. Be prepared to share your experience of applying these skills with the group to stimulate discussion and connection at the next session.

Module IV (Conscious Communication) Session 7:

How To Say No Skillfully and Gracefully ~ Applying Assertiveness Scripts

Suggested Opening Meditation ~ Facilitator's Choice: Choose a mediation that has resonated with you and your group.

Check-Ins and Q&A: Encourage participants to reflect over the past week and share examples of relationship challenges where the dynamic improved when they applied conscious relationship skills.

Handouts: Assertiveness Scripts & Integrating the Components of Being Assertive, Assertiveness Scripts Exercise, The Lighthouse ALIGN Guideline for Conscious Negotiations

How to Say No Skillfully and Gracefully

Have you ever been too quick to say yes when others ask you for a favor? We "helpers" have a tendency to say yes, even when it is not in our best interest or, as it often turns out, the other person's. It is an unhealthy habit and one that people (especially friends and family) can take advantage of, whether unconsciously or consciously. We can change that pattern by practicing how to say no in ways that are kind and respectful, both to ourselves and to the other person.

When we first practice setting healthy boundaries, it may feel uncomfortable, like walking around with one foot in a bucket--especially for those of us who unconsciously took on a helper role in childhood as our way to cope. We are programmed to make others feel supported, considered, and cared for. Secretly, we might want others to reciprocate our generous and supportive nature, which leads to feelings of disappointment and resentment. When those feelings bubble up within us, we can simply acknowledge them and recognize them as indicator lights. In this case, they are signaling us that we need to look at our core beliefs about how we relate to others. By noticing feelings as they arise, we can take responsibility for our own behavior and how we respond.

Years ago, I came up with a mantra to help me move out of my default helper programming and address feelings of guilt around saying no: *Self-care is not selfish; it is soulish.*

When I started to practice saying no, I would often notice how the body language or reaction of the other person was what I humorously call "sad face." Given my accommodating nature and helper role, I enjoy (and feel safer) getting a "happy face" reaction, but I have come to see that it is an addictive behavior and quick-fix reaction that does not support my wellbeing or the other person's in the long term. In my case, the addiction is codependency. Running a story in my mind about how someone should give me the supportive behavior I gave them or that they should *know* how to behave with more respect and consideration for me doesn't do either of us any favors.

My fear that the other person will abandon me because I rejected them is at the root of my desire to avoid "sad face." It is essentially a withdrawal symptom. To help build tolerance and move out of that default reaction, I continuously remind myself that it is okay to say no to someone, which brings me back to my mantra: self-care is not selfish, it is soulish. It is a more honest and loving way to be in a relationship with anyone, even if it means they are disappointed in the moment. Though we might be programmed to want and expect others (family members, partners, friends) to do it for us, it has to come from within. Looking to our own needs and desires is how we develop healthier relationships with others. The good news is, the more we practice, the easier it becomes.

In the same way that I might tell the group, *If you got really good at your addiction, you have the potential to be really good at recovery*, in this context, I'll say, *If you are masterful at helping others, you have the skills to be masterful at self-care. You simply need to direct that energy and effort inward.* It's a matter of prioritizing: Respect yourself by helping yourself first.

Practicing Your Way from Victim to Victor!

We cannot become fully aligned, mind, body, and spirit, until we fully come into a mindset of acceptance, understanding, and compassion. I have heard it said, "It's a house of mirrors out there!" For me, that sums up how, when we come from a place of victim consciousness, we set ourselves up to always be looking for someone or something to blame, rather than be accountable for ourselves. To become a victor, we want to look at our victim story as an indicator light that is flagging an underlying, negative core belief we hold, and then practice Reflective Inquiry in real time to understand why we keep playing that same story out. When we can acknowledge the role of our victim story and the lessons it might offer, we can begin to change it to a story of victory.

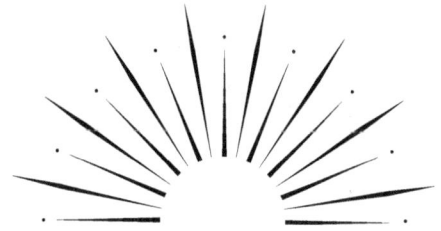

THE LIGHTHOUSE EFFECT
Assertiveness Scripts & Integrating the Components of Being Assertive

Applying assertiveness skills in our daily lives is a critical component in maintaining and formulating healthy long-term relationships, as they help us to avoid falling into passive or aggressive patterns that destroy the fabric of trust and intimacy. Assertiveness in this sense is about expressing our needs with calm clarity and in a manner that does not put the other person in defense mode.

Assertiveness is most easily learned by using a simple script. It gives us structure for what we want to say and keeps us focused. It also helps us to prepare for a conversation by practicing the script (on our own or with someone we trust) so that we can express ourselves with greater confidence. Importantly, we still want to be present in the moment and engage in active listening, and not get stuck in the script.

ASSERTIVENESS FORMULA: I THINK, I FEEL, I WANT, I PROPOSE

I THINK: Present the facts and your understanding of what is going on, without judgment, without making assumptions about the other person's motives, and without attacking or blaming the other person. Give a clear description of the events and experiences that you need to talk about and, perhaps, change. Notice that the "I think" statements below are not emotional and do not convey disapproval.

It seems we haven't spent much time together lately; I think it was just two nights last week, one the week before.

I think you may have billed me for a repair that I didn't authorize.

Checking in on the recent past, I think you've been late for most of our meetings.

I'm curious about some of these rules and I think I need to know more; could you help me understand this one?

I FEEL: Give a brief description of emotions triggered by the situation, in a way where you take ownership of your feelings. These are commonly referred to as "I" statements in the wellness field. We may not use them in all situations; for example, it would be beneficial to express our emotional experience to a friend or family member, but probably not with our auto mechanic.

I feel scared.
I feel lonely.
Lately, I feel sad about us.
I feel hurt, and that makes me want to give up on us.
I feel kind of lost and invisible, and more and more disconnected.
I feel rejected.

While "I" statements are about taking ownership of our emotions, "you" statements are likely to be perceived as accusations. When we use "you" statements, we are judging and blaming, and setting up a dynamic where the other person is defensive and less willing to listen to us or validate our experience.

You made me sad.
You don't care about us.
You're always late.

We need to be careful to not present a "you" statement as an "I" statement, where we are not really taking ownership about our emotional experience and are blaming the other person.

I feel that you're the cause of all of our problems.
I feel that you're being selfish.
I feel that you're manipulating me.

I WANT: This is the primary point of assertiveness. It is about asking for behavioral changes, not personality or attitudinal changes. We can't reasonably expect someone to change what they believe or feel, but we can ask them to change a behavior that is having a negative impact: we can ask them to change how they act and what they do. We don't want to give a laundry list, but, rather, ask for one change at a time and for something that can reasonably happen now or in the near future.

Avoid futurizing. For example, "The next time we go on vacation, I want you to ..." is a poor "I want" statement because it'll be long forgotten when the next vacation finally arrives. Be specific and concrete. Vague requests like "I just want you to be nicer" are not conducive to behavioral change because they are too vague. Describe what new behavior you expect, and say when and where you want it to occur. For example:

I want to experience a healthy relationship with you. When I say I want you to be "nicer" what I mean is, I want you to be aware of the manner in which you communicate with me. I ask that the next time we talk, please speak with a calm tone of voice and look directly at me, with curiosity and openness.

I want to feel that you are a safe person I can share anything with without being judged or advised. I am looking for emotional containment, where I feel like you have my back.

I want to experience confidence in our communications with one another where we both feel mutually supported and fully heard. I am asking that we both practice being conscious and present in our relationship by checking-in with ourselves at the beginning of the conversation the next time we talk, to both commit to having a meaningful conversation where we are able to be fully present with one another.

I want to experience love and connection with you in a way that we are both choosing to take good care of ourselves (mind, body, and spirit) so that we can demonstrate and reflect loving kindness for one another when we are together.

I Propose (Self-Care Solution): This is about protecting your rights and boundaries and is a way to demonstrate to the other person that you are capable of taking care of your own needs.

If you aren't prepared to leave for the party on time, I can take my own car and meet you there.

If you are unable to help with the cleaning, I can hire a maid and we can share the expense.

If you want to drive without insurance, I can transfer the title to your name and you can take over the payments as well.

INTEGRATING THE COMPONENTS OF BEING ASSERTIVE

Sample Script #1

I think: *It's been three years since we've had a cost-of-living raise, and prices have increased more than ten percent in that time.*

I feel: *I feel left out, because the convenience store is doing well and I'm not participating in that success.*

I want: *I would like a ten percent cost-of-living adjustment soon so my income can keep pace with inflation.*

I propose: *If we can't work this out, I'm going to have to look for something else so I can better support my family.*

Sample Script #2

I think: *I've been working against a deadline tonight and I think I won't have time to cook dinner.*

I feel: *I'm feeling pretty anxious and overwhelmed that I might not get my work done on time.*

I want: *Could you whip something together from leftovers, so I can keep going?*

I propose: *If that doesn't work for you, I can order pizza.*

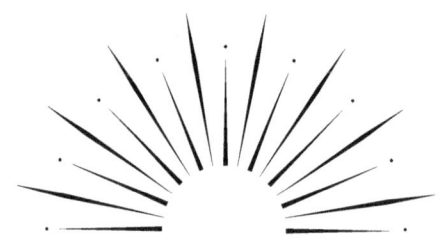

THE LIGHTHOUSE EFFECT
Assertiveness Scripts Exercise

STEP ONE: Identify three relationship dynamics where something feels wrong and you want things to change, and use them as opportunities to practice assertiveness.

Opportunity Example

Relationship issue: *My boyfriend is always late when he comes to pick me up and it triggers my sense that I'm not worthy.*

What I want to change: *I want him to know how I feel and I want to ask him to effort to show up on time.*

Opportunity #1

Relationship issue: _____
_____
_____

What I want to change: _____
_____
_____

Opportunity #2

Relationship issue: _____
_____
_____

What I want to change: _____
_____
_____

Relationship issue: _____
_____
_____

What I want to change:

_____

_____

_____

STEP TWO: Create an assertiveness script for each of the opportunities you've identified.

Opportunity #1

I think:

_____

_____

_____

_____

I feel:

_____

_____

_____

_____

I want:

_____

_____

_____

_____

I propose:

_____

_____

_____

_____

Opportunity #2

I think:

_____

_____

_____

_____

I feel:

_____

_____

_____

I want:

_____

_____

_____

I propose:

_____

_____

_____

Opportunity #3

I think:

_____

_____

_____

I feel:

_____

_____

_____

I want:

_____

_____

_____

I propose:

_____

_____

_____

Group Exercise ~ Assertiveness Scripts

Walk your group through the Assertiveness Scripts & Integrating the Components of Being Assertive handout and have them do the exercise together, using your whiteboard to reflect their responses.

The Lighthouse Effect Skillful Recovery program is about thriving--moving from survival to revival. Creating and maintaining conscious relationships is essential to moving toward wholeness and thriving in our lives. It takes a conscious choice and a willingness to commit to a daily practice to upgrade from our default survival patterns. It is an inside job that requires us doing our inner work, and to then model mindful presence and conscious behavior in our relationships. When we consider and reflect back others' perspectives while also conveying and advocating for our needs, we begin to build mutual trust and respect.

How to Negotiate

It is an art to effectively communicate and negotiate a resolution when a conflict arises. It requires being clear and firm about our own needs and desires, while being open and flexible to hearing and accommodating the needs and desires of someone else. It can be especially challenging when the other person's needs do not sync up with ours or even seem to be in direct opposition. It is an art--and one that we can develop with practice. It is also about being in alignment with our own morals and values, as in the Valued Living work we explored in Module II. To engage in conscious negotiations with someone, we need to be grounded, present, and mindful: in other words, in vertical alignment, mind, body, and spirit. Consider the following DBT-based solutions and compromises to common conflicts:

Balance of Power: *I'll deal with the realtor and bank on the sale of the house; you deal with the moving company.*

Take Turns: *I'm good to go hiking this weekend if we can go to the beach next weekend.*

Both/And: *You love Niam Leeson, go ahead and watch the movie again; I'm happy to dive into the book I just got from the library.*

Trial Run: *Let's try your way for two weeks, and then reevaluate. If it's working, great; if not, let's go back to the table.*

My Turn/My Way: *I know you love your stainless steel pan and the stir-fry you made us last night was delicious, but I'm cooking tonight and I love my cast iron, so I'll be doing my salmon dish in it.*

Take Turns: *I'll do the laundry and house cleaning this month, if you can mow the lawn and tend the garden; and we'll switch next month.*

Compromise: *I can give up on finding a hotel with a pool and hot tub, as long as there's a bathtub in the room.*

Split the Difference: *I advertised the sale of my car for $5500 on Craig's list and you are offering $5000. How about we split the difference, and make it $5250.00?*

Suggested Closing Meditation ~ I Am Worthy Meditation

Get into a comfortable position, and close your eyes or lower your gaze. (Sound chime or toning bowl.) Take three slow, deep breaths and allow a sense of stillness to penetrate your entire body. Feel this stillness clearing your mind. Tell yourself, *I am worthy*, as you take another slow, deep breath all the way into your belly; breathe out even more than before. Again, breathe in, *I am worthy*. Allow this sense of self-worth and self-value to penetrate every cell of your body; breathe out. Breathe in, *I am worthy*. Allow this deep sense of tranquility to penetrate your mind; breathe out even more fully than before. Breathe in, *I am grateful to know that I am worthy*. Allow gratitude to fill your body and clear your mind; breathe out slowly and completely. (Sound chime.) Slowly open your eyes, and return to the circle. Now carry this energy of worthiness with you and within you as you move through your day.

Suggested Homework: Reflect in your journal what you gained from this session. Review the ALIGN guideline and practice it in real time this week with your friends and family. Bring in your experiences of applying these skills to share with the group in the next session.

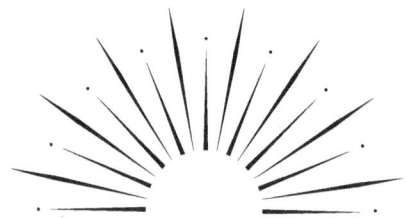

THE LIGHTHOUSE EFFECT
ALIGN Guide for Conscious Communication

A: ACCEPT. Radically accept conflict with the understanding that it isn't personal, or at least, it isn't against you; consider that, ultimately, it's for you. When we come from the perspective that conflicts are opportunities to practice conscious communication skills, we create healthier relationships. When we stand in alignment with our own morals and values, we are better able to accept others' views, even or especially when their values, needs, or concerns differ from ours. A simple way to come into alignment when a conflict arises is through the breath, mindful visualization, and taking "the lighthouse stance."

Take a long slow deep breath before you engage. Drop your shoulders and relax your jaw as you slowly exhale. Feel your feet planted firmly on the floor or ground—the bedrock of your lighthouse. Feel the stability of your feet grounding you there, right where you are. Straighten your spine, your lighthouse tower; feel how you are grounded and yet reaching toward the sky, connecting to spirit. Feel the calming energy of this integration of mind, body, and spirit.

L: LISTEN. Apply assertive listening to really hear, try to understand, and acknowledge the other person's perspective. Try to listen without judgment and without reacting emotionally or defensively. Be aware of your body; if it tenses up, take a slow, deep breath before you speak. Notice any urges or default reactions that send you into defensive mode and then turn your mind; focus on the other person from a place of compassion for them and their needs. Before responding, take a pause to avoid default responses, and instead, offer a considered, assertive response, speaking calmly and clearly.

I: INVITE. Be invitational and committed to hearing the other person. Use assertiveness skills as needed in the moment, paying attention to barriers to listening, asking questions to get clarity, inviting the other person to ask questions, and so on. Hold to your own values and needs, while being flexible and willing to compromise. Set an intention that the desired outcome be fair and mutually agreeable, where both of you benefit and get most of your needs met.

G: GUIDE. Be clear with yourself about your morals and values in the context of being in a conscious relationship. Guide your thoughts, emotions, and potential default reactions in accordance with Wise Mind, applying the practice of Reflective Inquiry as you go:

Is the reactionary thought I am having a Capital-T Truth, or a small-t truth arising from a fear or survival instinct? How do I want to be treated?

What is my vision for this relationship, or for the outcome of this conflict or potential conflict? What do I want to co-create in my relationship with this person?

Ask the other person what works best for them when a conflict arises. Let the inner light of your Authentic Self shine and guide you through the process.

N. NEUTRALITY. Be present and mindful. Take a neutral demeanor, which means to be neither forward nor aggressive, reserved nor passive. Be open to what transpires, with no agenda other than a mutually agreeable outcome. Practice balance and being in your "still point" within the eye of the hurricane.

Module IV (Conscious Communication) Session 8:
Group Mirror Work ~ Bringing Attention and Intention into Relationships

Suggested Opening Meditation ~ Tuning In Radio-Frequency Meditation

Get into a comfortable, receptive position and close your eyes or lower your gaze. (Sound chime or toning bowl.) Take three slow, deep breaths to bring yourself to this present moment. Now, as you continue to breathe deeply, imagine that your mind is a radio, giving and receiving signals. Imagine that your emotions are the radio frequencies or channels. Set your radio to the frequency you desire. Set it to love, or acceptance, or gratitude, whatever you desire in this moment; keep adjusting the dial until you get the frequency where the energy flows freely without static or distorted electronic sounds. Continue to breathe deeply. Notice how it feels in your physical body, your mind, your emotional body to be tuned in. Do you feel energized? Do you feel relaxed. Feel into your experience of being tuned in. Take one more deep inhalation, and one more full exhalation. (Sound chime.) Slowly open your eyes, and return to presence. Know that you can tune in to the frequency you want anytime!

Check-Ins and Q&A: Encourage participants to keep check-ins brief and to focus on how they are applying communications skills in their daily lives and challenging situations. Take the opportunity to point out progress when you observe it with the group. Comment on how challenging it is to do this work, yet at the same time, how rewarding and beneficial it is as a practice of self-acceptance, self-respect, and self-empowerment.

Handouts: Clearing Protocol for Bringing Attention & Intention into Relationships

The Clearing Protocol

The more we engage in inner work and apply our self-reflection skills, the higher our probability of experiencing healthier relationships with ourselves and with others. The Clearing Model or Clearing Protocol is a peer-to-peer process for engaging in dialogue. It serves as a process for conflict resolution, and I find it to also be a highly effective and transformative element of experiential therapy in terms of self-empowerment and self-mastery. As with Byron Katie's "The Work" and the practice of self-inquiry or what I call Reflective Inquiry, I have adapted the Clearing Protocol and woven it into The Lighthouse Effect Skillful Recovery Program as another process for deep inner work. As a role-playing exercise, participants can demonstrate and practice in real time what they have learned throughout the program about self-work, self-reflection, and the power of "knowing thyself."

How it works is that the facilitator invites someone to volunteer to do "a clearing" with another group member, either with the other group member playing the role of someone they are having a conflict or tension with in their life, or to work out tension or a conflict they have with that fellow group member. Because the latter is a deeper, more intense process, it's at the facilitator's discretion to proceed, taking into consideration the comfort level of the group. At this point, this far into the program, the group is likely to have established a strong, safe container for the deeper work, but again, it is up to you, the facilitator, based on your assessment.

If you have observed tension between members of the group or if someone has complained to you about another member, you might speak to each person privately prior to the next session, when the group will be doing a clearing in real time. Ask if they would be prepared to do a clearing, and if they say yes, ask if they would like to do it as themselves or as a role-playing exercise. If you have limited experience facilitating a Clearing Protocol, consider asking a colleague who has experience to co-facilitate to provide support for the process.

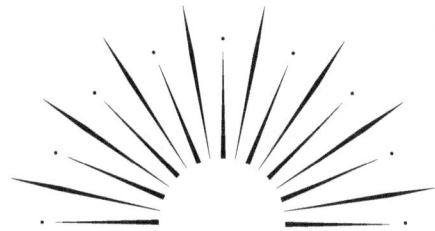

THE LIGHTHOUSE EFFECT
Clearing Protocol for Bringing Attention & Intention into Relationships

GROUP INTENTION: Our intention as a group is to work toward an integrated Self, and to support the members of our group who are engaged in a clearing in their process. The "Initiator" is the person initiating a clearing, and the "Mirror" is the person they invite to do a clearing with them. The Mirror might engage as their self or they night play the role of someone in the Initiator's life. Essentially, the Clearing Protocol provides the Initiator with their day in court. This process is not about passing judgment or blaming, but rather about acknowledging the other's experience, while being self-accountable at the same time. Essentially, the process reflects or mirrors the part or parts of ourselves that we deny or suppress. Clearing is a cathartic experience that ultimately helps both participants heal the wounds of negative core beliefs.

GROUP PURPOSE: Our purpose as a group is to create a safe container where we can learn how to be present with one another without losing our sense of self. Our purpose in coming together is to learn skills, techniques, and communication strategies that help us surf the waves of stress, conflict, addictive patterns, and seemingly uncontrollable emotions. Our purpose is to practice being more accepting and compassionate towards ourselves and others as we engage in our individual and collective healing processes and recovery journeys--from surviving to thriving!

TAKING THE OPPORTUNITY TO CLEAR: It is each person's choice to enter into the clearing process. This is deep inner work that takes courage and a willingness to heal. It is a universal truth in any tribe, family, or community system that we intuitively know when there are tensions or unresolved issues between members of the tribe. So, when we do enter into a clearing process, we help to build group cohesion by releasing some of that tension and empowering others to have the courage to do this intensive work.

THE INITIATOR & THE MIRROR: The "Initiator" is the person seeking to resolve an issue; the "Mirror" is the person the Initiator asks to do the clearing with them. When someone invites us to clear with them, it might (understandably) give rise to or trigger our own fears and bring up our defenses. It is vital that both people understand that the role of the person serving as the Mirror is to be a reflection, to allow the Initiator to address narratives, fears, and wounds that are surfacing for them; it is not personal to the Mirror. They did not create the Initiator's wounds! At the same time, it is an opportunity for the Mirror to hold up and reflect on their own fears. (It may be that the Mirror will then want to be an Initiator at another time to address what comes up for them.) Even so, it can feel rather intense when the Initiator might convey anger, blame, or judgment. The Mirror needs to understand the Initiator is in pain, which is an experience we can all relate to. It is the mirror aspect of this work. When we see how triggered the other person is, we can acknowledge our own pain.

It experientially teaches us how to be with pain, both our own and others' pain. For the other members of the group, observing the process is an intimate, emotional experience that fosters empathy, which can be profoundly healing for everyone and can serve to further strengthen group cohesion.

THE CLEARING DIALOGUE

1) Centering: This is about coming into balance, into your still point, by following the breath. Take three slow, deep breaths, following each inhalation through the nose and into your innermost core, and releasing tension and worry as you exhale through the mouth. Now, slowly and mindfully move your awareness out into the circle to embrace all group members. Know that you and every member of the group is valued and worthy of expressing your own voice and point of view without being judged.

2) Making Eye Contact: When speaking to another group member, it is always important to make direct eye contact with them to show respect for them and for yourself. It is especially important that the Initiator and Mirror make eye contact.

3) Clearing: Be clear and calm when you are inviting someone to clear with you and when you are responding to an invitation to clear. If you are the Initiator inviting someone to clear, you might say: *(Name), I want to do a clearing with you today. Would you accept*? The Mirror might reply: *Yes, I am willing to participate in a clearing with you.* The two participants in the clearing can ask members of the group to provide personal support during the process. Be specific about what you need and how they might support you. For example, Steve and Sally are doing a clearing, and Steve invites Joe to support him by standing behind him or to his side, while Sally invites Donna to support her by standing with her.

4) Ground Rules: Be careful to differentiate between a judgment and a feeling, and remember that our intention here is to bring our emotional experiences to the surface and validate them. For example, the Initiator might say, *When you did this, it made me feel this … .* OR, *When you said that, I felt … .* The Mirror simply listens and does not speak until the Initiator is finished speaking. The facilitator will check in with the Initiator to ensure they are "complete." It is up to the facilitator to remind the participants, as needed, that this is not about blame and shame, it is a process for resolving triggers and wounds that already exist, with the Mirror holding space for those wounds to be addressed.

5) Closing: The facilitator asks the Initiator if they are complete: *Did you feel heard*? *How do you feel*? The facilitator allows them time to not just say they are complete, but to feel and express that they are complete. Example of Completion Statement by an Initiator addressing a rejection wound: *I don't expect you to be my friend, or to like me, or to accept me for who I am. However, I want you to be my friend and to like me and accept me for who I am. What I truly need is for me to be a friend to me, to like myself, and to accept all of the parts of me that make me whole. I am the one I've always been waiting for.*

The facilitator asks the Initiator one more time if they are complete, and if they are, the facilitator invites the Mirror to respond with a clarifying statement to summarize what the Initiator said. Example of clarifying statements by the Mirror: *I heard you and I can imagine if I perceived what I said the way you did, I would feel the same way. What is not true for me about what you said is … . What I own about myself about what you said is … .*

Reframing: The Mirror might provide a reframing of what they heard, where they express accountability for what is true about the Initiator's complaint: *Had I been in a better place, I wouldn't have come on so strongly, I would have said it like this … . Now that I have heard your story and perspective, I am open and willing to be in this conscious growth process with you. Thank you for being in my life!*

Group Exercise ~ Understanding The Clearing Protocol

This is not a "live" exercise, where participants actually engage in a clearing process. That is the focus of the next session. This session is to introduce the concept. Walk your group through the Clearing Protocol handout, using your whiteboard to underscore key components and participants' reflections and insights.

It is essential when doing this work that we take responsibility for our own actions in order to move out of victim consciousness. Holding ourselves accountable for our mistakes actually gives us energy and helps us to feel lighter and more free: We can only be human, not perfect!

Suggested Closing Meditation ~ Tall Self Meditation

Sit comfortably in your chair and position your body to receive openly. Close your eyes or lower your gaze. (Sound chime or toning bowl.) Take three long, slow, deep breaths. Recall an experience when you were a child where you felt scared about something that wouldn't seem scary now. Maybe it was learning to ride a bike, or diving into a pool for the first time. Remember the feeling of fear you had about taking the risk to try something you had no experience in, and how *true* it felt that you couldn't possibly do it. Now, take another long, slow, deep breath, and step into your Tall Self; feel yourself getting taller, aligning vertically.

Breathe into this Tall Self version of you, the one who has had years or decades of experience taking risks, falling and getting up again, carrying on, developing the skills you need to ride a bike, drive a car, or dive into a pool, the one who is developing the skills you need to move from survival to revival. Now, take the hand of that small self, that child self, and reassure them: *We've got this*. Take another full inhalation, and full exhalation. (Sound chime.) Know that you can take the hand of the small self within you who is afraid, uncertain, or confused at any time. You always have the capacity to take three long, slow, deep breaths and align yourself with your Tall Self, the one who carries the wisdom of years and decades of experience. You have what it takes to listen to that tallest, wisest, and most resilient part of yourself no matter what challenges cross your path.

Suggested Homework: Reflect in your journal on what you gained from the session, focusing on what resonated and what you might find challenging about the Clearing Protocol. Remember that doing mirror work or any kind of inner work requires a willingness to "know thyself" on an emotional level; don't short-change yourself. This is the practice "from Victim to Victor" that we covered in an earlier session. Next week we are going to actually do a clearing! So come prepared to engage actively in a clearing, either as an Initiator, Mirror, or supportive group member.

Module IV Session 9: Role-playing & Clearing Protocol Practice

Suggested Opening Meditation ~ Eye of the Hurricane Meditation

Get into a comfortable, receptive position and close your eyes or lower your gaze. (Sound chime or toning bowl.) Breathe slowly and deeply, low into your belly and all the way into your back; engage your entire lung capacity. Exhale slowly and fully. Continue to breathe deeply, as you drop your jaw and shoulders. Notice any tension in your body and send your attention and your breath into those areas. Notice the tension leaving your body with each exhalation. Now, imagine that you are a lighthouse and there is a hurricane swirling about you; imagine how you stand within the eye of the hurricane--still, calm, and centered even as the storm rages around you.

Continue to be the lighthouse as you breathe. Feel the strength of your body. Feel your feet planted firmly on the ground where you stand, or your back against the chair where you sit. Notice how you are completely supported. Allow yourself to be held in the embrace of the present moment. Call in your higher power and take another full-body breath into this vision of you, the lighthouse. Imagine that higher power as warm light emanating from within you and from all around you. As you exhale, allow your entire body to feel the warmth and safety of this nonphysical connection within your physical being.

Continue to breathe deeply. Now, notice the sea, your emotional waters; simply notice from a distance, from your lighthouse tower; observe any worry-thoughts stirring the waters. Notice what happens when you send those thoughts loving attention. Notice the calming effect. Notice how it is easier to see and feel them from a distance. Continue to breathe deeply, as you allow yourself to simply be with them in this way, observing without resistance, without fear, and simply with loving acceptance. Now, slowly turn your attention back to your foundation, your lighthouse-self, and allow yourself to fully align with your center, your still point within. Notice how it feels to be sovereign--to stabilize and anchor your mind, in alignment with the moment, in alignment with your authentic power. Take one more deep inhalation, and one more full exhalation. (Sound chime.) Slowly open your eyes and come into the present moment. Carry this sense of yourself as the lighthouse, your own safe refuge, rooted in bedrock and sheltered from life's stormy seas with you. Call it up whenever you face challenges or sudden storms in your life!

Check-Ins and Q&A: Encourage group participants to focus their check-ins on current life situations that relate to the ALIGN handout, and field questions about the Clearing Protocol before entering the role-playing practice.

Handouts: Refer back to The Clearing Protocol handout from the previous session.

Group Exercise ~ The Clearing Protocol & Mirror Work

This session picks up from the previous session and provides the time and opportunity for participants to engage in a Clearing Protocol in real time. Use the Clearing Protocol and Clearing Dialogue handouts provided in the previous session to guide the process.

Ask for a volunteer to be the Initiator and to choose another member to be the Mirror. That person can accept or decline. *Yes, I accept*, or, *I pass*. Determine whether the Initiator has chosen that person to play the role of someone else in their life, or if it is to work out a conflict with that particular group member. The latter is more intense. Use your discretion as the facilitator to determine whether it might be more effective and appropriate to do the "role-playing" alternative. For example, if the Initiator says they want to clear with Brenda *"because she always cuts me off, just like my sister."* As the facilitator, you might ask both the Mirror and Initiator if it will work for Brenda to engage as herself, or if she might instead role play as the sister. It is essential that all participants are clear about and comfortable with their roles and how they participate. And, inside joke, it isn't a "comfortable" process.

Sample Prompt Questions:

Who wants to volunteer to be the Initiator?
Who do you want to be your Mirror?
Do you want the Mirror to play the role of someone in your life you are having a conflict or tension with? Or do you want to work out a conflict you have with the Mirror?

If the person invited to be the Mirror accepts the invitation, the process can begin. It's an opportunity for both participants to draw upon the skills they've learned in every module: mindfulness, building tolerance, emotional balancing, and conscious communication. And it helps underscore these skills and concepts for the other members of the group as they observe and hold space for the two people engaged in the clearing. Encourage participants observing the process and holding space to reflect on what resonates for them. It is an opportunity for mind-body-spirit integration, toward healing negative core beliefs from childhood and stepping fully into our Authentic Self.

Suggested Closing Meditation ~ The Mirror Meditation

Get into a comfortable position, and close your eyes or lower your gaze. (Sound chime or toning bowl.) Take three slow, deep breaths to come fully into presence. Think about all the times you are considerate, forgiving, and kind to others. Now, imagine you are looking in the mirror at yourself. Being perfectly honest, how do you treat yourself? Are you considerate, forgiving, and kind? How might it feel if you treated yourself the way you treat others? Continue to breathe gently and naturally, as you imagine telling yourself, *I will be considerate, I will be forgiving, I will be kind to me*. Notice how it feels in your body to give yourself permission to care for *you*. Let the feeling move through you.

Take one more full deep inhalation and exhalation. (Sound chime.) Slowly open your eyes and return to the room. Self-care is a process. Make a habit of looking in the mirror and committing to being considerate, forgiving, and kind to yourself no matter what is happening in your life. Afterall, it is a house of mirrors out there. Take care of your own reflection, it will serve you well!

Suggested Homework: In your journal, reflect on the Clearing Protocol and Mirror Work group exercise and what came up for you. Please be prepared to share your experience during check-ins at the next session.

Perhaps your challenges and your resistance to "change" were put before you to strengthen you, to help you grow, to support your transformation from a caterpillar into a butterfly—the metamorphosis of life, from surviving to thriving!

--Faith Burrington Jones

Module IV (Conscious Communication) Session 10:
Higher Power Alignment ~ Building a Relationship with your Higher Power

Suggested Opening Meditation ~ I Am of Light Meditation

Get into a comfortable, receptive position, and close your eyes or lower your gaze. (Sound chime or toning bowl.) Take three slow, deep breaths to bring yourself to the present moment. Now, take a deep breath and as you inhale, think, *I am of Light.* Breathe the thought all the way through you, and as you slowly exhale, allow your body to soften. Breathe in, *I am of Light, I am of Love.* Allow yourself to feel the energy of light and love flowing through your physical body, your emotional body, your mind. As you exhale, allow your body to soften even more. One more time. Breathe in, *I am of Light, I am of Love*, letting it seep into your core. Now exhale slowly, and allow your body to soften even more. (Sound chime.) Slowly open your eyes and return to the room and this present moment. Know that you can use the breath and "I Am" mantra at any time. Just breathe and really feel into it; feel the energy of the words permeating every cell of your body, every room in your mind. Allow your whole being to resonate with the energetic frequency that the words carry.

Check-Ins and Q&A: Encourage participants to focus on how they have been incorporating the clearing protocol work they did in the previous two sessions in their daily lives and interactions. Remind them to keep their check-ins brief so there is enough time for this session's content.

Handouts: Higher Power Activities & Practices, Connecting with your Higher Power Exercise

Higher Power Connection ~ Building a Relationship with your Higher Power

What does it mean to build a relationship with your higher power? What does that look like?

For some, the idea of a "relationship" with something so ethereal and intangible is a challenging concept. Even so, connecting to nonphysical reality, however we choose to define it or understand it, is essential to being in mind-body-spirit alignment. As many children do, as a child, I would ask my mother such unanswerable questions as, *where is God*? And, *if there is a powerful being named God, then why can't I go see him and meet him*? She would point skyward and tell me, "God lives in heaven." Though her explanation was difficult to conceptualize, I had a sense of *knowing* that she was somehow right. I could sense a connection to something that I couldn't physically see, and I could accept that "God" is a mystery that we don't need to *prove* exists. I also seemed to have an affiliation with the teachings of Jesus, about how to navigate life with all of its obstacles, unexpected twists and turns, and traumatizing events.

As an adult, I've come to appreciate that because we *can't* see or prove God (whatever or whoever God might be to us/the God of our understanding), our psyche is challenged to expand beyond physical reality and open us up to our spiritual nature. Whatever our language or understanding, we might simply think of our higher selves as the unseen guide posts or beacons that have supported us along the way; it might be the sense of peace or calm we feel in nature--being near water, hiking up a mountain, or walking in the woods. There are many ways to connect spiritually with the natural world and all that it has to offer.

When we are in recovery from anything that stops us in our tracks and holds us back--whether a traumatic event, a loss, or even a short illness or post-operative recuperation--we might see it as an opportunity to take a deeper look at the relationship between our mind, body, and spirit, or physical, psychological, and spiritual wellbeing.

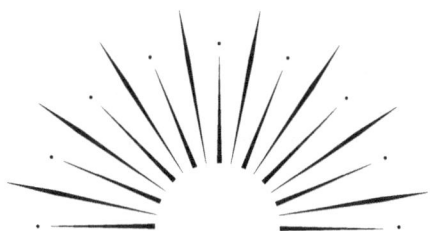

THE LIGHTHOUSE EFFECT
Connecting with Higher Power Activities & Practices

When we develop our connection to the nonphysical, Higher Power, Spirit, or God of our understanding, we gain an expanded perspective and capacity for moving from survival to revival.

MAKE CONNECTIONS. If you believe in the teachings of a particular religion or faith or are curious about one, consider exploring that community. Participate in events and/or gatherings. Reach out to the person who runs the services and other members and engage in conversations with them about the ways they move through challenges. Join support groups.

Ask people you trust what books they might recommend that would bring comfort, offer hope, and empower you on your journey to wellness. Find inspirational passages that resonate with you and keep them in close reach (wallet/phone/purse) so you can read them whenever you need a boost, wherever you are.

LOOK UP AT THE STARS. Feel the awe of the celestial expanse. Consider how the stars and planets you are seeing are millions of light years away, yet their light is reaching your eyes right now, here, this moment, on planet Earth. Consider that you and all that you see in the night sky are connected. Close your eyes and imagine that you are a conduit between the sky and the earth, channeling this flow of light, this Higher Power energy.

Take a slow, deep breath and imagine your legs are rooting downward, sending this star energy deep into the core of the earth. Feel the grounding power of the earth as you take another full breath, inhaling that earth energy up through your entire body, up through your heart, to the top of your crown, and out. Imagine beaming that light into the cosmos. Feel the power of the bioelectrical charge and fill your entire being with this Higher Power energy.

THINK ABOUT OUR PLANET. Earth is made up of the same elements that we are and held within the same energetic field. Consider how our bodies are sixty percent water and the earth's body is seventy percent water. Close your eyes and feel the life energy that flows within you and all around you. This life energy is present in the earth and every sentient being that lives upon her. Notice what happens in your body, your emotional body, and your mind, when you focus on this elemental truth. Do you feel more calm, more connected, more aligned with this living Higher Power energy?

IMMERSE YOURSELF IN NATURE. Walk in the woods, a park, a meadow, or up a mountain trail. Take notice of life all around you, the animals, plants, and insects that inhabit the environment and make up its ecosystem. Take pause; close your eyes, and breathe it all in. Breathe in the connection between everything that you are seeing; breathe it in with gratitude. Each living being is unique and special. There will never be another moment exactly like the one you are experiencing, the one you are breathing in; there will never be another moment when you are exactly as you are in *this* moment.

GO TO A BEACH OR IMAGINE BEING ON A BEACH. Consider the millions of grains of sand that make up the shore and how that sand is made up of shells, marine life, and minerals that have washed up from the ocean over millions of years. Sink your toes into the sand, take a deep full breath, and feel your connection within this vast expanse of time and our planet's history. Gaze across the ocean to where it meets the horizon, and feel its vastness and grandeur. Consider this Rumi quote: "You are not a drop in the ocean. You are the entire ocean in a drop." Breathe the wonder and truth of it into your being.

THINK ABOUT THE HUMAN BODY, ESPECIALLY YOUR OWN. Consider how your body is the vehicle that will carry you throughout your entire journey of life on this earth. Just like snowflakes, there will never be another body exactly like yours; it is as unique a creation as any work of art. Your DNA is specific to you, and carries forward from your lineage. In this way, your ancestors live within you. Your body is run by a powerful engine (Mind/Spirit) capable of extraordinary feats. Your body is magnificent. Invest in its wellbeing. Invest in your unique mind–body–spirit complex. Stand tall in your light: Embody the lighthouse effect!

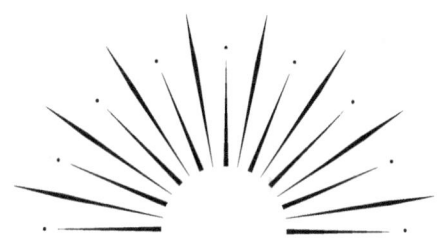

THE LIGHTHOUSE EFFECT
Connecting with your Higher Power Exercise

To come into alignment, mind, body, and spirit, we need to develop a relationship with the nonphysical, what we might call Spirit or our Higher Power. You may notice you have some resistance to engaging in exercises about spirituality or to using your creative imagination to connect to your Higher Power. You might be embarrassed and resistant to using your imagination if you grew up with caregivers who equated "imagination" with foolishness or childishness. We might trace any resistance to exploring spirituality back to our childhoods and how it impacted our belief systems, not just what we were taught by our caregivers, but what we picked up by their behavior, how they used language, what they conveyed about what was acceptable behavior and what was not. Explore whether the belief or the story around it that is causing resistance is valid. Is it true? Is it a Capital-T Truth?

1) What do you do to find inner strength, comfort, and peace? Close your eyes and imagine that sense of comfort and peace filling you. Breathe into the "felt sense" of that and consider that it is simply *you* connecting with your Higher Power.

_____

_____

_____

_____

2) Use your imagination to describe what you see and feel, whatever it may be, colors, shapes, energy, sounds, stillness.

_____

_____

_____

_____

3) What activities might you engage in that would nurture your connection with your Higher Power?

_____

_____

_____

_____

4) When you feel deeply into this connection, how does it influence how you feel about others, those you have good relationships with and those who challenge you?

_____

_____

_____

_____

5) What happens to your mind and body when you embrace this connection and spiritual perspective? Is there less tension? Fewer worry thoughts? Do you feel a sense of expansion and that you might be better able to face challenges?

_____

_____

_____

_____

6) Are you willing to bring connecting with your Higher Power into your daily practice? If so, how? What will that look like?

_____

_____

_____

_____

Group Exercise ~ Connecting with Your Higher Power

Walk the group through the handout, using your whiteboard.

Suggested Closing Meditation ~ River Wisdom Meditation

Get into a comfortable position and close your eyes or lower your gaze. (Sound chime or toning bowl.) Take three long, deep breaths and bring your attention inward. Visualize a winding river and watch as it flows downstream. Now, imagine you are the water, flowing smoothly and peacefully along, completely in harmony with your environment. Imagine you see an enormous rock up ahead, in the middle of the river. Continue to breathe gently and naturally as you observe the approaching obstacle. Notice how you intuitively flow around the rock; it does not stop you from moving forward. Think of a current challenge in your life; visualize it as another rock in the river. Simply notice that it is there, and then continue to breathe gently as you flow around it. Breathe in, slowly and deeply, letting this feeling of being river water move all the way through you. Breathe out, allowing your body to fully soften and relax. (Sound chime.) Slowly open your eyes and return to the group. Know that you can be as powerful, agile, and resilient as river water whenever you need to be; know that you can skillfully move past obstacles in your path.

Suggested Homework: Reflect in your journal what you gained from this session. Review the Higher Power Activities and Practices handout and commit to a daily practice of connecting with your higher power. Be prepared to share your reflections and insights at the next session.

Module IV (Conscious Communication) Session 11:
Stages of Change Reflection & Progress

Suggested Opening Meditation ~ The Five Senses Meditation

Get into a comfortable position, and close your eyes or lower your gaze. (Sound chime or toning bowl.) Take three long, slow, deep breaths to bring your attention inward. Now, as you slowly inhale, and slowly exhale, notice what you smell and continue to focus on your sense of smell as you breathe deeply. Now, bring your attention to your salivary glands; notice any taste sensations. Continue to breathe deeply, breathe in and breathe out, without judgment or commentary, focusing on any hint of taste. Move on to what you "see" behind your eyelids; notice shapes, colors, patterns, symbols, as you continue to slowly inhale and exhale. Now, as you continue to breathe deeply, move your attention to what you hear, in the room or outside of the room. Listen to the sound of your own breathing, hear the air moving in through your nose, and out through your mouth.

Continue to breathe slowly and deeply, as you move your attention to what you feel. Bring your attention back to the function of the breath. Breathe in through the nose, noticing how the breath feels as it moves down into your lungs. Feel the expansion of your diaphragm and allow your lungs to fill completely. Now, exhale, slowly and gently, following and feeling the sensation of the outflow of breath through your mouth. Feel into the deep peace of the breath. (Sound chime.) Slowly open your eyes and return to presence. Carry this felt sense of deep peace and relaxation throughout your day.

Check-Ins and Q&A: Have participants reflect on the homework from the previous session on Higher Power Alignment and/or any other aspects of this module they might want to reflect on.

Handouts: There are no new handouts for this session. You might choose elements or a handout from the upcoming Putting It All Together (PAT) chapter that would resonate with the group dynamics and underscore concepts that come up in the check-ins and Q&A. You might weave them into the upcoming closing session of this module (and of the program) too.

Group Exercise ~ Stages of Change Review, Repeat, & Reflect

As in the previous modules, bookend this module with a recap of Stages of Change. Review the SOC Model, and then have participants complete a new SOC Addiction/Recovery Pros & Cons Worksheet together as a group exercise, using your whiteboard, this time with the focus on conscious communications skills. Have them review the worksheets they completed individually as homework at the beginning of the module, reflect on notable changes, and share what progress they've made and what challenges they might still be facing. Invite them to also reflect on their Pros & Cons Worksheets from all of the previous modules and share their overall progress throughout the program.

If there is time, you might do a role-playing exercise around challenges participants indicate they are still facing or concepts they want more clarity on. This may include difficulty with the concept of "change" in general and how it manifests in their lives. I will often lead a group discussion on change and how we can look at it as *metamorphosis*, tying back to any previous discussions that might have come up in completing or reviewing the SOC Addiction/Recovery Pros & Cons Worksheets. You might want to ask them what they have learned about change, and how, though change may be challenging and scary, facing and moving through change leads to personal empowerment and healing into wholeness.

Suggested Closing Meditation ~ Metamorphosis Meditation

Sit comfortably with your eyes closed and your body completely open and relaxed. (Sound

335

chime or toning bowl.) Take three slow, deep breaths to breathe your way into this present moment. Imagine the process of transformation from a caterpillar into a butterfly, the magic and wonder of it all. Now consider the perspective of a caterpillar compared to the perspective of a butterfly. The caterpillar is unaware of the process of change that it is soon to experience, while the butterfly is the outcome of that change. Continue to breathe deeply, as you turn your mind's eye to the butterfly emerging from its cocoon and taking flight; imagine you are the butterfly. Breathe in; breathe out. Imagine the wisdom you carry now, having shed your old self and having completely changed your form. Breathe in; breathe out. Imagine what advice your butterfly-self could offer the caterpillar from this "higher" perspective.

Ponder what advice you might offer to comfort and encourage that caterpillar-self. Take another deep breath, and as you inhale, breathe in the courage and faith to face whatever changes are before you and view them from this higher perspective. As you exhale, release any resistance to change you might be holding. Take one more long, slow inhalation, and one more long, slow, exhalation. (Sound chime.) Slowly open your eyes and come back to the present moment. Allow yourself to be open and trust your personal journey of transformation and expansion. Consider how your butterfly-self feels, the power of your wings, and the liberty to fly free. Carry that feeling with you through your day.

Suggested Homework: Continue to practice and integrate all that you have learned in this module and commit to an ongoing practice of creating conscious relationships. Reflect on the major takeaways from the module and write about them in your journal. What were the highlights and what were the challenges? Be prepared to share your reflections with the group at the final session. Consider bringing art, poetry, a song, a story, or other works you created or that inspired you as you moved through the module to share with the group.

Module IV (Conscious Communication) Session 12:
Closing Ceremony & Graduation

Suggested Opening Meditation ~ Gratitude Meditation

Get into a comfortable, receptive position and close your eyes or lower your gaze. (Sound chime or toning bowl.) Take three slow deep breaths as you feel yourself come fully into this moment. Focus on the gentle lull of your breathing. Feel your body softening more and more with each exhalation. Now, using your creative imagination, breathe in the felt sense of the word "gratitude." What color is it? What does it feel like in your body as it flows through you? Continue to breathe gently and naturally. Now, think of the people, places, and things you are grateful for. See them in your mind's eye. Now, take another full, deep breath, as you reflect on simple daily pleasures that bring a sense of appreciation and gratitude into your life. Take another full, deep breath, and turn your attention to you. Reflect on the positive aspects of your personality and your unique way of being in the world. Take one more full deep inhalation, breathing gratitude all the way into your being; one more full exhalation, as you fully relax your body. (Sound chime.) Slowly open your eyes and return to the present moment. Commit to a daily practice of gratitude, not just for others and what is outside of you, but for you. Reflect in your Gratitude Journal all the ways you are grateful for yourself; acknowledge your willingness to practice, your willingness to forgive yourself for being human; your willingness to let go of the past and allow the energy of gratitude to heal you. Carry this high frequency practice throughout your day and shine your light, best as you can.

Check-ins and Q&A: Open up the check-in by sharing your gratitude to the group for their trust in you to provide a safe container and to guide them through their process of discovery and recovery as they moved through the program. Encourage group participants to focus their check-ins on their appreciation, reflection, and takeaways from the module and the entire program. What were the highlights? What were the challenges?

Handouts: The Six-Pointed Star Model, Module IV Completion Certificate, LHE Program Completion Certificate, The Lighthouse Effect Putting It All Together (PAT) Packet

TIP: If your facility/agency does group evaluations this would be the time to have the group complete them and offer any feedback they believe would improve the group experience.

The Six-Pointed Star

What I have come to understand as heart-mind coherence is demonstrated in The Lighthouse Effect Six-Pointed Star Model. It is where mind, body, and spirit are fully integrated and in complete alignment. The ego and the soul have merged through the heart, and this integration is fully felt and realized throughout the entire human energy field. The upper triangle represents the Soul Self and unity consciousness, where the lower, inverted triangle represents victim consciousness. When they merge, they become a six-pointed star, symbolizing the integrated self and unity consciousness. Collectively, I see this integration process as an evolutionary process, where the human race might transcend separatism to be fully awakened into our essence as "spiritual beings having a human experience." Individually, we are called to fully step into our sovereignty. We might embrace the notion that this idyllic model is a visual map and that we, as humans, are constantly fluctuating around this ideal because we are emotional beings. Just like a ship at sea, we have to accept what is out of our control and focus on navigating through stormy waters, changing the things that we can, in other words, doing the best we can and going with the flow of what life presents.

THE LIGHTHOUSE EFFECT
THE SIX-POINTED STAR MIND/BODY/SPIRIT INTEGRATION MODEL

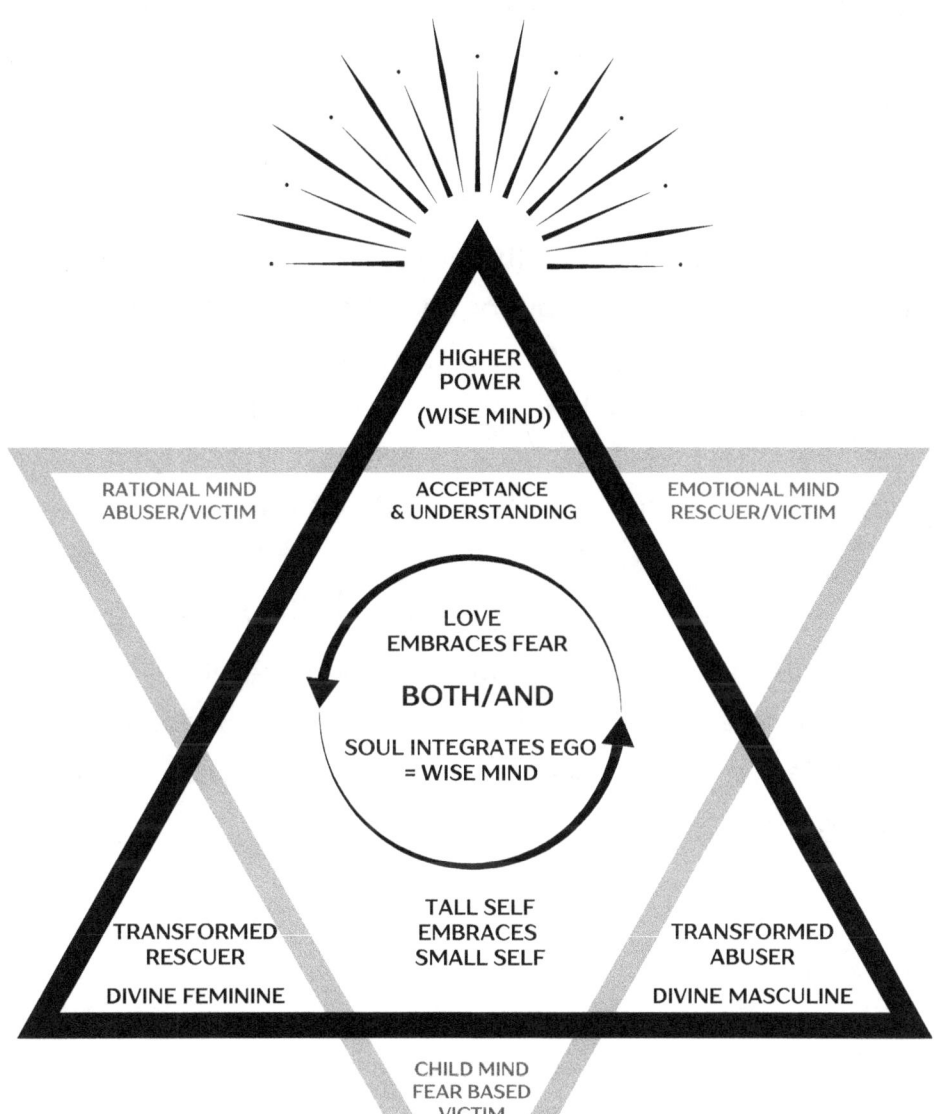

Group Exercise ~ The Six-Pointed Star

Use your whiteboard to draw The Lighthouse Effect Six-Pointed Star Model. Discuss how this symbol demonstrates and encompasses the integration of all four modules, how the concepts and skills presented in each module come together and can be integrated into a comprehensive practice for self-mastery in our healing journey.

If you have the time in the session, walk the group through the Twelve Commitments for Moving from Surviving to Thriving handout or one of the other handouts in the PAT Packet that you intuit would best work for your group. Otherwise, encourage your group to review the handouts in the packet as part of their ongoing daily practice.

Closing Ceremony & Closing Out the Module & Program

Present completion certificates to the group for Module IV and for the year-long program. Provide your group with the Putting it All Together (PAT) packet. If you will be facilitating a month-long Bookending Your Day challenge (using the *Bookending Your Day: The Lighthouse Effect 30-Day Self-Care Challenge* workbook), invite them to join you and provide the date and time it will begin.

THE LIGHTHOUSE EFFECT SKILLFUL RECOVERY PROGRAM

Certificate

This certifies that

_____

has successfully completed The Lighthouse Effect Skillful Recovery Program
Module IV Conscious Communication
The Visible Shine of Your Lighthouse ~ Transmitting Your Light

_____   _____
FACILITATOR   DATE

THE LIGHTHOUSE EFFECT SKILLFUL RECOVERY PROGRAM

Certificate

This certifies that

_____

has successfully completed
The Lighthouse Effect Skillful Recovery One-Year Program

_____   _____
FACILITATOR   **DATE**

THE LIGHTHOUSE EFFECT PUTTING IT ALL TOGETHER (PAT) PACKET

"At a time of crisis in any civilization certain individuals turn from the outer world to the inner life of the psyche and, discovering there a new way of life, they return to the outer world to form a creative minority, which acts as a leaven for the renewal of that civilization."

-- Arnold Toynbee

Understanding the Human Condition & the Authentic Self

I believe that we must confront and heal the crisis that is happening in our own hearts and homes before broader change in the world can happen. To reset core-belief systems and reactions that keep us in suffering, we can look to our relationships, especially those that challenge us. By looking at the ways in which we relate to others, we can better understand ourselves and begin to heal the patterns that have kept us from becoming whole or stepping fully into our Authentic Self. As we heal ourselves from within, we shine our light outward, to our families, friends, inner circles, and communities, radiating outward throughout the planet like rays of healing light: *the lighthouse effect*. Refer to this PAT Packet to support you in your daily practice as you continue on your healing journey.

The Lighthouse Effect PAT Packet Handouts:

Bookending Your Day: The Lighthouse Effect Self-Care 30-Day Challenge
Increasing Vibrational Frequency: The Power of Words
Twelve Commitments for Moving from Surviving to Thriving
Conscious Compassion: The Authentic Self
The Lighthouse Effect ALIGNMENT Buoys

Bookending Your Day: The Lighthouse Effect Self-Care 30-Day Challenge

Take the challenge! If you have the opportunity to do this with your group or others, sign up for it, or do it on your own to create a daily practice for healing into wholeness. You can order the *Bookending Your Day: The Lighthouse Effect Self-Care 30-Day Challenge* workbook or download the free PDF from innerfaiththerapy.com, or order from Amazon and other online booksellers. This daily mind-body-spirit practice reinforces the concepts and skills you've learned throughout the program, all of which foster emotional wellbeing, increase vitality and resilience, and help you to cultivate healthy relationships with yourself and others. It is a self-empowerment practice that raises our frequency and moves us from surviving, to reviving, to thriving as our Authentic Self.

BOOKENDING YOUR DAY

From The Lighthouse Effect™ by Faith Burrington Jones

choose you!

**CREATE YOUR OWN
SELF-CARE PRACTICE**

MIND

BODY

SPIRIT

**SIGN UP!
GET YOUR FREE
BOOKENDING YOUR DAY
WORKBOOK**

www.innerfaiththerapy.com

Self-care is not selfishness
It is soulfullness

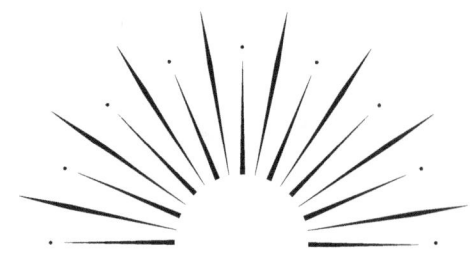

THE LIGHTHOUSE EFFECT
Increasing Vibrational Frequency ~ The Power of Words

Change your words, uplift your mood!

Low Frequency Words & Phrases	High Frequency Words & Phrases
I have to clean my house/car/room.	I choose to clean my house/car/room.
I can't do this anymore.	I can find a way to move through this.
I can't seem to lose weight.	I can choose to eat healthy.
I can never get ahead.	I can focus on what I have achieved.
They are judging me.	I accept them and myself.
I hate my life.	I choose to enjoy my life.
There is so much darkness.	I choose to see the light.
I always feel not good enough.	I am enough just as I am.
I am so overwhelmed.	I am grounded and stable.
I am a loser.	I am a winner.
Death and taxes are all there is.	Life and my sovereign being are birthrights.
I feel so resistant.	I am resilient.
Life is one problem after another.	Life is an adventure.
I never seem to get what I want.	I am grateful for what I have.

Consider the vibrational frequency of words in terms of both/and, and how we can choose words that convey acceptance of what is and at the same time acknowledge and commit to changes we can make.

Example: *There is so much darkness* (low vibration) *but I choose to see and radiate light* (high vibration).

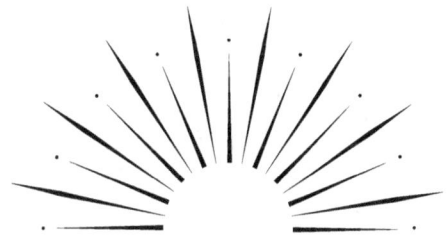

THE LIGHTHOUSE EFFECT
Twelve Commitments for Moving from Surviving to Thriving

1) Live in the present. We are here, and we are now. (The past and future do not really exist!) Life happens in the now; be present with life and trust what happens. (The "how" is in "the now!")

2) Make peace with grievances. Holding on to grievances is living in the past. It only weighs you down and lowers vibrational frequencies. Let those grievances go, and lighten up!

3) Inquire within. Focus on you. Ultimately, what other people think of you is none of your business; it's about them. (Think: Reflective Inquiry.)

4) Be happy. Happiness is an inside job! Take charge of your own happiness; when you depend on other people, events, life itself to make you happy, you give up your power to choose happiness, to radiate your own light.

5) Don't compare. Don't compare yourself to others. It is disrespectful to you, to them, and to both of your unique expressions of creation. Shine your light!

6) Accept what is. Accept what is beyond your control. Acceptance of "what is" and of all parts of the Self is how we heal and move toward wholeness. Recovery is an ebb and flow process. Accept that you will have setbacks, and when you do, take three deep breaths, and start again.

7) Change perspective ~ Zoom out. Step back (Observer Self) and simply observe your thoughts and narratives. Shift from "figuring it out" to "feeling it through," without judgment or commentary.

8) Embrace challenges. Challenges cultivate greater resilience and provide opportunities for change. Instead of seeing a challenge as against you, think, *How is this for me? What is this teaching me?*

9) Be human. Accept that you are human and allow yourself to be human. It's about practice, not perfection; mindfully and patiently practice your way from survival to revival.

10) Let your Soul Self drive. Be guided by your soul/spirit/higher self. Let Soul take the wheel and send Ego on vacation. (It works too hard.) Trust your Soul Self.

11) Align vertically. Align your mind, body, and spirit vertically; stand in alignment with your own values and higher self. Be the lighthouse!

12) Commit to love. Cultivate loving connection with yourself and in all of your relationships!

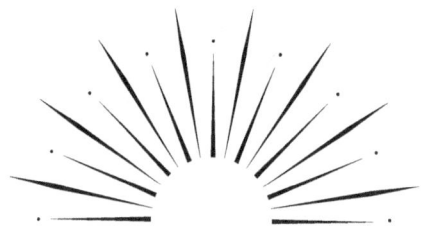

THE LIGHTHOUSE EFFECT CONSCIOUS COMPASSION
The Authentic Self ~ Meeting the Self with Understanding

Notice when you are being critical and judgmental towards yourself, and agree to be softer. Take slow, deep breaths to soften your muscles, release tension, and come into alignment.

Find Three Strengths: List three qualities or strengths that you possess. If it is difficult to think of them, ask a supportive friend if they can help point them out. Take time to write them down in your journal and reflect on them. Trust your own internal guidance system; you can depend on these attributes to carry you through challenging times and draw on them when you feel down or are being hard on yourself.

Consider positive character traits; acts of service; how you treat people in your relationships (family, friends, co-workers, neighbors); physical attributes or athletic abilities; education, career, or creative accomplishments. Recall your positive qualities when you face challenges within yourself, with others, or with whatever life throws at you. Know that you have everything you need to access Wise Mind, to be in full alignment with your Authentic Self, and to shine with your own unique light.

Cultivate a Supportive Environment: Choose to surround yourself with friends, family, and community who will support and encourage you, while patiently and kindly holding you accountable to your healing journey and life goals. Move away from people who trigger you and who have a tendency to reinforce the negative core beliefs you are working to release and heal from. Create a living space that brings you joy and a sense of coziness. Be clear about what you like and what you dislike. Wherever you spend most of your time (work, school, home, home-office), make it a supportive environment: place, post, or hang inspirational quotes or mantras by spiritual teachers, messages from loved ones, paintings or photographs, books that you love.

Radical Self-Acceptance: Be willing every day to practice radically accepting of all parts of you. Self-acceptance does not mean you need to like every aspect of yourself or a particular aspect that has been triggered. It's about meeting it with understanding and kindness. Radical self-acceptance is about acknowledging your humanness; it's part of the human experience to possess both strengths and weaknesses. Having compassion for your human nature *is* radical self-acceptance. Practice being open and nonjudgmental with yourself by treating yourself as kindly as you want to be treated and as kindly as you treat others. Be careful to not frame "acceptance" in ways that reinforce negative self-assessments; for example, *I accept that I am never going to be good enough.* If you find yourself framing acceptance in that self-defeating way, reframe it. For example: *I accept that I feel like I am never going to be good enough, and I see that it is a feeling and not a Tall Self or Capital-T Truth.*

Become Your Own Best Friend: You were born alone and you will leave this physical reality alone, so all the more reason to develop a healthy relationship with yourself. Practice the conscious compassion suggestions above. Meet yourself with understanding for being human. Focus on your strengths and radically accept your short-comings. Choose to live and work in a healthy environment and create conscious relationships with yourself and others. Remind yourself that being your own best friend is the best way to support you in your healing journey. Remember you are healing from the inside out!

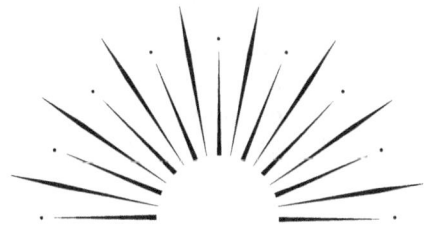

THE LIGHTHOUSE EFFECT ALIGNMENT BUOYS

LIGHT
Your true essence, authentic self, soul

HOUSE
Your body ~ the physical form that channels your light

EFFECT
The energetic life force (qi) that moves your light through your mind-body-spirit complex,
radiating outward, connecting to all that is, within your sphere and beyond

A: ACCEPT. Accept "what is:" Coming into acceptance is the ultimate wisdom for moving from survival to revival. It is about acknowledging and letting go of what you cannot control, which doesn't mean you have to like or be in agreement with whatever it is. It simply means making the choice to not fight what you cannot change, so that you can focus on and put energy into what you can change.

L: LISTEN. Listen deeply, to yourself and others. It is a precious gift to give and receive. It is essential to creating and maintaining conscious relationships with yourself and others.

I: INQUIRE. Inquire within: The practice of Reflective Inquiry helps you get clear about what is true and what is a fabrication or a programmed belief. It is about discernment, separating facts from feelings and releasing negative core beliefs that are not reflective of your authentic self so that you can step into the "Capital-T Truth" of who you are.

G: GRATITUDE. Be in gratitude for what you have and what is working in your life. Acknowledge the positives so that you can put mindful energy into changing what isn't working by engaging in self-care practices. Notice that gratitude is nonphysical, and therefore carries a higher vibration. (Think Wise Mind, with Emotional Mind and Rational Mind in balance and in vertical alignment.)

N: NONJUDGMENT. Taking a nonjudgmental stance with yourself and others is to step out of victim consciousness and into oneness consciousness. It is essential to moving toward wholeness, as it releases negative assumptions, beliefs, and programming.

M: MINDFULNESS. Mindfulness is an essential practice or state of being for mind/body/spirit health, as it aligns you with nonphysical reality and develops inner peace. It brings you to a neutral stance, to the still point of your being. Use such practices as meditation or self-affirming mantras to focus your mind and bring yourself into alignment with your higher self, higher consciousness, or God of your understanding.

E: EMOTIONAL BALANCE. To be in emotional balance is to acknowledge and accept all parts of the self. Your Tall Self (authentic adult) sees and takes the hand of your small self (inner child) rather than letting them lead. You might consider intervention techniques such as Emotional Freedom Technique (EFT) and "havening" to energetically rewire neural pathways and repattern negative and/or trauma memories and imprinted (false) core beliefs.

N: NURTURE. Take care of yourself by attending to your mind, body, and spirit. "Bookend your day" with morning and evening self-care routines, as presented in the *Bookending Your Day: The Lighthouse Effect 30-Day Self-Care Challenge* workbook.

T: TRUTH. Seeing the "Capital-T Truth" of things is about being honest and clear with yourself, to stand in the integrity of your Authentic Self. Truth resonates at a high vibration, which elevates your consciousness and *conscientious*ness! (The Lighthouse Effect Mind States Model.)

E: EMOTIONAL BALANCE. To be in emotional balance is to acknowledge and accept all parts of the self. Your Tall Self (authentic adult) sees and takes the hand of your small self (inner child) rather than letting them lead. You might consider intervention techniques such as Emotional Freedom Technique (EFT) and "havening" to energetically rewire neural pathways and repattern negative and/or trauma memories and imprinted (false) core beliefs.

N: NURTURE. Take care of yourself by attending to your mind, body, and spirit. "Bookend your day" with morning and evening self-care routines, as presented in the *Bookending Your Day: The Lighthouse Effect 30-Day Self-Care Challenge* workbook.

T: TRUTH. Seeing the "Capital-T Truth" of things is about being honest and clear with yourself, to stand in the integrity of your Authentic Self. Truth resonates at a high vibration, which elevates your consciousness and *conscientious*ness! (The Lighthouse Effect Mind States Model.)

Dear Facilitator,

I want to thank you for being a "lighthouse" in facilitating The Lighthouse Effect Skillful Recovery program, whether you facilitated one module or the whole program. As the program is the result of twenty-plus years of my life's work you can imagine how much gratitude I have that you made a commitment to facilitate it.

I underscore again how important it is to develop a daily practice of self-care; it is the core takeaway of the program. It takes awareness and willingness to not fall back into old patterns and habits, which can happen all too easily, even after we've moved through the year-long program and built our Lighthouse Effect toolkit. It seems to me that the mind, body, and spirit aspects that make up our whole self, our Authentic Self, need to be acknowledged and nurtured in our daily lives in order to thrive through the rest of our lives.

I encourage you to contact me and provide any feedback that you think would be helpful to improve or evolve The Lighthouse Effect program. You are the boots on the ground bringing this skillful recovery program out into the world of recovery, and beyond.

Many blessings to you as a "beacon of light" and wayshower!

With much gratitude,

Faith

TIP: As for my final tip to you, I encourage *you*, dear facilitator, to please engage in a daily self-care practice yourself, so that you will be less likely to burn out. It isn't easy to hold space and guide others through the challenges of addiction and trauma. Remember, you can't give from an empty cup. Fill yourself up with self-love, self-respect, and self-compassion through your own daily practice, one day at a time, one moment at a time!

REPEAT HANDOUTS

The Lighthouse Effect Group Rules

Stages of Change: Metamorphosis from Survival to Revival Lifestyle

Stages of Change Addiction/Recovery Pros & Cons Worksheet

The Role of an Accountability Partner & How to Give Constructive Feedback

Relapse Prevention Plan Worksheet

Post-Acute Withdrawal Syndrome (PAWS) Self-Assessment

How to Manage Emotional Denial

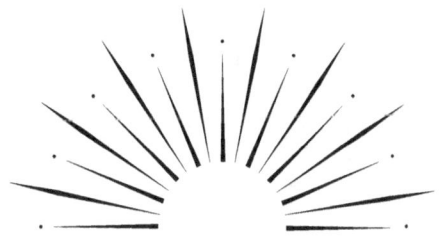

THE LIGHTHOUSE EFFECT
Skillful Recovery Program Group Rules

1. Confidentiality. What is shared in this group stays in this group. You can share your story with your personal support network, but please don't share anyone else's.

2. Respect for Others and Yourself.

- Attend group sessions clean and sober ∼ Abstinence is the goal!
- Arrive on time.
- Use "I" statements.
- Do not talk over one another.
- Use good hygiene and refrain from wearing strong scents.
- Turn off cell phones.
- Call the group facilitator if you are not able to attend a session.

3. Practicing. Commit to practicing skills and completing homework and exercises.

4. Sharing. Share with honesty and heart.

5. Support Network. Make use of your support network to hold yourself accountable to your stated goals and commitments. Be sure to engage at least one sponsor or feedback person who can be available to support you through your recovery process.

6. Value all Members. Understand that each group member is worthy of being heard and being valued, just as they are, and all group members are integral to the group process.

7. Check-ins. Keep check-ins brief; practice being concise. If you are comfortable sharing, practice sharing more concisely. Those of you who are less likely to share, practice sharing more.

8. Commit to the Practice. Be prepared to work at recovery by practicing the skills you learn. This program is all about practicing your way through recovery: practice, not perfection. It is about applying the skills you are learning in your daily life to support your healing process and journey to wholeness. Be prepared to develop your "Observer Self" as an integral component of the program and your daily practice.

9. Welcome All! You are all welcome here, each of you individually, and all of the parts of you that make up your unique and Authentic Self: Shine your light!

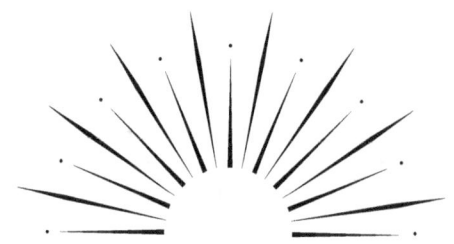

THE LIGHTHOUSE EFFECT
Stages of Change: Metamorphosis from Survival to Revival Lifestyle
(Based on Prochaska & DiClemente's Model of Change and evolved Transtheoretical Model)

Stages of Change

Precontemplation Stage: Denial
Contemplation Stage: Ambivalence (Addiction vs. Recovery)
Preparation Stage: Research and Exploration of Recovery Lifestyle
Action Stage: Practicing Recovery Lifestyle
Maintenance Stage: Practicing, Consistently Applying Skills, Utilizing Support Network
Relapse Phase (Returning to Short-term Relief/Old Crutches)

Precontemplation (Denial): I am not considering change.

- Is treatment a priority? *Not today*!
- What were my previous experiences with drugs or alcohol/my attachment/habit/behavior? *It was never a problem before.*
- What is good about using/my attachment/habit/behavior? *I don't think I'll gain anything by changing or even considering that something is wrong.*
- What are the benefits of not using or changing my attachment/habit/behavior? *It doesn't really matter.*

Contemplation (Maybe/Maybe Not): I am considering change, but I am ambivalent.

- What are the cons of using/dependency/codependency?
- What are the advantages of having a clear mind/independence/interdependence?
- What are my reasons for changing my lifestyle or changing my perspective or narratives?
- What are my barriers to success? What programming, fears, and negative core beliefs limit my growth and inhibit my conscious awakening?

Examining Potential Barriers to Change: Opportunities for Self-Reflection

Belief System: Am I sticking to old narratives or "small-t truths," or am I expanding my awareness and looking outside the box of my comfort zone, physically, psychologically, and spiritually?

Personal Choice: Am I accepting the consequences of not changing an unhealthy lifestyle? Am I content with following default programming and narratives, or will I choose to break away from them? Am I using critical thinking and thinking independently from what I've been taught?

Denial (Unconscious): Am I blind to the truth about the long-term negative consequences?

Defiance (Conscious): Am I refusing to see and stand in my own truth; am I making my own decisions?

Fear of Failure: Am I sticking to a failure story? Narrative: I always fail. Negative Core Belief: I am a failure.

Fear of Success: Am I afraid of change? Narrative: Things will change if I succeed, and the unknown terrifies me. Negative Core Belief: I am familiar with identifying as being a failure; I am afraid of success because I don't know success.

Preparation (Ready to Change):
I have begun to explore making changes in my lifestyle.

- I have had moments standing in alignment with my Authentic Self.
- I have had periods where I've been abstinent, changed my behavior, practiced independence and interdependence, and I felt better at those times.
- I am motivated and have a supportive network of people who want a different lifestyle, just like me.
- I am able to choose and make decisions about potentially successful strategies based on my personality, strengths, past successes, and willingness to try.
- I can work with a therapist to decide the safest and best treatment plan for me; I continue to build my recovery network, and can turn to them for suggestions and support.
- I am willing to assertively listen to myself and others about the benefits of moving out of survival and into revival; I am willing to learn more skills and interventions to help me make conscious choices, in the moment, for a life worth living.

Action (Consistent Experience):
I am practicing a lifestyle of recovery and revival and I am experiencing the benefits.

- I am inspired and committed to applying the various interventions, skills, and practices that I am learning; I am fully engaged in my recovery and revival lifestyle.
- I am focused on identifying emotional triggers, applying recovery-based strategies, and developing my own customized daily practice for dealing with them.
- I am choosing to make incremental positive changes to build my foundation, the base of my lighthouse, one moment and one day at a time!

Maintenance (Stable Abstinence):
I am consistently living a lifestyle of healing into wholeness.

- I am able to identify relapse triggers and behavior patterns, and I am able to apply intervention skills with confidence and consistency.
- I will try to identify self-defeating behaviors with my support network and resources, such as my Lighthouse Effect Skillful Recovery group, AA, NA, Refuge Recovery, Smart Recovery, and others.
- I will set specific goals for recovery with my sponsor/recovery coach/therapist.
- I will explore personal growth issues with my sponsor/recovery coach/therapist.
- I am noticing that other disempowering addictions/addictive behaviors such as unhealthy eating habits and relationship attachments are coming to the surface; I am now open to looking at them.

Relapse (Short-Term Comfort) Phase:
I reverted to the short-term comfort of my addiction after stable abstinence.

(The risk of relapse increases if recovery support has decreased, recovery skills have not been consistently practiced, or when a traumatic or significant life event occurs.)

- I will reflect on my complacency and review what I have learned.
- I will not be complacent with my recovery and my daily practice. I will continue to address feelings of shame and guilt with my recovery network.
- I will review what my barriers to success are, based on my relapse pattern and trauma programming history.
- I will thoroughly explore relapse triggers and the events around the relapse with my sponsor, recovery coach, therapist, recovery network, or accountability partner.
- Most importantly, I will forgive myself and hold myself accountable with compassionate action; I will challenge myself to commit to a higher level of self-care and enhanced daily practice to get me back on track. (See *Bookending Your Day: The Lighthouse Effect Self-Care 30-Day Challenge*.)

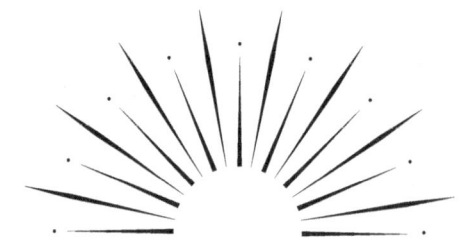

THE LIGHTHOUSE EFFECT
Stages of Change Addiction/Recovery Pros & Cons Worksheet

The example below is from a real group session. The thing we focused on wanting to change was self-talk.

What seems beneficial about my addiction?
What is detrimental about my addiction?

What is beneficial about recovery?
What is challenging about recovery?

ADDICTION PROS	ADDICTION CONS	RECOVERY PROS	RECOVERY CONS
Familiar	Keeps me stuck	Upgrades my self-talk	Unknown
Self-preservation	Spinning my wheels	Broader perspective	Uncertainty
Survival	Energy drain	More clear-headed	Fear of failure
Short-term relief	Self-medicating	Better overall health	Fear of future
Easier to berate	Not sustainable	Builds confidence	What will I lose?
Get to feel bad	Enslavement	Reclaim my spirit	What will I do instead?
What I deserve	Steals my soul	Return to my true self	Who will I be?

Notice the correlation between Addiction Pros and Recovery Cons in the example. Fill in the columns below with what you see as pros & cons at this moment in your recovery process. Then apply Reflective Inquiry: Is it true? Is it a Capital-T Truth?

ADDICTION PROS	ADDICTION CONS	RECOVERY PROS	RECOVERY CONS

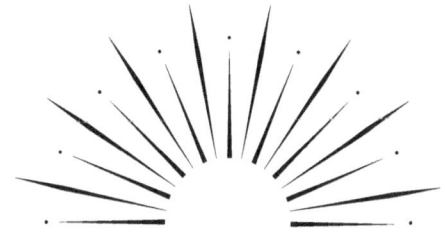

THE LIGHTHOUSE EFFECT
The Role of an Accountability Partner ～ How to Give Constructive Feedback

In conscious relationships, constructive feedback that is given in a respectful manner encourages the other person to become more aware of their behaviors, and to then practice "relating" in a more skillful and positive way. And it helps the one delivering the feedback to continue to model skillful behavior. Delivering feedback in this way helps the other person understand how their behavior affects others, helps them build the confidence to learn how to be more considerate and mindful in social interactions, and leads to self-empowerment and personal growth.

When feedback is given unskillfully, it is more likely to cause the other person to feel critically attacked or blamed, which only serves to disempower them. When the other person feels attacked, it creates a dynamic of one-upmanship and provokes a power struggle, which in turn, reinforces negative behavioral patterns. In conscious relationships, setting an example and modeling a healthy way to offer constructive feedback means modeling good intentions to prevent conflict, to not blame, and to not disconnect or disengage. The goal is to offer feedback skillfully enough that the other person can hear it as an act of support, and therefore, take it seriously and give it careful consideration.

Ten Points for Providing Conscious Constructive Feedback

1) Plan When: Set a time for the constructive feedback to take place that will work for both of you, and be sure you allow ample time to complete the conversation.

2) Plan Where: Arrange to have the conversation in a private setting that works for both of you. Avoid settings where others can hear your conversation; this shows respect to the person receiving feedback.

3) Set Intentions: Make your intentions clear by first sharing what benefits you think will come of the conversation before you begin offering the other person your constructive feedback. Speak with a kind and supportive tone of voice.

4) Describe, Don't Judge: When you introduce the event that you want to offer feedback about, stick to descriptive details and avoid making judgments, labeling their behavior, or blaming the other person.

Unconscious feedback example: *You were so rude when you left me out of the conversation you were having with the new group member.*

Conscious feedback example: *I felt hurt when you didn't include me in the conversation you were having with the new group member.*

5) Avoid Generalizations: Avoid phrases and generalizations, such as "you always" or "you never," and focus instead on that one event, or maybe two, where the same thing occurred. This reduces the risk of the other person becoming defensive.

6) Use "I" Statements: Offer constructive feedback about how you were personally affected, as with the example above in number 4: *I felt hurt when you didn't include me*. Don't assume what their intention may have been. For example, the way the word "purposely" is used in the following assumes they intended to hurt you: *You made me feel rejected when you purposely excluded me*. Don't "bandwagon" by inferring or stating what other people's experiences are. For example: *I'm not the only one you've hurt by making them feel rejected*.

7) Make A Reasonable Request: If you are asking for a change of behavior, don't judge the other person for having a different communication style than yours, simply request the change you would like to see in a respectful manner.

Examples of judging communication styles: *You are too expressive. You need to calm down*.

Example of respectful, reasonable request: *Can you speak to me with a calm voice, and can you please not slam your fist on the table?*

8) Be Invitational: When making a request for a behavioral change, ask in an invitational way that reassures them that your intentions are to improve the relationship and connection. For example, *I really want us to be able to communicate in a way that builds on the trust we've been trying to create in our relationship.*

9) Check In: Ask the other person if they clearly understand what you are trying to convey. Ask them to summarize in their own words the constructive feedback. For example, *Can you share with me what you've heard about what I'm trying to convey?*

10) Apply Conscious Listening: Just as you want the other person to hear you, be prepared to really listen to them and hear them. Be open to their response and experience; be open to learning something about your part in the relationship and be prepared to admit if you have misunderstood or made a mistake with your interpretations.

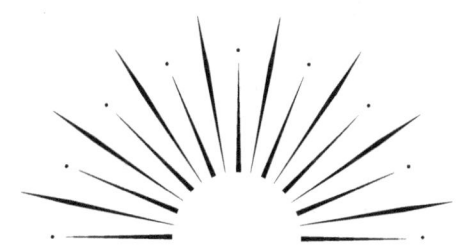

THE LIGHTHOUSE EFFECT
Relapse Prevention Plan Worksheet

Three Triggers I have Identified:

_____

_____

_____

My Choice of Action (Skill or Practice) to Address Trigger #1:

_____

_____

My Choice of Action (Skill or Practice) to Address Trigger #2:

_____

_____

My Choice of Action (Skill or Practice) to Address Trigger #3:

_____

_____

Initiating Action Plan for Relapse Prevention Support

1. If I am experiencing "triggers" that cannot be managed alone, how can my accountability person help me come into alignment with my lighthouse?

_____

_____

_____

2. What can my support person do to help redirect my thinking? What skills have been effective in the past to help me prevent a relapse?

_____

_____

_____

3. What reminder or example can my support person give me about ways that have worked for me, for integrating Emotional Mind (reactivity) and Rational Mind (skill set) to access Wise Mind (higher thinking) to effectively prevent a relapse?

_____
_____
_____

4. What could this person remind me to do that has helped me ride the temporary wave of urges or cravings?

_____
_____
_____

5. What if my contact person tries to get me back on track and I resist? What moves me out of resistance and into receptivity? What would be the most effective strategies to prevent a relapse?

_____
_____
_____

6. What are common life situations or events (holidays, family gatherings, work scenarios) where I might need more support? What do I need to plan for in advance?

_____
_____
_____

7. My Action Plan (Be specific):

I will: _____
I will: _____
I will: _____

My Support Network Contact List (Recovery Coach, Sponsor, Accountability Partner, Trusted Friends)

Name	Phone Number	Email Address
_____	_____	_____
_____	_____	_____
_____	_____	_____

_____   _____
SIGNED   DATE

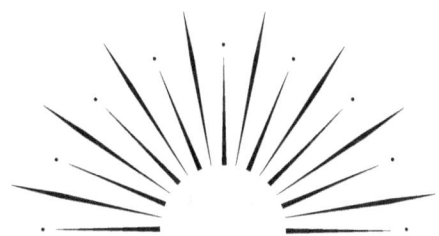

THE LIGHTHOUSE EFFECT
Post-Acute Withdrawal Syndrome (PAWS) Assessment

Self-Assessment of Mind, Body, and Spirit with Self-Care Guidelines

The Post-Acute Withdrawal Syndrome (PAWS) assessment is a standard mental health protocol for substance addiction, and beneficial to recovery from any addiction, addictive pattern, or trauma, which is why it is a key tool in The Lighthouse Effect Skillful Recovery Program.

It can take a year or longer of abstinence for the brain and other major organs to heal from drug (illicit and prescribed) or alcohol dependency. While the brain-body complex is healing, it is common to experience detoxification symptoms of both the mind and the body, as they are interconnected. We also experience hormonal changes (cortisol and oxytocin levels, for example) when we move into a period of abstinence, suffer a trauma, or experience a sudden life change, such as a breakup. These brain/body detoxification symptoms cause short-term lapses in brain function. Such symptoms can be completely disabling and impact daily life; they can be especially challenging in maintaining recovery, which makes the risk of relapse relatively high. (Thus, the significance of the evolved Stages of Change model, which indicates relapse as a potential or probable phase of recovery.)

The Lighthouse Effect Skillful Recovery Program was developed to educate and engage participants in classic recovery healing processes. While the program focuses on second stage recovery, it is essential to understand that second and third stage recovery build off of basic skills we gain in taking that first step and moving through the first stage. Thus, understanding PAWS symptoms benefits us at whatever stage we are in and helps us to monitor our progress. (It also helps us to be supportive of others in our recovery network who might be struggling.)

Common PAWS Symptoms:

1) Difficulty thinking clearly
2) Inability to manage feelings
3) Poor memory or recall
4) Sleep disturbances and insomnia
5) Lack of physical coordination
6) Difficulty managing stress
7) Difficulty being/staying grounded in reality

PAWS Self-Assessment Exercise and the Mind/Body Connections. Use the following scale to rate the symptoms presented in each of the Assessment segments.

0 = Not at all
1 = Sometimes
2 = Several days a week
3 = Consistently

(1) DIFFICULTY THINKING CLEARLY (MIND/BODY)

Are you experiencing any of the following, and to what degree?

___ Poor concentration, feeling drugged.
___ Cognitive clouding, brain fog.
___ Ruminating, repetitive thinking, negative-feedback loops.
___ Difficulty putting words together, needing to see or touch things in order to put things together in my mind.
___ My thoughts are running all over the place. I feel like it's almost impossible to be positive.
___ I'm unable to get to the root of a problem.
___ My priorities seem all messed up. I am unorganized in my brain.
___ I can't predict the logical consequences of my own behavior or others' behaviors.
___ I can't take appropriate action based on my judgment, or do what I tell myself I need to do. I seem to be unmotivated.
___ I can't stop doing things that I know will hurt me or others. I seem to not be in control of my mind or my behaviors, as if someone else is controlling my mind.

Clarifying Notes: Are symptoms more prevalent during the day or at night?

_____

_____

_____

How well do you function when you are having trouble thinking clearly?

___ I can effectively function, without extra energy.
___ I can effectively function, but it takes extra energy.
___ I can't effectively function, even with enough energy.
___ I can't function, whether I have energy or not.

Name and rate stressors or triggers that impact your ability to think clearly. (Add more to the list.)

—— When someone criticizes me.
—— When I see someone else lapse in their recovery.

—— _____

—— _____

Name and rate the symptoms you experience in your body. (Add your own to the list.)

___ Tightness or tension in my body
___ Rapid heart rate
___ Headache
___ Shortness of breath
___ Fatigue

___ _____
___ _____

Self-narratives (self-talk) in times of high stress versus low stress: Are interventions being applied?

What are the narratives I am running that may be negatively affecting my focus? What narratives increase or decrease stress levels?

Example: *When I am abstaining from using or trying to detach from attachments or addictive behavior and I'm really stressed, my thinking is foggier and more fearful. I start running stories that I am not worthy, and I notice more urges and cravings. When I "move a muscle" by taking a walk or being in nature, I notice my thinking is more positive, and I am better able to function; I am more present.*

Write your own example of your experience of focusing and thinking clearly when you are highly stressed:

_____
_____
_____
_____

Consider intervention skills that work for you when you are having difficulty thinking clearly. (Apply these interventions when you are having difficulty thinking clearly, to help you focus and be present.)

Move a Muscle/Change a Thought

_____
_____
_____

(2) DIFFICULTY MANAGING EMOTIONS (MIND)

Are you experiencing any of the following, and to what degree?

___ I find it challenging to comfort myself or others
___ I am feeling discomfort
___ I feel lost
___ I feel powerless
___ I feel numb

___ I feel emotionally overwhelmed
___ I can't seem to feel love or know what love is, as if it is foreign
___ I seem to jump from emotional overreaction to feeling numb
___ I am unable to tell people what I am feeling
___ I am out of touch and can't seem to pinpoint what I feel

Clarifying Notes: Are symptoms more prevalent during the day or at night?

_____

_____

_____

How well do you function when you're having trouble managing your feelings?

___ I can effectively function, without extra energy.
___ I can effectively function, but it takes extra energy.
___ I can't effectively function, even with enough energy.
___ I can't function, whether I have energy or not.

Name and rate stressors or triggers that impact your ability to manage your emotions. (Add your own to the list.)

___ When I haven't slept well.
___ When my partner, or a friend or family member gets mad at me.

___ _____

___ _____

Name and rate the symptoms you experience in your body. (Add your own to the list.)

___ Tightness or tension in my body
___ Rapid heart rate
___ Headache
___ Shortness of breath
___ Fatigue

___ _____

___ _____

Self-narratives (self-talk) in times of high stress versus low stress: Are interventions being applied?

What are the narratives I am running that may be negatively affecting my ability to manage my emotions? What narratives increase or decrease stress levels?

Example: _I notice when I negatively ruminate about the past or fearfully project into the future, my emotions get out of control and my stress level increases. When I turn my mind to the present and drop past and future narratives and focus on the positive, I naturally calm down._

Write your own example of your experience managing your emotions when you are highly stressed:

_____

_____

_____

_____

Consider intervention skills that work for you when you are having difficulty managing your emotions. (Apply these interventions when you are having difficulty managing your emotions.)

Meditating
Turning the Mind
Opposite Thought/Opposite Action

_____

_____

_____

(3) DIFFICULTY WITH MEMORY LOSS (MIND)

Are you experiencing any of the following, and to what degree?

___ I have difficulty retaining what I have just learned (short-term memory).
___ I have difficulty now remembering things I have known for years (long-term memory).
___ I have difficulty remembering important childhood experiences.
___ I have difficulty remembering important events in adulthood.

Clarifying Notes: Are symptoms more prevalent during the day or at night?

_____

_____

_____

How well do you function when you're having trouble remembering?

___ I can effectively function, without extra energy.
___ I can effectively function, but it takes extra energy.
___ I can't effectively function, even with enough energy.
___ I can't function, whether I have energy or not.

Name and rate stressors or triggers that impact your ability to manage your emotions. (Add your own to the list.)

___ Following directions when I'm driving.
___ Not remembering a conversation.

___ When I think someone notices I'm having memory issues.

___ _____

___ _____

Name and rate the symptoms you experience in your body. (Add your own to the list.)

___ Tightness or tension in my body
___ Rapid heart rate
___ Headache
___ Shortness of breath
___ Fatigue

___ _____

___ _____

Which of the following statements most accurately describe the relationship between stress and the concerns you have about your memory challenges?

___ I have trouble remembering things only when I'm really stressed. When I am not stressed, I don't have any difficulty with my memory.
___ It makes no difference if I am really stressed or not stressed, I still have memory loss issues.
___ It seems like when I abstain (from the substance or behavior) I have a more difficult time with memory loss.
___ It seems that when I abstain, I have better memory recall.
___ It makes no difference whether I abstain or not, I still have memory issues.

How long does this difficulty remembering things usually last? (Be specific: minutes, hours, days)

_____

_____

_____

Self-narratives (self-talk) in times of high stress versus low stress: Are interventions being applied?

What are the narratives I am running that may be negatively affecting my memory? What narratives increase or decrease stress levels?

Example: *This memory loss that I'm experiencing will never get better; nothing ever gets better for me.*

Write your own example of your experience with memory challenges when you are highly stressed:

_____

_____

_____

Consider intervention skills that work for you when you are having difficulty remembering. (Apply these interventions when you are having difficulty remembering.)

Reflective Inquiry
Is it Capital-T True?

_____

_____

_____

(4) DIFFICULTY WITH PHYSICAL COORDINATION (BODY)

Do you experience any of the following, and to what degree?

__ Dizziness/vertigo
__ Trouble keeping my balance
__ Poor hand/eye coordination
__ Slow reflexes
__ Clumsiness
__ Being accident prone

__ _____
__ _____

Clarifying Notes: Are symptoms more prevalent during the day or at night?

_____

_____

_____

How well do you function when you're having challenges with your physical coordination?

___ I can effectively function, without extra energy.
___ I can effectively function, but it takes extra energy.
___ I can't effectively function, even with enough energy.
___ I can't function, whether I have energy or not.

Name and rate stressors or triggers that impact your physical coordination. (Add your own to the list.)

___ When I'm tired.
___ When I don't drink enough water.

__ _____
__ _____

Name and rate the symptoms you experience in your body. (Add your own to the list.)

__ Tightness or tension in my body
__ Rapid heart rate
__ Headache
__ Shortness of breath
__ Fatigue

__ _____
__ _____

Which of the following statements describe the relationship between stress and the difficulty with your physical coordination?

__ I have difficulty with coordination when I'm really stressed. When I have no stress, I have no difficulties with coordination; my physical coordination is normal.
__ It makes no difference if I am really stressed or have no stress at all, I still have physical coordination difficulties.
__ When I am abstinent, I have difficulty with physical coordination.
__ It seems that when I abstain, I have better physical coordination.

Self-narratives (self-talk) in times of high stress versus low stress: Are interventions being applied?

What are the narratives I am running that may be negatively affecting my physical coordination? What narratives increase or decrease stress levels?

Example: _It doesn't matter if I'm clean and sober or not, my body doesn't seem to physically function as well as I want it to._

Write your own example of your experience with physical coordination challenges when you are highly stressed:

_____
_____
_____

Consider intervention skills that work for you when you are having difficulty with physical coordination. (Apply these interventions when you are having difficulty with your physical coordination.)

Meditating
Yoga
Qigong

_____
_____
_____

__

(5) SLEEP DISTURBANCES AND/OR INSOMNIA (BODY)

Do you experience any of the following, and to what degree?

___ Difficulty falling asleep
___ Difficulty staying asleep
___ Unusual or disturbing dreams
___ Wake up frequently during the night
___ Wake up exhausted no matter what time I went to bed
___ Always feel tired
___ Inconsistent sleep patterns
___ Sleeping longer than normal

Clarifying Notes: Are symptoms more prevalent during the day or at night?

_____
_____
_____

How well do you function when you're not getting adequate sleep?

___ I can effectively function, without extra energy.
___ I can effectively function, but it takes extra energy.
___ I can't effectively function, even with enough energy.
___ I can't function, whether I have energy or not.

Name and rate stressors or triggers that impact your sleep. (Add your own to the list.)

___ When I watch the news before bed.
___ When I have an unresolved conflict.
___ When I'm sad.
___ _____
___ _____

Name and rate the symptoms you experience in your body. (Add your own to the list.)

___ Tightness or tension in my body
___ Rapid heart rate
___ Headache
___ Shortness of breath
___ Fatigue
___ _____
___ _____

Which of the following statements describe the relationship between stress and the difficulty with getting sufficient sleep?

___ I have difficulty with sleep when I'm really stressed. When I have no stress, I have no difficulties with sleep; my sleep pattern is normal.
___ It makes no difference if I am really stressed or have no stress at all, I still have sleep issues.
___ When I am abstinent, I have difficulty with sleep.
___ It seems when I abstain, I have less difficulty with sleep.

Self-narratives (self-talk) in times of high stress versus low stress: Are interventions being applied?

What are the narratives I am running that may be negatively affecting my sleep? What narratives increase or decrease stress levels?

Example: *It doesn't matter what I do to improve my health, I can't seem to get a good night's sleep.*

Write your own example of your experience with sleep issues when you are highly stressed:

_____
_____
_____
_____

Consider intervention skills that work for you when you are having difficulty with sleep. (Apply these interventions when you are having difficulty sleeping.)

Sound therapy (listening to soothing music)
Gentle Movement (gentle stretching)

_____
_____
_____

(6) DIFFICULTY MANAGING STRESS (MIND/BODY/SPIRIT)

Do you experience any of the following, and to what degree?

___ I have difficulty noticing minor signs of stress
___ I have difficulty relaxing when I become aware that I'm under stress or anything stressful happens
___ I'm often tired or fatigued
___ I worry that stress will "overtake" me physically
___ I worry that stress will "overtake" me mentally
___ I have difficulty functioning normally when I am really stressed
___ I feel overwhelmed by my stress level

Clarifying Notes: Are symptoms more prevalent during the day or at night?

_____
_____
_____

How well do you function when you are stressed?

___ I can effectively function, without extra energy.
___ I can effectively function, but it takes extra energy.
— I can't effectively function, even with enough energy.
— I can't function, whether I have energy or not.

Name and rate stressors or triggers that impact your stress level. (Add your own to the list.)

___ When other people are stressed.
___ When I have too much on my To-Do list.
— _____
— _____

Name and rate the symptoms you experience in your body. (Add your own to the list.)

___ Tightness or tension in my body
___ Rapid heart rate
___ Headache
___ Shortness of breath
___ Fatigue

— _____
— _____

Which of the following statements most accurately describes the relationship between stress and your difficulty with stress management?

___ I have difficulty managing my stress levels only when I'm under high stress. When I have less stress my ability to manage my stress returns to normal.
___ I have difficulty managing stress regardless if my stress levels are high or low.
___ When I am abstinent, I have more difficulty managing my stress levels.

Self-narratives (self-talk) in times of high stress versus low stress: Are interventions being applied?

What are the narratives I am running that may be negatively affecting my ability to manage stress? What narratives increase or decrease stress levels?

Example: *It seems like my stress levels have been increasing since I have been abstaining from my addiction.*

Write your own example of your experience managing stress:

_____
_____
_____
_____

Consider intervention skills that work for you when you are having difficulty managing stress. (Apply these interventions when you are having difficulty sleeping.**)**

Radical Acceptance
Opposite Thought/Opposite Action
Half-Smile

_____
_____
_____

(7) DIFFICULTY STAYING GROUNDED IN REALITY (MIND/BODY/SPIRIT)

Do you experience any of the following, and to what degree?

___ I can become confused about who I am.
___ I can become confused about the people I'm with and who they are.
___ I can become disoriented and don't know where I am.
___ I can become confused about what time or day it is.
___ I can become confused about what I need to do.
___ I can feel dissociated or disconnected from my body.

Clarifying Notes: Are symptoms more prevalent during the day or at night?

_____
_____
_____

How well do you function when you're feeling ungrounded?

___ I can effectively function, without extra energy.
___ I can effectively function, but it takes extra energy.
___ I can't effectively function, even with enough energy.
___ I can't function, whether I have energy or not.

Name and rate triggers that impact feeling ungrounded. (Add your own to the list.)

___ When people around me are upset.
___ When I feel alone or isolated.

___ _____
___ _____

Name and rate the symptoms you experience in your body. (Add your own to the list.)

___ Tightness or tension in my body
___ Rapid heart rate
___ Headache

___ Shortness of breath
___ Fatigue

___ _____

___ _____

Which of the following statements most accurately describe the relationship between stress and the difficulty you can experience staying grounded in reality?

___ I can have difficulty staying grounded in reality, especially when I'm really stressed. When I am not stressed, I am fully grounded in my mind and body.

___ I can have difficulty staying grounded in reality no matter if I am really stressed or not stressed.

___ When I'm abstinent, I am challenged with staying grounded in reality.

Self-narratives (self-talk) in times of high stress versus low stress: Are interventions being applied?

What are the narratives I am running that may be negatively affecting my sense of being grounded? What narratives increase or decrease stress levels?

Example: *It seems like since I've maintained abstinence for several months, I am having difficulty being present; I don't feel grounded or normal without my drug of choice.*

Write your own example of your experience of not being grounded when you are highly stressed:

_____

_____

_____

_____

Consider intervention skills that work for you when you are not feeling grounded in reality. (Apply these interventions when you are feeling ungrounded.)

Body Meditations (Be the Mountain)
Move a Muscle/Change a Thought

_____

_____

_____

PERSONAL EVALUATION SUMMARY & MIND/BODY/SPIRIT SELF-CARE PLAN

What are some key takeaways you learned about yourself by completing this PAWS and Mind/Body/Spirit assessment and evaluation?

MIND: _____

_____

_____

_____

_____

BODY: _____

_____

_____

_____

_____

SPIRIT: _____

_____

_____

_____

_____

How does this self-assessment process help you with knowing what to look for and what sort of challenges might come up that could put you at risk of relapse?

_____

_____

_____

_____

_____

What skills and practices do you know or have you considered that can support your healing and recovery process, for moving from surviving to reviving to thriving?

_____

_____

_____

_____

_____

Use your answers to create your personal self-care daily practice and when you fill out the Relapse Prevention Worksheet. Share your assessment with your therapist and/or accountability partner, a trusted friend or family member, or person in your recovery network.

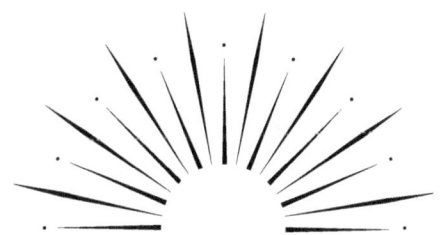

THE LIGHTHOUSE EFFECT
How to Manage Emotional Denial

What is emotional denial? It is a survival instinct fueled by fear, a maladaptive coping mechanism for avoiding physical or emotional pain that we seem unable to navigate. The nature of denial is to ignore, avoid, deflect, or even protect the thing that feels like a threat to our wellbeing, though it's the very thing the pain is signaling us to pay attention to. Instead, we seek to self-medicate to get short-term relief and numb the pain or pretend it doesn't exist. We might deny that we have an issue, deny that the issue isn't serious, deny that we are responsible for the issue, or that we have a responsibility (ability to respond) to face our issue. When we are in denial, we are not in our integrity and we are not being accountable to ourselves or others.

Am I In Denial?

Denial can be tricky, so how can we tell whether we are in our integrity or in denial? By applying Reflective Inquiry! Ask yourself the following three questions, monitor your feelings as you contemplate them, and then mindfully write your answers.

1) *What is the story I'm telling myself that may not be true*? (Assess whether you are trying to make an excuse, trying to fool yourself, or attempting to skirt the truth. Notice what you feel and how your body responds.)

2) *How does this story and my feelings about it keep me from confronting my challenges and addiction or addictive behavior*? (Notice any internal conflicts that arise or sound off in your mind.)

3) *What behaviors are tied to my story that protect me or prevent me from facing the truth*? (Consider how you react: is it with intention or default programming?)

Denial is an automatic, unconscious reaction that distorts our clarity of mind and creates erratic emotions. The issues that we neglect or deny often harbor shame, guilt, or embarrassment. Identifying and naming the thing that we are avoiding helps us to respond consciously. The relief we experience when we air our fears and acknowledge the truth can be felt on a deep visceral level. Through mindfulness practice and developing our Observer Self, we can learn to detach from our fears and repressed issues, instead of denying them.

Denial and the Feelings that Fuel It

Primary feelings that fuel denial are pain, anger, fear, guilt, shame, and humiliation. When we repress the truth, we get caught in a feedback loop of false narratives that perpetuate being in denial. Examples: *I feel pain because I am running a narrative that makes me feel overwhelmed, out of control, and hopeless; I don't know what to do. I feel anger because the challenges I am facing seem so unjust and there is seemingly nothing that can be done to change the reality of my life situation.*

I feel fear because my perception of this life situation is so out of control that I am at a loss to know how to navigate it.

I feel guilty because I believe that I am responsible for another person's pain, or I am experiencing these painful issues because I am to blame.

I feel shame because I have internalized and identified with being "bad," and so I am cursed with these relentless challenges.

I feel humiliated because I believe I should have been stronger or smarter than to have succumbed to the addiction and/or dependency.

Ultimately, denial is futile, as the repressed feelings that we are trying to ignore will inevitably surface. Better to address them through mindfulness practice and consciously move out of denial.

Denial as a Human Condition

Denial is part of the human condition, part of our survival instinct, which is a normal human response to challenging life experiences. We need to understand the function of denial in order to move out of it. Though it may be our intention to always be honest, we all have the human tendency to cover our mistakes or "save face." Childhood programming causes us to feel embarrassed, hurt, and disappointed in ourselves when we make mistakes. To protect ourselves from experiencing such feelings when we make mistakes and avoid the emotional pain, we go into denial and essentially lie to ourselves. When we lie to ourselves and others, we eventually come to believe that what we are telling ourselves is true.

When we habitually revert to denial to avoid experiencing pain, guilt, and shame, it becomes all the more difficult to change the behavior and learn how to face our emotional pain. While it is part of the human condition, we also have the capacity to learn and engage in healthier ways for managing emotional pain and making conscious choices about our behavior.

Understanding the Pros and Cons of Denial Management & Making Conscious Choices

We can look at the principles of the coping strategy of denial and lay out the "pros" and "cons," to then either continue to use the maladaptive coping strategy or develop skills to manage our emotional pain and give our feelings the attention they deserve.

1) Denial is an instinctual psychological defense that can be functional and dysfunctional.

2) The primary feelings that fuel denial are pain, anger, fear, guilt, shame, and humiliation.

3) A primary benefit of using denial is that it protects us from feeling emotional pain caused by life challenges and memories that are overwhelming and fear-inducing.

4) A primary dysfunction of denial is that it blocks and blinds us from attending to our vulnerable inner selves and meeting our emotional needs, thus, from moving from survival to revival.

5) Though denial is an unconscious coping strategy, we can break free from it. Shining the light of truth on underlying negative core beliefs is key to dismantling the denial mechanism and reprogramming or updating them with truer narratives. By being "true to ourselves" we sedate the nervous system, reduce stress levels, and release all of the negative feelings that went with the outdated narrative.

6) Remedies for moving out of denial: accepting that life has become unmanageable using the current strategies; being willing to learn healthy and effective coping strategies; applying and practicing interventions, techniques, and skills to gain a healthier perspective; seeing challenges and mistakes as growth opportunities for developing confidence and resilience.

When we are honest with ourselves, responsible for our behaviors, and address our emotional pain, we strengthen our foundation, and step fully into alignment to radiate the unique light of our Authentic Self.

Becoming Aware of our Denial Behaviors

Becoming aware of our denial behaviors is the first step towards changing them. And that requires willingness and the desire to change. Once we make the choice, we can begin to recover our power and detach from our addiction and/or addictive pattern. Admitting that we have a serious dependency (dependency traits) opens us up to all of the various interventions that are available. Remember that our default, maladaptive coping strategies and the narratives we run mask what is really going on below the surface. Review the checklist below and notice which denial strategies resonate with you.

1) Avoiding (Distracting/Deflecting): *I'll distract myself to escape facing life challenges.*

2) Indignant Denial: *Who, me!? I don't have any issues.*

3) Minimizing (Convincing Self/Others): *My issues aren't that serious, trust me.*

4) Rationalizing & Justifying: *I can provide reasons for my challenges, so I can justify not having to pay any attention to them.*

5) Blaming (Lacking Accountability): *My issues aren't my fault, so I don't have to pay attention to them.*

6) Comparing & Justifying: *Proving that others are far worse than me shows that I don't have serious issues. At least I still can drive and haven't lost my license like they did.*

7) Compliance (Subservience): *If you promise to leave me alone, I'll pretend to do what you want and keep it to myself.*

8) Manipulating (Child Mind): *If you can solve my life situations, I won't have to admit I have them.*

9) Temporary Health (Pink Cloud): *I feel better for the moment, so I must be cured.*

10) Recovery by Fear: *I can stick my head in the sand; I'm scared of my problems and if I hide from them, they will go away.*

11) Learned Helplessness (Strategic Hopelessness): *Because nothing works, I don't have to try.*

12) Democratic Deception: *I have the right to destroy myself and no one has the right to stop me.*

Take time to reflect on the twelve "denial principles" above before moving on. Now, zoom in on your own life. What denial behaviors do you use? Practice mindfulness in the moment to be fully present, while you consider the question. Take several slow, deep breaths to relax and be receptive to whatever insights arise. Write them down here and in your recovery journal.

_____

_____

_____

_____

Gaining Clarity & Personalizing your Denial Coping Strategies

1. Deflecting (Avoiding/Distracting): *I know I'm using the denial strategy when I refuse to directly answer a question and keep trying to change the subject.*

2. Saying It Isn't So (Indignant Denial): *I know I'm using denial when I tell people that I don't have a problem even though I know deep inside that I do.*

3. Saying It Isn't That Bad (Minimizing): *I know I'm using denial when I admit that I have a problem, but try to tell people that it isn't as bad as they think it is.*

4. Giving Good Reasons (Rationalizing & Justifying): *I know I'm using denial when I try to convince people that there are good reasons for me to have the problem and that because there are good reasons, I shouldn't be responsible for having to deal with it!*

5. Saying It's Not My Fault (Blaming/Lacking Accountability): *I know I'm using denial when I try to blame someone else for my problem and deny that I am ultimately responsible for dealing with it.*

6. Criticizing Others (Comparing): *I know I'm using denial when I point out how bad other people's problems are and use that reasoning for why my problems aren't so bad.*

7. Being a Good Child (Compliance/Subservience): *I know I'm using denial when I start telling people exactly what they want to hear to get them off my back.*

8. Getting One Over on Others (Manipulating/Child Mind): *I know I'm using denial when I try to get other people to handle my problems for me.*

9. Suddenly Cured (Pink Cloud/Temporary Health): *I know I'm using denial when I believe that my problems have suddenly gone away without me doing anything to solve them.*

10. Scared Straight (Recovery by Fear): *I know I'm using denial when I tell myself that I could never use alcohol or drugs again because I'm so afraid of what will happen if I did.*

11. Why Bother? (Strategic Hopelessness/Learned Helplessness): *I know I'm using denial when I tell myself that I can never solve my problems and that other people should just leave me alone.*

12. I Have My Rights (Democratic Deception): *I know I'm using denial when I tell other people that I have a right to use alcohol, drugs, or any other addiction or addictive behaviors, regardless of what happens, and that nobody has a right to try and stop me!*

Practice Personalizing Coping Strategies

1) Write down a primary personal denial narrative. **2)** Write a corrective response that aligns with your morals and values (how you would like another person to be responding to you if the situation were reversed and they were the one in denial). **3)** Write a reinforcement statement.

Examples of Personalized Coping Strategies

1) Denial Coping Strategy & Narrative: Blaming the Partner. *What would you do if you were in my situation? You have no idea what it's like to be me. It's the only thing that helps me sleep at night! Leave me alone!*

2) Conscious Communication Reflection/Response: *I realize that I feel victimized by my life circumstances and I have treated you unfairly. I'm sorry, you are just trying to be a supportive partner and I have not taken ownership for my emotional pain; it is not yours to fix and I shouldn't use it to get you to feel sorry for me. My emotional pain is my responsibility and me rationalizing my pain by comparing it with yours is unfair and unhealthy for our relationship. Thank you for being a mirror for me and reflecting back the care I need to give myself, with support and not comparison.*

3) Reinforcing Personal Creed (Aligning with Morals & Values): *The truth is, I need to make changes in my life to be able to face challenges in ways that support my wellbeing, mind, body, and spirit. I want to navigate life by making conscious choices.*

Projecting my incredibly painful situation onto you or attempting to place that burden on you isn't healthy for me or you. Denying my experience only makes it worse! I notice that I end up disrespecting you, disrespecting myself, and violating my own relationship values. It's time to change my narratives to "I" statements. I choose to live my life with intention and in alignment with my own values.

Denial Coping Strategy & Narrative:

_____

_____

_____

_____

Denial Coping Strategy & Narrative:

_____

_____

_____

_____

Denial Coping Strategy & Narrative:

_____

_____

_____

_____

The "Lighthouse Effect" is about shining a light into the dark shadows and recesses of repressed trauma and old wounds that carry emotional pain. By practicing and applying intervention skills, we develop resilience, can better manage our emotions, and make conscious choices to support us in moving from survival to revival. Be sure to add your denial intervention skills to your Lighthouse Effect toolbox!

Mindfulness Practice: Awareness is the key. Be present, here, now, this moment!

Observer Self: Detach from your fears by stepping back and observing them without judgment, instead of denying and repressing them.

Reflective Inquiry: Is the narrative I'm running really true? Is it a Capital-T Truth?

DBT: Apply Dialectical Behavior Theory (DBT) skills such as "Radical Acceptance" and "Both/And" in real time when you notice you are in emotional denial.

Daily Practice: Bookend your day with a morning routine and evening routine that supports your wellness and recovery process. (See *Bookending your Day: The Lighthouse Effect 30-Day Self-Care Challenge* workbook: www.innerfaiththerapy.com.)

www.ingramcontent.com/pod-product-compliance
Lightning Source LLC
Chambersburg PA
CBHW082246120626
46555CB00009B/2984